Springer

London
Berlin
Heidelberg
New York
Barcelona
Hong Kong
Milan
Paris
Santa Clara
Singapore
Tokyo

A.T. Wood-Harper, Nimal Jayaratna and
J.R.G. Wood (Eds)

Methodologies for Developing and Managing Emerging Technology Based Information Systems

Information Systems Methodologies 1998, Sixth International Conference on Information Systems Methodologies

Proceedings of the Sixth International Conference of the British Computer Society Information Systems Methodologies Specialist Group, held on 25-27th August 1998

British Computer Society
Information Systems Methodologies
Specialist Group

 Springer

Trevor Wood-Harper, PhD, MBCS, MA
University of Salford, Manchester, UK
and University of South Australia, Adelaide, Australia

Nimal Jayaratna, PhD, MSc, MBCS, MIFIP
Sheffield Hallam University, Sheffield, UK
and Curtin University, Perth, Australia

Bob Wood, MSc, BSc, MPhil
University of Salford, Manchester, UK

ISBN 1-85233-079-1 Springer-Verlag London Berlin Heidelberg

British Library Cataloguing in Publication Data
Methodologies for developing and managing emerging
   technology based information systems : Information Systems
   Methodologies 1998, Sixth International Conference on
   Information Systems Methodologies
   1.Information storage and retrieval systems - Congresses
   2.System design - Congresses
   I.Wood-Harper, A. T. II.Jayaratna, Nimal III.Wood, Bob
   IV.International Conference on Information Systems
   Methodologies (6th : 1998)
   004.2'1
   ISBN 1852330791

Library of Congress Cataloging-in-Publication Data
A catalog record for this book is available from the Library of Congress

Typesetting: Camera ready by contributors
Printed and bound at the Athenæum Press Ltd., Gateshead, Tyne & Wear
34/3830-543210 Printed on acid-free paper

JK

Chair and Committees

Conference Chair: Trevor Wood-Harper, Salford University

PROGRAMME COMMITTEE

Trevor Wood-Harper
David Avison
Richard Baskerville
Frances Bell
Gro Bjerknes
Mike Cavanagh
Louise Chan
Roger Clarke
Jean-Pierre Claveranne
Gilbert Cockton
Brian Fitzgerald
Guy Fitzgerald
Bob Galliers
Goran Goldkhul
Debra Howcroft
Jim Hughes
Patrik Holt
Nimal Jayaratna
Jean-Michel Larrasquet
Graham MacCloud
Tom McMaster

Enid Mumford
Peter Nielsen
Anders Nilsson
Hans-Erik Nissen
Graham Perven
Stephen Probert
Jan Stage
Nahed Stokes
Steve Smithson
Paula Swatman
Julie Travis
Duane Truex
Richard Vidgen
Lisa von Hellens
Sam Waters
Dave Wastell
David Wilson
Russel Winder
Bob Wood
Pak Yoong

ORGANISING COMMITTEE

Bob Wood (Chair)
Frances Bell
Debra Howcroft

Tom McMaster
David Wilson

ACKNOWLEDGEMENTS

Salford City Council, IT Services Directorate
GEMSIS
School of Computing and Mathematical Sciences, Salford University

Editorial

This is the Proceedings of the 6th International Conference of the BCS Specialist Group on Information Systems Methodologies. This year's conference attempted to bring together papers on methodology issues based on emerging technology i.e. internet, WWW, multimedia. There is considerable organisational change brought about by the recent developments in IT and yet methodologies for engaging these technologies are running behind the ability to utilise the concepts embedded in the technology. Innovation has become a primary characteristic of emerging technology based applications. If we are to benefit from this technology then not only should its capabilities be captured but also the social and ethical consequences of using the technology need to be understood.

We hope that the conference proceedings contain interesting ideas for your perusal and look forward to your participation in future conferences.

Nimal Jayaratna
Trevor Wood-Harper
Bob Wood

Contents

Using SSM and Software Prototyping: an Emergent Methodology for an Ethical Information System

Frances Bell & Robert C Davis
Information Systems Research Centre, University of Salford,
Salford, M5 4WT
F.Bell@cms.salford.ac.uk

Abstract

We examine one particular example of multi-paradigm methodology - the combination of Soft Systems Methodology and software prototyping - to identify its strengths and weaknesses when used in the analysis of an 'ethically sensitive' information system. A range of theories and concepts is used to explore the emergent methodology, and the issues of boundary setting and participation are addressed in the context of this case study. The methodology is found generally effective but the ethical issues are seen to be privileged at the expense of the organisational analysis.

Introduction

In this paper, we ask the question, "Can Soft Systems Methodology [1] and software prototyping be usefully combined in the analysis of an ethically sensitive information system?"

The problem situation was the Detention Management Unit (DMU) within the United Kingdom Immigration Service, and the client with whom the project proposal was developed was the Detention Co-ordinator (DC). One of the responsibilities of the DMU is to track those immigrants detained by the Immigration Service for all or part of the time that their requests for asylum are being processed. The then Detention Co-ordinator for the Detention Management Unit was interested in how technology might improve the operations of the unit.

The analysis of the problem situation took place in two parts:
- (major part) analysis by a final year undergraduate (Davis) for his project and dissertation (one third of his final year work)
- subsequent analysis by the supervisor (Bell).

To answer the question above, (loosely guided by the NIMSAD framework [2]), we discuss the problem situation, the methodology user and the methodology itself (i.e. the particular combination of methodologies used in the analysis). Our discussion of the methodology is broadly organised into four phases: the formation of the project; the first part of the student project; the second part of the student project; and analysis since the formal completion of the student project and dissertation.

Throughout these phases, the following means of recording knowledge and reflections were employed:

- regular meetings between supervisor and student
- meetings between client and student/supervisor
- shared electronic workspace for supervisor and student, containing plans, models and records of meetings and client sessions
- hand written notes
- formal documents (Project Proposal in October 1997 [3], Interim Report in January 1998 [4], Final Report in April 1998 [5], and this paper in first written in July 1998)

A previous potential supervisor had highlighted the ethical issues in this project and had been unhappy to countenance the use of software prototyping in advance of significant analysis. Davis was particularly keen to have a practical element to his project, and favoured the use of Lotus Notes for prototyping, particularly as an asset to his curriculum vitae.

The objectives of the project were identified as [3]:

- a better understanding of requirements of any computer-based detainee tracking system that is developed,
- an exploration of any ethical issues that may arise in tracking detainees and the identification of any questions that may need to be answered before development of a production system could proceed,
- an investigation of the use of one candidate technology in the implementation of a prototype detainee tracking system

Davis completed the project in April 1998, and presented his findings to an audience including the client and the supervisor (Bell), since when further analysis of the problem situation and the problem-solving process has taken place.

We use Midgley's notion of marginalisation to discuss the use of boundaries within the analysis and evaluate the emergent methodology in terms of its treatment the technical, organisational and personal perspectives [6], [7], discussing reasons for any perceived deficiencies.

Discussion of Methodology

No doubt influenced by his experience of Systems Analysis on his course so far, Davis considered using structured techniques [8] as well as other approaches.

"These could include Entity Relationship (or Object) Modelling, Data Flow Modelling and Requirements Cataloguing. In addition, problem-solving techniques such as Soft Systems Methodology (SSM) will be used. A challenge will be in fitting these two approaches together in a cohesive way." [3]

The rather off-hand reference to SSM (Soft Systems Methodology [1]) as a problem-solving *technique* confirms that the analyst was somewhat less enthusiastic at that stage about using SSM than was the supervisor, who had suggested the use of SSM as a way of promoting the social and organisational issues to balance the functional / logical view offered by prototyping.

	Problem Situation - Knowledge of / treatment of (focus)	Methodology User	Methodology
Before Jun - Sep '97	(Context Local to DMU) problem perceived with processing of information related to the management of detained immigrants. (Political Context) New (Labour) government in power.	(RD as analyst, FB as commentator) awareness of social/human issues strong focus on technical	• strands identified but planned process unclear • prototyping approach adopted
During Oct97-Jun98	Rich picture (secondary boundary) permits wider consideration of problem context (identifying stakeholders) - *Zooming Out* Initial conceptual model and prototype itself improve understanding of functioning of the DMU (primary boundary). - *Zooming in*	(RD as analyst, FB as commentator) • major concern at this time is the logical stream of analysis using SSM • prototype used to mediate discussion between DC and analyst • recognises stakeholders	• embedding approach to SSM [9], [10] • SSM's logical stream of analysis + exploratory prototyping
After – Conclusion of "Project" Feb 98- Apr 98	Area between primary and secondary boundaries is explored via root definitions of relevant systems. Better understanding gained of customer - supplier relationship between IND and Group 4 in detention of immigrants. - *Zoom to medium*	(RD as analyst, FB as commentator) • Cultural stream of analysis is major concern • Experience gained in use of SSM range of tools, concepts, theories learned and used for ethical analysis • personal ethical position developed	• SSM found to be good for mapping out cultural stream of analysis., supplemented with ethical theories
After – Further analysis May 98-July 98	Existence of IND/Siemens Caseworking Project emerges and "asylum seeker" issue increasingly becomes subject of media and parliamentary debate. *Zooming out again*	(FB as analyst, RD as commentator) • Further analysis of problem situation • Critique of project methodology	Project methodology is evaluated here, using additional theories / concepts

Table 1 - Methodology summarised using NIMSAD framework, Jayaratna 1994

Davis says himself,

"... at the start of the project, the reason I was sceptical about using SSM was because I was of the (mistaken) belief that it was a toy for academics" [11]. The planning schedule included with the report reveals a little more about the analyst's intentions. SSM is included within "Produce Feasibility Document" and "Human/Legal Issues" two activities to be conducted in Weeks 8-11 of the 27-week project.

We have an included an overview of the methodology (see Table 1) influenced by the NIMSAD framework [2].

However as you will see, Davis became an enthusiastic exponent of SSM and used it alongside Software Prototyping to analyse the problem situation, an example of method integration [12]. His approach was influenced by the idea of 'embedding', whereby additional techniques or methodologies are introduced at an appropriate point but SSM still guides the intervention [9], [10]. This type of approach is elsewhere described as *methodological imperialism* [13] and *methodology enhancement* [14]. In fact, the process that emerged was fluid: at times the prototype predominated, and other techniques and concepts were drawn on as seemed appropriate at the time. For example, although SSM loosely structured the ethical analysis, the main support was from theories and ideas about ethical issues, not declared in advance. Additionally Wood-Harper et al's ethical analysis approach was used to post-rationalise the ethical analysis process [15].

SSM, Prototypes and Boundaries

We can use the notional boundaries identified to examine the role of methodology (including prototyping) in the analysis process. Initially when Davis envisaged the project, a boundary was drawn around the Detention Management Unit itself and the perspective was primarily technical.

When the first rich picture was drawn up (for the initial discussion with the client), the wider perspectives were evident in two ways:

- within the drawn boundary which represented the "scope" of the Detention Management Unit, other organisational and extra-organisational elements can be seen (e.g. Prison Governor, the hostels, etc.)
- outside of this drawn boundary we can see other organisational players (e.g. Immigration officers at the point of entry) and stakeholders (Parliament, Amnesty International, Local Authority, detainees' families, etc.) [1]

Davis' use of this boundary within the rich picture emphasises his perceived need to bound the project, for practical reasons of time and limited access to the organisation, and because he was required to do so by the project guidelines formally expressed in a student handbook.

Discussions with the client, based on this rich picture and use of the first prototype, enabled Davis to gain a much richer understanding of the management of the detainees. This management was from the perspective of the DMU and thus

---

[1] It is interesting to note that the detainees figure mainly as arrows, only appearing as a person at the point of entry to the country.

was more concerned with their placement and tracking than their day to day supervision. Other issues which emerged were the need for detention centre governors to have improved information about the people in their care, and the treatment of any possible conflicts arising from the use of that information.

Observation of the second rich picture reveals that the increased understanding of the organisational context appears as increased detail *within* the DMU boundary and the pushing of some elements *beyond* this boundary. Detainees still appear as arrows flowing (like physical goods) across the boundary.

Midgley contends that when a boundary is set, it can be a grey area between the light of what we include in our system definition and the dark of what we exclude [6]. He uses this concept to discuss *marginalisation* where marginal elements are those lying between the primary and secondary boundaries set. In the rich pictures of Figures 1,2, we can see that Davis has specified a primary boundary (the scope of the DMU). The secondary boundary can be seen to include anything within the rich picture itself. Thus elements considered to be outside the scope of the DMU can be seen to be marginalised, some (e.g. Police, Courts, Prison, etc.) *becoming* marginalised in the development of the rich picture from version 1 to 2.

The most developed conceptual models are those relating to the work of the Detention Management Unit, and specifically those elements seen to be amenable to support by information technology. Davis commented that

"SSM has proved to be a revelation in identifying logical activities required to perform tasks, stakeholders, and potential areas of disagreement. In fact, it was used much more extensively than the more traditional tools, and conceptual models were used in place of data flow diagrams for development of the second prototype" [4].

At this stage, other stakeholders and relevant systems were identified but not explored in great detail i.e. they remained in the grey area between the primary and secondary boundary. The competing demands of the prototype and the SSM study began to conflict at this point. A more traditional SSM study might have progressed the root definitions and conceptual modelling immediately. However, the client had responded enthusiastically to the first prototype and was keen to see his suggestions incorporated [3].

Such a use of prototyping is commonly called exploratory, where the prototype is used as "a learning medium between developer and user to help them converge on an adequate set of requirements", [8]. In commercial software product development, the prototype can become the finished product and the specification develops in tandem.

Schrage compares the reflexive relationship between specification and prototyping with that between theory and experiment in physics, where each takes a turn at driving the agenda [16].

6

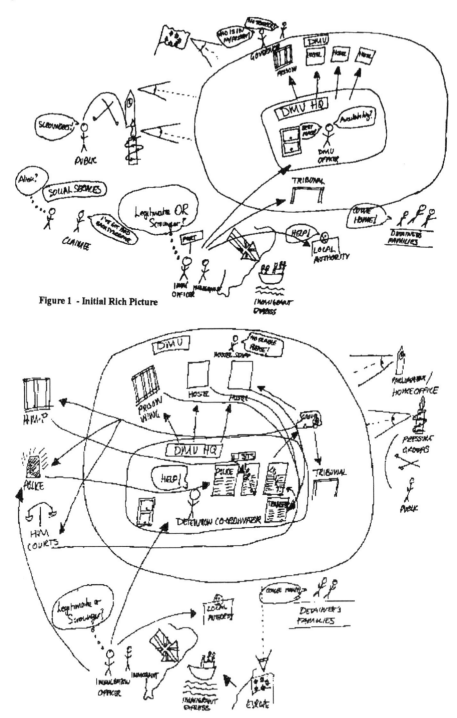

Figure 1 - Initial Rich Picture

Figure 2 - Second Rich Picture

Both schools of thought recognise that
1. prototypes can raise unrealistic expectations about functionality and resource efficiency, and
2. there is a tension for the analyst between maintaining user commitment and retaining some control over the analysis and development process.

The former was not a major issue in this project, since there was no expectation of a delivered system but the latter did apply. As this tension became evident within the project, Davis took action by suspending development work on the second prototype and concentrating on a wider analysis. Thus the effect was that the first half of the project was dominated by the logical stream of analysis and the second half by the cultural stream of analysis in SSM, and the prototype was influential at the *beginning* and the *end* of the project period.

The grey area between the primary and secondary boundaries set **first** began to be explored via root definitions of relevant systems relating to the wider set of stakeholders than the DMU itself. (See Table 2 for treatment of relevant systems, and, Figure 3, Figure 4 for examples of root definitions of relevant systems)

Relevant System	Conceptual Models	CATWOE	Future Analysis
1. Immigration Service (Overview)	✓	✗	✗
2. DMU	✓	✓	✓
3. Welfare of Detainees	✓	✓	✓
4. Stopping detention of non-criminals	✗	✓	✗

Table 2 - Relevant System and Extent of Modelling

SSM proved to be very useful in identifying stakeholders and the transformations in which they were involved (as actors, clients, owners and/or elements of the environment). The sources were the rich pictures, the root definitions and CATWOE summary (Client, Actor, Transformation, Weltanschaunng (or Worldview), Owner, Environment) produced for each of the relevant systems, summarised in Table 3.

Davis also engaged in future analysis to explore the possible uses of technology, influenced by the use of the prototype. He found that SSM helped identify areas for investigation in the cultural stream of analysis.

Each relevant system can be considered to have its *own* primary and secondary boundary but we can regard modelling of relevant systems as shedding some light on the **initial** primary and secondary boundaries set. For example, the analysis did consider one group of those marginalised by the primary boundary, namely the detainees themselves. Consideration of their *welfare* (rather than aspirations) was consistent with the approach adopted and was also important to the Detention Co-ordinator himself for the rational reason that if the detainees were happy, then it was less likely that disturbances would break out.

A Government owned system operated by the Immigration Service to monitor the welfare of detainees, by means of Government resource, in order to ensure that detainees are treated humanely and given maximum access to relatives and legal representation.

C:	Detainees and their families
A:	DMU; Immigration Officers; Parliament; European Union
T:	Need to be 'looked after' → That need met
W:	Detainees have in most cases not committed a crime (other than illegally entering the country or overstaying a visa) and deserve to be treated with consideration and humanity
O:	Parliament / Government
E:	Public opinion (British)

Figure 3 - Root Definition and CATWOE Analysis – A System to Monitor the Welfare of Detainees (Relevant System 3)

A system to prevent immigrants who have not committed a crime (other than illegally entering the country or overstaying a visa) from being imprisoned, by means of public support and pressure on the Government, in order to uphold the principles of natural justice.

C:	Society; Immigrants
A:	Amnesty International; Government; Lobby groups
T:	Need to stop detaining non-criminals (that need met
W:	Immigrants who have not committed a crime (other than illegally entering the country) should not be detained.
O:	Government
E:	Perception of economic difficulties (unemployment); perception of political difficulties (racial tensions)

Figure 4 - Root Definition and CATWOE Analysis – An Alternative View (Relevant System 4)

Stakeholder	Relevant System 2	Relevant System 3	Relevant System 4
Detention Co-ordinator / DMU	Actor	Actor	
Immigration Service	Client	Actor	
Detention Centre Staff			
Group 4 Security	Actor		
Her Majesty's Prisons			
Police	Actor		
Detainees and their families	Client	Client	Client
Local Authorities			
Parliament	Environment	Actor, Owner	Actor, Owner
Home Office	Owner		
EU	Environment	Actor	
Pressure Groups (e.g. Amnesty International)	Environment		Actor
British Public		Environment	Client, Environment

Table 3 - Stakeholders and their role in relevant systems modelled

Ethical Analysis

An ethical analysis was always planned for this project but the process was not initially clear. From the use of SSM, relevant systems and stakeholders concerns with ethical implications were highlighted but this did not constitute a satisfactory analysis of the ethical issues (see summary in Table 4)

Principal Stakeholder(s)	Transformation	Worldview
Immigration Service / Parliament	Need for immigration control met	Immigration control is necessary
Detention Management Unit	Need for detention management met	Immigration detention is necessary in certain circumstances
Detainees / Detention Co-ordinator	Need for detainees to be looked after met	Immigrants deserve to be treated fairly
Amnesty International	Need to prevent immigration detention met	Non-criminals should not be detained

Table 4 - Summary of Ethical Perspectives

To supplement SSM's cultural stream of analysis, Davis studied the work of various authors in the field of Information Systems Ethics [19], [20], [7], and [23]. His application of his study to this particular problem situation enabled him to:

- develop a personal ethical position

- identify the moral agent(s)
- identify the alternative courses of action and discuss their likely results
- explore further the stakeholders and their concerns.

He also used the Wood-Harper et al's ethical analysis process model to organise the models and relevant systems already identified, and to progress his analysis [15].

Davis states his personal ethical position (arrived at as an outcome of the ethical analysis) as follows:

"My own position on this issue is that in this country the law comes from the people (through the election of parliamentarians). Those working in the Detention Management Unit are officers of the law and therefore any involvement with them in developing a new system would be morally acceptable in principle. However, the law can be used to suppress minorities and blind conformance may not be ethical."

The first and second sentences are not surprising since an analyst with deep reservations about the need for immigration control would have been unlikely to take on this particular project. Davis found that Mumford's suggestion of an "ideal" solution was untenable [21]:

"In this case none exists, since there are two polar arguments: one which holds that immigration detention is a fundamental and unacceptable breach of human rights; and another (dominant) view that it is necessary to maintain political and economic stability." [5].

Most of the ethical analysis is concerned with the final sentence in Davis' personal ethical statement. Davis' use of theories to explore the current and possible future problem situation was effective. His vision of the future was helped by his dialogue with the Detention Co-ordinator (sometimes mediated by the use of the prototype) and his study of Amnesty International publications.

He identified a feature of modern information technology systems (such as Lotus Notes) that, in enabling end-users to develop functions themselves, we give them the capability to use the technology to support what we may regard as ethically unsound decisions.

"The current Detention Co-ordinator is keen to ensure that the system is an ethical one and that detainees obtain maximum benefit from it, but there is no guarantee that the next incumbent will be so detainee-oriented." [5].

Thus, he distinguishes between ethical analysis and ethical operation or action, and stresses the role of the Detention Co-ordinator as moral agent, in addition to his own (the analyst), [22].

Further Analysis

The student project concluded with a formal presentation attended by the client, the supervisor and other assessors of the student's work. After the meeting, the client, supervisor and student held a meeting to progress reflection on the area of action and the methodology used for the project. A chance remark by the client revealed that currently under development for the Immigration and Nationality Directorate (IND) was a substantial Information Technology project (called the IND

Caseworking Programme) to support the process of deciding on immigrants' claims for asylum and/or nationality. This revelation provoked a new phase of analysis, this time with the supervisor Bell playing the role of analyst, and Davis playing the role of commentator.

The further analysis has uncovered some interesting facts and raised even more interesting questions about the progress (or lack of it) of the IND Caseworking Project but these are beyond the scope of this paper. Were the DMUIS analysis to be progressed, it would need to be extended to take account of this parallel development for the following reasons:

- both projects shared a need to know personal details and the whereabouts of detainees
- the delay in processing of immigrants' cases adds to the pressure on places in detention centres and may affect Immigration Officers' decisions on where (or even if) to place detain an immigrant
- (to our knowledge) no analysis associated with the IND Caseworking Project has involved participation by officers in the DMU.

Analysis of Perspectives

We can critique Davis' analysis using the technical, organisational (or societal) and personal perspectives [7].

Technical Perspective

The use of the prototype to mediate discussion between himself and the client helped to build requirements for the possible future use of information and communications technology (ICT) provided a useful technical perspective. Not only was discussion of the current situation and future requirements facilitated but also raised were the ethical issues raised by the use of ICT, e.g. searching of demographic data and security across different locations.

Personal Perspective

Interviewing and use of the prototype with only one user (the Detention Co-ordinator) certainly promoted his personal perspective over those of other potential users within the Detention Centres. As these users were more junior and/ or from a different organisation, it is likely that they had quite different personal perspectives. The perspective of the "immigrant" was addressed (e.g. their *welfare* was considered) but this was a less personal perspective. Immigrants themselves had no direct voice in the analysis: the Detention Co-ordinator (directly) and Amnesty International (indirectly via their publications) spoke for them. The analyst also addressed his own perspective in the analysis: in identifying himself as a stakeholder at the outset (e.g. his desire to learn Lotus Notes), and in his development of a personal ethical statement. The supervisor likewise has become a stakeholder, as she publishes this research into the process.

Organisational Perspective

The organisational perspective did not fare so well. Although aspects of work process are evident in the rich pictures and in some of the conceptual models, geographical distribution of work between the DMU and Detention Centres, and organisational distribution of work between the Immigration Service and the Contractors (Group 4 and Wackenhut) are not clear in Davis' analysis.

To what can we attribute this perceived lack of organisational analysis?

1. Checkland and Holwell [23] point to the "conventional wisdom" learned by students which tends to generalise, and to trivialise the need to understand each organisation as essentially different. Certainly, on Davis' course, there was relatively little study of the organisational context.
2. His supervisor could have insisted on a more robust analysis of the organisation. In reviewing the process of the project, we can see that the first half was dominated by the wider view (e.g. the rich picture) and the personal view provided by the Detention Co-ordinator. The response to the perceived technical dominance of the prototype was to concentrate on the ethical analysis (a priority). Had the ethical implications been less present, perhaps the organisational analysis would have assumed importance earlier than it did. If we compare Tables 3 and 4, we can see that the "principal stakeholders" identified in Table 4 are privileged at the expense of others e.g. Group 4 and Detention Centre Staff to the detriment of the organisational perspective.

Conclusions

We can look at the methodology from the analyst's perspective and examine the relationship between the quality of the analysis and the methodology adopted. SSM was of benefit in three ways:

*   the use of rich pictures and modelling of relevant systems (combined with stakeholder analysis) helped to surface ethical issues
*   the use of conceptual modelling to help understand the logical dependencies of activities, some of which were further explored using the prototypes
*   the methodology was used as a template for analysis (consistent with the findings of Fitzgerald [24],[25] for developers who have had educational exposure to methodologies).

The software prototype was effective in the understanding of functional requirements and the surfacing of ethical issues associated with the introduction of ICT.

We have found that some personal perspectives were "missing". In exploring why this should be so, we find that possible reasons include the narrow scope of the project definition and the very limited range of participation. In this respect, the methodology is not the guilty party but rather we can look at the circumstances surrounding the project. Indeed, were this project to continue, these omissions could be rectified with no contradiction to the chosen multi-methodology.

The reasons for the perceived lack of organisational analysis include developer-embodied factors [24], the initiation of the project, time constraints and the distraction posed by the pre-eminence of "ethical issues".

The major outcomes of this project were learning by those involved - student, client and supervisor: learning about the problem situation, the methodology used and about themselves, participating as actors in human activity systems. In answer to the question posed in the first paragraph of this paper, we believe that SSM can be usefully combined with prototyping in the analysis of an ethically sensitive information system, provided that the technical perspective offered by the prototype does not eclipse the organisational perspective. A significant realisation was that, although it is important to consider the ethical implications when introducing technology, the technology itself is no guarantor of a particular ethical behaviour - that is bound up between the technology and the human actor who uses it.

A pertinent question to ask is why we identified in advance this information system as "ethically sensitive". What information system is not ethically sensitive? In doing so, we may have privileged glaring ethical issues (associated with immigration and detention) over other organisational issues (e.g. sharing of work managed by the DMU between the Immigration Service and contractors) which are important and have their own ethical implications.

The authors wish to thank Bob Wood, Briony Oates and Mark Jones for their helpful comments on a previous draft of this paper.

References

1. Checkland P, Scholes J. Soft Systems Methodology in Action, Wiley, UK, 1990

2. Jayaratna N. Understanding and Evaluating Methodologies: NIMSAD A Systemic Framework, McGraw Hill, 1994

3. Davis R. Detention Management Unit information system (DMUIS) Project Proposal, Unpublished Document, Department of Computer and Mathematical Sciences, University of Salford, 1997

4. Davis R. Detention Management Unit information system (DMUIS) Interim Report, Unpublished Document, Department of Computer and Mathematical Sciences, University of Salford, 1998.

5. Davis R. Detention Management Unit information system (DMUIS) Final Report, Unpublished Document, Department of Computer and Mathematical Sciences, University of Salford, 1998.

6. Midgley G. The Sacred and Profane in Critical Systems Thinking. Systems Practice 1992; 5(1): 5-16

7. Mitroff I, Linstone HA. The Unbounded Mind, Oxford University Press, Oxford, 1993

8. Goodland M with Slater C. SSADM Version 4: A Practical Approach, McGraw Hill, 1995.

9. Miles RK. Combining 'Soft' and 'Hard' Systems Practice: Grafting or Embedding. Journal of Applied Systems Analysis 1988; 15.

10. Miles RK. Combining 'Hard' and 'Soft' Systems Practice: Grafting and Embedding Revisited. Systemist; 14(2).

11. Davis R. Private email communication with F. Bell, 1998.

12. Bell F, Oates BJ. A Framework for Method Integration. In: Jayaratna N., Lissoni C. (eds) 2nd BCS Conference on IS Methodologies. September 1994, Edinburgh.

13. Flood R, Jackson M. Creative Problem-Solving, Wiley, London, 1991

14. Mingers J. Multi-paradigm methodology. In: Mingers J, Gill A (eds) Multi-methodology. John Wiley, UK, 1997.

15. Wood-Harper T, Corder S, Wood JRG, Watson H. How We Profess: The Ethical Systems Analyst. Communications of the ACM 1996; 39(3).

16. Schrage M. Cultures of Prototyping. In: Winograd T. (ed,). Bringing Design to Software, Addison Wesley, 1996.

17. Langford D. Practical Computer Ethics. McGraw-Hill, UK, 1995.

18. Bommer M, Gratto G, Gravander J, Tuttle M. A Behavioural Model of Ethical and Unethical Decision-Making. Journal of Business Ethics 1987; 6, Kluwer Academic Publishers, US

19. Mason R. Four Ethical Issues of the Information Age. MIS Quarterly, March 1986, Vol. 10, No. 1.

20. Mason R. Applying Ethics to Information Technology Issues. Communications of the ACM 1995; 38(12).

21. Mumford E. Systems Design: Ethical Tools for Ethical Change, Macmillan, 1996, UK.

22. Walsham G. Ethical Issues in Information Systems Development: The Analyst as Moral Agent. In Proceedings of the IFIP WG 8.2 Conference at Noordwijkerhout, The Netherlands, May 1993.

23. Checkland P, Holwell S. Information, Systems and Information Systems: making sense of the field, pp118-124, John Wiley, 1998.

24. Fitzgerald B. Formalized systems development methodologies: a critical perspective. Information Systems Journal 1996; 6, 3-23.

25. Fitzgerald B. The use of systems methodologies in practice: a field study, Information Systems Journal; 1997; 7, 201-212.

A Critical Analysis of the Practical Relationship Between Soft Systems Methodology, Husserlian Phenomenology and Systems Development

Stephen K. Probert
Computing and Information Systems Management Group
Cranfield University
RMCS Shrivenham
Swindon
SN6 8LA
United Kingdom

Abstract

It is argued that the epistemology proffered by the SSM advocates does not provide a practical basis upon which to conduct team-based systems development; this is because the SSM advocates over-emphasise the need for subjective certainty and meaning, thus rendering their epistemology over-idealistic. It is concluded that the need for effective communication between team members necessarily implies abandoning the search for subjective certitude and supplanting it with the search for practical "working knowledge" of the actual situation in which IS development occurs.

1 Phenomenological Ambitions

Edmund Husserl (1859-1938) developed *phenomenology*, which supposedly provides the foundation of SSM's *epistemology*. According to Checkland, "Soft systems methodology implies ... a model of social reality such as is found in the ... (phenomenological) tradition deriving sociologically from Weber and philosophically from Husserl." [1] (p. 19). Consequently, the arguments put forward in this work will be based on Husserl's phenomenological works [2,3,4,5]. Although it has been argued that many of Husserl's substantive arguments have been virtually ignored by the SSM advocates [6], certain traits of his key ideas do seem to map neatly to some of the key epistemological assumptions of the SSM advocates[*]. This, it is argued, is no accident – because (at the *theoretical* level) both Husserl and the SSM advocates have similar

---

[*]   A more thorough discussion of the SSM advocates' epistemological assumptions can be found elsewhere [7].

motives for adopting the positions that they hold. Ultimately, these motives relate to the real world conditions in which they have to operate. Essentially, what is intended herein by the phrase 'theoretical level' is a body of doctrine *not* concerned with how the world is, *but* is concerned with how statements about the world must be linguistically formulated. In the case of SSM, they must be formulated such that they do not violate the ontological assumptions made by subjective idealists.

An examination, of the reasoning behind the relevant aspects of the SSM advocates' stated (epistemic) position, is undertaken. This examination will be based on a critical analysis - in order to develop a critical interpretation – using arguments that have been adopted (and modified slightly) from Adorno [8]. Essentially, the argument is that:

> "Not least because it was reminiscent of psychology, did proud philosophy since Husserl reject psychology. Dread of psychology leads philosophy in quest of the residuum to sacrifice everything for which it exists." [8] (p. 16).

A practically-oriented (critical) interpretation will be provided below to indicate the SSM advocates' motivations for adopting the position that they hold; this will be characterised as the result of a perceived need to attain "epistemic altitude" (this concept will be explained). Further considerations concerning Husserl's search for certitude will inform the pragmatic recommendations, which will be discussed at this point. The practical conclusion drawn is that, whilst not attempting to sanction "sloppy" systems analysis, epistemic certitude is not attainable - therefore the demand for it can only be counter-productive – when undertaking systems development.

2 Epistemic Altitude

Essentially, SSM advocates hold that statements about the real (i.e. objective) states of affairs in the social world are unwarranted and untenable. Consequently, discourse about mental states is *elevated* to a position of high (or higher) epistemic significance, whilst statements about the real world are denigrated as having a low - or even insignificant – epistemic status [9,10]. It is precisely this *elevation* (of discourse about mental / ideal states of affairs) which constitutes the common ground between the SSM advocates and Husserl; this (generic) approach is criticised by Adorno for what he characterises as its *imaginary altitude*. *Prima facie* the (crude) positivists' position is that sense-data puts us in immediate contact with external reality (although considerable variations on this theme can be found in the writings of the so-called positivists). At any rate, it is this (arguably a "straw man") version of positivist thought that both Husserl and the SSM advocates take umbrage at. The SSM advocates have often proffered the view that, as ideas, *human activity systems* have properties, characteristics, etc. which may be examined; whereas – on the contrary – *human activity systems* as real world occurrences are (strictly-speaking) unknowable; therefore they cannot be modelled. In this respect, Husserl's ideas and those of the SSM advocates (subjective idealism) are strikingly similar. Adorno argues that the motivation for idealism is a ("theoretical") belief that unless a thought (or a judgement) about some aspect of experience admits the possibility of being *certain* (whether true or false) then that thought is epistemologically worthless:

"The thesis of the perceptibility of the purely possible as a doctrine of *essential insight*, or as Husserl originally called it, *categorial intuition*, has become the motto of all philosophical approaches which evoke phenomenology. The fact that the new method should guarantee ideal states of affairs the same immediacy and infallibility as sense-data in the received ["positivist"] view, explains the influence which Husserl exercised over those who could no longer be satisfied with neo-Kantian systems and yet were unwilling to blindly hand themselves over to irrationalism." [8] (p. 200 [emphases added])

The "altitude" supposedly gained by taking such a view (i.e. the idealism adhered to by both the SSM advocates and Husserl) is achieved by, as it were, "rising above" the real world into an ideal world (or worlds) – in a search for greater epistemic security. Of course, the "price to be paid" is the removal ("elevation") of oneself from the real world within which one may be attempting to act. However, and in agreement with Adorno, it is not being suggested here that an alternative position of naïve positivism should be adopted:

"[C]ategorial intuition is the paradoxical apex of his [Husserl's] thought. It is the indifference into which the positivistic motif of intuitability and the rationalistic one of being-in-itself of ideal-states-of-affairs should be sublated. The movement of Husserlian thought could not tarry at this apex. Categorial intuition is no newly discovered principle of philosophizing. It proves to be a sheer dialectical moment of transition: imaginary altitude." [8] (p. 201)

Similarly, it might be argued that the SSM advocates in fact hold the position that thought is not *so* detached from the real world as the above account would imply. Indeed, the SSM texts contain many references to an unfolding flux of ideas *and* events. However, it is also made clear – in the various SSM texts (e.g. [1,9,10,11]) that "perceived events" are – for the SSM advocates - just (precisely) *subjective perceptions* of events. Adorno cogently distinguishes between epistemological accounts of experience given in terms of *sense-data of* and (ephemeral) *encounters with* the real world:

"In a certain way categorial intuition was devised by the doctrine of propositions in themselves … If these are truly to be more than creations of thought, then they cannot really be products of thought but must simply be encountered … by it. The paradoxical demand for a merely encountering thought arises from the claim to validity on the part of logical absolutism*. The doctrine of categorial intuition is the result of this on the subject side." [8] (pp. 201-202).

---

* The term 'logical absolutism' is introduced by Adorno to connote Husserl's general view of logical statements as being in no way dependent on events occurring in the real world for their truth-values; this is an important aspect of Husserl's conception of *eidetic* sciences.

However, it should be noted that Husserl felt compelled to extend his idealism to cater for "object-correlates" of thought. Put bluntly, Husserl considered that if there are perceptions of objects, then there must be real objects "out there" somewhere. As Adorno stresses:

> "Only if categorial moments of meaning copy some objective-ideal being and 'correspond' to it instead of just producing it, can objective-ideal be intuited in any sense at all. Thus Husserl is forced, in spite of his own critical discernment, to plead positively for the 'object correlates' of categorial forms and thus for an intuition which fulfils them and is non-perceptible in principle, so that the fundamental thesis of propositions in themselves does not collapse." [8] (p. 204)

It is concluded that, to date, the SSM advocates have not felt similarly compelled. Indeed, SSM advocates *prima facie* would hold that the world is constituted by and through subjective perceptions. Ostensibly, the reason for this position is *epistemological rigour* (i.e. what should more properly be understood as *imaginary altitude*).

3 Subjective Certitude and Epistemological Rigour

The question that must now be asked is: why should so much emphasis be placed on (the need for) *subjective certitude* in the SSM advocates' formulations of the epistemological problems of systems analysis? The demand for subjective certitude – inherent in the epistemology proffered by the SSM advocates – would *prima facie* seem to generate immediate problems for the use of (soft) systems epistemology in practical endeavors. One might think that practical IS development work should, minimally, be more concerned with getting a practical working knowledge of a situation in order to take positive action – rather than getting embroiled in "epistemologically purist" issues and concerns. Of course, to take this literally would be to proceed uncritically. In order to operate in a critically aware manner, epistemological considerations will be important – but it will be argued here that "epistemological purism" is not the best way to proceed. Further discussion of an appropriate epistemological framework with which to undertake critical systems analysis lies outside the scope of this paper, but an introductory discussion can be found elsewhere [12].

3.1 Adorno's Structural Argument

Now to return to the question raised above (why should so much emphasis be placed on the need for *subjective certitude* in the SSM advocates' formulations of the epistemological problems of systems analysis?). According to Adorno, the answer is to be found in the actual circumstances in which academics find themselves, i.e. (what he calls) *middlemen* – the social grouping that we might characterize today as the *middle class*. Interestingly, Adorno's argument would appear to hold *a fortiori* for the likes of SSM practitioners, consultants, etc.

Adorno's argument can be applied as follows. The source of the subjective idealism - inherent in the SSM advocates epistemological accounts – may be found in *practice* (i.e. *experience*) rather than in *theory*. The accounts of epistemology given in the SSM texts are supposedly based on (or supported by) the practical experiences of using systems ideas in organisations. In all such accounts (encountered by the author at any rate), the Soft Systems Practitioner does not claim to be the *owner* of the system. Indeed, the impression one usually gets is of the SSM practitioner being rather unceremoniously "dumped" into a conflict-ridden and potentially hostile social situation, of which he or she has little prior knowledge – and little power to control. Might this explain the perceived need for (or the motivation for seeking) certitude? Adorno makes the following comments about subjective idealists (in general) in the introduction to his *Against Epistemology – A Metacritique**:

> "The open or secret pomp and the totally unobvious need for absolute spiritual security – for why, indeed, should the playful luck of spirit be diminished by the risk of error? – are the reflex to real powerlessness and insecurity. They are the self-deafening roar through positivity of those who neither contribute to the real reproduction of life nor actually participate in its real mastery. As middlemen, they only commend and sell to the master his means of lordship, spirit objectified … into method [or methodology, for that matter]… They use their subjectivity to subtract the subject from truth and their idea of objectivity is as a residue." [8] (p. 15)

However, there is another aspect to the search for certitude; this is bound up with the desire to "attribute meaning" to one's experiences – another central tenet of SSM. The search for certitude begins with Descartes – in particular with his "cogito ergo sum" proposition. This is normally understood as "I think therefore I am." although there are other interpretations, and Descartes himself used a variety of formulations of what has come to be known as *the Cogito* [14]. Kolakowski argues:

> "[I]t is plausible to suspect, on the basis of the development of European philosophy from Descartes onward, that if we start with Cogito, we can reconstruct the world only as somehow correlated with subjectivity … The converse relation is probably valid, too.

---

* The title of this book is somewhat misleading; Adorno was conducting a critical analysis of subjective idealist epistemology as a (sort of) groundwork for an alternative epistemology, "Criticizing epistemology also means … retaining it." [8] (p. 27 - N.B. the three dots are included in the original text). Some aspects of what such an alternative epistemology might look like are discussed elsewhere [13].

If we start with the thing ... the categories applicable to it do not enable us to describe the irreducible subjectivity, this "miracle of miracles" (Husserl), this being-directed-toward-oneself, this act of experiencing oneself ... It is very doubtful if anybody has succeeded in producing a language jointly encompassing these two viewpoints: one directed toward Cogito and the other directed toward things."* [15] (pp. 82-83)

Ultimately, most modern-day systems development is a social activity, and it is *groups* who must ultimately conduct effective systems development in organisations, e.g. Griffiths and Probert point out the importance of teamwork in the development of Electronic Payment Systems [16]. Groups imply a need for individuals to communicate, and communication implies a need for the interpretation of what is being said by others in the social settings that systems development takes place. However, as Kolakowski argues:

"[A] certitude mediated in words is no longer certitude. We gain or we imagine to have gained access to certitude only as far as we gain or imagine to have gained perfect identity with the object, an identity whose model is the mystical experience. This experience however is incommunicable; any attempt to hand it over to others destroys the very immediacy that was supposed to be its value – consequently it destroys certitude. *Whatever enters the field of human communication is inevitably uncertain, always questionable, fragile, provisory, and mortal.*" [15] (pp. 83-84 [emphases added])

Philosophically-speaking, other people's experiences are "outside" of our immediate subjective experience, therefore reports about them are essentially uncertain (for the recipient).

3.2 "Meaning-attribution"

One final important point in the context of this discussion is that, ultimately, the drive for subjective certitude has strong religious or crypto-religious ("meaning-endowing") overtones. It is, precisely because science (and, arguably, most other intellectual pursuits) have abandoned the search for absolute certitude in their methods [17,18], that the search for certitude must direct itself (or "take its cues") from elsewhere as a consequence. One "avenue open" in this respect is that of (allegedly) "pure" or "unmediated" subjective experience. Kolakowski summarises thus:

"This search [for certitude] has little to do with the progress of science and technology. Its background is religious rather than intellectual; it is, as Husserl perfectly knew, a search for meaning. It is a desire to live in a world out of

---

* This analysis can provide us with an insight into the reasoning behind the proffered arguments that soft systems thinking is fundamentally different from hard systems thinking; however, this issue lies outside the scope of this paper.

which contingency is banned, where sense (and this means purpose) is given to everything. Science is incapable of providing us with that kind of certitude, and it is unlikely that people could ever give up their attempts to go beyond scientific rationality." [15] (p. 84)

However, the actual demands made upon systems development teams require that they proceed in an epistemologically uncertain (practical) manner.

4. Conclusion

So, to conclude, there are two plausible explanations for the drive towards epistemic altitude: firstly, one that arises from the psychological insecurity engendered by the social situations in which most soft systems projects (and no doubt many systems development projects) take place. Secondly, the more general psychological effect that - despite the remarkable progress that some essentially uncertain enterprises, e.g. the physical sciences, have had - an unsatisfied demand for meaning in many practitioners' subjective experiences persists (why this is so is an interesting question – which lies outside the scope of this paper). However, it need not follow that a desire to take purposeful action implies a search for some kind of ultimate and/or certain meaning to life.

Also, it is concluded that – whatever the motivations for desiring it – epistemic certitude is not attainable, therefore the demand for it can only be counter-productive when undertaking systems development work. Our understanding of the real world in which systems development must take place may often be partial, confused and even bigoted. Essentially, critically-minded vigilance will provide some defence against the latter – as will openness to the critical comments and suggestions of others. For the former – the epistemological problems – we had best learn to make do with whatever understanding of the problem situation can be obtained, given the time and resources available. This is *not* to sanction sloppy analysis! The alternative - only to sanction (unattainable) epistemological rigour - can only force us to withdraw our attention from the real world and into our (subjective) selves. Few practical problems are amenable to solution solely by introspection - although this is not to deny the value and importance of critical reflection. Moreover, the need for effective communication between systems development team members necessarily implies abandoning the search for subjective certitude and supplanting it with the search for practical "working knowledge" of the salient aspects of the actual situation in which IS development takes place.

It is easy to imagine why IS practitioners (and particularly systems analysts) find themselves in positions of daunting epistemic insecurity.* Complex organisational structures, procedures, cultures, etc. - all have to be understood in a relatively short space of time if emerging technology is to be fruitfully exploited to provide real benefits for organisations. But the very complexity of the environment may well engender a (counter-productive) tendency to withdraw into an "inner realm" of subjective epistemic certainty. Practitioners need to resist this temptation. Of course,

---

* As a practitioner once myself, I can clearly recall being in such situations .

there will always be technical aspects of the models to attend to; here subjective (introspective) rigour is both possible and desirable (notwithstanding the fact that attempting to be too rigorous can sometimes be unproductive). But the main point of this discussion is to argue that practitioners need to produce *models of the actual situation* (and understand that that is what they should be attempting to produce!) – although these will almost certainly be poor (factually incorrect) models in the early stages of analysis. Although poor models can be refined, it will probably never be the case that they can be refined until they are 100% accurate (even if a model was 100% accurate we could probably never know it!). Moreover, if the IS practitioners are working (sensibly) as a team, each model produced by the different practitioners will inevitably be only a part of the picture. Therefore, as Kolakowski argues, any certainty about the models will be destroyed once they have been communicated to other members of the team [15]. Consequently, all models built by teams are inherently (subjectively) uncertain – and this is something which, as humans, we must simply endure. In practice, sensible project management will be needed to allow sufficient time for iterative modelling to be carried out - relative to the needs of the IS development project. Perforce this depends on the nature of the project, as some projects have rigid time constraints whilst others have looser time frames but a greater need for accuracy, and so forth.

References

1. Checkland PB. Systems Thinking, Systems Practice. Wiley, Chichester, 1981
2. Husserl E. Ideas. George Allen and Unwin, London, 1931
3. Husserl E. Logical Investigations. Routledge and Kegan Paul, London, 1970
4. Husserl E. Phenomenological Psychology. Martinus Nijhoff, The Hague, 1977
5. Husserl E. The Idea of Phenomenology. Kluwer Academic Publishers, Dordrecht, 1990
6. Probert SK. Should Soft Systems Methodology be taught to all our information systems students? In: Jayaratna N, Fitzgerald B, Wood-Harper T, Larrasquet JM (eds) Training and education of methodology practitioners and researchers. Springer-Verlag, London, 1998, pp 289-300
7. Probert SK. The metaphysical assumptions of the (main) Soft Systems Methodology advocates. In: Winder RL, Probert SK, Beeson IA (eds) Philosophical aspects of information systems. Taylor and Francis, London, 1997, pp 131-150
8. Adorno TW. Against epistemology: A metacritique. Basil Blackwell, Oxford, 1982
9. Checkland PB. Towards the coherent expression of systems ideas. Jnl of Appl Syst Analysis 1991; 18:25-28
10. Checkland PB. Systems and scholarship: The need to do better. Jnl of the Opl Res Soc 1992; 43(11):1023-1030
11. Checkland PB, Scholes J. Soft Systems Methodology in action. Wiley, Chichester, 1990

12. Probert SK. Subject and object in IS development. In: Gupta JND (ed) Proceedings of the 3rd Americas conference on information systems. Association for Information Systems, Pittsburgh, 1997, pp 315-317

13. Guzzoni U. Reason – a different reason – something different than reason? wondering about the concept of a different reason in Adorno, Lyotard, and Sloterdijk. In: Pensky M (ed) The actuality of Adorno. State University of New York Press, Albany, 1997, pp 23-42

14. Williams B. Descartes: The project of pure enquiry. Penguin, Harmondsworth, 1978

15. Kolakowski L. Husserl and the search for certitude (2nd edition). University of Chicago Press, Chicago, 1987

16. Griffiths DM, Probert SK. Development methods for electronic payment systems: The need for methodology research. In: Jayaratna N, Fitzgerald B, Wood-Harper T, Larrasquet JM (eds) Training and education of methodology practitioners and researchers. Springer-Verlag, London, 1998, pp 137-146

17. Popper KR. Objective knowledge (2nd edition). Oxford University Press, Oxford, 1979

18. Quine WV, Ullian JS. The web of belief (2nd Edition), Random House, New York, 1978

A First Step in Developing a Web Application Design Methodology: Understanding the Environment

Nancy L. Russo
Northern Illinois University and University College Cork
Cork, Ireland

Brian R. Graham
Motorola Information Technology Services
Chicago, USA

Abstract

The development of applications for the World Wide Web is different from the development of applications for traditional information systems environments. Not only do the applications themselves differ in terms of audience and scope, but the individuals developing these applications are also quite different from traditional system designers. A study of web application designers indicates that a large percentage of "information-providing" web applications are developed outside of the IS function, by individuals with little or no knowledge of traditional IS development methods, and with no organizational guidelines or standards in place. To determine what might be useful in a web application design method, a web development project was studied and a suggested design methodology was identified.

1 Introduction

The Internet is the world's largest computer network, composed of over 25,000 connected networks with over 6.6 million computers and 40 to 50 million users worldwide [1]. Traffic over the Internet grew over 80% in 1995, and shows no signs of slowing down [2]. The World Wide Web, an Internet resource that allows users to locate and retrieve information from computers around the world, is the fastest growing resource on the Internet. In two years, the web grew from 100 sites to 100,000 sites that house more than a million web pages [1]. It is estimated that over 80% of US Fortune 500 companies have a web application of some sort [3].

Web applications range from something as simple as an on-line course syllabus to sophisticated sales ordering and tracking systems. Although many web applications serve primarily as sources of information, others are fully-functioning applications with dynamic interaction with databases and other information systems.

applications with dynamic interaction with databases and other information systems.

The proliferation and high visibility of web applications have raised concerns in some business (and educational) organizations. Because a web site may be the initial contact a potential customer has with the organization, it is important that the information presented be accurate and timely, and reflect the objectives of the organization. However, most web applications are developed with little or no control, and without formalized processes.

The solution to the lack of formalization and control in traditional system development environments has been the implementation of formalized system development methodologies. The use of an appropriate development methodology has been considered essential when designing and building computerized information systems. The failure to follow an appropriate methodology has been linked to poor quality systems, low levels of user acceptance, and high development costs. However, current research evidence indicates that existing system development methodologies are insufficient to support the development process required for today's systems. Methodologies are used in a piecemeal fashion, adapted on a project-by-project basis, or ignored altogether [4] [5] [6]. Developers today are faced with a multitude of hardware and software environments. For example, a recent study [7] found that 85% of the organizations surveyed were developing systems on three or more hardware platforms. Thus it is not surprising that existing methodologies are not able to support the variety of development environments found in many organizations.

In addition to limitations in existing methodologies, differences between web applications and traditional information system applications may prevent the use of these methodologies in the web environment. Web applications differ from traditional information systems in terms of the purpose and audience for which they are developed, their use of communications technology and multi-platform accessibility, and their non-sequential nature, due to their reliance on hypertext links to other web documents. Another difference has to do with who is developing web applications. Our study indicates that many web sites are initiated and developed outside of the IS function. In addition, the users of web applications are likely to be outside of the organization, and typically cannot be identified or included in the development process. The issue of "user-friendliness" is taken to extremes; often the web designer has to consider methods of drawing users to the site, so promotion of the web site becomes a new task.

Although there are many differences between web application development and traditional information system development, this is not to say that there is a totally different process at work. Whereas the ability to instantly publish a web application appears to "trivialize" the need for planning and design [8], experience has shown that as far as web applications are information systems, systems development principles remain applicable [9].

Based on the data collected regarding web development and our experiences with the design of applications for the web, many of the tools and techniques that make up traditional methodologies are not applicable and the set of existing tools is not sufficient to meet the needs of web developers. The nature of web applications is such that it requires a different support structure. Therefore, new methodologies are needed to support the development of web applications.

It is proposed that a new methodology can be developed which more appropriately represents and supports the development process and activities in the web environment. As a first step in identifying the requirements for a web application design methodology, some information regarding the characteristics of web development is needed. In this study, we looked specifically at who is developing web applications, and how they are doing it. To provide additional insight into web design, one of the researchers evaluated various traditional design techniques in the process of developing a web page, and from this process identified a potential web application design methodology.

2 Studying Current Web Application Development

The research reported here is part of an on-going study of web development methods [10]. As an initial step, we sought an understanding of how web applications are being developed today.

2.1 Research Methodology

The first phase of the study was an electronic survey of web developers. To identify a broad group of web developers, five hundred web sites were randomly selected from the 1997 *Internet & Web Yellow Pages*. An electronic questionnaire was e-mailed to the webmaster of each of these web sites. This questionnaire examined the who and how of web application development. It specifically addressed the background, experience, and knowledge of web developers and the methods they used for developing their web applications. (A copy of the questionnaire is available from the authors.)

2.2 Results

Responses were received from 70 of the sites contacted; however, only 57 of these were usable, resulting in a response rate of just over 10%. It should be noted that upon examination of the web applications developed by the respondents, we learned that nearly all of these sites are what we would call "information providing" sites; that is, they are not full blown IS applications, but instead are a series of linked pages to provide information on a product, service, or organization. Therefore, the results should be interpreted in light of this particular sample, and may not apply to large corporate web-based applications development.

2.2.1 Web Developers

Less than one third (32%) of the web developers studied were employed in an IS department. Their job titles included president, programmer, web coordinator, costume designer, and many others. The formal educational background of the responding web developers varied. All had some college, and approximately one third had master's degrees. Most did not come from traditional computer science/IS backgrounds, although a few had some prior programming knowledge (not necessarily work experience). The programming languages which were most commonly known (and in some cases used) by the responding web developers were BASIC, C, Visual Basic and COBOL. Less than 15% of the respondents received formal training in using hypertext markup language or other web development tools/languages. Those who did have some training were most likely to report having received it during a one-day seminar or workshop. Approximately half of the web developers had been involved in the development of computerized information systems in the past (non-web applications). Of these developers, very few indicated that they had used any type of systems development methodology while developing previous computerized information systems.

2.2.2   Web Development Background

Respondents were asked to indicate the motivation(s) for developing the web site. The most common motivation was the desire to have a presence on the web, followed, in order of importance, by the development of a totally new type of application, applications to replace existing computerized systems, and those to replace existing manual systems (respondents could indicate more than one reason). Most web development projects (60%) were initiated by the developer rather than by a manager or customer. The number of web applications developed by respondents ranged from one to thirty, and the amount of time it took to develop the applications ranged from a few days to over one year. An average of five web applications were developed in the last six months by the respondents and their most recent web application took an average of one month to complete (although most agreed that development was never completely finished due to the need to keep pages current).

2.2.3   Systems Development Methods

Only 29% of the developers worked as part of a formal development team in developing their web applications. More often the developer worked alone, on 39% of the sites, or worked informally with users (32%). The majority (68%) of the respondents indicated that their organizations have no standards or guidelines for web development. Some organizations are in the process of developing standards, and several developers indicated that they have their own informal guidelines or "rules of thumb" that they follow. These guidelines typically involved activities such as looking at other web sites (including those of competitors) and more pragmatic concerns such as insuring that the application met net browser and screen display standards. None of the developers used a formal system development methodology. However, a small number of the developers did report using traditional development tools and techniques, such as entity-relationship diagramming, prototyping, decision tables, and flowcharting. Half of the respondents prototyped a version of their web application before doing the full development. This, however, was not necessarily a formalized use of prototyping but may have been used to test out designs and flow informally.

2.3 What Did We Learn?

Web applications are being developed by a diverse group of people, many of them working outside the formal information systems function, and with little or no background or training in systems development principles. Most of these developers are doing web design completely on a trial and error basis, with no standards or methodologies to guide them. Whereas we would not want to downplay the importance of creativity and aesthetics in web page design, there are possible benefits of using some type of methodology, even informally. For example, a methodology could provide some structure for the process, could be used to promote organizational standards, and could allow designers and others to more easily document and communicate about the design.

3 Web Application Development Methodology

In addition to studying what others are doing in terms of web application design, we also sought to "learn by doing" web design. A web development project was initiated by one of the authors, who worked with a small development team to produce a functioning application. The application centered on a database containing information regarding a manufacturing process. The goal of the web application was to provide easy access to the information in the database from a variety of locations.

While going through the development process, the team was asked to try to apply any traditional development tools or techniques with which they were familiar. When no familiar tool or technique appeared to fit the design and/or documentation requirements of the project, the team was asked to develop their own. In addition, the team was asked to describe the process they followed in the design and development of the web application.

3.1 The Process

The process described by the team was not very different from a traditional lifecycle process model. The process is viewed as circular and iterative, with a number of feedback points and looping back to previous phases if necessary. Each of the steps will be described below, including a discussion of how the activities might be undertaken in a web development process. Information from the survey responses will be incorporated as well.

3.1.1 Identification of the Problem

The survey data indicated that a large number of web applications are developed primarily because the initiator saw a need to have a presence on the web. Therefore, many of these applications are not the outcome of a formal strategic planning process, nor are they responses to specific problems. Very frequently they are not part of a corporate information systems architecture at all.

Because many of the web developers who responded to the survey were also the initiators of the application, the survey responses gave little attention to feasibility analysis. It is so quick and easy to put together a simple web page that very little justification is required. However, feasibility does remain an issue. If the organization does not own or have access to the hardware and software to support the desired web application, or if the external users don't have the hardware/software environment for which the application was designed, then the ultimate implementation will not be successful.

3.1.2 Analysis

Whereas in a traditional information systems development project, analysis often focuses on the processes or functions that must be performed by the new system, in the world of web applications, the focus is more likely to be on the information content of the site. A number of survey respondents described their analysis process as looking at company brochures and other web sites. In traditional IS development, we are likely to focus on various techniques to get information from users regarding what they want and need in the new system. However, when a web application is developed, we may not know exactly who our users will be. Therefore more responsibility is placed on the designer to decide what will meet the users' needs.

3.1.3 Design of the Application

In this phase of the web application development process, the look and feel of the application is designed. Databases and processing functions would also be designed at this stage. Design techniques which were used in developing the manufacturing application included entity-relationship diagramming and a set of new documentation symbols, which are discussed briefly in a later section. Survey respondents reported using tools such as FrontPage and Word for design as well as for building their applications.

3.1.4 Resource Gathering

The necessary resources, including hardware, software, communications links, and personnel skills, must be available. Because there are many languages and packages available to develop web applications, and several may be needed, integration issues must be part of the resource selection process.

3.1.5 Design Review

The design team believed that a specific phase was required to reconcile the chosen design with the resources available. If these are incompatible, then the two previous phases are revisited. This may take several iterations as design ideas and technology change.

3.1.6 Coding

Once the final design review is complete, the application itself is created. The pages are developed and linked. Databases are built, and any necessary code (Java, CGI, etc.) is written or imported and modified. It is quite common for nearly all the code to be acquired from on-line libraries or other sources.

3.1.7 Testing

Testing in some ways is even more difficult in the web environment than with traditional IS development. When a traditional information system is developed, it is typically for a known group of users and a known hardware/software/network environment. Web applications, however, many times are developed for an almost infinite group of users, working in vastly different environments. An important aspect of the testing, therefore, is to ensure that the site works as intended from all the types of users. In addition, many web applications are hyperlinked to other applications, both internal and external. Not only must all of these links be tested before implementation, but they must be tested frequently throughout the life of the application to ensure viability of the links.

3.1.8 Implementation

The actual installation of the web application may be as simple as loading it onto a server. With traditional applications software, we would expect there to be a set of users waiting to use the system. This may not be the case with a web application. An important component of implementation for many web sites is making the site known to the target audience. Some type of advertising or promotion of the site might be required.

3.1.9 Post-Implementation Review & Maintenance

Because many web applications are developed to serve as important sources of information for current and/or potential customers, it is essential that the information provided be up to date. Content and links must be monitored continuously to ensure that they remain current. To assist in this effort, many web sites provide a format for feedback concerning the site.

3.2 The Tools

As mentioned earlier, the design team was asked to try to apply traditional IS design tools and techniques to the web development process, and when those didn't work, to develop new ones. For this particular project, one traditional system design technique was found to be useful. Entity-Relationship diagramming was used to design the relational database that was at the core of this application.

No existing documentation techniques were considered adequate to document the overall design of the application. A method was needed to illustrate pages and links (internal and external) between pages and other information pertinent to web applications. Symbols to represent pages, frames documents, tables, and local and remote links were created. Additional information provided on the documentation included the programming language(s) used, the server address, the browser standard for which the application was designed, and the standard screen resolution required. Examples of these are available from the authors.

3.3 Evaluating a Web Application Development Methodology

The proposed methodology is by no means considered to be a finished product. It is merely a "first draft" that needs to be applied and refined through numerous iterations. Once a viable methodology is identified, it must be validated in use. The methodology should be evaluated by a variety of web developers on a range of web projects. The process identified in this study was suggested by traditional IS developers; however, from the survey we learned that a majority of web application developers do not fit this profile. Therefore, it is essential that a methodology be tested across the broad spectrum of developers. Criteria for evaluating a web application development methodology might include: its ability to support (but not confine) the entire web application development life cycle, from initiation to maintenance, its impact on the time required to develop the web application, and its flexibility to fit with the variety of environments and activities required to develop web applications.

4   Conclusions

As the importance of web-based applications grows, organizations will increasingly seek to formalize and improve the development of these applications. It is therefore essential that we understand how these applications are developed, and what types of methods, tools, and techniques are used or are needed to support this process. Existing methodologies, tools, and techniques are poorly accepted in traditional development environments; they are even less relevant to web development. Although web application development appears to be a more unstructured, creative process than is traditional systems development, there is still a need for tools and guidelines to support the development process.

Web developers are inventing their own methods on the fly, with little evaluation or sharing of information. In this paper we have presented an outline of a possible web application development methodology. The web application development methodology presented in this paper was developed by a team trained in structured tools and techniques. The types of methods they found useful may not produce the same benefits for different web developer communities. Due to the large number of web developers are who are not part of the IS function, it is particularly important to study the processes they use for web design and development. Case studies in which non-IS web developers are asked to document their design processes would be especially useful. The role of context and designer characteristics may be important factors in determining methodology requirements. Continuing research is needed to bring together the knowledge and experiences of web developers in order to create and evaluate methods, tools, and techniques for this changing environment.

In addition to modifying and evaluating web application development methodologies, there are other significant issues regarding web development that should also be addressed. One of these issues concerns the quality of web applications. What makes a web site "good"? Another area which needs exploration is the creative side of web development. How important is it to include artists, graphic designers, etc. in the design of web pages? The web provides a rich new area for exploration by methodology researchers.

References

1. Neubarth M. Let's go to the videotape. Internet World 1996; January:8

2. Caron L. Web applications evolve. Sybase 1996; July-September:24-28

3. In search of the perfect market. The Economist 1997; May 10:3-6

4. Fitzgerald B. The systems development dilemma: whether to adopt formalized systems development methodologies or not. In: Baits W (ed) Proceedings of Second European Conference on Information Systems, Nijenrode University Press, 1994, pp 691-706

5. Hardy C, Thompson J, Edwards H. The use, limitations and customization of structured systems development methods in the United Kingdom. Information and Software Technology 1995; 9:467-477

6. Russo N, Wynekoop J, Walz D. The use and adaptation of system development methodologies. In: Khosrowpour M (ed) Managing Information & Communications in a Changing Global Environment: Proceedings of the Information Resources Management Association International Conference. Idea Group Publishing, Hershey, PA, 1995, p 162

7. Russo N, Hightower R, Pearson, J. The failure of methodologies to meet the needs of current development environments. In: Jayaratna N and Fitzgerald B (eds), Lessons Learned from the Use of Methodologies: Proceedings of the Fourth Conference of the British Computer Society's Information Systems Methodologies Specialist Group. BCS Publications, Swindon, 1996, pp 387-394

8. Balasubramanian V, Bashian A. Document management and web technologies: Alice marries the mad hatter. Communications of the ACM 1998; 7:107-115

9. Dennis A. Lessons from three years of web development. Communications of the ACM 1998; 7:112-113

10. Russo N, Misic M. Web applications: A whole new world of systems development? In: Khosrowpour M (ed) Effective Utilization and Management of Emerging Technologies: Proceedings of the Information Resources Management Association 1998 International Conference. Idea Group Publishing, Hershey, PA, 1998, pp 843-844

A Meta Modelling Approach for Unifying Soft Systems and Information Systems Modelling

Quan C Dang[*], Dilip Patel[†] and Shushma Patel[†]

[*] Department of Computing and Information Systems,
University of Paisley, Paisley PA1 2BE, Scotland
[†] School of Computing, Information Systems and Mathematics,
South bank University, London SE1 0AA, England

Abstract

This paper presents an approach based on meta-modelling techniques for unifying soft systems and information systems models in information systems development. The object-oriented conceptual modelling language Telos is utilised to specify SSM and other information modelling concepts together with their relationships. As a result, the meta model, which is in the format of Telos classes, represents the unified modelling language. These Telos classes can then be instantiated with objects that represent models of problem domains. These objects inherit all the properties of the classes (i.e. the modelling concepts and their relationships) specified in the meta model. Furthermore, the meta model can be flexibly defined and extended by the modeller to meet specific requirements of a particular modelling project.

Keywords: Conceptual modelling, Soft systems, Information modelling, Meta modelling, Telos, Information systems methodology.

1.   Introduction

It is well-recognised that the appreciation of the problem situation, in particular its relevant human activities, plays a crucial role in successful development of information systems (IS) (see e.g. [1; 2; 3]). Given this, Soft Systems methodology (SSM) [4] is advocated to provide the IS analyst with a powerful methodology to obtain a rich understanding of the problem situation for which an information system is built [1; 3]. Effectively, applications of SSM in information systems development (ISD) ranges from the planning of IS strategies (e.g. [5]), IS requirement analysis (e.g. [6]), IS analysis and design (e.g. [2]), to evaluation of IS methodologies (e.g. [7]).

In this paper, we focus on the use of SSM in the context of information systems modelling [8, page 61; 9; 10]. Specifically, we are concerned with the fashion in which soft systems models, and/or knowledge gained from soft systems analysis, are linked to information models, such as the data/structural model and process/behavioural model (for a review of these models, see e.g. [8]).

We begin by discussing issues inherent to the linkage of SSM to information systems modelling and drawbacks of the current approaches. Subsequently, we propose an approach to unify SSM and information modelling based on meta modelling techniques; the language Telos utilised to implement the approach and a method for constructing a meta model that unifies SSM and information models are outlined. This is followed by a section that presents an exemplary application of the method to build the meta model. Benefits of using the meta model in modelling problem domains are highlighted. The final section gives an appraisal and discusses relationship of the proposed approach to other work.

2. Background: Linking SSM and Information Systems Models

In soft systems practice, work that utilised SSM in helping information systems development was reported as early as in 1970 [11]. Following the publication of [4] a great many papers on using SSM in ISD appeared (see e.g. [12; 13; 3; 14]). According to [1], these approaches can be classified into two main streams. The first stream involves linking SSM to well-established information systems design methods (e.g. [15; 16; 17]). The second stream explores SSM in creating an information strategy in an organisation (e.g. [5]). The work in both stream faces the problems of making links between SSM's models and the data-oriented considerations or information systems models (hereafter called information models for short). The issues and problems related to linking SSM to ISD are highlighted and discussed in numerous publications, from both methodological and technical viewpoints. Detailed discussions can be found in e.g. [18], [19], [20] and [21].

This research has observed that none among the current approaches has provided a model combining SSM's and IS models which has a uniform formalised representation. For a review of these approaches see e.g. [20]. In fact, the issue of uniform and formalised representation of the combined model has not been addressed by most of the approaches. In [22], a method for representing SSM conceptual models using Prolog is described. However, this method does not address the general issue of the representation of the knowledge captured by soft system analysis. Specifically, the knowledge captured by the rich picture is not included in the final Gregory and Merali's model. In other approaches, such as [15], [17], [2], it is not unusual for combined models to be represented using several languages. These approaches just provide frameworks in which different (sub-)models are conceptually combined/linked, but the original languages of the constituting sub-models are still utilised as such. This results in the following drawbacks: (a) the links between the constituting models are not explicitly present in the final model, though they may be stored in the modeller's head or documented in an informal format; (b) the resultant models, or the knowledge captured by the modelling, are difficult to manage. Because the models are represented in different formats, which may be both formal and informal, there is no formalised way to impose and check the model in terms of its consistency and (meta-)data redundancy over the entire model; (c) modelling activities are difficult to support by a software tool.

These drawbacks may be overcome with a uniform and formalised representation of the combined model, provided that such a representation is capable of representing aspects captured by soft systems and information models as well as links between the aspects. In addition, the representation formalism used should not impose any extra structure on the soft systems modelling in order to foster the exploratory nature of soft systems enquiry. The SSM incremental modelling process should also be supported when using the formalism.

In the next section, an approach that implements these ideas using the conceptual modelling language Telos [23] is presented.

3.   An Approach Based on Meta Modelling

3.1   Meta modelling

Meta modelling is an activity of building a model of a model [23; 24; 25]. It allows one to specify the semantics of, and structural relationships between, the modelling concepts of a model. The resultant meta model can then be exploited as a modelling language to represent the real world abstracted using the model.

A meta model allows modelling languages to be specified in a meta modelling language, which facilitates the interoperability and communication among the constituting models [10; 25; 8]. On the basis of a meta model, a CASE tool can be built to support modelling activities, maintaining the consistency and integrity constraints of the overall model.

In order to achieve a uniform and formalised representation of the SSM models and information models we have utilised meta modelling techniques. Our approach is to represent the set of modelling concepts of both SSM and information models along with their relationships using a meta modelling language. This language should meet the requirements indicated in the previous section. It is worth noting that the application of the meta modelling techniques is not straightforward because there is no universal meta modelling language. Most of existing meta modelling languages have been developed to support a pre-determined set of models, modelling formal and structured knowledge [25; 10]. The language to implement our approach needs to be capable of representing both formal and informal knowledge and supporting incremental modelling.

3.2 The Conceptual Modelling Language Telos and the Concept Base System

Several languages have features that satisfy the indicated requirements, such as OMEGA [26], CLASSIC [27], and Telos [23]. In comparison to OMEGA and CLASSIC, Telos is a conceptual modelling language that is specifically designed to represent the knowledge of categories that pertain to information systems development (for more details see [23]).

Telos is capable of representing informal knowledge that is represented in the natural language, as in soft systems models, because it implements the *semantic network* knowledge representation scheme (see e.g. [28]). Besides, being an *object-centred* knowledge representation language (see e.g. [29]), Telos supports various formal abstraction mechanisms such as *classification, generalisation-specialisation* and *aggregation* [30]. A *typed first order assertion sublanguage* is offered in Telos as a means of specifying *integrity constraints* and *deductive rules*.

The other reason for choosing Telos is that it is fully implemented in the ConceptBase system [31; 25]. ConceptBase is a deductive object base manager with a graphical user interface that allows Telos objects to be created, stored, retrieved, visualised and queried in both textual and graphical formats.

3.3 Specification of Modelling Languages as Meta Models in Telos

A meta model of modelling languages can be constructed using the primitive objects of the Telos kernel object model [25]. This kernel model can be extended with objects that define new modelling constructs. Structural and semantic constraints among the constructs are specified as Telos objects, assertions and abstraction mechanisms. The resultant meta model's collection of objects can then be employed as a modelling language to represent application domain models.

Given the expressive power of Telos, it can be used to build a meta model that is a modelling language that unifies SSM's models and information models.

4. An Exemplary Application

In this section, an exemplary application is presented in order to show the operationalisation of the proposed approach. In other words, the example demonstrates the use of Telos to build a meta model of a model that combines SSM models and information models. The meta model is then used as a unifying modelling language for modelling a problem domain, resulting in a model with uniform and formalised representation.

The SCORE model [32] is chosen for the purpose. However, it is worth noting that the presented method of building meta models is equally applicable to other models that combine SSM and information models.

4.1   A Bird's Eye View of the SCORE Model

The SCORE model is designed with an aim to capture both human activity and information related aspects of an office environment in an integrated manner. In the model, an office environment is conceived as a problem situation with relevant human activities, and is modelled with soft systems. Resultant soft systems models are then enriched with events, entities, rules and constraints that are involved in the relevant activities. The constructs of event, entity, rule and constraint are deliberately chosen to capture the dynamic, structural and declarative knowledge of a problem domain respectively. These are principal bodies of knowledge required to be captured by an information model [2; 10; 8; 9]. Thus, the SCORE model represents the models that attempt to combine soft systems model and models of information modelling.

4.2   A Meta Model of the SCORE Model

A meta model of the SCORE model has been built using Telos and fully described in [32]. The meta model defines all the modelling constructs of the SCORE model (namely, *rich picture, human activity system, conceptual model, entity, event, entity life cycle, rule and constraint*) and the links between the constructs in the form of *Telos object specifications*.

The meta model's specifications capture explicitly the semantics of the SCORE modelling constructs, which are of both soft systems and information modelling. This is illustrated by the object specification of the construct of *conceptual model* of a human activity system and the object specification of the construct of *entity life cycle*.

The specification of the object ConceptualModels (Figure 1) indicates that a conceptual model is built based on a root definition (see the attribute

```
Individual ConceptualModels in ScoreObjects,MetaClass,Class isA SSMConstructs with
   attribute,necessary,single
      systemDefinition : RootDefinitions
   attribute,necessary
      subActivity : HumanActivitySystems;
      logicalLink : Links
   attribute
      monitorAndControl : HumanActivitySystems
   attribute,constraint
      containsTwoDifferentSubActivities : $ forall m/ConceptualModels
a1/HumanActivitySystems (m subActivity a1) ==> exists a2/HumanActivitySystems ((m
subActivity a2) and not (a1==a2)) $
end
```

Figure 1: The specification of the *conceptual model* construct `systemDefinition`) and is composed of sub-activities linked by logical links (see the attributes `subActivity` and `logicalLink`). Moreover, the specification requires that at least two sub-activities must be specified in a conceptual model (see the constraint `containsTwoDifferentSubActivities`).

In comparison with the specification of the construct of conceptual model, the

```
Individual EntityLifeCycles in ScoreObjects,MetaClass,Class with
  attribute,necessary
      consistOf : ELC_elements
  attribute,constraint
      noCrossLink_in_a_lifecycle : $forall e/ELC_elements sq1,sq2/Sequences
it1,it2/Iterations sl1,sl2/Selections not(exists elc1/EntityLifeCycles (elc1
consistOf e) and ((elc1 consistOf sq1) and (elc1 consistOf it1) and (sq1 seq e)
and (it1 iter e)) or ((elc1 consistOf sq1) and (elc1 consistOf sl1) and (sq1 seq
e) and (sl1 sel e))   or ((elc1 consistOf it1) and (elc1 consistOf sl1) and (it1
iter e) and (sl1 sel e)) or ((elc1 consistOf sq1) and (elc1 consistOf sq2) and
(sq1 seq e) and not(sq2==sq1)) or ((elc1 consistOf it1) and (elc1
consistOf it2) and (it1 iter e) and (it2 iter e) and not(it2==it1)) or ((elc1
consistOf sl1) and (elc1 consistOf sl2) and (sl1 sel e) and (sl2 sel e) and
not(sl2==sl1)))$
end
Individual ELC_elements in ScoreObjects,MetaClass,Class
end
Individual Events in ScoreObjects,MetaClass,Class isA ELC_elements with
  attribute
      underlyingActivity : HumanActivitySystems;
      precondition : Proposition;
      participatingEntity : Entities;
      effect : Proposition
end
Individual NullEvents in ScoreObjects,MetaClass,Class isA Events,ELC_elements
end
Individual Sequences in ScoreObjects,MetaClass,Class isA ELC_elements with
  attribute,necessary
      seq : ELC_elements
  attribute
      timeOrder : TemporalLinks
  attribute,constraint
      containsTwoDifferentElements : $ forall s/Sequences e1/ELC_elements (s seq
e1) ==> exists e2/ELC_elements ((s seq e2) and not (e1==e2)) $;
      needsTimeOrder : $ forall s/Sequences e/ELC_elements (s seq e) ==> exists
l/TemporalLinks (s timeOrder l) $
end
Individual TemporalLinks in ScoreObjects,MetaClass,Class isA Links with
  attribute,necessary,single
      followedBy : ELC_elements;
      precededBy : ELC_elements
  attribute,constraint
      needsTwoDifferentElements : $ forall l/TemporalLinks e1,e2/ELC_elements ((l
followedBy e1) and (l precededBy e2)) ==> not(e1==e2) $
end
Individual Iterations in ScoreObjects,MetaClass,Class isA ELC_elements with
  attribute
      condition : Proposition
  attribute,necessary,single
      iter : ELC_elements
end
Individual Selections in ScoreObjects,MetaClass,Class isA ELC_elements with
  attribute
      condition : Proposition
  attribute,necessary
      sel : ELC_elements
  attribute,constraint
      atLeastTwoChoices : $  forall s/Selections e1/ELC_elements (s sel e1) ==>
exists e2/ELC_elements ((s sel e2) and not (e1==e2)) $
  end
```

Figure 2: Telos objects necessary for representing the *entity life cycle* construct

specification of the construct of entity life cycle is more complex (see Figure 2). In the SCORE model, the entity life cycle is represented using the *program structure diagram* [33]. The specification is composed of a collection of related objects, namely, `EntityLifeCycles`, `ELC_elements`, `Events`, `NullEvents`, `Sequences`, `Iterations`, `Selections` and `TemporalLinks`. The specifications of these objects embrace not only three basic control flow structures (i.e. *sequence*, *selection* and *iteration*) and temporal order of events of an entity life cycle, but also commandments that must be conformed when constructing an entity life cycle. For instance, the commandment that cross-links are not allowed in an entity life cycle's tree [33] is captured the constraint `noCrossLink_in_a_lifecycle` in the specification of `EntityLifeCycles`.

In addition to the semantics of individual modelling constructs, links between the constructs are explicitly embedded in the meta model. These links are (meta) modelled in several ways: (a) by using attributes in specifications of modelling constructs, for example, the specification of the construct HumanActivitySystems includes the attributes involvedEntity, involedEvent and governedBy, which indicate what entities, events, rules and constraints are involved in an activity; (b) by defining aggregate objects, for example EntityLifeCycles and RichPictures; (c) by defining special objects to represent particular types of relationships between modelling constructs. For example, the constructs Links, Boundaries, BinaryLinks and DirectedLinks are useful for representing lines/arcs, circles, and arrows between elements of soft systems rich pictures and conceptual models, as well as for representing specific relationships between arbitrary objects of a problem domain.

From the specification of the construct `HumanActivitySystems` given in Figure 3, it can also be seen that the meta model captures not only links that relate constructs belonging to an individual model (e.g. the *relevance* of a human activity to a *problem situation* and a *conceptual model* in a soft systems model). However, it also captures cross-model links that connect soft systems and information modelling constructs (e.g. the *involvement* of an *entity* in the execution of a *human activity*).

```
Individual HumanActivitySystems in ScoreObjects,MetaClass,Class isA SSMConstructs with
    attribute
        involvedEntity : Entities;
        involvedEvent : Events;
        governedBy : RulesConstraints;
        relevantTo : ProblemSituations;
        hasRD : RootDefinitions;
        hasCM : ConceptualModels
    end
```

Figure 3: The specification of the *human activity system* construct

Furthermore, because Telos allows the meta-model to be adjusted and extended, new objects can be defined to meet specific modelling requirements, particularly to represent the knowledge that is not amenable to the pre-defined set of modelling constructs. This feature is useful, given the fact that the knowledge learned from a soft systems analysis is usually more than that is scripted using rich pictures, root definitions, conceptual models. In addition, using the ConceptBase system, the model's consistency and integrity are easier to maintain. That is, in a ConceptBase object base, deductive rules and integrity constraints defined in objects' specifications are automatically checked when a new object is added to the object base. Thus this supports soft systems incremental modelling.

Once the meta model has been built, the modeller can employ the collection of the meta model's objects as a unified modelling language to model problem domains.

5. The Use and Benefits of the Meta Model

The goal of building the meta model is to use it as a unifying modelling language to model a problem domain, which is abstracted with a combined set of SSM and information models' constructs.

Continuing the SCORE model example, the use and benefits of the proposed approach can be shown. In a case study, the SCORE meta model is utilised to model the problem domain of the admission of students for university courses (for more details of this case study see [32]). The Telos objects that represent the SCORE meta model and the resultant model of the university admission can be seen as a hierarchy (see Figure 4). Figure 4 illustrates the Telos feature that there is no limitation of the classification/instantiation hierarchy, i.e. classes can belong to other (*meta-*) classes which can also belong to other (*metameta-*) classes. It is this feature that imposes the problem domain model to inherit the semantic and structural properties of the modelling language defined by the meta model.

To build a model of a problem domain, the objects of the meta model (e.g. `HumanActivitySystems`, `Entities`), which are metaclasses, are instantiated with objects to represent the problem domain's concepts (e.g. `Applicants` and `Courses`). The resultant objects are simpleclasses that contain only tokens as their instances. Tokens are objects that have no instances. Tokens are employed to represent concrete objects of a problem domain, e.g. the applicant `John` and the course `B.Sc. Computing`, which are

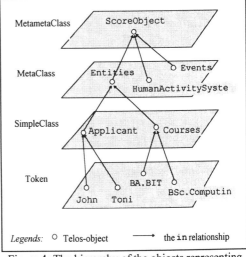

Figure 4: The hierarchy of the objects representing the SCORE model

abstracted using the problem domain's concepts (viz. `Applicants` and `Courses` in this example, see Figure 4). Altogether, the SCORE meta model (i.e. the unified modelling language), the problem domain model (i.e. the abstraction of problem domains in terms of concepts) and the concrete data of problem domains are uniformly represented as Telos objects.

The uniform and formalised representation of the meta model and the problem domain model as Telos objects, which can be stored in the ConceptBase system, enables the modeller to manage the knowledge captured by the model. A model's objects can be retrieved not only in the textual format of Telos object specifications but also in graphical format (see [31] and [32] for details).

Using the described method, the linkage between SSM's and information models becomes seamless because their links have been incorporated in the meta model, whose objects are subsequently instantiated to model problem domains. The explicit capture of links in the model is seen by the fact that questions (about the knowledge captured by the model) like the ones listed below can be answered, getting data from the problem domain's model object base.

- Which entities share a given event?
- Which human activity systems share a given event?
- Which events happen in the performance of a given human activity system?
- Which entities are involved in the performance of a given human activity system?
- In which human activity systems does a given entity participate?
- Which rules and constraints govern the performance of a given human activity system?

Answers to these questions can be automatically obtained using Telos query classes and the *Display Queries* tool of ConceptBase. Figure 5 on the following page illustrates the use of a query to retrieve the events, which are modelled and stored in the ConceptBase knowledge base, involved in the human activity `Handle_applicants_enquiries`.

6. Summary and Discussions

In this paper we have proposed an approach for unifying SSM's models and information systems models. The approach is based on the idea that the linking of SSM's and information models can be enhanced by the explicit capture of the links by a final model that has a uniform formalised representation. The idea is implemented using meta modelling techniques and the conceptual modelling language Telos.

In comparison to other approaches that attempt to link soft systems and information modelling, our approach has several advantageous features. First, it is capable of uniformly representing the knowledge gained from the soft systems analysis as well

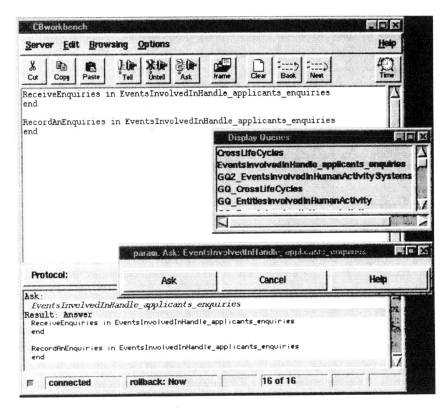

Figure 5: An example of a query class and its returned objects

as the knowledge captured by information modelling concepts. Second, the approach does not reduce SSM into a reductionist method. But it supports the soft systems model's extendibility and SSM incremental learning. Finally, the representation of the unified model is formal in the form of Telos objects, resulting in a model that can be maintained and exploited using a knowledge base management system (viz. ConceptBase). Having these features, the proposed approach has thus overcome the drawbacks highlighted in the second section of this paper.

Referring to the 'grafting' and 'embedding' taxonomy [19], the meta modelling approach belongs to neither of the classes of approaches. This is because our approach does not address the issues of linking SSM models with an information modelling approach or design method *at the conceptual level*. The meta modelling approach deals only with the *representation* of models that combine SSM and information models. It takes a combined model as given and provides a method to produce a unifying modelling language derived from the given combined model. Thus the method to generate a unifying modelling language of a combined model is applicable to models of both 'grafting' and 'embedding' approaches.

In terms of the links between SSM and information models, the method outlined in the paper deals with the representation of only those links between SSM's and information models that have been purposively established by the modeller at the conceptual level. As such, the meta modelling method proposed by this approach may be utilised as a complementary component to achieve a uniform formalised representation of models combining SSM's and information models at the conceptual level proposed by other approaches such as Multiview and Savage and Mingers' [17].

Finally, because the use of the unifying language of a combined model requires the knowledge about Telos and the supporting software tool, it might be difficult for the modeller to use the language in lieu of the SSM conventional modelling language. However, the unifying language may be used to create a model's objects repository. The model stored in the repository can subsequently be exploited using the software tool for the analysis and reference purposes.

References

1. Checkland PB. Soft Systems Methodology and its relevance to the development of information systems. In: [3], pp 1-17
2. Avison DE, Wood-Harper AT. Multiview: an exploration in information systems development. Blackwell, Oxford, 1990
3. Stowell F (ed). Information systems provision - the contribution of Soft Systems Methodology. McGraw-Hill, London, 1995
4. Checkland PB. Systems thinking, systems practice. John Wiley & Sons, Chichester, 1981
5. Galliers R. Soft systems, scenarios, and the planning and development of information systems. Systemist 1992; 14:146-159
6. Stowell F, West D. Client-led design, a systemic approach to information systems definition. McGraw-Hill, London, 1994
7. Jayaratna N. Understanding and Evaluating Methodologies, NIMSAD: A Systemic Framework. McGraw-Hill, Maidenhead, 1994
8. Avison DE, Fitzgerald G. Information Systems Development: Methodologies, Techniques and Tools, Second edition. McGrawHill, London, 1995
9. Flynn DJ, Diaz OF. Information Modelling, an international perspective. Prentice-Hall, London, 1996
10. Loucopoulos P, Zicari R (eds). Conceptual modeling, Databases and CASE: an integrated view of information systems development. John Wiley & Sons, New York, 1992
11. Checkland PB, Griffin R. Management information systems: a systems view. Journal of Systems Engineering 1970; 1:29-42
12. Stowell F (ed). Systemist, Special Edition on Information Systems, Volume 14, Issue 3. Word Publications, 1992
13. Avison DE, Fitzgerald G (eds). Journal of Information Systems, Volume 3, Issue 3. Blackwell, Oxford, 1993
14. Jayaratna N, Fitzgerald B (eds). Proceedings of the 4th Conference of the British Computer Society Information Systems Methodologies Specialist Group, September 1996, Cork, Ireland, 1996
15. CCTA (Central Computer and Telecommunication Agency). SSADM Version 4 Reference Manual: Feasibility - Soft Systems Methodology. CCTA, Norwich, 1991

16. Prior R. Deriving data flow diagrams from a "soft systems" conceptual model. Systemist 1990; 12:65-75
17. Savage A, Mingers J. A framework for linking Soft Systems Methodology (SSM) and Jackson System Development (JSD). Information Systems Journal 1996; 6:109-129
18. Checkland PB. SSM in information systems design: history and some current issues. Systemist 1992; 14: 90-92
19. Miles RK. Combining "soft" and "hard" systems practice: grafting or embedding? Journal of Applied Systems Analysis 1988; 15:55-60
20. Mingers J. Using Soft Systems Methodology in the design of Information Systems. In: [3], pp18-46
21. Checkland PB, Howell S. Information, systems and information systems: Making sense of the field. John Wiley & Sons, Chichester, 1998
22. Gregory F, Merali Y. Inductions, modality and conceptual modelling. Warwick Business School Research Bureau Research Paper 79. Warwick University, 1993
23. Mylopoulos J, Borgida A, Jarke M, Koubarakis M. Telos: a language for representing knowledge about information systems. ACM Transactions on Information Systems 1990; 8:325-362
24. Kottemann JE, Konsynski BR. Dynamic metasystems for information systems development. In: Proceedings of the 5th International Conference on Information Systems, Tucon, Arizona, 1984, pp 187-204
25. Jeusfeld MA, Jarke M, Nissen HW, Staudt M. ConceptBase: Managing Conceptual Models about Information Systems. In: Bernus P, Mertins K, Schmidt G (eds) Handbook on Architectures of Information Systems. Springer-Verlag, Berlin, 1998 (in press)
26. Attardi G, Simi M. Consistency and Completeness of Omega, a Logic for knowledge representation. In: Proceedings of the 7th IJCAI Conference, Vancouver, 1981, pp 504-510
27. Brachman RJ, Borgida A, McGuinness DL, Patel-Schneider PF, Resnick LA. The CLASSIC Knowledge Representation System, or, KL-ONE: The next generation. In: Proceedings of the International Conference on Fifth Generation Computer Systems, Tokyo, 1992, pp 1036-1043
28. Minsky M (ed). Semantic Information Processing. MIT Press, Cambridge, MA, 1968
29. Nilsson NJ. Principles of artificial intelligence. Springer-Verlag, Berlin, 1982
30. Brodie ML, Mylopoulos J, Schmidt JW (eds). On conceptual modelling: Perspectives from Artificial Intelligence, Databases, and Programming Languages. Springer Verlag, New York, 1984
31. Jarke M (ed). ConceptBase V4.1 User Manual. RWTH Aachen, Aachen, Germany, 1995
32. Dang QC. A soft-systems-conceived model with knowledge representation for information systems in the office environment. PhD thesis, South Bank University, London, 1997
33. Jackson MA. Systems Development. Prentice Hall, Hemel Hempstead, 1983

A Methodology and Maturity Critique of an Intranet Development

David W Wilson
Birkbeck College
Camelot Lecturer in MIS
Department of Computing Science
University of London
Malet Street WC1E 7HX
London
United Kingdom
dave@dcs.bbk.ac.uk

Abstract

This paper describes the development of a small intranet which is a major communications facility of the Information Systems and Management Honours programme at Birkbeck College.

The development is critiqued in the light of a well known framework for Computer Supported Co-operative Working and various well known methodological frameworks of Information Systems Development. Whilst those frameworks throw some light on the practice there are other questions which reflective practice throws up and these are also surfaced.

This paper reviews the development of the intranet site used to communicate to students seeking the BSc (Hons) in Information Systems & Management (IS & M) award at Birkbeck College, University of London. The development is critiqued in the light of a number of Information Systems Development Methodologies and Maturity Models of Information Systems Development.

Keywords: Information Systems Development Methodologies, intranets, web-based development

1.   The Development

The BSc IS & M is a double honours Degree awarded jointly by the Department of Computer Science with the Department of Management. The initial impetus for the development was an urgent need to review and publish the "Options Booklet".

Students entering the third year of the course require the information in this booklet on completion of the second year in order to support their selection of optional courses. Students are credited in the award with no fewer than four options. They may select those from an approved set detailed and described in the booklets provided by the Departments of Management and Computing Science. Alternatively they may request the Course Director to be allowed take any one other course from the undergraduate offerings of the college.

Previously, a paper booklet had been produced for the Computer Science offerings to the IS & M Course. However, in 1997 the Management Department, who provide approximately 50% of the course had produced a Booklet covering all the course units which they offered. It would be complicated for students to use that booklet as many of the courses have been developed for particular Courses and others require pre-requisites. It was thought there should be a web page through which students could navigate to descriptions of each of the options suitable for students on the Course. This page should have a form which ideally students could submit electronically.

On reflection, it soon became apparent that there should be two such pages, one for each of the third and fourth years. Optional courses which clashed with core courses for a particular year would not be shown on that year's page making it easy for the students to make appropriate selections. Since the students would require navigating to the appropriate page the merit of a Course Home Page became apparent and it was decided that Bulletin Boards for each cohort should also be set up.

The Site structure is show at Figure 1.

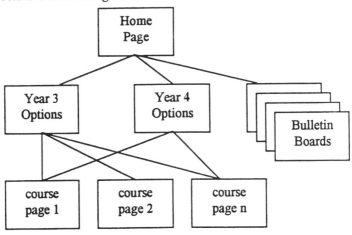

Figure 1. Structure of the intranet site. Note course 2 clashes with a Year 4 core course and so there is no link from the Year 4 options page to the course 2 course page

It was not intended that the site should be in the public domain but no security was set up on the site initially. Care had to be taken that the information on the intranet site did not conflict with the Course Home page on the Department of Computer Science's internet site.

There were protracted discussions with the Department's Systems Manager who had responsibility for maintaining the Course's Home Page on the internet site. Since there was a duplication of information between Course's the internet site and the Course's intranet site. The Courses internet Home Page is primarily aimed as a shop window for prospective candidates to the Course. The Course intranet site is primarily for students already on the Course. The Systems Manager seemed to have difficulty appreciating this difference and pressed strongly for responsibility for the internet Home page to become the responsibility of the Course Director.

1.1 Sources informing the development

1.1.1 Synchronicity, Proximity and the environmental issue

From the outset it was clear that the aim of the development was to enable asynchronous and "a-proximous" communication between the Course Director and specific groups of students. Figure 2 shows an adaptation for Course delivery of DeSanctis and Gallupe's (1985) taxonomy of communication, their original intention being to inform the development of Group Decision Support Systems.

	Same Time (synchronous)	Different Time (asynchronous)
Same place (proximous)	Lectures Seminars	Pigeon Holes Notice Boards
Different Place ("a-proximous")	Telephone tutoring Teleconferencing	Web based course notes Bulletin Boards

Figure 2. Various means of communication between faculty and students.

The choice of a-proximous, asynchronous communication was guided by the nature of the Students. Birkbeck's historic mission is to provide opportunities for people in work, who for some reason or another have missed traditional opportunities to obtain recognised qualifications, particularly degrees. Since many of the students on the course have access to the world wide web from work it was expected that they would view the Course intranet from work. Analysis of hits has shown that many hits are made during lunch breaks and from employer's sites but similar numbers come from college terminal rooms and there are a number of hits from the curious, some interestingly from institutes of education. The "a-proximous" need is clearly being met. The asynchronous choice is not so clear cut. The real need is for "nearly synchronous" rather than asynchronous. It is desirable that students should be informed of developments concerning the course such as Exam Timetables and lecture room changes as soon as possible but not so urgently as to interupt their work.

Whilst the considerations of synchronicity and proximity are important the real benefit is in the saving of paper and paperwork. Much of the information on the site arrives with the Course Director in electronic ascii form and can usually be easily placed onto web pages. Both the Course Director and the Course Secretary have taken the trouble to develop HTML skills but so far most of the posting has been done by the Course Director.

1.1   Maturity in Information Systems Development

Figure 3 assess the development against the Summa Maturity Model of Information Systems development (Wilson,1997). This model normally examines an organisation's IS development practice through a number of dimensions. However, it is instructive to view this single development through the model. The **Scope** of the problems in this case was solely the communication between Course administration and the student. A sound technological infrastructure was already in place. Computer technicians in the Department of Computer Science and the College provided a technical environment which required very little enhancement to establish Course Administration to Student communication via the internet. Communication in the other direction is problematic. Whilst the options form can be easily transmitted to the college through a program which has been specially written, problems that students might send large numbers of forms have caused the Course management to consider that a paper based form is preferable until some experience is gained with less critical feedback. Despite the limited scope of the project the third box for scope is shaded in Figure 3. There was an analysis of the needs prior to implementation and the design reflected the user's desire that the site should be future proof.

There was a high degree of **User involvement** in that the Course Director was the user and the developer. Frequent feedback was sought from the students who pointed out some unnecessary complication in the early structure. The developer has been involved in many projects, mostly using **Methodologies** such as or similar to, SSADM (Ashworth, 1989; Avisson & Fitzgerald, 1988). Clearly a Methodology designed for large transaction processing systems would be inappropriate. The areas of insight brought from this methodological discourse for the intranet project were the need to preserve archives and lay down back-up. The concept of developing a flexible future compatible structure is largely attributed to previous immersion in this discourse. The underlying principles of DSDM (1995), however, proved the most useful guide. There were frequent jumps forward in development in the manner described by Gilb (1988). This meant that before commitment to a particular kind of complex page attempts were made to mount and test the "fiddly bits" first so that time wasn't wasted developing things which could not be completed.

The degree of **Automation** in the practice is assessed as being fairly high. In the early days most of the pages were hand-crafted in HTML and Perl. However, these were mounted in a ready environment provided by the Department of Computer Science. Latterly, much use has been made of pages generated from the Office Suite favoured by the department. To facilitate the ease of maintenance the Course Secretary has recently taken a short course on Web Technology and it is hoped that this will lead to removing much of the maintenance of the site from the Course Director.

Another dimension of the model is the concern of the practitioners for **Measuring** the quality and effectiveness of their work. No attempt has been made to measure the time, effort or skill development which has gone into the development of the site. Because the technology was developing rapidly time was spent in gaining basic skills. Many of these skills have been made redundant by tools now on the market. Collecting data on these developments therefore would also have been a redundant exercise. The null position is therfore appropriate for this dimension in relation to this project. Points on the dimensions are shown in figure 3. which is presented in the sequence in which the dimensions have been found to be most useful (Wilson, 1996)

Dimension	Stage 1	Stage 2	Stage 3	Stage 4
Scope Life Cycle	-a piece-meal contingency approach -focus mainly on Implementation -Problems likely to be carried forward	-implications of designed change catered for -most attention paid to Design and Implementation	focus mainly on Analysis, Design and Implementation	activity flows from a process of strategic planning
Scope System Boundary	solutions usually contained in one Department or Organisation	solutions frequently cross Departmental boundaries but never organisational boundaries	solutions frequently cross organisational boundaries	
User involvement	developer dominates the design process	user involvement tacit	mechanisms for involving the user frequently invoked	mechanisms for involving the user always invoked

Methodology sequence	stages visited sequentially in a single pass	stages visited sequentially with some backward iterations	stages visited sequentially with jumps forward	situation apparently chaotic with iterations forward and backwards
Methodology paradigm diversity	single paradigm dominates all phases	each phase dominated by a particular paradigm	multiple paradigms used and reconciled in some phases	multiple paradigms used and reconciled in all phases
Automation	no automation other than compilers	Word Processors, Drawing tools used in a disintegrated manner	toolset integrated for development	toolset integrated with the operational databases, communications processors etc.
Metrics and Quality Control	quality control procedures in place	metrics collected	management use made of metrics	an approval scheme in place

Figure 3 - The SUMMA Maturity Model shaded to show where the activity of the project would be placed.

52

References

Ashworth C & Goodland M,1989.*SSADM: A Practical Approach*. McGraw -Hill.

Avison D. E. and Fitzgerald G., 1988.*Information Systems Development; Methodologies, Techniques and Tools*. Blackwell Scientific Publications. Oxford.

DeSanctis, G., & Gallupe, B. 1985. *Group decision support systems: A new frontier*. Data Base, 16(1), 3-10.

DSDM Consortium, 1995. *Dynamic Systems Development Method,* Tesseract Publishing, Kingsnorth, Ashford, Kent.

Gilb T, 1988. *Principles of Software Engineering Management*. Addison-Wesley

Wilson D. W. 1997. *SUMMA : A New Maturity Model of Information Systems Development*. Business Information Technology Conference. Manchester Metropolitan University. November.

---

[i] The terms "course" and "course" is used in the College to mean an Award consisting of a number of courses. In order to avoid confusion, in this paper where the term course is used to mean a prolonged course of study leading to a degree award the word is used capitalised e.g. "Course". Where it is used to mean the teaching which takes place on a particular subject, normally for a period of 13 weeks in two terms, contributing only in part to an Award the term is used without capitals e.g. course.

A New Methodology for New Systems Technology: How Lotus' Accelerated Value Method is Addressing Groupware Systems Development

Susan Trost
Computer Applications
Montgomery College
Rockville Campus, USA
strost@mc.cc.md.us

A. Abu-Samaha
ISRC
The University of Salford
Salford, UK
a.m.abu-samahia@cms.salford.ac.uk

Abstract

This paper explores the fundamentals of Lotus Consulting's Accelerated Value Method (AVM) a groupware systems methodology released in 1995. Each of the five modules; Process Innovation, Collaborative Development, Enterprise Deployment, Transformation Management and Engagement Management are described in a context highlighting the unique aspects of groupware systems development. The authors provide a critical account of the framework showing its weakness as well as its strength.

1. Introduction

Developed by Lotus Consulting for four years before its release in 1995, the Accelerated Value Method (AVM) enables a flexible framework for designing and redesigning business processes and implementing results oriented systems. AVM focuses on the unique issues associated with a rapid development collaborative computing environment. Formal training in this methodology consisting of five modules is in an instructor led workshop environment. Training tools used include case study analysis, role play, practical individual and group learning exercises, use of management tools, and integration of teams, tasks, and technology.

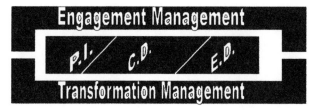

Figure (1) The AVM Framework

Every methodology has its own unique qualities and AVM is no exception. In comparison to other formal systems development methodologies AVM focuses as much, if not more, on people and their human relationships than on the technology of delivering collaborative systems. A set of collaborative computing best practices has evolved through the years and AVM captures and documents those found in organisations where collaborative systems implementation have been successful. AVM is a proprietary methodology developed by Lotus Consulting primarily for assisting in delivering successful systems based on Lotus groupware products which result in increased sales, support and services revenue. As such, a heavy emphasis is placed on picking and delivering applications can be developed and implemented quickly. Resulting benefits can be promoted within an organisation to spawn further application development. Henry Blum and Salloway (1992) has identified early success and momentum as a critical element to widespread success of implementing groupware systems on an enterprise or extended enterprise level [7]. Finally, AVM addresses management of organisational change necessary for successful system implementation as an important module of the framework. These characteristics are in addition to the standard framework found in many other methodologies that support services from identifying opportunities to system delivery and maintenance.

2.0 Why AVM?

Why do groupware systems merit a specialised methodology? In the past, organisations tended to be hierarchical, used linear processes, had clear departmental boundaries, were internally focused and individuals were concerned with their own productivity. Systems were designed with these characteristics in mind and, in general, the life expectancy of systems was longer. Today, many companies and industries have experienced a radical shift to flexibility and in order to be flexible as an organisation, flexible systems have to be in place. New challenges are created by customer demands, competitive pressure, and changing markets. Companies are being forced to be flexible in order to stay in business. The ability to innovate and respond quickly to opportunities and changes in the environment, to reduce time to market, to improve customer service, and to enhance the quality of products is more important [2]. In organisations that are successfully managing this rate of change we see cross-functional work-groups, customer driven products and services, empowered workers who can enable responsiveness and individuals at all levels of a shrinking hierarchy all working toward the same goals.

Lotus is known for its innovation in collaborative computing technology in the form of its Lotus Notes and Lotus Domino products. AVM as a methodology has a certain instant measure of credibility based on the merits that Lotus Consulting had access to the Notes installed client base on a global scale and the Lotus Consulting Group could exploit the knowledge of the developers of the Notes core product group. However, few people within Lotus, and the parent IBM Corporation who purchased Lotus in a hostile turned friendly take-over in 1995, can use or discuss AVM in detail. The authors suspect part of the reason for this is that Lotus Consulting is a small division of Lotus whereas IBM's consulting services divisions form a larger part of its business and IBM views AVM as a methodology best kept proprietary and used only by its own consultants or replaced by its other broader scooped methodologies.

The general philosophy behind AVM is that consultants have a responsibility to ensure companies are improving their business practices as they implement collaborative computing technologies and to accomplish this a holistic approach is necessary. Since many people are likely to be effected by change they should be involved in the process. To help ensure full participation, AVM recommends project teams include representatives from all parts of the organisation that will be affected. Further, as organisations learn how to work in this new flexible and collaborative environment their system requirements will, and are expected to, change. This is quite different from Andersen Consulting's Method/1 or other standard approaches where requirements are agreed and the system developed and many changes are handled post implementation. A real key here is to successfully manage these changing requirements so that companies can have changes implemented 'on the fly' but not to point where the implementation goals of the system are compromised. AVM uses the concept of Value Frames to manage change and minimise risk by delivering value in modular, iterative, discrete, time-bounded cycles. By using Value Frames, people, processes, and technology can evolve together.

3.0 AVM's Structure

As mentioned previously, AVM is comprised of five integrated components which together form a structured framework for designing and developing groupware systems. The five components are:

- Process Innovation
- Collaborative Development
- Enterprise Deployment
- Transformation Management
- Engagement Management

3.1 Process Innovation

Process Innovation focuses on business processes and redefining and redesigning them. Davenport, (1992) discusses this concept thoroughly in his book *Process Innovation: Reengineering Work Through Information Technology*. A comprehensive understanding of business strategies and the competitive environment drives process innovation objectives while knowledge of enabling technology stimulates and facilitates process redesign. Process Innovation can occur within or across an organisation and can be single function or cross-functional. Process Innovation can occur in an extended organisation breaking through traditional business boundaries.

Process Innovation is managed through facilitated workshops that involve project team members from both business and technical perspectives. A primary design consideration is enabling technology contrary to other traditional reengineering methodologies where enabling technology is handled later in the methodology - perhaps in the application design phase or as an implementation detail.

AVMs Process Innovation module defines the business process as the activities involved in accomplishing a defined business outcome. AVM also identifies attributes of business processes including:

- Has customers
- Generates a resulting product or service
- Has a strategic purpose
- Is event-driven
- Has an associated time element
- Has decision points
- Has associated performance measure associated with the process
- Crosses functional/organisational boundaries

AVM's Process Innovation module aims to set a business context and define value for the organisation. An existing process is assessed by taking a clear snapshot of the process by measuring costs, time, bottlenecks and developing a process map on paper. Once the existing process is assessed then priorities defined and steps for designing the new business process including setting benchmarks for measuring change improvement are undertaken. Benchmarks must be discrete. As an example, reducing work order processing from 12 to 4 days. Workshops to facilitate business process redesign are an AVM tool used to achieve a multitude of Process Innovation objectives including gaining consensus, fostering collaboration, promoting project ownership, and developing the foundation for Structure Iterative Prototyping.

AVM employs 10 basic principles of Process Innovation:

1. Focus on the customer of every process
2. Ensure all activities in a process add value
3. Design around desired results and outcomes, not tasks
4. Appoint team or person who is accountable for the process
5. Capture information one time only, as close to the source as possible
6. Build Error proofing into processes as part of the new design
7. Enable decision-making where the work is performed
8. Justify all checks, controls and reconciliation activities
9. Design processes for flexibility
10. Break down complex processes into a number of simpler processes

Creating an appropriate environment is crucial to the success of Process Innovation exercise. Participants should be in a frame of mind where they can think freely and look for ways to break rules like "work should be done in an office" or "learning should take place in a classroom." In AVM, periodic value assessments are used to keep the project moving forward and act as a guide to ensure participants stay focused on objectives.

Choosing the process to innovate is critical in groupware applications since quick success and benefit help perpetuate the growth of further groupware applications. Process Innovation relies on participation from an interdisciplinary team of key players and stakeholders early on. The team chooses the right process to improve with a groupware application and uses workshops and prototyping to validate any new process design.

> "Process is the most important element... (in Reengineering the corporation, and yet it) gives most corporate manager the greatest difficulty. Most business people are not process oriented: the are focused on tasks, on jobs, on people, on structures, but not on processes" [6].

The mix of this team will often determine the success or failure of a system. Diverse stakeholders may have inconsistent frames, which may lead to difficulties in implementing or using the technology [5]. When this occurs, some technologies may fail to achieve the intentions held by technology designers or management sponsors [10], as shown by a case study of one firm's adoption of the Lotus Notes groupware product [11]. AVM helps facilitate bringing the right stakeholders, key players and processes to innovate into the project but there is no guarantee that the team is comprised of the right mix.

3.2 Collaborative Development

Collaborative Development is the AVM module which delivers technology applications to support the new business processes derived from the Process

Innovation module. Development involves rapid, structured prototyping and is iterative in nature. Including structured iterations in the methodology helps ensure that new business requirements generated from the co-evolving people, processes and technology can be incorporated into the new application as it is developed.

The approach relies on collaboration, with users (who do not need to be competent with the technology up front) actively involved with designing their applications using business object modelling techniques.

> "Collaborative effort... is an active, explicit, joining of minds, people working together... (and) combining individual achievements into a sequence of actions that achieve a goal" [13].

Users design their application with coaching type help from consultants. By involving the users so closely, they can evolve to achieve a greater understanding of the underlying potential of new technology and consequently expand their business requirements to exploit the technology. One of the techniques used to help users understand business object modelling is to have them "wear their business object," for example, a sales order. The users are then asked "if you are a sales order, which processes do you affect and which ones affect you?" Another by-product of close user involvement during development includes smoother prototype reviews since users and developers are working from a shared framework and objectives for the project.

With users actually responsible for specifying their requirements, there is no need for outside requirements engineers. Macaulay (1995) illustrates problems requirements engineers and systems designers face when trying to understand users and their work intricacies when designing systems [9]. Rather than bringing outside designers into the user group, AVM focuses on the users learning to become designers.

Structured Iterative Prototyping enables rapid response to needs, increases business satisfaction, and helps gain user commitment since users can visually see their contributions in the prototypes. Again, Value Frames are used in Collaborative Development to reduce risk and keep the project on track. Business objectives in the Collaborative Development phase include:

- Proving the concept:
- Business
- Technical
- Organisational
- Accelerate the learning curve
- Deliver maximum business and technical value quickly
- Ensure smooth application deployment

The Collaborative Development Phase starts with application design workshops. During the initial design workshop the first Value Frame objectives will be agreed.

In addition, iteration cycle lengths are specified. During each iteration the following occurs as necessary:

- Design and build prototype
- Test prototype
- Update documentation & training materials
- Train users
- Conduct value assessment at the end of each iteration

After a number of iterations, the application will be ready to pilot. During pilot planning the following tasks are undertaken:

- Select the pilot group
- Plan the pilot
- Deploy/train work-groups using the application
- Solicit constructive feedback
- Conduct value assessment

When objectives are reached during the pilot phase then the application is taken into pre-production status. Bringing a pilot application to production ready is can be difficult and key success elements include agreeing change management processes, holding firm to application functionality enhancement freeze dates, planning to unit, system and acceptance testing and devoting at least one iteration to readiness including system clean-up, testing, and documentation.

> "Building a ground swell, through pilot projects in the field, with line operators as champions, simply turns out to be the most effective – and efficient – way to implement anything…. The best news of all is that this piloting / chunking / testing mind-set, far from creating expensive and time-consuming chaos, actually creates inexpensive order and powers the way to rapid success" [12].

3.3 Enterprise Deployment

AVM's Enterprise Deployment module creates a groupware environment infrastructure that is robust and scaleable and supports current and evolving business needs. Enterprise Deployment emphasises the "planning big and starting small." The Enterprise Deployment module is conducted in parallel with the iterative Process Innovation and Collaborative Development modules.

During Enterprise Deployment the following tasks are undertaken:

- Architecture design
- Network topology design

- Creating hardware standards
- Creating software standards
- Planning and testing pilot and production environments
- Defining ongoing support policies and procedures

By planning big and starting small, a project has more chance for success than an ad hoc implementation which usually falls over when the system infrastructure fails to support the project. By starting small, the concept of incremental function and value is introduced. Incremental deployment objectives are synchronised with development iterations. During deployment, the iterative approach is even applied to infrastructure testing. Applications usually are test piloted within work-groups first and then perhaps to a regional or national level and finally – enterprise wide or global.

Since Enterprise Deployment is a daunting module, at best, for organisations who are new to this type of system implementation, an online guidebook is part of the deliverable package developed for this module. The Guidebook contains architecture design information, network topology maps and configuration, systems assurance documentation, security guidelines, and application development standards. The Enterprise Deployment Guidebook can be customised for different organisation needs.

Operations and support issues are considered during the Enterprise Deployment module. Service level agreements, charge-back policies, skills and competency assessments, support procedures, training requirements, administrative costs, problem logging and resolution, and documentation requirements are some of the operations and support considerations addressed in this module.

3.4 Transformation Management

The AVM Transformation Management module creates strategies to support the implementation of behavioural and cultural changes required for a successful collaborative computing environment. Groupware environments can enable radical business transformation. Transformation can also be a shocking experience for any organisation and resistance to change is a normal human response, particularly when it affects the way people work and incompatible corporate culture exists.

> "One of the most fundamental assumptions made in planning any IT system(:)... if you build it, people will use it" [3].

Transformation Management plays a larger role in AVM than other standard systems development methodologies due the culture shock an organisation can experience when implementing groupware systems. For example, issues such as fear of sharing knowledge or learning to navigate online information sources are common in implementing groupware systems. In some cases, projects fail because resistance to change is underestimated. Workshops and interviews with key stakeholders are conducted during this module to help an organisation anticipate organisational and cultural issues and develop strategies and plans to manage changes associated with a collaborative computing environment. Resulting strategies for handling change fallout include designing new reward, compensation, and incentive programs that support desirable new behaviour within the organisation.

3.5 Engagement Management

The AVM Engagement Management module is conducted throughout the client relationship and usually spans multiple projects. The objective of Engagement Management is to ensure the overall success of a project, as measured by business results, through comprehensive project and risk management. Engagement Management couples traditional project management activities – work breakdown structures, resource management, and status reporting – with relationship management skills. With unique characteristics of heavy user involvement and the potential for a distributed user base and developer base - groupware systems project management can be even more difficult than traditional systems management. AVM is built with these requirements in mind. AVM projects require a sophisticated management of expectations as well as project deliverables. This is because many activities happen in parallel, projects typically have users with different needs, and requirements analysis and development efforts are iterative. AVM adopts the approach of managing by influence rather than control.

Once a project plan is complete, individual work plans for each Value Frame are created. Key activities in Engagement Management include defining the scope of successive Value Frames, and scheduling Value Assessments at the end of every Value Frame. Value Assessments are formal project reviews with clients, typically every four to eight weeks, which ensures business value, as defined by the client, is being delivered rapidly and effectively.

4.0 Theory

Having thoroughly described AVM, the authors will now provide a critical account of the method trying to link AVM to theory and to other development methods used in Information Systems Discipline. In order to do that, the authors will look at two important aspects of any Systems Development method, these being Synthesis and Role of Developers.

First of all looking at the Synthesis or building blocks of the method, the following can be said:

- AVM uses Prototyping as an analysis and development approach from the early stages.
- AVM makes use of the Participative philosophy in which it tries to involve users in the design and development of the chosen process and related applications from stage one.

- Technology enabled and driven.
- Uses some of the latest management tools like Business Process
Reengineering and Process Innovation.

From the description, we can see that many of the ideas used in AVM are not new. On the contrary, AVM developers scoured existing methods, tools, philosophies adopted practices best suited for the collaborative applications development environment.

Secondly, Role of Consultants or Developers, the consultants are seen by AVM as a hybrid of Facilitators of change and Technical Experts who is knowledgeable about both Technology and Business.

In order to position AVM amongst other Information Systems Development methods and techniques, the authors decided to adopt the grid developed by Hirschheim & Klein in their paper 'Four Paradigms of Information Systems Development'[8]. It became evident from the description of AVM and the subsequent analysis of its building blocks, that such a method should be positioned in the Functionalist paradigm as shown in figure (2). Taking into account that the authors has situated AVM at the far end of the Functionalist paradigm and nearer to the Social Relativist paradigm.

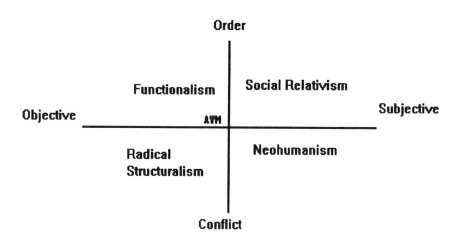

Figure (2)
AVM within other ISD methods/methodologies

A number of reasons has led to such belief. First of all, AVM like other functionalist methods look to the world as ordered and objective. Issues like consensus and agreement is perceived as essential and sought throughout the development effort. AVM does not acknowledge the fact that people may disagree and conflict can arise between different groups and parties of people. On the other hand, AVM makes use of participative approach to ISD by involving the users in the design and development of the new process and applications, which made the authors push AVM nearer to the social relativist paradigm. Taking into account that Lotus developers have not made the effort to provide a paradigmatic shift.

Other issues had led to positioning AVM within the functionalist paradigm like extracting a process and dealing with it as isolated from and independent of its context. A great emphasis has been given for both Technology and Business throughout the whole method without paying attention to the social and cultural issues associated with such a technological change. Although AVM deals with change and its consequences, not enough effort has been made to show how organisations can confirm with technology or the other way around.

Other issues can be brought to question here as well, like AVM's focus on the users learning to become designers. Is it achievable? Is it ethical? Are the users trained enough to do so? And others more.

Probably it is important as well to establish how successful AVM has been in producing systems that really meet users' specifications?

5.0 Conclusion

It can be argued that AVM is not a pure methodological approach to systems development because achieving only 80% of system requirements is considered a success. AVM falls short when developing complex applications because of its general simplicity. It can be too fluid and when used in practice it is easy to get caught in iterations that lose sight of system objectives. Further, the value of AVM to those who study information systems methodologies is limited since this method is proprietary. AVM's future is uncertain in the hands of IBM.

Despite its problems, AVM is still a refreshing addition to the information systems methodologies arena because it concentrates on groupware and collaborative systems, is real-world oriented, business focused and accommodates human behaviour and relationships which can go unaccounted for in other methodologies. AVM can be a valuable tool for enabling and managing controlled incremental change which we see more often in systems development – particularly in web based applications. Further, unlike some other systems methodologies, the AVM framework and modules are easy to understand and work with. It is possible to develop a one page checklist of tasks and activities for each module that could encompass AVM. One of the authors previously worked for a large consulting firm where their proprietary methodology took years to fully comprehend let alone apply in a client engagement. Training was given in small increments over a period of years and full documentation for the methodology exceeded 20 ring binders. AVM, on the contrary, is quick to learn. Professional training in all five AVM modules can be completed in two weeks and skills learned can be applied immediately.

References

1. Accelerated Value Method, AVM, Value Frames, Value Assessments, the AVM logo, Lotus Notes and Lotus Domino are all trademarks of Lotus Development Corporation.

2. Bjorn-Andersen, N., and Turner, J. "Creating the Twenty-First Century Organization: the Metamorphosis of Oticon." Prepared for the IFIP Working Group 8.2 Conference, Michigan, USA   August 1994.

3. Davenport, T. H. "Saving IT's Soul: Human-Centered Information Management." Harvard Business Review, March 1994.

4. Davenport, T. H., Process Innovation: Reengineering Work Through Information Technology. Boston: Harvard Business School Press, 1992.

5. Gallivan, M. J. "Contradictions among Stakeholder Assessments of a Radical Change Initiative: A Cognitive Frames Analysis," Images of Practice: Business Processing Reengineering. 1995.

6. Hammer, M., and Champy, J. Reengineering the Corporation: A Manifesto for Business Revolution. New York: Harper Business Press, 1993.

7. Henry, J.,   Blum, P., and Salloway, S. "The Impact of Lotus Notes on Organizational Productivity: Evidence from Customers," Telesis, 1992.

8. Hirschheim & Klein, 'Four Paradigms of Information Systems Development', Communications of the ACM, Vol. 32, No 10. 1989

9. Macauley, L. "Requirements Engineering," part of The Applied Computing Series for Springer-Verlag London Ltd., 1995.

10. Orlikowski, W. J. "The Duality of Technology: Rethinking the Concept of Technology in Organizations." Organizational Science, Volume 3, Number 3, 1992a, pp. 398-427.

11. Orlikowski, W. J. "Learning from Notes: Organizational Issues in Groupware Implementation." In Turner, and R. Kraut (Editors), Conference on Computer Supported Cooperative Work, Toronto, Canada, 1992b, pp. 362-369.

12. Peters, T. *Liberation Management*. New York: Alfred A. Knoph, 1992.

13. Seybold, P. "Patricia Seybold's Notes on IT." July 1994

A Preliminary Account of a Case Study Approach to Understanding Factors that Shape the Requirements Process in an NHS Hospital

Zahid I Hussain and Donal J Flynn
Department of Computation, UMIST,
Manchester, M60 1QD, UK
flynn@umist.ac.uk, zh@acm.org

Abstract

The research we are currently conducting concerns a large NHS hospital in Yorkshire. Our research goals are to apply theories of social behaviour relevant to IT to seek to explain the factors which, in this hospital, shape the structure and process involved in obtaining the requirements for an information system. The theories in which we are currently interested are: (1) the four paradigms for developing information systems (Hirschheim, Klein and Lyytinen 1995), (2) metaphors of organisation (Morgan 1997), and (3) structuration theory (Giddens 1979). We are carrying out the research using an interpretivist approach (Walsham 1993). No results are available from the research as yet: we only show our intended approach.

Keywords. Case study, interpretivist approach, requirements, user, social factors, structuration theory, information systems paradigms, organisational metaphors.

Introduction

The research we are currently conducting concerns a large NHS hospital in Yorkshire, UK and will spread to other hospitals in the near future. The hospital is seeking to merge several day clinics into one clinic in a single location; part of this integration process is concerned with the development of an information system (IS) to support certain aspects of the new clinic's procedures. We are interested in developing and testing theory to support social aspects of this integration process.

Our research goals are, firstly, to apply theories of social behaviour relevant to IT to seek to explain the factors which, in this hospital, shape the structure and process involved in obtaining the requirements for the information system. We anticipate

involved in obtaining the requirements for the information system. We anticipate that by focusing more on the social rather than the technological nature both of the requirements development activity as well as that of the eventual system, we will generate proposals for newer methods for requirements development that will better satisfy users of IT systems. We use several theories in an attempt to present several points of view, in the belief that any one theory may result in too narrow an account. Secondly, we aim to refine theory through practical experience of its applicability.

Two theories in which we are currently interested, and which are quoted widely in IS research, are: (1) four paradigms for developing information systems [10], (2) structuration theory [8]. A third theory concerns metaphors of organisation [17] which we have selected as, although it is not widely used in an IS context, we believe exhibits a number of interesting features that may be applicable to requirements development. Our approach is to ascertain, for key stakeholders in the requirements activity, for theory 1, paradigmatic assumptions held concerning systems development and, for theory 3, metaphors which underpin stakeholders' views of organisations. We will then link these assumptions and metaphors to the results of stakeholder interviews in an attempt to investigate the extent to which they shape stakeholders' views of the requirements activity. Such "psychological" factors may contrast nicely with the more "sociological" approach of theory 2, structuration theory. We are carrying out the research using an interpretivist approach [25]. The aim of this paper is not to discuss results of the research, which has only recently begun, but to discuss the approach we are taking in terms of the operationalisation of the theories and their likely applicability to the research setting.

In the next section we discuss the hospital background and context, followed by a short section contrasting interpretivist and positivist approaches to research. We then describe the three theories which we are seeking to use, followed by a short conclusion.

Background and Context

The hospital in question is a large well-established hospital employing over seven and a half thousand workers and treats half of the total patient population of its city. It has a very good national and international reputation. It is located over a number of sites with its central location being the biggest. Over the past a few years the hospital has faced a number of problems, such as:

- Long waiting lists   - Patients sent elsewhere for treatment
- Increase in the number of complaints - More workload for staff
- Shrinking levels of finance   - Pressure from Audit Commission

Such problems are common in NHS hospitals but this hospital wishes to take radical steps to eliminate or minimise them. On the other hand, there is a growing amount of pressure from the government and public to improve patient care and service. As a result, the hospital has project teams headed by a project manager, which are responsible for projects and training schemes to increase efficiency and effectiveness.

This research focuses on a Day Clinic project, which is a potential improvement area. The project was initiated to integrate all Day Clinics of the hospital into a single Day Clinic. These clinics are located over a number of sites and have their own ways of operating and some also have their own (small) computer systems. Some reasons for this integration are to reduce administration inconsistency, reduce customer dissatisfaction and achieve economies of scale.

After high level discussions, top management decided to integrate all seven Day Clinics. This is planned to be done in short phases, the first and the biggest phase would bring together majority of clinics, with later phases bringing in clinics which required more preparation. The clinic is to be housed on an entire floor of a large building that became vacant two years ago. The actual need for integration was realised in 1995 but it had been postponed a number of times. The project finally resumed in July 1997 and the real work began in September 1997. The targeted move in date or the initiation of the first phase was set for June 1998. In order to meet the deadline the management decided to form four groups/teams (consisting of workers from the clinic question) who would plan this change. These teams are:

IT Team - responsible for finding, modelling, applying, implementing and maintaining IS for the newly integrated day clinic.

Operational Team - responsible for formulating the operational policy that would reflect the new (common) ways of working. This is done by brainstorming ideas, discussing, investigating into areas, and then making final decisions on the process and system requirements.

Administrative Team - responsible for deciding on the new administration system, which works for all the new specialities in the clinic. Effective administration is important in improving customer service and satisfaction. The administration system will be used together with the information system.

Documentation Team - responsible for designing, drafting documents and forms that can be used by all specialities in the new Day Clinic and its specialisms.

These teams are independent of each other, but a few individuals participate in more than one team to communicate decisions. Only the IT team contains IT personnel. The status of the teams and those involved in them varies depending on the size and importance of the decisions being accomplished. All these teams are productive and are perceived generally as having produced good results to date.

As the project moves towards completion, the teams will merge. On completion two objectives should have been achieved: a well planned change and well planned requirements for the IS. Thus, the outcomes generated by the teams are crucial. We have documented many factors that are involved in implementing the IS, some of which are:

Decision making	Need for the system and requirements
Standards	Information System being purchased

Shortages (and surpluses)	System architecture
Reaction towards change	Usability
Conflict	IS vendor and their project understanding

Interpretivism and Positivism

The nature of this research is interpretivist which was chosen to suit the research situation, as discussed in Galliers and Land [6], Newman and Sabherwal [19], Knights and Morgan [13]; we were interested in discovering views of the individuals in the hospital concerning the social process whereby Day Clinic integration has taken place. The research strategy selected was the case study approach of the field study type [3]. Access to the hospital arose from a personal contact between one of us (ZIH) and a senior member of hospital management.

It is important to distinguish between the interpretivist and positivist approaches and we put forward our own view on this in Table 1. This explanation and comparison of the approaches sets out some fundamental differences and contrasts the paths that a researcher following one of these two approaches could take.

Theory

In this section, we highlight some of the theoretical frameworks used in this research. We use the theoretical frameworks of Hirschheim, Klein and Lyytinen [10] (Assumptions), Morgan [17] (Metaphors) and Giddens [7, 8] (Structuration Theory). The first two frameworks will be operationalised to evaluate their relevance to this research and structuration theory will be applied and evaluated.

Table 1. Distinctions between interpretivist and positivist approaches to research.

	Interpretivism	*Positivism*
Social phenomena /consciousness	Symbolic	Concrete
Reification	Reification in the form of human interaction	Reify social process by creating structures
Social boundaries	Individuals control their own environment	Individuals are products of their environment People are controlled in a mechanistic way
Organisations	Have a diverse purpose and are coalitions of individuals	Co-operative systems, pursuit of common goals/interests

| *Communication* | Social reality is made up of words/symbols created by actors | Horizontal/vertical flow of information. Network and frequency of communication is important. |
| *Method of study* | Subjective, here & now approach | Natural science approach. |

Operationalisation will involve drawing up a checklist characterising the essential notions of these frameworks and/or their sub-components. The checklists will then be used in the hospital to evaluate framework relevance. The checklists may be agreed between the original authors of these frameworks and we the researchers in due course. The operational checklists will be used to ask questions of the key stakeholders in the hospital change process, with a view to establishing whether the concepts within these frameworks are useful in explaining the attitudes or behaviour of these stakeholders within the requirements activity.

Hirschheim, Klein and Lyytinen framework

Firstly, we shall focus on the framework of Hirschheim, Klein and Lyytinen [10], referred to subsequently as HKL. Since many readers will be familiar with their work it will only be discussed very briefly. In applying their work to this hospital we seek to identify the basic assumptions held by stakeholders. According to HKL, system developers approach the development issue with a number of explicit and implicit assumptions. For example, they write:

"depending on the assumptions adopted, different systems development approaches are identifiable and each of these leads to different system outcomes" (p119)

Assumptions relate to the attitudes adopted towards the world and how we store and communicate knowledge about it [2]. There are many writers in this area such as Dagwell and Weber [4]. Hirschheim and Klein [9] and HKL [10] explore the importance of developer assumptions and their importance to the success or failure of a system. They profoundly illustrate the different origins of assumptions that are used in making choices concerning the development and implementation of IS.

HKL analyse assumptions and beliefs about the nature of social phenomena as revealed in a number of design methods and approaches that have been proposed for ISD. For example, they write that:

"Different sets of assumptions are likely to yield very different approaches to information systems development. Yet this kind of philosophical analysis of an applied field is a genre which has not received much attention in IS literature" (HKL:3)

In fact, all assumptions can lead to radically different approaches to IS. They attempt to develop a philosophical and conceptual foundation to analyse and discuss representation of IS development. They build a critical syntheses of current approaches and discuss the implications of their debate for possible theoretical improvements. Our view on the assumptions of HKL are summarised in the chart in Appendix 1.

We aim to investigate the extent to which these assumptions are held in the hospital context, and to do this we intend to operationalise the assumptions by asking stakeholders a set of questions, examples of which are provided below:

How do you see management intervention?
What form of authority is used in your organisation?
How are workers perceived?
Does your organisation have a physical or conceptual existence and why?
What are normal conflicts and how are they resolved?
Are changes regular in this organisation?
How do people react to change?
What are the management views towards employees?

Using these questions, and from stakeholder interviews, we will build a map of the assumptions held by different stakeholders and investigate the extent to which these appear to shape the requirements activity.

Morgan's metaphors

Morgan [17] views metaphors as conceptual tools for the communication of ideas and beliefs. They are used in our everyday life, and they affect the way we interpret and make sense of the world. One can establish a relationship between metaphors and organisations. Metaphor can be used as language and help us to interpret the world in certain ways and assign meaning to it. Therefore, it can be said that metaphors are hermeneutical equivalents of the phenomenological assigning of meaning to language Morgan [16]. The role relationship of hermeneutics into phenomenology has concerned philosophers such as Heidegger and Husserl who sought to interpret language and assign certain meaning to it.

Metaphors create pictures in our minds, using assumptions and analogies. We assign literal meaning to situations such as organisational settings [23]. After we have been given certain analogies and assumptions we are then invited to use them in a particular context, such as in looking at an organisation as a soap bubble. On the other hand, writers such as Lackoff and Johnson [14] and Morgan [17] highlight the psychological impact of metaphor, where they propose that metaphors affect our cognitive learning and structure. They also make up our everyday language/communication. Ortony [22] provided three theses on the use of metaphors. These are:

. Compactness thesis - metaphors are quick, precise and effective.
. Inexpressibility thesis - metaphors help to say things that are not expressible in

normal language.
. Vividness thesis - metaphors build on experience and enhance cognitive and
   emotional impact.

Metaphors are embedded in our daily lives and enforce our interpretations of the world, because they open up ways of seeing situations. However, the metaphors are constructed from a set of assumptions that can help to distinguish the role of developers and users. They help in defining the approaches used in developing IS in organisations. These metaphors will be considered before proceeding to look at the effects on IS stakeholders. Metaphors can also be used in viewing an organisation and the attitudes of its work. For example, a worker may see his/her organisation as a social entity, in which case they may discredit a more technical perspective. We see certain advantages associated with operationalising metaphors at the hospital, as they may clarify issues, help in expressing issues that can not be expressed verbally, can be used for motivating workforce, and may help in putting ideas into perspective.

A preliminary set of questions to be used in eliciting stakeholders' metaphors is provided below:

How are orders given and executed?
Who makes decisions and has responsibility?
What is the main objective of management?
How are conflicts managed?
What reactions are held towards change?
In which of the following categories does the hospital fall: autocracy, bureaucracy, technocracy, representative democracy, direct democracy?
How well can the organisation handle change?
How is IS seen?

The presence of these metaphors will be elicited by stakeholder interview and we will attempt to link them to attitudes or behaviour in the requirements activity.

Structuration theory

Structuration theory is an attempt to explain the relationship between human action and structure, since it focuses on implications of an individual's action on structure and vice versa, as discussed in Giddens [7], Riley [24], Macintosh and Scapens [15], Orlikowski [20] and Orlikowski and Robey [21]. The relationship between the two is provided in Figure 1. As shown in the diagram, structure becomes established through action, and it can be used or modified as required. A simplified analogy of this is a standardised company document, which is used and modified as the company's needs and customer base change.

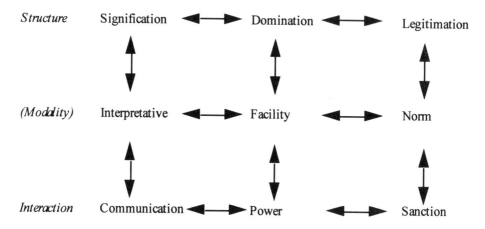

Figure 1. Relationship between interaction and structure (Walsham, p61 taken from Giddens, 1984).

Structuration theory is concerned with the individual's interaction that over time and space "creates" institutions, by linking micro variables (individual beliefs) to macro variables (eg, structure and procedures. For example, Riley [24] notes that a central concern of structuration theory is the identification of the condition which manages the continuity or transformation of structure and reproduction of system. It is an attempt by Giddens [7] to link macro level organisational issues (structure) with micro level individual issues (agency). This inter-subjective theory provides a holistic framework for constructing rules and taking actions. Two of the most important aspects of this theory are structure and agent.

The notion of structure is at the heart of this theory. A way of looking at structure is that it contains action. Structure is made up of rules and resources that people use to interact, as a company document will be based on grammatical rules as well as linguistic rules which determine its level of formality. This is referred to as duality of structure, which acts as "medium" and is the final result of the actor's interaction; just as the formal company documents will be the operator's input which s/he decides upon after interaction with others. They are referred to as "mediums" or "modalities" because the structure provides them with rules and resources that they use for interaction. Outcomes, rules and resources only have an existence through their application and with reference to interaction, so they do not have an existence beyond social reality and are dependent upon the rules of social practice.

Giddens [7] writes that structuration theory concerns re/production of social systems through application of rules and resources. They are regularised relations in interaction, rather than a functional link between parts within a whole. Giddens [7:65] refers to this as "structural totality"; he states that structures do not exist in time and space, apart from their role in creating social systems such as organisations. Organisational structures are constructed by people involved with(in) them. In applying this theory it is important to pay particular attention to "individual" because s/he re/creates action by using stores of knowledge (language, grammar, rules social norms, values) and combines that with the knowledge of specific organisations (procedures, organisational structure, resources,. For example, in the hospital situation the decisions made by an individual will depend on their norms, values and social background as well as NHS rules and procedures. Ideally, their decisions will contain a good combination of both, with, sometimes a greater proportion of the latter in order to gain greater credibility. Every individual attempts to achieve their own goal, and in doing so structure or parts of it may be re/produced.

Table 2 shows a preliminary analysis of the types of structure and interaction associated with each team in the hospital. This is a very simplified account of the application of structuration theory partly because a full account is not possible as the research is only halfway through its development. However, the above illustration of structure and interaction highlight interdependence of one over the other. We will use the theory for sense making of stakeholder interviews concerning the nature of the requirements activity.

Table 2. Preliminary analysis of structure and interaction for teams.

Structure	**Signification**	**Domination**	**Legitimation**
Operational	Operational codes, discourses	Authoritative, Allocation of clinic resources	Operational policy, clinic code of conduct, rules & procedures, norms
Documentation	General documentation standard	Make it obligatory for groups to fill in parts of forms	Documentation portfolio for the clinic, documentation standard norms
Administration	General ways of operating, codes of operating the admin system	Assign certain admin. tasks to certain workers	Clinic admin standard
IT	Perception	Allocate IT resources	System architecture, application portfolio, clinic IT strategy

Interaction	Communication	Power	Sanctions
Operational	Ideas about the change, issues concerning the change	Individuals use their power to safeguard their interests	Operational issues have to be acceptable to all involved and also satisfy NHS guidelines, operational policy guidelines
Documentation	New procedures, new factors that need recording, who is to record these factors	Individuals attempt to safeguard their interests	NHS doc standards binding over all other documentation types
Administration	New administration procedures, who will carry these out	Emphasis on importance of good admin system, particularly for improving patient service	Other admin systems in the hospital, admin standards at the hospital
IT	The need for IT, what IT is needed, who will use it, when will it be used	Technical superiority, IT centrally controlled by IT dept	All IT systems proposed and policies formulated must adhere to NHS IM+T strategy which is centrally coordinated

Conclusion

We have described our intended approach to examining key factors in shaping the development of IS requirements in the hospital. The Day Clinic integration was scheduled for June 1998 and our study is continuing beyond this into the hospital's evaluation phase. We anticipate that our approach, based on the application of the three theories discussed above, will yield novel and interesting results on the nature of the social process of requirements development. We anticipate that our approach, based on the application of the three theories discussed above, will yield novel and interesting results on the nature of the social process of requirements development, will lead to proposals for modifications to requirements methods that place more emphasis on social factors and will critically comment on the applicability of the three theories used in this research for sense-making in the requirements context.

Appendix 1. Assumptions underlying four paradigms of Hirschheim, Klein, Lyttinen

	Interpretative scheme	Functional scheme	Radical Structuralism	Radical Humanism
Organisation	Made up of human actions	Concrete entity	Concrete oppressive entity	Made up of human actions that change constantly
Management/Organise change	Social interaction	Pre-defined/well planned	Oppressive	Management styles change rapidly
Authority	Personal influence/created	Well established	Used for oppression	Depends on the subordinates
Individual/Worker	An independent agent	Assigned a role	Oppressed by those in power	Independent agent
Decision-Making	Mutual agreement/freedom	Structured decision making	Made by those in power	Consultation between management and worker
Politics	Result of interaction	Formalised politics	Favour the owners	Geared up to deal with change
Conflict/work relations	Very high	Standard way of resolving	A lot of conflict	Conflict quite apparent
Method of work	Self selected or agreed	Well defined	Maximise the output	Flexible
Efficiency/effectiveness	Agreed with management	Well planned and controlled	Exploit workers & machinery	Flexible
Notion of change	Positive/needed	Strategic targets	Common but troublesome	Most common
Employee reward	Personal fulfilment	Well defined by management	Minimal fulfilment	Agreed with management
Employee need	Personal fulfilment	Well defined by management	Not fully met	Carefully considered

References
1. Attlewell P and Rule J (1984) Computing and organizations in what we know and what we do not know, *Communications of the ACM,* **27**(12), December.
2. Burrell G and Morgan G (1979) Sociological paradigms and organisational analysis, Heinemann, London.
3. Cavaye A L M (1996) Case study research: a multi-faceted research approach for IS, *Information Systems Journal* 6, 227-242.
4. Dagwell R and Weber R (1983) Systems designer's user models: a comparative study, *Communications of the ACM,* **26**(11).
5. Galliers R D (1995) Information Systems Research, Blackwell Scientific Publications, Oxford.
6. Galliers R D and Land F F (1987) Choosing appropriate information systems research methodologies, *Communications of the ACM,* **30**(11), November.
7. Giddens A (1979) Central Problems in Social Theory, Macmillan Press, London.
8. Giddens A (1984) The Constitution of Society, Polity Press, Cambridge.
9. Hirschheim R, Klein H K (1989) Four paradigms of information systems development, *Communications of the ACM,* **32**(10), October.
10. Hirschheim R, Klein H K and Lyytinen K J (1995) Information Systems Development and Data Modeling: Conceptual and Philosophical Foundations, Cambridge University Press, Cambridge.
11. Keen P G W (1981) Information systems and organisational change, *Communications of the ACM,* **24**(1), January.
12. Kling R (1980) Social analysis of computing: theoretical perspectives in recent empirical research, *Computing Survey,* **12**(1), March.
13. Knights D and Morgan G (1991) Corporate strategy. Organizations and subjectivity: a critique, *Organization Studies,* **12**(2).
14. Lackoff G and Johnson M (1980) Metaphors We Live By, University of Chicago Press, Chicago.
15. Macintosh N B and Scapens R W (1990) Structuration theory in management accounting, *Accounting, Organizations and Society,* **15**(5).
16. Morgan G (1980) Paradigms, metaphors and puzzle solving in organization theory, *ASQ,* 605-622.
17. Morgan G (1986) Images of Organization, Sage Publications, USA.
18. Mowshowitz A (1981) On approaching the study of social issues in computing, *Communications of the ACM,* **24**(2), March.
19. Newman M and Sabherwal (1996) Determinants of commitments to information systems development: a longitudinal investigation, *MIS Quarterly,* March.
20. Orlikowski W J (1992) The duality of technology: rethinking the concept of technology in organisations, *Organization Science* **3**(3), 398-427.
21. Orlikowski W J and Robey D (1991) Information technology and the restructuring of organizations, *Information Systems Research* **2**(2), 143-169.
22. Ortony A (1975) Why metaphors are necessary and not just nice, *Educational Theory* 25, 45-53.
23. Palmer J and Taylor D (1995) Total quality in Rolls Royce plc, *OR Insight,* **4**(3), London.
24. Riley P (1983) A Structurationist account of political culture, ASQ, **28**(3).
25. Walsham G (1993) Interpreting Information Systems in Organizations, Wiley, Chichester.

A Preliminary Investigation of Rapid Application Development in Practice

Brian Fitzgerald

Executive Systems Research Centre, University College Cork, Cork, Ireland

Abstract

Rapid Application Development (RAD) has been proposed by some as the latest 'silver bullet' to address the software crisis, while others have likened it to 'old wine in new bottles', suggesting that it doesn't really provide anything new in terms of tools or techniques. Researchers have noted that while much has been written on the subject, there is a paucity of empirical research on the concept in practice. This paper discusses the rationale behind the emergence of RAD and the fundamental principles underpinning it. The findings of a preliminary study which investigated the RAD phenomenon in practice are presented. Briefly, the study findings focus on the profile of RAD usage, suitability criteria for using RAD on development projects, and how RAD is used to deliver its mission of faster development, within budget and without sacrificing system quality.

1 Introduction

The term Rapid Application Development (RAD) was introduced to the literature by James Martin in his 1991 book [1]. Martin drew on the development experiences of Scott Shultz at the Dupont corporation in 1984. Shultz described a particular development approach, Rapid Interactive Production Prototyping (RIPP), which was clearly the forerunner to the RAD approach proposed by Martin. Earlier antecedents in the literature include that of Gane [2]. However, as illustrated by its emergence in actual development practice, it is a concept which has resonances for practitioners. Indeed, the Dynamic Systems Development Method (DSDM) Consortium who are elaborating their own RAD method [3] currently have around 200 affiliated organisations in the UK and Ireland.

This paper is structured as follows: The next section discusses the rationale behind the emergence and current popularity of the RAD concept. The difficulty of defining RAD is discussed, and in light of this, the fundamental principles that characterise the RAD approach are identified and discussed. Following this, the results of a preliminary field study which investigated the application of RAD in practice are presented. The study findings focus on the extent of RAD usage and the profile of companies who are using it; the project suitability criteria for determining whether

RAD should be used for development; and the manner in which RAD is implemented so as to deliver its mission of faster development, within budget and without sacrificing system quality.

2 Rationale for RAD

Early efforts at software development in the 1950s and 1960s often relied on unsystematic and random methods. However, at a conference in 1968, the term 'software crisis' was coined to refer to a number of fundamental development problems which were universally acknowledged by conference participants [cf. 4]. Simply stated, the software crisis referred to the fact that systems took too long to develop, cost too much, and did not work very well. As the complexity of the systems which needed to be developed was actually on the increase, the situation would inevitably be further exacerbated. The initial response to the software crisis was to endeavour to introduce engineering principles to software development. Over the last 30 years or so, these engineering principles have been enshrined in the many software development methodologies that have been proposed. Indeed, recent estimates suggest that more than a thousand such methodologies are in existence [5].

However, the software crisis has not abated. In relation to development time-scales, different estimates have been made as to completion times for systems development. For example, Flaatten et al. [6] estimate development time to be about 18 months on average—a conservative figure given that other estimates put the figure at about three years [7] or even up to five years [8]. Also, a recent IBM survey estimated that 68 percent of projects overrun schedules [9]. In relation to cost, the IBM study suggested that development projects were as much as 65 percent over budget [9], while a Price Waterhouse study in the UK in 1988 concluded that £500m was being lost per year through ineffective development. Finally, in relation to performance, the IBM study found that 88 percent of systems had to be radically redesigned following implementation [9]. Similarly, a UK study found that 75 percent of systems delivered failed to meet users expectations. This has led to the coining of the term 'shelfware' to refer to those systems which are delivered but never used. Thus, the problem has not been solved. However, given the increasingly complex nature of systems that are being developed and the rapid pace of change characteristic of today's organisational environment, traditional monolithic development approaches are clearly inappropriate [cf. 10]. Indeed, it has been estimated that development productivity needs to increase tenfold to satisfy demand [11]. Table 1 provides a summary of evidence which indicates the nature and extent of the problems inherent in the software crisis.

Average completion times for systems development projects range from 18 months to five years
68 percent of projects overrun schedules
65 percent of budgets exceed budget estimates
75 percent of projects face major redesign following initial implementation
Development productivity needs to increase tenfold to keep up with demand
Productivity differences of 10-to-1 have been reported among individual developers with same level of experience
Productivity differences of up to 5-to-1 have been found among different development teams
Average developer in the US works 48 to 50 hours per week
75 percent of development organisations have inadequate project management practices
Requirements errors cost 200 times as much to fix if not discovered prior to implementation
Less than 3 percent of developers interviewed at Microsoft could accurately explain the fundamental design concepts of modularity and information hiding
Development projects which have experienced excessive pressure to complete on schedule have been found to have four times the normal number of defects
35 percent of companies have at least one runaway development project
Based on a comprehensive study (4000 projects), the overall rate of efficiency for the software industry is estimated to be 35 percent

Table 1 Evidence of the Software Crisis

As already mentioned, over the past 30 years various solutions have been proposed, ranging from tools and techniques to overall methodologies. Brooks [12] suggests that these have often been offered as 'silver bullet' solutions, and concludes that they typically do not address the essential and inherent difficulties of software development. At first glance, RAD might be dismissed since it does not offer anything radically new in terms of tools or techniques. However, the real potential of RAD arises from the synthesis of currently-available tools and techniques, coupled with fundamentally different management principles that serve to overcome bureaucratic obstacles to faster development. Thus, the mission of RAD is the simple but powerful one of increasing development speed at a reduced cost without sacrificing quality.

3 Fundamental Principles Underpinning RAD

It is probably inevitable that definitions are elusive with any emerging concept that is being shaped through practical experiences, and RAD is no exception. Definitions of RAD vary in terms of it being characterised as a tool, methodology or lifecycle [cf. 13, 14, 15]. Given this definitional quagmire, the approach taken here is to document the fundamental principles underpinning RAD, thus allowing a clearer picture of the concept to coalesce. These principles include active user involvement, small empowered teams, frequent delivery of products which focus primarily on satisfaction of business functionality, iterative incremental development, top-down approach, and the use of integrated CASE wherever possible. These principles are complementary in many respects, and as a whole are extremely powerful. They are discussed in turn below:

3.1 Active User Involvement

The schism between users and developers in traditional development approaches has rightly been condemned—indeed, it is almost an axiom that user involvement is necessary for successful development. However, several studies have found that user involvement is not a simple issue, and the link between involvement and success is not a simple one [cf. 16]. The RAD approach recognises that user involvement is necessary for intellectual reasons—to reduce costly requirements elicitation problems, for example—and for political reasons—users may reject systems outright if they have not been sufficiently involved in development. However, the RAD operationalisation of the user involvement concept is a very rich one. At the heart of the RAD approach are joint application design (JAD) and joint requirements planning (JRP) workshops. These are extremely intensive sessions of short duration which serve to identify more completely problematic requirements analysis and systems design issues. All relevant parties are co-located thus leading to synchronisation in the communication process. Also, RAD recognises that users are not homogeneous and identifies a number of different roles that users may play.

3.2 Small Empowered Teams

Again, the concept of development teams is not a new one. However focusing on each of the words, *small*, *empowered* and *teams* in turn, the advantages which accrue can be seen to be considerable. Firstly, communication channels increase exponentially in relation to team size. Thus, *small* team size ensures that the potential for communication distortion and conflict is kept to a minimum. Secondly, the *empowerment* element helps ensure that bureaucratic delays and shirking of decision-making responsibility, so inherently characteristic of the traditional requirements signoff, are minmised. Teams are empowered to make vital design decisions (although changes are reversible—an issue which is discussed again below). Finally, the *team* aspect serves to ensure that all the vital skills for successful development are present. As already mentioned the team issue has already been proven to be useful. For example, the Chief Programmer Team (CPT) under Harlan Mills which developed the New York Times system achieved incredible results—83,000 lines of code written in 22 months, after implementation, the system ran for 20 months before the first error occurred [17]. Successful development requires that many varied roles be accommodated, e.g., project manager, technical co-ordinator, developer, tester, scribe, user, executive sponsor. The fulfilment of these roles is facilitated by team composition, and their importance has been acknowledged by Microsoft who organise their software development around various development roles in a similar manner [18].

3.3 Frequent Delivery of Products

As already mentioned, traditional development projects can take from 18 months to five years to complete—an issue increasingly problematic given the rapidly-changing nature of today's competitive market-place. RAD, by definition, seeks to reduce development time-spans. Thus, shorter time-boxes for development—typically 90 days—are an important feature. These shorter time-boxes make project management more straightforward in that it is easier to focus on necessary activities, and be more accurate in what can be achieved. Also, this principle is concerned with delivery of *products*. Rather than being focused on *process*, RAD is premised on delivering products which satisfy the essential criterion of addressing some business function.

3.4 Iterative Incremental Development

Another fundamental principle of RAD is that systems evolve incrementally and are never complete. Rather, new requirements emerge which are then built into the system. Thus, systems emerge through iterative prototyping, with iteration seen as useful and necessary, not as rework delaying development. It is recognised that requirements specification is a heuristic or learning process which greatly benefits from the deeper insight that both developers and users get from realistic experience with an actual prototype system. Users may not be able to specify in advance exactly what they want in a system but are able to recognise it when they see it—an example of a well-known psychological phenomenon, namely, that recognition is a far easier process than recall. In traditional development, errors in requirements which are not identified before coding or implementation are extremely costly to correct [19, 20]. In fact, it is now commonly accepted that since the system produced by the traditional life-cycle undergoes a significant maintenance phase, it may be more properly viewed as a prototype anyway.

3.5 Top-Down Approach

As already mentioned, the RAD philosophy accepts that requirements cannot be completely specified in advance. Rather, they are specified at a level appropriate to the knowledge available at the given time. These are then elaborated through incremental prototyping. Similarly, products fit for business purpose are produced according to an application of the Pareto principle—that is, approximately 80 percent of the functionality may be delivered in 20 percent of the time. Systems are then elaborated and finessed as knowledge grows, from broad outline to precise detail. Also, being a top-down approach characterised by short time-boxing, all decisions are assumed to be fairly quickly reversible. This also contributes to developers feeling more empowered to assume responsibility and being less likely to shirk decision-making.

3.6 Integrated Computer Assisted Software Engineering (I-CASE)

If dramatic increases in development productivity are to be achieved, it is vital that the more routine and time-consuming aspects of development be automated. These include code generation and documentation, for example. The automation of these tasks may be achieved through the use of I-CASE. The latter provides a single electronic repository for project-related data. Change control and configuration management features—vital in an environment of iterative prototyping—are also provided. Additionally, I-CASE facilitates reuse by providing access to previously designed and tested elements. Thus, by increasing the granularity of the development building block, productivity improvement is further enhanced.

4 The Research Approach Adopted for the Study

Beynon-Davies *et al.* [21] note that while much has been written on the concept of RAD, there remain a paucity of empirical studies which have investigated the RAD phenomenon in actual practice. The work of the aforementioned authors represents a notable effort in redressing this imbalance [21, 22]. This study, albeit a preliminary one, also attempts to provide further empirical evidence on the RAD concept in practice.

Given that RAD is relatively new, a significant difficulty exists in relation to getting access to organisations who are experienced in the concept. This was addressed in this study by constructing a sample drawn from three specific groups: firstly, those organisations who were registered members of the DSDM consortium; secondly, a number of consultancy companies/software houses identified in the National Software Directory; and finally, a number of companies from the Top 100 database of Irish companies. On this basis, a sample of 100 organisations were selected and sent a survey questionnaire [cf. 23]. The researchers were aware that the sampling strategy very much represents a purposeful one rather than a random one. However, as already mentioned, this study was a preliminary and exploratory one which sought to investigate the nature of RAD in practice. Thus, it was not intended to apply sophisticated statistical analysis to the data, and so sample randomness was less of a concern. In order to elaborate and elucidate the findings, personal interviews were subsequently conducted with experienced RAD practitioners in eight companies selected from the respondents to the survey. Respondents had been asked to indicate their willingness to participate further in the research study, and those who expressed willingness were candidates for the interview phase. However, since a larger number were willing to participate than could be accommodated in the time available for the study, eight companies who had provided the richest survey responses were selected. The findings are discussed next.

5 Study Findings

While traditional development approaches were still the norm in the organisations studied, there was evidence of an increasing trend towards the use of RAD approaches. In this section the relevant findings are presented in three broad sections. Firstly, some evidence is provided in relation to the extent of RAD use and the types of organisations adopting the approach. Following this, the suitability criteria for using RAD on a development project are discussed. Finally, the manner in which organisations attempted to achieve the RAD mission—that of faster development within budget and without sacrificing system quality—is discussed.

5.1 Extent of RAD use

The survey found that 43 percent of respondents were knowledgeable about RAD and using it for development in some manner, whereas 57 percent were not using a RAD approach for systems development. The newness of the concept can be gauged from the fact that only 14 percent of respondents had been using RAD for more than 2 years. In terms of predicting use of RAD, no clear pattern emerged. Industry sector, for example, was not found to be significant. Organisation size proved to be interesting in so far as RAD was equally likely in both small (less than 100 employees) and large organisations (more than 500 employees). However, it was less common in medium size organisations (100-500 employees). One possible explanation for this is that small organisations are less bureaucratic and have less administrative overhead, and thus may be more willing to practice a RAD approach. On the other hand, large organisations are likely to have large IS departments, and thus are more capable of establishing small teams which can pioneer the use of new concepts, such as RAD.

5.2 Project Suitability Criteria for a RAD Approach

A number of criteria were identified as rendering a development project suitable for RAD. The factors are summarised in Table 2 and are briefly explained here. Firstly, application size was frequently cited, with RAD perceived as better suited to small projects with few developers and a small user base. By contrast, large projects with a large user base and thus more complex requirements were not viewed as suitable. Similarly, RAD was typically adopted in less complex applications which were perhaps targeted at a single department, and perhaps an interim solution, rather than for enterprise-wide applications which were expected to have a longer service life. Additionally, mission-critical systems were not seen as suited to a RAD development approach; rather RAD tended to be used in novel application areas where the emphasis was on discovering and surfacing user requirements. Finally, RAD projects differed in relation to the languages being used (typically 4GLs), the amount of documentation (less in RAD, with responsibility for producing it delegated to users).

5.3   Nature of RAD Implementation

As already mentioned, the mission of RAD is to increase development speed at a reduced cost without sacrificing quality. The study focused on the manner in which organisations actually achieved this. A number of factors were found to be important: Briefly summarising:

- The use of CASE tools and high-level languages which could also be used directly by users, helped to reduce tedious and time-consuming low-level coding, and allowed parallel, modular development to take place.

- Increased delegation of development tasks to users was also important. Thus, in addition to the coding task mentioned above, users were also given more responsibility for producing documentation and for maintenance of the systems developed.

- The task of requirements specification, one of the most lengthy in traditional development projects, was also greatly altered. Typically, less effort was devoted to an initial formal specification of requirements; rather, a high-level listing of requirements served to initiate development. A high level of user participation and the use of prototyping ensured that requirements were fully addressed as development proceeded.

- Reuse of modules wherever possible helped to improve both development speed and quality, as coding was again greatly reduced, and the modules reused were already fully-tested. This issue was quite revealing in the organisations studied. Those who were most succesful in increasing the level of reuse had formally assigned the responsibility for it to a high-ranking individual, thus ensuring that reuse was taken seriously. The issue of automated testing was also one which interviewees felt had great potential, and practically all interviewees thought they should be leveraging this aspect to a greater degree.

Suitable for RAD	Unsuitable for RAD
Small project. Few developers. Small user base.	Large project. Many developers. Large user base with complex requirements.
System for a single department.	Enterprise-wide application.
Interim or temporary solution. Not mission critical.	Long service-life expected. Mission critical.
4GLs used. Emphasis on user interface, information presentation.	3GLs. Application area more algorithmically complex.
Less formalised documentation. Responsibility for it delegated to users	Traditional formalised documentatic pattern.
Novel application area. Emphasis on surfacing user requirements.	Traditional application areas.

Table 2 Project suitability criteria for a RAD approach

6 Conclusion

RAD methodologies are now beginning to emerge, prominent examples being a variant of Information Engineering [1] and the DSM methodology [3]. However, much needs to be done to elaborate the concept. Problems may be anticipated in the areas of management and control, raised user expectations, half-hearted implementation of the concept, and so on. Also, the issue of RAD suitability—is it appropriate for use in the development of safety-critical systems—needs to be further investigated. Indeed, it may be the case that traditional development approaches may be more appropriate in some circumstances. Clearly, more empirical studies of the concept, as advocated by Beynon-Davies *et al.* [22] are necessary.

The question also arises as to the extent to which RAD is a fad. For example, productivity was the buzz-word in the 1970s, with quality perhaps being that of the 1980s. Both are incorporated into the RAD concept. However, the issue of whether development speed and quality can be increased and cost reduced has yet to be proven. Certainly, there is no royal road to RAD, and companies will not find it to be the 'silver bullet' solution. Rather, as much work needs to be done in changing traditional mind-sets as overcoming technical issues.

As already mentioned, this study was very much a preliminary, exploratory one. The intention is to follow up with a more comprehensive study, using a large-scale survey and several in-depth case studies. However, the preliminary results from the study reported here will be drawn upon to provide a more realistic background for the in-depth study.

References

1. Martin, J. (1991) *Rapid Application Development,* Macmillan, USA

2. Gane, C. (1989) *Rapid Systems Development*, Prentice-Hall, USA.

3. DSDM (1995) *Dynamic Systems Development Method*, Tesseract Publishing, UK

4. Naur, P. Randell, B. and Buxton, J. (1976), Software Engineering: Concepts and Techniques, Charter Publishers, New York.

5. Jayaratna, N. (1994) *Understanding and Evaluating Methodologies*, McGraw Hill, London.

6. Flaatten, P., McCubbrey, D., O'Riordan, P. and Burgess, K. (1989) *Foundations of Business Systems*, Dryden Press, Chicago.

7. Business Week (1988) The software trap: automate—or else, *Business Week*, May 9, 142-154.

8. Taylor, T, and Standish, T. (1982) Initial thoughts on rapid prototyping techniques, *ACM SIGSOFT Software Engineering Notes*, 7, 5, 160-166.

9. Bowen, P. (1994) Rapid Application Development: Concepts and Principles, IBM Document No. 94283UKT0829.

10. Fitzgerald, B. (1997) Systems Development Methodologies: Time to Advance the Clock, in Wojtowski, G. (Editor) *Systems Development Methods for the Next Century*, Plenum Press, New York.

11. Verity, J. (1987) The OOPS revolution. *Datamation*, May 1, 73-78.

12. Brooks, F. (1987) No silver bullet: essence and accidents of software engineering. *IEEE Computer Magazine*, **April**, 10-19.

13. Baum, D. (1992) Go totally RAD and build applications faster, *Datamation*, September, pp.79-81.

14. Card, D. (1995) The RAD fad: is timing really everything?, *IEEE Software*, September.

15. Mimno, P. (1991) What is RAD?, *American Programmer*, **4**, 1.

16. Butler, T. And Fitzgerald, B. (1997) A case study of user participation in the IS development process, *Proceedings of the 19th International Conference on Information Systems*, Atlanta, Georgia.

17. Yourdon, E. (1979) *Classics in Software Engineering*. Yourdon Press,New York.

18. Sinha, M (1997) Development Practices at Microsoft, Seminar given at the Sixth International Conference on IS Development, Boise, Idaho, 11-14 August 1997.

19. Boehm, B. (1981) *Software Engineering Economics*. Prentice Hall, Englewood Cliffs, New Jersey.

20. DeMarco, T. (1978) *Structured Analysis and System Specification*, Yourdon Press, New Jersey.

21. Beynon-Davies, P. Tudhope, D. and Mackay, H. (1997), Integrating RAD and participatory design, in Avison, D. (Ed) *Key Issues in Information Systems*, McGraw-Hill, UK, pp.317-330.

22. Beynon-Davies, P. Carne, C. Mackay, H. and Tudhope, D. (1998), A comparison of seven RAD projects, in Avison, D. and Edgar-Nevill, D. (Eds) Matching Technology with Organisational Needs, McGraw-Hill, UK, pp.127-140.

23. O'Connor, A. (1996) *An Empirical Investigation of the Implementation of the Rapid Application Development Approach*, Unpublished MSc Thesis, University College Cork.

A Team-Based Process Model for UML

Kari Kivisto

MSG Software
P.O. Box 28
FIN-90101 Oulu
Finland
Phone: +358-8-8155333, Fax: +358-8-8155339
eMail: kari.kivisto@msg.fi
http://www.msg.fi

Abstract

This paper suggests a team-based process model to be used with the Unified Modeling Language (UML). This team-based Object-Oriented Client/Server model (OOCS) has its background in the same sources as the modeling language, and it has been used in practical projects for some years. Before the UML appeared, the model combined use case analysis, the Object Modeling Technique and client/server architecture with an iterative/incremental development process. In addition to this, the OOCS model defines the roles of the developers and their tasks in each phase. The roles are described and their use in practice is discussed in this paper.

KEYWORDS: Process model, modeling language, object-orientation, client/server architecture, role, team.

1. Introduction

The idea of a team-based Object-Oriented Client/Server development model is to combine three dimensions:

1. **Organizational dimension** (structure of a project, management of the project, roles of the project members)
2. **Technological dimension** (client/server architecture consisting of three sub-architectures)

3. Process dimension (process model, phases, activities, deliverables, methods)

The OOCS model consists of a process model that stresses client/server architecture and project organization. The client/server architecture consists of three sub-architectures: technological architecture, data architecture and application architecture [10] (lower part in Figure 1). In addition, the client/server application architecture divides the application into presentation, business logic and data management (upper part in Figure 1).

A Team-Based role model (TB model) defines the roles of a development team. The idea is to develop the application in small teams, with each team being responsible for at least one business object or component (Figure 3).

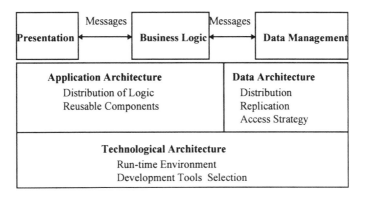

Figure 1. The three-tier client/server architecture.

The OOCS and TB models combine the roles of the developers and the activities and artifacts in the process. The OOCS and TB models are used in some Finnish IT departments. They have been adapted to the needs of these organizations. Experiences with the adaptation process can be read from Kivisto [9], where the reader will also find descriptions of versions 1.0 of the OOCS model and the TB model.

The Unified Modeling Language [13], [14], [15] has been accepted as a standard by the Object Management Group (OMG) and it is aimed at a common meta model and a common notation ([15], p. 9), but it does not include process model. The authors, including Booch [1], [2], [3], Rumbaugh et al. [14], and Jacobson et al. [7] favor a process model that is use-case driven, architecture centric, and iterative and incremental ([13], p. 9). Development of the OOCS model was started several years ago with these requirements in mind.

90

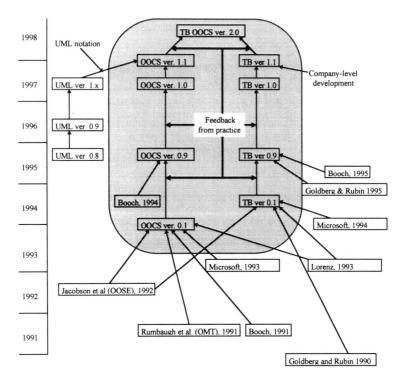

Figure 2. Evolution of the OOCS model, the TB model and the UML.

Figure 2 captures the evolution of the OOCS and TB models and the UML. The TB model and the OOCS model are briefly introduced next, the roles in each phase are focused, and the use of the UML as a modeling language is described.

2. Team-Based Process Model

The team-based Object-Oriented Client/Server application development model (the OOCS model) was developed with the following requirements in mind:

1. **The applications must be client/server applications**
   - user-centric, i.e., most of the system's functions are carried out using user interfaces
   - data-centric, i.e., most of the system's functions use databases
   - operative systems as opposed to embedded systems
   - tailored applications, not off-the-shelf products
2. **An object-oriented paradigm and related methods are used in application development:**
   - concepts, notation

- object-oriented methods and techniques in all phases
3. **The life cycle development model covers all relevant phases of development**
    - model includes phases from system definition to deployment
    - iterative/incremental development process is used in appropriate places
    - prototyping is used whenever needed
    - artifacts are exactly defined, including document templates
4. **Team organization is used in development, with exactly specified roles and responsibilities**
    - the number of roles is kept to a minimum
    - roles refer to both the object-oriented paradigm and client/server architecture

Team organization issue (item 4 above) is discussed first in section 2.1. The rest of the items are dealt with in section 2.2.

2.1 The Team-Based Role Model

The idea of the TB model stems from two points: 1) the client/server application architecture divides the application into three tiers (presentation, business logic and data management) and 2) object-oriented methods and techniques can be used in each tier (Figure 3). When the project is big, the project group is divided into small teams [11] with each team having the roles of a Team Leader, a Business Object Developer, an Application Developer and probably a Database Developer.

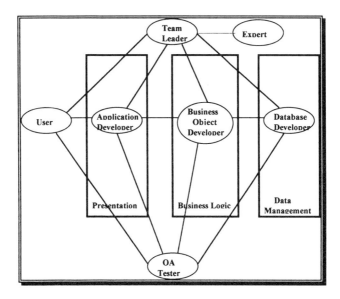

Figure 3. Roles of the team and client/server application architecture.

The roles in the TB model are:

Project Manager (PM)
The Project Manager is responsible for management of the project's resources (human and technical), tasks, deliverables, schedule and planning.

Team Leader (TL)
The Team Leader is responsible for directing the application development process. The Team Leader manages the application development, while the Project Manager manages the project.

Business Object Developer (BO)
The Business Object Developer designs, develops and maintains reusable business objects, and will 'own' some business objects. If there is more than one team in the project, each team will have at least one Business Object Developer.

Application Developer (AD)
Application Developers analyze, design and develop the requested application using reusable components whenever possible. They may design and develop new reusable components or drafts of them during the project.

Database Developer (DB)
This role is responsible for data modeling and database design, and he/she acts as an expert in data architecture definition.

Quality Assurancer/Tester (QA and TE)
The Quality Assurancer is an outsider in the project, who comes from the QA department and reviews, inspects and audits the quality of the project. The Tester is an insider, who is responsible for making test specifications and testing. Both roles are relevant parts of quality.

User (US)
Users are an elementary part of the development team. They take part in system definition, analysis and testing. With a little training, users are capable of writing use cases, on-line helps and user's manuals.

Expert (EX)
There are at least two categories of Experts, namely domain experts and technical experts. Domain experts work with Business Object Developers, while technical experts take part in activities in the Architecture phase.

The activities of each role are described next as a part of the OOCS model.

2.2 The OOCS Model

The OOCS model joins well-known object-oriented models and client/server architecture (recall Figure 2). Figure 4 depicts the OOCS model in the form it has been in for the last three or four years. The roles described in section 2.1 can be found from the figure. The model is based on three-tier client/server architecture, i.e., in each phase there are activities for presentation, business logic and data management. For instance, the Analysis phase includes use case analysis and user interface design (presentation), class/object modeling and design of operations (business logic) and data modeling (data management). Appropriate roles and artifacts (outputs from each activity) are assigned to these activities. In this way the project plan and development model are more tightly linked together. We further believe that the role approach could be used successfully with other development models, too.

The Architecture phase has been very useful, especially in projects dealing with emerging technologies (for instance, client/server and internet platforms). This phase has helped companies which select new technological strategies. Usually, architecture design, evaluation and testing proceed in parallel with the Analysis phase. The chosen architecture is then described in the documents of the Architecture phase.

Before the UML was introduced, the OOCS model included use case descriptions by Jacobson et al. [7] to capture users' functions, and OMT notation by Rumbaugh et al. [12] for object modeling (classes, operations, communication between classes, internal behavior of the class) and common ER notation for data modeling. The UML has been a great help in unifying the artifacts by providing notation and diagrams. In particular, the new Component and Deployment diagrams support documentation in the Architecture phase. The UML lacks data modeling diagrams, although class diagrams may be used instead. However, this may confuse Database Developers and cause problems in documenting.

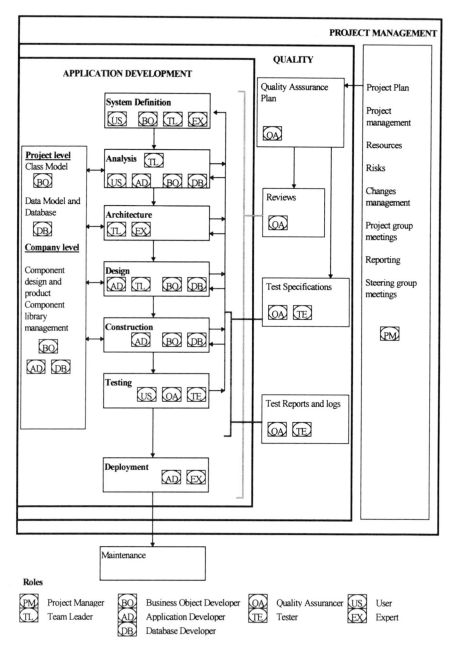

Figure 4. OOCS model including roles.

The first three phases are described next in order to give the reader an idea of the model. The overall description of the model is designed so it can be adopted into a quality system. It consists of a model description, techniques to be used and document templates.

2.2.1 The System Definition Phase

This is the first phase of the model (Figure 5). The System Definition phase serves as a starting point for later activities. The user roles and their main functions are input to use case analysis, the business object modeling is input to object modeling and the architecture draft to the activities in the Architecture phase.

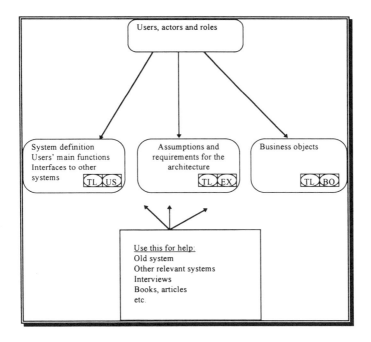

Figure 5. System Definition Phase.

Table 1 summarizes the roles and their activities, the artifacts and the UML diagrams that can be used.

Table 1. System Definition Phase.

Roles	Activities	Artifacts	UML Diagrams
US & TL	Define the system, users' main roles and functions	System definition, roles of the users, main functions	Use case Diagram Activity Diagram
BO & TL	Define business objects	System's business objects	Class diagram
TL & EX	Define Architecture draft	Architecture draft	Deployment diagram
TL & EX	Define interfaces to other systems	System's boundaries and interfaces	Deployment diagram

As can be seen from Table 1, the Team Leader plays the main role. He/she receives requirements from different user groups, consults Business Object Developers about existing business objects and Experts about architectural issues. The Team Leader uses this information to shape the overall system. He/she has to have a clear vision of the system to be built and be able to share this vision with the developers and users.

2.2.2 The Analysis Phase

The three-tier client/server approach in the Analysis phase can be seen in Figure 6, where the presentation is described by use cases and interfaces, business logic by an object model and operations, and data model by a data model description.

Iteration and prototyping are used in the analysis phase as much as possible. Feedback from users is a critical factor for the success of the project, and the best feedback is guaranteed via user interfaces. Thus, the first drafts of the user interfaces should be ready soon after the analysis phase has started.

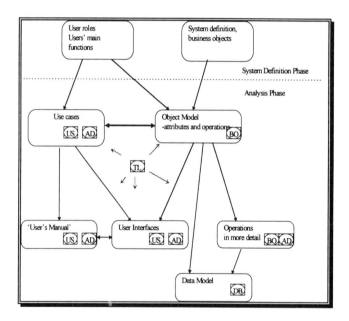

Figure 6. Analysis Phase

Figure 6 attempts to express also that the link between the use cases and the object model is a very tight one, and to point out that the user interfaces are defined after both the use cases and the object model have been designed. This does not mean the use cases and the object model have to be ready before going on, however, as the process is iterative in nature. On the other hand, the use cases should be available for the user interface design and the object model for data modeling, not vice versa. It must be remembered that one use case may lead to different kinds of user interfaces, depending on the developer.

Table 2. Analysis Phase.

Roles	Activities	Artifacts	UML Diagrams
US & AD	Use case analysis	Use case descriptions	Use Case Diagram Activity Diagram
US & AD	Write user manual draft and on-line help texts	User manual and on-line help draft	
US & AD	Define user interfaces and reports	User interfaces and reports descriptions	
BO	Define Business objects	Class descriptions	Class Diagram
AD & BO	Define operations	Operations descriptions	Class Diagram
DB	Carry out data modeling	Data model description	Class Diagram

The UML lacks a data modeling notation and diagram. A Class diagram can be used for data modeling, but one would expect the presence of a specific data modeling diagram in the UML. Fortunately, tools that implement the UML include usually data modeling capabilities, for instance, mapping of a class model to the data model and the data model to the database model can be found from those tools.

Users are part of the project group in the TB model. Their main work load is carried out in the Analysis phase when the use cases and user interfaces are designed. The use cases have been tested in reality and they have shown their power when user needs are gathered. Use cases were adopted into the OOCS soon after Jacobson et al. published their book (Jacobson et al. [7]) There were some practical problems at the beginning, since the OMT was the best known method (in Finland, at least) and it did not have use cases. Furthermore, the OMT included scenarios as design time artifacts, which confused the developers (see, Kivisto [8], pp. 61-62). Practice has shown us that most users can adopt use cases after a short training period and they are able to write and update use cases whenever necessary.

2.2.3 The Architecture Phase

The Analysis phase is normally followed by the Design phase. The OOCS model emphasizes the Architecture phase before designing begins. Technological architecture is changing rapidly nowadays, and both the technical infrastructure (workstations, servers, network, operating systems, etc.) and the tools (CASE, I-CASE, application development tools, etc.) are evolving faster and faster. Two things must be ensured: the application is rational and it can be built with the chosen technology, and that the technology will be valid and usable in future years, too. So, the development and run-time environments are defined in this phase. (Recall also Figure 1).

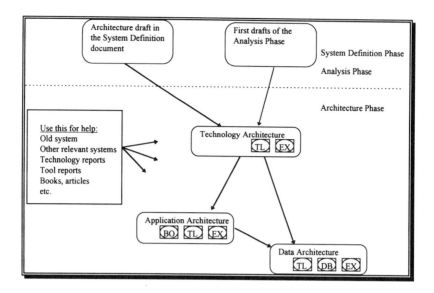

Figure 7. Architecture Phase

The application architecture describes the structure of the application and how it will be divided into presentation, business logic and data management. If the business logic is to be divided between client and server, this division is decided here. Other relevant parts here are the reusable components, which means that one should look for parts in the system that should be constructed with reusability in mind. These parts could later be moved into a company's reusable component library. Parts that could be constructed either from the company's own reusable libraries or bought from vendors should also be looked for.

Table 3. Architecture Phase.

Roles	Activities	Artifacts	UML Diagrams
TL & EX	Define Technology architecture	Technology architecture description	Deployment diagram
BO & TL & EX	Define Application architecture	Application architecture description	Component diagram
DB & TL & EX	Define Data architecture	Data architecture description	Deployment diagram

The Component and Deployment diagrams are a good addition to the UML. So far, the architectural descriptions have been more or less company-specific, with each company having its own description standards. The diagrams mentioned can be used in the OOCS model as shown in Table 3, with texts, lists and other diagrams fulfilling the document.

This phase, if any, calls for expertise. The Team Leader is again in the main role when he/she designs the architecture together with other experts. Although this phase usually increases the work load of the overall project, it pays back later when there are less problems in the Design and Construction phases. We have also been in projects where about half of the time from the System Definition phase to the Architecture phase is spent on architecture selection, evaluation and testing. However, in large projects (around 10 developers, lasting two years, in emerging technologies) the benefit has been seen in the Construction phase: the client/server architecture, including all three sub-architectures, has been tested in advance and there have been less technical problems than in projects that have used new tools without prior testing.

3. Discussion and Conclusions

This paper gave one solution to the problem of how to organize developers when they develop object-oriented client/server applications. The Team-Based role model and the OOCS process model were defined. The roles and their activities in the three first phases of the process model were illustrated. Although the OOCS model was taken as an example of the process models, there is no reason to doubt that other models would not benefit from the same kind of approach. The roles are an extra link between the project plan and the development model. Project members can view the tasks they have in the project via their roles. They can concentrate on these activities each role includes. Users are also part of the project team in the TB model. They can also see from the OOCS model where and when they are needed and what tasks are assigned to them. The OOCS model emphasizes that users can take part in activities like use case analysis, object modeling and user interface design. Users and Application Developers establish mini teams which combine domain expertise and software engineering.

The TB model is sometimes criticized by those who do not accept the idea that Application Developers both design and code, although this stems from the iterative development (design-code-test) approach more than from the role model itself. This is also a social question (status of designer). In the TB model, there are Business Object Developers that may not code, but usually the Application Developers code the parts they design. The role of the Database Developer includes also coding, usually database classes (i.e., the database is used via database classes, not directly using SQL), but in the case of object-relational or pure object-oriented databases, also part of the business logic may be coded into the database. The TB role model underlines the ownership of the business objects and the distribution of component libraries. The idea is to establish teams around the Business Object Developers, i.e., owners of business objects. This kind of company-level component development (see Figure 1 and 4) has been started in one company and the first results are encouraging.

The OOCS model has been developed in the last four years and it is based on same sources as the Unified Modeling Language. Before the UML was released, the OOCS model combined use case descriptions from Jacobson et al. [7] and OMT from Rumbaugh et al. [12]. The data modeling part has always been present as to fulfill the three-tier client/server architecture. Common data modeling notations have been used, since the object-oriented world has underestimated the role of databases in application development. The OOCS model is devoted to application development in the three-tier architecture. It also emphasizes the strong connection between the roles of the developers and the responsibilities they have. When the roles are linked to the project members at the beginning of the project, each member can find his/her activities from the OOCS model and concentrate on them. The model has been used in projects developing applications for client/server, internet and cooperative (distributed) architectures. The model has been very stabile during the last years and the biggest change lately has been the adoption of the UML, which has only affected documentation. The UML eases the use of the OOCS model, because the UML unifies the notation and there is no need to combine several notations anymore. The Component and Deployment diagrams are a good addition when the architecture of the application is designed. The usefulness of the UML will be tested in practice in the near future, when companies begin using the UML.

The team-based Object-Oriented Client/Server development model combines three dimensions (organization, architecture, process). Normally, these dimensions are kept separate, but the OOCS and TB models have shown in practice that they can be successfully combined.

References

1. Booch G. Object-Oriented Design. Benjamin/Cummings, Menlo Park, CA, 1991.
2. Booch G. Object-Oriented Analysis and Design with Applications.Benjamin/Cummings, Redwood City, CA, 1994.
3. Booch G. Object Solutions: Managing the Object-Oriented Project. Addison-Wesley, Menlo Park, CA, 1995.
4. Goldberg A, Rubin K. Talking to Project Managers - Case Studies in   Prototyping, Part 2. HOTLINE on Object-Oriented Technology, June 1990.
5. Goldberg A, Rubin K. Talking to Project Managers - Project team job descriptions. HOTLINE on Object-Oriented Technology, November 1990.
6. Goldberg A, Rubin K. Succeeding with Objects. Decision Frameworks for Project Management. Addison-Wesley, Reading, Mass., 1995.
7. Jacobson I, Christerson M, Jonsson P, Övergaard G. Object-Oriented Software Engineering - A Use Case Driven Approach. Reading, MA: Addison-Wesley; New York:ACM Press, 1992.
8. Kivisto K. Team-Based Development of Object-Oriented Clien/Server Applications: The Role Perspective. Licentiate thesis. Institute of Information Processing Science, University of Oulu, Finland, 1997.

9. Lorenz M. Object-Oriented Software Development: A Practical Guide. Prentice Hall, Englewood Cliffs, NJ, 1993.
10. Microsoft Corporation. Analysis and Design of Client/Server Systems. Course Material, 1993.
11. Microsoft Corporation. Seminar Material. 1994.
12. Rumbaugh J, Blaha M, Premerlani W, Eddy F, Lorensen W. Object-oriented modeling and design. Prentice Hall, Englewood Cliffs, NJ, 1991.
13. UML Notation Guide, ver 1.1. Rational Software Co., 1997.
14. UML Semantics, ver 1.1. Rational Software Co.,1997
15. UML Summary, ver 1.1. Rational Software Co.,1997.

Active Interfaces to Facilitate Network Based Cooperative Work

Roose Philippe, Dalmau Marc, Aniorté Philippe

Laboratoire d'Informatique Appliquée de l'UPPA
IUT Informatique de Bayonne
Place Paul Bert
64100 Bayonne
France

Abstract

This paper proposes to extend the concept of activity used in Active DataBases (ADB) to the interface domain. The objective is to obtain interfaces adapted to distributed functionalities and, as in cooperative work, a high autonomy is needed for them. Using our experience in the Active DB domain, we propose to transpose these concepts to interfaces in a cooperative environment using a network (intranet).

1. Introduction

This paper proposes to extend the concept of activity used in Active DataBases (ADB) to the interface domain. The objective is to obtain interfaces adapted to distributed functionalities and as in cooperative work, a high autonomy is needed for them.

The mechanisms that we propose will allow the user to make active interfaces become the central node of the cooperative activity. These interfaces of course keep their traditional role but can also generate and receive events. Events that they generate provoke actions in the application, those they receive allow users to view the progress of the work [1]. We hope that the interfaces will become sensitive to the totality of the cooperative activity on the network in order to reflect its state. Similarly, user's manipulations on their own interface have to be able to provoke actions in any part of the network.

This poses new conceptual problems as we need to delimit the frontier between what is application dependant (under its control) and what is interface dependent. Moreover, we have to extract key events of the cooperative application, and define how to react to these events. It will also be necessary to define events composed from other events. If detection mechanisms of such events are available [2], the definition of composed events linked to an application remains a delicate problem.

Using our experience in the Active DB domain, we propose to transpose these concepts to interfaces in a cooperative environment using a network (intranet). We will begin by detailing our cooperative work view, the manner in which we want to manage it and the place of the interface in such applications. In a second part, we will present the concept of Active DB which is the basis of our work, and we will link it to active interfaces for cooperative work. We will then present some primitives allowing the matching of the new functionality of this kind of interface and the implementation of the necessary mechanisms. Finally, we will present a concrete example.

2. Interfaces in Cooperative Work

We focus on the problem of shared interfaces adapted to cooperative work. They need to represent the whole activity of an application managed in a cooperative way and of course this problem is not trivial [3].

2.1. Cooperative Work

Cooperative work allows people and machines to achieve a common task. It is defined by the automation of procedures where documents, information, and tasks are shared between participants. All of them conform to a set of rules which contribute to a common goal [4]. The first objective of cooperative applications is to propose a medium where the space and time dimension disappear. We cannot speak about cooperative work without introducing the concept of group, this allows us to define a set of entities as one virtual entity, which gives possibilities to call all the members of a group by the same name. This allows communication with all of them using only one address. Among these groupworks, links of dependance may be introduced, allowing us to define hierarchies and canvas of services. Moreover, the task network can evolve dynamically as it is running (addition, exit) even if the system functions and messages circulate on the network. Dynamic management of groups is required, as is the inclusion of an adapted handler. This evolution of groups will oblige us to create human-computer (and human-human) interfaces depending on their activities, their needs and adapted to this evolution in the time.

The principal tasks are collectives (needing organized, simultaneous or alternative interventions) or individualized but with a collective objective. In this context, mutual ignorance of participants must give away to some awareness of the group (a group is a set of individuals or services). Therefore, it is necessary to propose a new generation of multi-user interactive systems allowing cooperation between participants and allowing appropriate ergonomics to collective and individual tasks. It appears necessary for us to know and manage interventions of different users. We can distinguish two appropriate solutions. The first using synchronous communication is the possibility of being informed in real time of the progress of the work . It is the principle of triggered actions thanks to rendez-vous which will be developed later. The second is the implementation of an asynchronous communication mechanism (for actions whose time criterion is less crucial) allowing the exchange of information even if the addressee is absent. For example, when the service is momentarily closed.

We therefore have the following schema : a cooperative application is composed of a set of modules (applications realizing a simple task) cooperating between each of them to realise more complex tasks. They are composing a groupwork. These groupworks move dynamically with time to answer requests coming from users and applications. They have synchronization possibilities by giving each other some points of rendez-vous. These rendez-vous are taken when events are produced in the application environment.

Each of these modules can be interactive when associated to an interface allowing the user to participate in the cooperative work. The rendez-vous principle allows real time reaction of these interfaces, and knowledge synchronization between modules. We will use the principle of ECA rules : when an event E occurs, if the condition C is verified, then the action A is executed. In fact, the condition is an algorithm allowing, for example, consultation of a state (the interface is updatable or not), a value or any condition algorithmically expressible [5]. If the condition is true, the action is triggered causing, for example, the update of the interface. Thus, this solution allows also the implementation of the ECAA (Event Condition Action Alternative) mechanism : when an event occurs, if the condition is true, the action is done, if false, the alternative action is triggered [4].

The information exchange between modules has been made with an asynchronous communication mechanism using messages. We notice that it is sometimes necessary to communicate with modules not present on a machine (when the application needs services not present on the same site). A groupwork can be spread on the whole network including modules not actually running. The messaging mechanism ignores the geographic limits. Thus, we have the following schema representing 3 sites supporting 12 modules consisting of 4 groupworks.

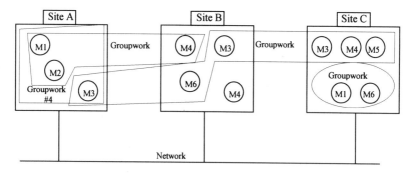

Figure. 1 : Multiplace groupwork

2.2. Distributed Interfaces

With the Web, a new way of developing interfaces has appeared. Distributed aspects have become the object of new research in this domain. These new interfaces have to be totally adapted to the cooperative work which badly needs them. Some work in this direction has been made and, most of the time, in collaboration with cooperative research teams. Projects such as [6] show the necessity of using tools adapted to this kind of development. This project, like ours, shows the essential links between cooperating modules and evokes the ECA principle.

Our proposition for an active interface is based on the concept of events. It generates events depending on user actions (mouse events, loss focus, ...) and it is also able to receive events. When an event is received, if it is recognized, a rule (a task) will be activated to achieve an action (functionality update, information update, aspect modification, ...). Including the interface in a module of the application will remain impossible because of the problem of taking into account external events. The interface not only reflects the state of the associated module, but in general, the state of all the modules making up the application (and its context). To respond to all of these criteria, it seems necessary to separate the interface from the application itself. Having an autonomous interface presents three main advantages : management of views, personalization and modularity.

For the same application, programmers have to provide different views depending on the user's competence. For example, it allows, some important manipulations, to restrain or, alternatively to increase functionality of an application. It can avoid bad manipulations by making somebody aware of his responsibilities. These restrictions will be defined stating who is able to do what and when. Indeed, an operation achievable for a user at the moment t will not necessarily be achievable at the moment $t+1$. We need to define access rights according to the membership or otherwise of a groupwork, to the level in the hierarchy of groups. It will, therefore, be necessary to have primitives allowing the definition of rights for the action directly concerning the interface. This management of rights will therefore only allow the interface to be updated by the groupwork for which they have been defined . Some common data may not have to be seen by individual applications (for confidential reasons for example). This creates a problem of views management. We need to provide mechanisms (groupwork managing) allowing different persons to have access only to a specific part of data and functionality. As these views are dynamic, we have to foresee definition commands for the access rights as : what can be seen, who can see it, when can it be seen. As the group management is dynamic, the rights management s has to be dynamic too. A groupwork will not necessarily have the same rights all through its life. Therefore, rules triggered by some events will modify the aspect of the interface, and the data displayed (update, period of refreshment, etc), but they also modify the commands available.

Personnalization is always better for productivity. It allows each person to move with the time on their own work space (interface) which can be parametrized (update delay for some informations, granularity of received informations...). This parametrization can be done according to the environment using rules, as in

Computer Aided Learning. Indeed, conditions of ECA rules allow us to verify many parameters concerning the user interface. If these conditions are verified, they will trigger actions allowing, for example,adaptation to functionality.

Finally, modularity provides a best programming language independence between the application and the interface, facilities of debugging, updating and good reuse possibilities.

3. Active Databases : Introduction

" Classical " DBMS manipulate data in response to explicit demands of a user or an application. This " passivity " influences directly interactions with these datas and therefore systems which will use them [7], requiring the inclusion of control of the application or the user requests. The main defaults are the loss of modularity and time reaction problems which prevent control in time.

The active behavior is obtained integrating ECA rules [8]. ECA rules are inspired of expert systems production rules, they allow the DBMS to be reactive to what happens in the DB and its environment. The activity idea is not new, it has been proposed in the R system [9] as an assertion and exists as triggers in many systems (SQL 3, Sybase, Oracle 7). Nevertheless, this kind of activity is limited to actions allowing operations to be abort in particular those which cause inconsistency in the DB.

Active DBMS are able to recognize specific situations and to manage them without explicit requests from the user or the application. They associate actions (programs) to situations (e.g. database operation occurences). Therefore, activity allows separation of control from the application itself to obtain more modular applications, which are easily modifiable, but also answer automatically and more quickly to specific situations. Moreover, reactions to temporal events are easier to achieve.

4. Active Interfaces for the Cooperative Work : Mechanisms

Our experience is the Active-DBMS domain. We hope to transpose our work to the interface and the cooperative work domain. We will present briefly the ADACTIF's basic principles [10]. We will concentrate on the notion of parallel tasks and rendez-vous. Next, we will present the architecture needed to elaborate an active interface for the cooperative work.

4.1. Active Interfaces with the ECA Model

The interface creates/receives events. As events are received, some rules will be activated. They will modify the interface (the aspect, the functionalities). This is the same philosophy as in ADACTIF : some basic operations trigger events activating specific rules, but in a cooperative environment, this is the main difference. It will therefore, be necessary to manage events which are not local. In addition, a set of cooperative work characteristics; groupwork management, access rights (reading, updating, creating, ...) and messaging will be added.

4.2. Local Events - Distant Events

We distinguish two kind of events. Locally produced events on the site where they are detected, and distant events recognized on a site but produced on another. Every defined event has to be qualified, that means, when it is defined, its origin and destination have to be specified. Thus, we can ensure the correct diffusion. For example, we want some modules of a specific groupwork (destination) to be informed when a specific event occurs on a precise site, module or group (origin). Events allow the synchronization between modules and groupwork.

4.3. Condition-Action

When an event is detected, a rendez-vous is taken with one or several rules on the site where it is detected. When this event is a distant one, it is broadcast on the network towards one or several sites. Then, it is processed as a local event, the condition is evaluated and the action is eventually executed on each site where this event has been received. The rendez-vous principle was inspired by ADA language. It allows parallel execution of the different active rules. The activated rule will evaluate the condition and, if verified, execute the action which will modify the interface. At this level, the sending or reception of messages will be also managed. So, activated rules will use a messages exchange (DB requests, context...) to gain all data needed to their correct execution.

4.4. Composed Events and Detection Principle

Elementary events (for example, a simple interaction between the user and the interface as a mouse-click) are of too low level to express the behaviour of the cooperative application. Therefore, we have to detect more complex events composed of simple or already composed events.

The solution we propose has been developed in ADACTIF [10] and is: when the first event of the composition occurs, we activate the detective rule. This will achieve the composition operation. Events taking part in the composition (they can be composed themselves) take a rendez-vous with it. When all necessary occurences are detected and, if the composition operation is finished, the rule raises the composed event. Detective rules are present on each site where a composed event has to be detected. The programmer of the cooperative application will then have to be able to define relevant events to be detected and their eventual composition with other to achieve composed events. When these events are identified, it is necessary to associate them with the corresponding conditions and actions. This is the center of the activity operation.

4.5. General Architecture

We will define ECA triggered rules when changes occur on displayed data, or when a specific action is detected. To achieve that, we need an active environment which will describe graphic objects to manage. The chosen mechanism is similar to [11]'s work in the sense of all the activity is locally managed on each machine by a set of mechanisms. All information goes through the active system which dispatches them. The interface is seen as a generator event which informs the active system of changes. These events are taken into account locally and will be broadcast on the network to ensure synchronization with other modules or groupworks. Therefore, we need to provide mechanisms allowing the local/distant managing with the ECA rule principle described previously. Here is our proposition :

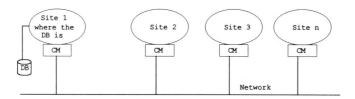

Figure. 2 : General architecture principle

Each site on the network will include a Communication Manager (CM) allowing us to communicate using a system similar to system mail with all the other sites and to take rendez-vous with distant rules. The CM manages all the synchronous (events) and asynchronous (messages) communication. Furthermore, each site will have an Event Manager (EM) and a Rule Manager (RM) :

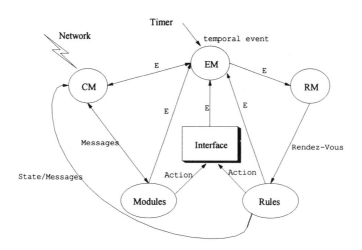

Figure. 3 : Architecture on each machine

When an event occurs on a site, it is sent to the Event Manager (EM) of this site. If this event is recognized (in the list of known local events), it will be transmitted to the Rule Manager (RM) which will take a rendez-vous with the appropriated rule(s). If the event has to be sent, it is transmitted to the Communication Manager (CM) which will broadcast it to the sites concerned. Once the rendez-vous is made with a rule (task), this will evaluate the condition, if satisfied, the action is executed. We have to realise that each of the modules and rules may raise new events. The interface is in the center of our schema because it raises all events caused interactively by the user or caused by specific situations. Furthermore, rules act on this interface to modify it (update). The modules manage the operational part of the application and its interface. The CM also receives messages (thanks to the message passing technique [12]) from the network and broadcasts them toward the modules or rules concerned.

5. Specification Langage

We have presented the operative mechanisms. Now, we will describe the associated specification langage. We will express the different primitives needed to specify events and rules (conditions and actions).

5.1. Events

Events have to be qualified by the groupwork and module which have produced them (origin). Therefore, we need to distingish an event E produded by a module M of the groupwork G of an event E' produced by another module of the same group or from another identical module of a different groupwork. Events will be broadcast on the network, so, we need to specify which modules and groups to inform (targets). The event specification syntax is the following.

```
DefineEvent <EventName> [from origin] [to target] [kind]
```

The origin of an event describes which module (if specified) of which group (if specified) has raised it. Symmetrically, the destination of an event can be all modules, the modules of a group, one specific module or some different modules.

5.2. Rules

There are two kind of rules. Standard rules achieving the CA (Condition-Action) part of the the ECA mechanism, matching to an event E. Detective rules allow the detection of composed events (cf. 5.3.).

5.2.1. Standard Rules

They can evaluate conditions relative to the global activity of the system. They can also generate actions (acting for example on the interface) implementing, for example, the communication between modules thanks to a mail like system (asynchronous communication).

5.2.1.1. The Condition

The condition is evaluated by the rule when a triggering event occurs. It allows decisions regarding the execution of an action. In our system, the condition may reflect the state of the interface, the DB or be evaluated from the local state of the application. However, it is sometimes necessary to evaluate the general state of the application in term of modules, and group participation with the cooperative work.
It therefore appears necessary to implement a mechanism to determine which modules constitute a group. In this way it will be possible to adjust actions in function of the real activity on the network. We will use the primitive memberOf(GroupName) to obtain the list of the module in the precise group. The system will maintain an up to date information base concerning all modules participating in the cooperative work. It will be informed by the modules of theirstart, end and also participation of a group (or their exit)

5.2.1.1. The Action

The action will be triggered as a reaction to an event.. It can achieve all kind of operations (calculation, DB access, ...) but also operations on the interface (updating, functionality evolution, appearance modification, ...).

In the context of a distributed application, it will be neccessary to communicate with other modules. So, we offer a messaging mechanism allowing the transmission of information to anybody on the network. The addressee will be identified by the name of the module and the group to which it belongs .
We introduce the following primitives :

```
sendMessage (message, [destination])
```

If the target parameter is omitted, the message is broadcast to all modules. In the opposite case, it is interpreted as the event destination designation (cf. 5.1.).

```
getMessage (message, [origin])
```

If the origin parameter is omitted, the message is received wherever it comes from. In the opposite case, it is interpreted as in the event origin designation (cf. 5.1.).

Moreover, the general state of the application can be examined when condition evaluation is done (cf. 5.2.1.1.). It can also be modified when the action is executed. In this way, a module can inform the system of its participation (or none participation) to a groupwork.

We use the following commands :

```
joinGroup (group name) and quitGroup (group name)
```

5.2.1.2. Rules Specifiaction and Association to Events

This specification concerns the behavior model which refers to the associated rule. Here is the syntax of these declarations :

```
createRule <ruleName> as <activityModel>
Activity model :
void activityModel () {
    if condition
        action;
}
```

Here is the definition of how to take a rendez-vous with the rule when an event occurs :

```
fire <ruleName>  when <eventName>
```

And to raise an event :

```
raise <eventName>
```

5.2.2.   Detective rules for Composed Events

It will sometimes be necessary to compose events in order to to create a new one; a Composed Event (CE). Unlike the main Active-DBMS developed (HiPAC, REACH, SAMOS) which achieve the composition with logical operations, we have chosen to use detective rules. Indeed, this solution allows more freedom to achieve truly complex composition algorithms. Furthermore, this choice is more efficient when in a distributed event environment. To trigger a composed event, we need a rule (a detective rule) which will receive events coming into the composition of the CE and trigger it when the condition is verified. The detective rule becomes active only when a rendez-vous is taken after the occurrence of the first triggering event.
The association between the detective rule and component events will be created by the primitive *fire ruleName **when** eventName* as explained previously, whereas the detected event will be triggered with the primitive ***raise** eventName*. As this event receives an origin definition, it will have to be detected on each place corresponding to this origin.   An instance of the detective rule will be present on each site where

the event may be detected. Each detective rule will produce a different event because it will come from a different site. Rendez-vous are taken across the network. It is not the same with standard rules because they are always active where the triggering event takes place.

6. Example

Let us consider a production workshop made up of cells composed of a computerized command system and a robot making spare parts for the manufactured product. Each cell do several manufacturing phases per element. Cells are part of an assembly line in order to make a finished product. A supervision quarter takes place in the workshop and watches the work in progress and controls the production. From our point of view, we consider each cell as a module. The supervision software will be considered as a module too. The organisation of cells in the production chain corresponds to the notion of groupwork.

Each module (production cell or supervisor) is placed on a distinct site. All of these sites are linked by a network. The supervision quarter has an interface allowing knowledge of :

For each cell :
- the state of the cell (out of order or not),
- the number of producted elements since the beginning of the series.

For each cell of the group :
- the number of finite products achieved since the beginning of the series.

Moreover, this interface offers a set of buttons. Each of them controls the activity of a group and includes stopping. We will show the pertinent events.

6.1. Events to Provide

Now, we have to consider all the relevant events of the applications. They will be identified and qualified according to their role.

6.1.1.   Events whose Origin is the Supervisor

Interface button activation. We will have as many distinct events as buttons on the control panel. These events are generated by the interface and remain local to the supervisor module.

```
defineEvent ActivatedButtonB1from Supervisor interface
                                  // as much as buttons
```

Group stop request. We will have many distinct events as groups in the activity. These events are managed by the supervisor and have to be broadcast to each cell of the group.

```
defineEvent StopGroup1 from Supervisor to Group1
        interface                    // as much as groups
```

6.1.2.   Events whose Origin is a Cell

End of a manufactuing phase on an element in progress. This event is created by the robot when it reaches the end of a sequence of operations constituting a complete phase. It has to be broadcast to all other cells of the group to ensure their synchronization in order to make the finished product.

```
defineEvent FinPhasec1 from CellC1 to Supervisor
        abstract                    // as much as cells
```

Breakdown detection. This event is created by the robot and sent to the supervisor

```
defineEvent Breakdown from CellC1 to Supervisor abtract
                                    // as much as cells
```

End of element manufacturing. This event is not directly detected by the robot which does not know the sequence of phases but only activates the commands according to received orders from the control of the cell. Therefore, it is a composed event which will be detected when *n* successive occurences of the simple event of a factoring phase have been produced. Of course, the number *n* is different on each cell. Thus, we have to define for each cell, a detective rule to generate this event. This event will be broadcast towards the supervisor and the cells of the group.

```
defineEvent EndElementC1 from CellC1 to Supervisor
        abstract
defineEvent EndElementC1 from CellC1 to Group1 abstract
```

For example, the detective rule for the composed event on the cell C1 is defined as follows :

```
createRule <endingPhaseC1> as <instanceEndPhaseP1>
void instanceEndPhaseP1 ( ) {
   getRendezVous(EndPhaseP1);
     if (nbEndP1 == n)
         raise EndElementC1;
}
```

The rule triggering is done with the primitive fire.

```
fire EndingPhaseC1 when EndPhaseC1
```

6.2. Actions to Provide

When an event occurs on a module, it will trigger one or several rules. These rules will achieve some associated actions. They are described by an algorithm evaluating whether a condition has been met and executing the action associated with the triggering event.

6.2.1.   Rules on the Supervisor's Site

Interface button activation event. The button has to be active (this is the condition). The associated action consists in generating the group stop request event for the corresponding group.

Breakdown detection event. For this event, two rules are triggered on the supervisor quarter :

1/ The first one is for the interface updating in order to display the new state of the cell where the event comes from. There is no special condition for this rule.
2/ The second one is for the production supervision in the eventuality of a breakdownDepending on the seriousness of the breakdown it triggers an event " group stop request " for the group which the breakdown cell belongs to.

End of element manufactoring event. Two rules are also triggered by this event on the supervisor quarter.
1/ The first one is for interface updating. It counts the number of manufactured element by the event's source cell since the beginning of the series.
2/ The second one is for finished products. If the event's source cell is the one which makes the last operation on the element, the information concerning the number of finished products made by the group in which the cell belongs will be updated on the interface. The element becomes a product, otherwise nothing happens.

6.2.2.   Rules on each Cell Site

Each cell has a detection rule for the composed event (already described). Moreover, it has the following rules :
Group stop request event. The associated rule will immediately stop the robot. This event, automatically broadcast to all others cells in the group, will stop the whole assembly line.
End of element manufacturing event. The associated rule allows the command organ of the cell which receives it to know that it has an element waiting to be manufactured. Indeed, the cell supplying it will indicate with this event that it has terminated its work. The rule will verifiy that the cell which created the end of element manufacturing event is the one which supplies it. In this case, the action will authorize the start of a new manufacturing cycle.

Note: In this example, groupworks are not involved dynamically. We should have proposed a dynamic assembly line. We neither manage users' profiles, different views, nor DB. It should however be possible to imagine an automatic update of a DB for each new element producted (stock managing). The user interface should be modified to add a view of the stocks. So, the user may have the possibility to stop momentarily the production of an assembly line.

7. Conclusion

With Internet and intranet, the work can be easily decentralized. It becomes necessary to strengthen the collaboration between persons working together. Applications have to provide more user-friendly interfaces, adapted to this kind of work. Developing applications for the cooperative work has to solve a number of problems (to be aware of the cooperative activity, consistency of informations displayed, coordination of actions, ...) which force us to provide synchronous and asynchronous mechanisms of communication [13] [14]. We think that the presented architecture provides a number of qualities for this kind of application. Its main advantage is the use of the task principle and the rendez-vous mechanism to achieve the activity. Indeed, this principle is very general and may be easily implemented with Java/CORBA [15] which has many internet facilities. This allows us to exploit the possibilities of parallelism and synchronisation across a network. Furthermore, it appears important to offer to the cooperative application developer some low level tools (tasks algorithms, detection operations, event triggering, ...) allowing precise control of the system behaviour. We now have to define an adapted design method using these simple mechanisms which allows the definition of the different parameters they will need.

The conceptual problems touched on at the beginning of this paper are still the center of our concerns (the border between interface and application, which are the relevant events of the cooperative application, ...). Otherwise, it appears necessary to us to define simple but powerful tools which will constitute the base. They are the first step to the creation of cooperative applications because they allow, in particular, the concept of cooperative active interfaces resolving many problems involved with this kind of application. Following this study of problem identification and providing solutions to solve them, we will focus more precisely on the methodological aspects. Studies concerning creation and implementation of Active DB have been made with the IDEA methodology and a formal specification langage [16]. Our aim is to study this kind of methodology to extend it to cooperative work and to active interfaces.

References

1. Roose P. Réalisation d'un prototype d'interface active en Java, Rapport de DEA du LIUM, Le Mans, France, 1997.
2. Tawbi C., Jaber G., Dalmau M. Activity specification using rendez-vous, proc. of the second Int'l Workshop on Rules in Database Systems RIDS'95.

Springer, Lecture Notes in Computer Science, Vol. 985. Athens, September 1995.

3. Diaz O. Diaz, Arturo J., N.W. Paton, al-Qaimari G. Supporting Dynamic Displays Using Active Rules, ACM SIGMOD- Vol 23(1), pp 21-26, 1994.

4. Jagannath M. K. A workflow management and simulation system and its supporting object-oriented knowledge base management system, thesis of the university of Florida, 1997.

5. Aniorté P., Dalmau M., Roose P. Supporting laborative work in Intranet using an Active DBMS implemented with Java, WebNet'97, Toronto (Canada), November 97.

6. OSAKA Project , Trigone Laboratory, Lille 1 University, www.univ-lille1.fr

7. Barros de Sa J. État de l'art des Bases de Données Actives, Laboratoire PRISM - Université de Versailles, technical report, 1994.

8. Dayal U. Active DBMS, Proc. of 3rd Int'l conference on database and knowledge base, Jerusalem, June 1988.

9. Eswaran K.P. Spécification, implementation and iterations of a trigger subsystem in an integrated DB system, IBM Research report RJ1820, August 1976.

10. Tawbi C. ADACTIF : Extension d'un SGBD à l'activité par une approche procédurale basée sur les rendez-vous – PhD Thesis of the Paul Sabatier University - Toulouse III - 1996.

11. Lebastard F. CERMICS/INRIA, CHOOE project presentation, www.inria.fr/cermics/dbteam.

12. Tagg R., Freyberg C. Designing distributed and cooperative information systems, Thomson computer press, 1997, pp. 280-297.

13. Amit.P. Sheth A. From Contemporary Workflow Process Automation to Adaptive and Dynamic Work Activity Coordination and Collaboration, Keynote talk at the Workshop on Workflows in Specific and Engineering Applications, Toulouse - France - September 1997.

14. Geppert A., Tombros D., Dittrish K.R. Semantics of Reactive Components in Event-Driven Workflow Execution, Proc. of the 9th int'l conference on Advanced Systems Engineering, Borcelona, Spain, June 1997.

15. The Common Object Request Broker : Architecture ans Specificartion -Revision 2.0, The Object Management Group (OMG), Juillet 1995.

16. Ceri S., Fraternali P. Designing Database Applications with Objetcs and Rules, IDEA Methodologie, Addison Wesley, 1997.

Adapting the OPEN Methodology for Web Development

M. Lin and B. Henderson-Sellers

School of Information Technology
Swinburne University of Technology,
Hawthorn, Victoria, Australia

Abstract

Information systems methodologies for web-based developments are crucial for largescale commercial software. Indeed, even though small projects can be apparently accomplished successfully without use of a formal methodology, these projects will become less of the norm as web-based development is integrated into commercial organizations as one of their major platforms for delivering business solutions to their customers. In the context of object-oriented web development, the third generation methodology, OPEN, is linked with the needs of web-based development. Extensions needed are evaluated and recommendations for future work given.

1. Introduction

Methodologies are essential for rigorous software development, particularly when teams are large and software mission-critical. However, arguments have been made (e.g. Thomas, 1996) that when developing "in web-time", a methodology is irrelevant. This paper takes the opposite view. Whilst we acknowledge that a comprehensive, "one-size-fits-all" methodology designed for a team of 100 is overkill for a development team of 2, we maintain that using a flexible, carefully tuned methodology is vital for achieving high quality in all project sizes and types.

In this paper, we describe a tailorable and flexible methodology which is useful for a wide variety of project sizes and scopes, including these very small webtime developments. The methodology adapts and extends the first third-generation OO lifecycle methodology, OPEN (Graham *et al.*, 1997b; Henderson-Sellers *et al.*, 1998). We identify first the current limitations in web development approaches and then make some tentative recommendations on how OPEN can and should be adapted to cater for the emergence of web development.

2. What is Web Development?

The web and the internet relate to networks using higher level protocols such as HTTP, FTP, SMTP, as well as various other technologies all based on underlying TCP/IP and physical hardware layers. These terms thus apply equally to both the public internet, as well as internal corporate intranets.

Some of the benefits of using web development (even in its current embryonic state) include:

- An organizational structure able to allow widely dispersed, disparate and transient teams to work on large, complex projects
- The common and encouraged use of open standards
- Production of high quality software with little or no formal QA process
- Large amounts of documentation written by developers notorious for their resistance to producing it.

It can also be argued that web development is matched by a highly iterative, 'customer-focussed', RAD-like development process in which end-users can be considered as members of the software development team (Raymond, 1997).

Booch (1996) discussed three aspects of web usage in OO:

(1) 'Development of the Web' is the most prominent. However, it soon becomes clear that there is little in the way of software development in this area, with most of the work being carried out by skilled graphic artists to create visually effective web sites.
(2) 'Development for the Web' — in fact there is little difference between developing applications for the web and other types of software development. The features of web development such as distributed computing, client/server architecture, database interfacing, hypertext user-interfaces, use of scripting and OO programming languages are all present and well known in other areas of software development (see discussions in Henderson-Sellers et al., 1998).
(3) 'Development by the Web'. Booch (1996) notes "the tremendous value to be gained by using an intranet to manage the products of development". This use of the web, as an *environment* for software development holds the most promising future use of this technology for the software development world.

From the above discussion a concise definition for the term web development can be given as:

The development of applications (which may or may not be deployed on the web) using web based technologies to create the development environment for the project.

3. Experiences from Successful Web Development

One of the most successful web development projects to date has been that of Linux. Essentially still organized and coordinated by one person, the core Linux operating system (the kernel and related drivers) is now made up of a source tree some 23 megabytes and 2000 files in size and with close to 200 listed contributors and some 50 odd active maintainers/developers (Torvalds, 1998). Yet the pertinent fact in this is not that one person has been able to manage the project, but that the project *did not require* any appreciable amount of management (in comparison to commercial software projects of comparable size) and that the whole development team was able to coordinate their efforts, while being geographically dispersed and only loosely coordinated by a single individual. This suggests that some projects can be successful without the use of a formal methodology. What it does not demonstrate is whether the development relied on an *implicit* methodology — at the very least, version control, configuration management, testing, design and implementation techniques must have been used in some organized fashion!

Taking the approach used by Linux one step further, the Apache HTTP server project's software is being developed by a group without even a permanent coordinator (let alone a project manager). Again, this project has produced not only a high quality product, but one that reportedly dominates the market over equivalent commercial products (Fielding and Kaiser, 1997)!

However, outlining here the successes of these (and other smaller, less well known) web development projects in the free-software community cannot (and should not) be taken as advocating that *commercial* software developers should switch to this method of development. In fact, while it has been successful, the current web development methodology and process has many shortcomings. Some of these were outlined by members of the Apache project in Fielding and Kaiser (1997), while others are discussed below.

4. Current Problems with Web Development

While the web development process of the informal style has been very successful in the projects mentioned above, it has also had some lesser known failures. However, they might not be classified as such by the standards of many commercial projects where even the successful delivery of most required features (with no continued development and minimal support and maintenance) is all too rare. But even in the success stories, there are areas where the business (and definitely the IS) community would consider them inadequate or incomplete.

So what are these areas of deficiencies of the web development process as it now stands?

4.1 Lack of documented process

Probably the most obvious is the lack of a documented process. Arising as it does out of a hacking culture [1], web development projects have not (until recently) had any documented process, instead relying on 'release early, release often' attitude identified by Raymond (1997). While this has not, to date, been a hindrance web development projects, it will become an increasing problem as commercial organizations start to use web-based software development environments. Their need to understand and integrate any web-focussed process into their existing practices will require at least a minimal documentation of the new process. In addition, any adoption of the process for internal use by an organisation will require a much more substantial amount of formal documentation.

4.2 Lack of non-code deliverables

While the current web development process has managed to produce copious amounts of *good quality* user documentation and usually well commented code (Gleditsch and Gjermshus, 1997 for a good example of this), there has been a tendency not to produce similar amounts or quality of technical documentation. This has probably been due to the availability of source code together with the assumption that anyone working on these projects would be proficient enough to gain all the information they required by simply reading the source code. This assumption, even in the case of coding 'gurus', is probably incorrect since, although the free availability of source is a great boon to developers, it should be considered a final resort, with good technical documentation being the primary objective.

4.3 Lack of object orientation

This is probably the greatest fundamental problem with current web development. While penetration of OO has not yet been great in commercial software development, it is virtually non-existent in web development projects — surprising since much of today's focus on web exploitation is through the object-oriented programming language Java. The dearth of usage of OO programming languages, whilst surprising, can probably be attributed to most web development projects originating in UNIX environments, where C and various scripting languages have long dominated. With the rising popularity of Java, it might be anticipated that this will soon change. What will probably not occur so readily is the adoption of OO techniques at levels above the source
code implementation. This is the focus of the OPEN/WWW project described here.

4.4 Lack of metrics

With most projects being carried out in the developers' spare time or as part on academic projects, there has been little interest in collection of metrics of these

---

[1] Nielsen (1995) refers to hacking as: Software products created by programming directly from loosely formulated requirements specifications.

projects. This is hardly surprising, especially given the status of metrics collection and use on many commercial projects.

4.5 Lack of CASE/support tools usage

The lack of good *free* CASE tools is undoubtedly the reason for the rare usage of CASE tools in web development, as the use of small, code-level automated tools is widespread. This, of course, will not be a problem for any commercial adoption of this process (though customization to the process will be required), but projects involving commercial/open-source or multi-organizational collaboration will face the problem, though in the guise of standardizing on one tool or interoperational difficulties between different tools.

5. What is OPEN?

OPEN (standing for Object-oriented Process, Environment and Notation) is a third generation, public domain[2], process-focussed OO methodology (Graham *et al.*, 1997; Henderson-Sellers, 1998). It is flexible and designed specifically to be tailored for specific domain types (e.g. MIS, realtime) and different project sizes. OPEN is essentially a framework, providing strong support for, *inter alia*, process modelling, analysis and design models, requirements capture and migration strategies. It also has a strong business focus as well as supporting
links to human relations issues (see Unhelkar, 1998). A prime concern of OPEN is software quality and the use of metrics.

OPEN was created and is maintained by the OPEN Consortium — a non-profit organization consisting of over thirty members drawn from the OO methodology, research and training communities worldwide. OPEN was initially created by a merger of MOSES (Henderson-Sellers and Edwards, 1994), SOMA (Graham, 1995a) and the Firesmith (1993) methods commencing at the end of 1994 when it became clear that (i) there were too many first and second generation methods in the marketplace and that their scopes were too limited; and (ii) the philosophies underlying these three methods were almost completely compatible.

In addition to synthesizing the best ideas and practices from MOSES, SOMA and Firesmith, OPEN also utilizes concepts from BON, Mainstream Objects, Martin/Odell, OBA, RDD, Syntropy, UML and others. OPEN also offers a set of principles for modelling all aspects of software development, across the full life-cycle. Individual methods may conform to it by applying its principles and adopting all or part of the OPEN framework specification: management and technical life-cycle processes, techniques and modelling language (metamodel plus notation). OPEN will continue to evolve as new techniques are developed and enhanced by working methodologists, users and researchers. The OPEN/WWW project is just one example.

The lifecycle process in OPEN is described by the contract-driven lifecycle model (Graham, 1995b; Graham *et al.*, 1997b). This is complemented by (a) a set of

---

[2] See website http://www.csse.swin.edu.au/cotar/OPEN/

Techniques (Henderson-Sellers *et al.*, 1998) and (b) a formal representation using a modelling language such as OML (Firesmith *et al.* 1997) or UML (OMG, 1997a,b). Techniques permit tailoring of the process, this tailoring being a major Task within the overall OPEN architecture (Figure 1). Tasks are carried out by agents (people) using Techniques. A two-dimensional matrix (Figure 2) links the Task (which provides the statement of goals i.e. the 'what') to the Techniques (which provide the way the goal can be achieved i.e. the 'how'). Techniques range across project management, inspections and so on through to detailed theories and practices for requirements engineering and system modelling. OPEN provides a large repository of Techniques (Henderson-Sellers *et al.*, 1998), many taken from existing methods including traditional, non-OO sources such as Soft Systems Methodology

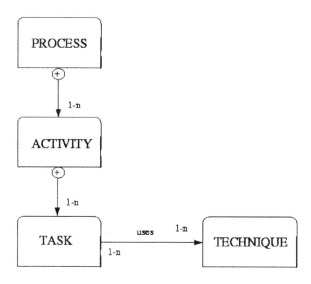

Figure 1   OPEN's Activities have Tasks which themselves are accomplished by the use of Techniques (after Graham *et al* , 1997b).

One of the greatest technical advantage of an OO lifecycle process is that of (almost) seamlessness. "Objects" [3] are used as the basic concept and unit of consideration during requirements engineering, systems analysis and design and in the OO programming language and future maintenance. "Objects" are the common

---

[3] Here, we do not want to enter into any arguments regarding the use of the words object, type, class, rôle and instance, collectively called CIRT in OPEN, and will just use "object" in a truly generic and formally undefined sense.

language of users as well as technical developers. Of course, the notion of seamlessness causes concern for project managers more used to being able to clearly delineate the end of the analysis phase and the end of the design phase.

In this seamless, iterative lifecycle in which incremental delivery is the norm — and highly advantageous in keeping the user "in the loop" providing immediate feedback, always a currently viable version for use and evaluation and producing higher quality software — the elements which comprise the lifecycle describe the high level Activities which must be undertaken in order to produce the software product(s). The Activities are linked together in an organization's tailoring of the contract-driven lifecycle — which produces their organizationally-specific process. The way in which Activities are linked together depends on the organization and the problem.

Finally, OPEN embodies a set of (object-oriented) principles. It permits enhanced semantics for object models based on the contributions of methods such as SOMA, BON, Syntropy, etc. Furthermore, OPEN is fully object-oriented in that encapsulation is a basic principle. To this end, bi-directional associations rarely occur and are strongly discouraged (Graham *et al.*, 1997a). It is a logical consequence of this that class invariants are not an optional extra in the modelling semantics. Rulesets (which generalize class invariants) can be used to model intelligent agents as objects.

Tasks

Techniques				
M	D	F	F	F
D	D	F	F	D
D	D	O	O	D
F	O	O	O	F
F	M	O	D	F
R	R	M	R	O
D	R	F	M	O
D	F	M	D	D
R	R	D	R	R
O	D	O	O	R
F	M	O	F	D

Figure 2 A core element of OPEN is a two-dimensional relationship between techniques and the tasks. Each task may require one or several techniques in order to accomplish the stated goal of the task. For each combination of task and technique, an assessment can be made of the likelihood of the occurrence of that combination. Some combinations can be identified as mandatory (M), others as recommended (R), some as being optional (O), some are discouraged (D) but may be used with care and other combinations that are forbidden (F) (after Graham *et al.*, 1997b).

In OPEN, OO principles are basic and should be adhered to. These include:

- object modelling as a very general technique for knowledge representation
- encapsulation
- polymorphism

together with
- clear, jargon-free and well-founded definitions of all terms
- extensive use of abstraction techniques, a foundation for semantically cohesive and encapsulated "objects"

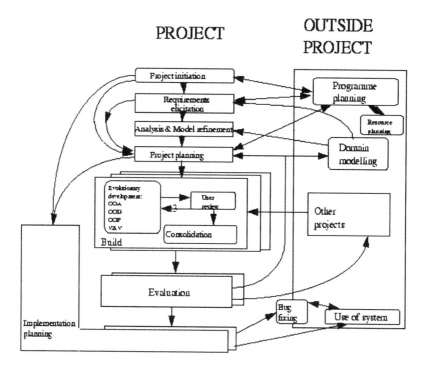

Figure 3 Contract-driven lifecycle process model (after Graham *et al.*, 1997b).

The contract-driven lifecycle, as used in OPEN, is shown in its most up-to-date form in Figure 3. The model is, in essence, very simple. In summary, a development programme may be decomposed into a network of projects that produce deliverable, working software products. Projects are composed of activities.

Each OPEN Activity is shown as a box, either with rounded corners (an unbounded Activity) or with rectangular corners (Activity tightly bound in time). Since we are modelling these activities as objects, when we can associate contracts with each Activity object (hence the lifecycle name of "contract-driven"). These are expressed primarily by pre- and post-conditions; in other words, constraints that have to be met before an Activity can be commenced and final conditions that have to be met (and signed off) before another Activity can be initiated (triggered). Testing is an integral part of these exit conditions. Activities include well-specified testing activities and should deliver test results against both task scripts (a higher form of use cases — see Graham, 1997) and a technical test plan of the normal kind; i.e. tests that answer the questions: Does an enhancement leave previous things that worked working? Does the system work well under stress and high volume I/O? These Activities thus provide a large scale structuring in time. Different configurations, chosen to reflect the needs of different problems and different organizations, can be constructed from this flexible framework. Each combination of Activities and interconnecting paths defines a software engineering process (or SEP). Once chosen, the lifecycle process is fixed — although still, at least in an OO project, highly iterative, flexible and with a high degree of seamlessness.

The progression order is neither prescriptive nor deterministic. Rather, the contract-driven lifecycle permits (1) ordering in an iterative and incremental fashion and (2) the tailoring by a given organization to its own internal standards and culture. We indicate in this figure some of the likely routes between Activity objects. But remember, the main governing constraint on the routes are whether you do or do not meet the pre-conditions of the Activity to which you wish to transition.

6. Making OPEN "Web-Friendly"

Having admitted that shortcomings exist in the web development process as it now stands, it is our intention to examine these inadequacies and show how using OPEN can help to overcome them and allow an 'OPEN-ised' version of web development to be feasible for use by both commercial software developers and the free software community. To do so, we are currently developing and testing an instantiation of the OPEN framework to cater for and improve the current process of web development. From this work, we anticipate several new additions (most probably in the form of new Tasks and/or Techniques: although, due to the large and fairly generic nature of the currently available Tasks and Techniques, this may prove to be unnecessary.

Having identified in Section 4 what is missing from the current 'version' of the web development process, in the following, analogously numbered subsections, we identify how the use of OPEN can help to address these deficiencies.

6.1 A documented process

The need for documentation of the process will of course be served through the creation of a process specification document, utilizing the OPEN framework. Because of its thorough nature, use of the OPEN framework allows the process to be documented as rigorously as required by the context. Thus a 'light' version can be used for open-source projects, while a more comprehensive version can be prepared for commercial use within an organisation.

6.2 Deliverables

OPEN describes a very large number of possible deliverables that may need to be produced as a part of the software development lifecycle. This represents an extremely large amount of documentation that is not intended to be used in full (except on extremely large and complex projects). The problem is, however, that even in the area of web development, it is conceivable that any of these deliverables may be required for a given project. One of the OPEN Tasks supports the tailoring of the OPEN methodological framework to the current project — choosing appropriate deliverables is just one element of this.

Table 1. Some possible deliverables for an OPEN–web-based development

- Project Proposal
- Requirements specification
- Project plan
- Configuration/version management plan
- Unit test plan, integration test plan, acceptance test plan
- CRC cards (object, cluster and rôle CRCs)
- Static graphical models (semantic nets) — context diagrams, layer diagrams, configuration diagrams, cluster diagrams
- Inheritance diagrams
- Deployment diagrams
- Dynamic graphical models — state transition diagrams, collaboration diagrams, sequence diagrams
- Test harness — test cases for classes, clusters and for acceptance testing
- Prototypes — user interface and model code
- Source code (class code, cluster code, release code, application code)
- Potentially reusable components

A typical set of deliverables for a web-based development is shown in Table 1. This list would probably be even shorter in the case of open-source developments, where the need for rapid development and less stringent organizational/management requirements would allow for a more technically-focussed set of deliverables.

6.3 Object orientation

The use of OPEN intrinsically solves the problem of the lack of OO in web development projects since OPEN is a 100% object-oriented method. OPEN also already provides a number of OO techniques which can be used in web development projects.

6.4 Metrics

In OPEN, the collection of metrics is considered an integral part of the software development process. Although OPEN provides extensive guidance in this area, the distributed nature of web development is likely to make metrics a difficult area to address in web development. (No serious research, to the best of our knowledge, has been done in the area of metrics for truly distributed applications). However, the current development of automated tools may improve the situation, by removing much of the burden for metrics collection from developers. The collection of metrics in web development will also be important for examining the effectiveness of using OPEN for web development.

6.5 CASE tools

Although there are a number of tools which support OPEN (both notation and process), that does not really provide much of a benefit to the process if it is to be used in web collaborations where there is no standardization on one of these tools. Also, web development requires the use of several types of communication tools which cannot readily be integrated into these existing tools, even if they were to be used. Thus the need remains for a specialized CASE tool to better support the web development process. One possible way that this need may be met is through the integration of a number of small, existing tools.

7. Recommendations for Future Work

After the publication of the OPEN-web development process specification, the next step will be to create some test cases in which to study its use. Existing ongoing projects such as those identified above, as well as the recently announced Netscape Communicator project, will provide a baseline from which to gauge the success of projects using this modified process.

At this stage, it is planned that both an open-source and commercial project will be undertaken using the process. To provide a suitable 'testing ground' for the process, the open-source project will involve the development of a large and fairly complex Java-based application, hopefully involving (eventually) a large number of widely dispersed and varied developers and users.

The many techniques available in OPEN to address the human element of software production, from human problem solving to successful team creation, will permit this study also to evaluate scale differences (in project and team size) in relation to the individuals and groups participating in these case study web developments.

8. Conclusions

With the emergence of the web, an environment has been created which allows widely dispersed developers to work together on software development projects. From the initial projects that have been carried out in this environment, a number of discerning features of the development process have been identified. However, despite the success of these projects, the web development process they utilize does have significant deficiencies, originating from its ad hoc evolution. These deficiencies can be addressed, in most part, by adapting the process using the OPEN methodological framework.

9. Acknowledgements

This research was funded in part by grants from the Australian Research Council. This is Contribution no 98/10 of the Centre for Object Technology Applications and Research (COTAR).

References

Booch, G., 1996, Development of the web, by the web, for the web, *Object Magazine*, **6(6)**, 96–95

Checkland, P., 1981, *Systems Thinking, Systems Practice*, John Wiley and Sons Ltd., Chichester, England

Fielding, R.T. and Kaiser, G., 1997, The apache http server project, *IEEE Internet Computing*, **1(4)**, 88–90

Firesmith, D.G., 1993, *Object-Oriented Requirements Analysis and Logical Design: A Software Engineering Approach*, J. Wiley and Sons, New York, 575pp

Firesmith, D., Henderson-Sellers, B. and Graham, I. 1997. *OPEN Modeling Language (OML) Reference Manual*, SIGS Books, NY, 271pp.

Firesmith, D.G., Hendley, G., Krutsch, S.A. and Stowe, M., 1998, *Object-Oriented Development Using OPEN: A Complete Java ™ Application*, Addison-Wesley, London
Gleditsch, A.G. and Gjermshus, P.K., 1997, Cross-referencing linus, URL: http://lxr.linux.no/

Graham, I.M., 1995a, *Migrating to Object Technology*, Addison–Wesley, Wokingham

Graham, I.M., 1995b, A non-procedural process model for object-oriented software development, *Report on Object Analysis and Design*, **1(5)**,10–11

Graham, I.M., Bischof, J. and Henderson-Sellers, B. 1997a. Associations considered a bad thing, *Journal of Object-Oriented Programming*. 9(9): 41–48.

Graham, I., Henderson-Sellers, B. and Younessi, H., 1997b, *The OPEN Process Specification*, Addison-Wesley, London, UK, 314pp

Henderson-Sellers, B., 1998, OPEN: Object-oriented Process, Environment and Notation. The first full lifecycle, third generation OO method, chapter for *Handbook of Object Technology* (ed. S. Zamir), CRC Press (in press)

Henderson-Sellers, B. and Edwards, J.M., 1994a, *BOOKTWO of Object-Oriented Knowledge: The Working Object*, Prentice Hall, Sydney, 616pp

Henderson-Sellers, B., Simons, A.J.H. and Younessi, H., 1998, *OPEN's Toolbox of Techniques*, Addison-Wesley, UK, 425pp

Nielsen, K., 1995, *Software Development with C++: Maximizing Reuse with Object Technology*, Academic Press, Cambridge, MA, USA

OMG, 1997a, UML Semantics. Version 1.1, 15 September 1997, OMG document ad/97-08-04

OMG, 1997b, UML Notation. Version 1.1, 15 September 1997, OMG document ad/97-08-05

Raymond, E.S., 1997, The cathedral and the bazaar, URL: http://www.opensource.org/

Thomas, D., 1996, Keynote at TOOLS Melbourne 1996

Torvalds, L., 1998, Credits and maintainers text files in linux source tree. URL: ftp://sunsite.anu.edu.au/pub/Linux/kernel/v2.0/linux-2.0.tar.gz

Unhelkar, B., 1998, Transactional analysis (TA) as applied to the human factors in OO projects, Chapter 42 in *Handbook of Object Technology* (ed. S.Zamir), CRC Press, Boca Raton, FL, USA (in press)

An Expectation-Perception Gap Analysis of Information Systems Failure

Linda, SL LAI

Department of Information Systems, City University of Hong Kong, Kowloon, Hong Kong

Abstract

This primary objective of this paper is to investigate new ways to tackle the old problem of organisation failure of information systems (IS) development. IS failure is defined as a gap between what the users expect from an information system and how well these expectations are met by the perceived performance of the delivered system. Problems leading to this expectation-perception gap are identified and modelled as five interrelated discrepancies or gaps throughout the process of IS development. The antecedents pertaining to each gap and corrective measures to close the gaps are also suggested. Success in IS development could be achieved by closing the five interrelated gaps and thus closing the expectation-perception gap.

I Introduction

The subject of information systems grew out of computer science to fill a gap created by the failure of machine-code programmers to understand and solve user problems [1]. As pointed out by Stamper in 1973 [2]: 'On the one side, stand the technologists, most of whom have no idea of the complexity of organisations. On the other side, stand the managers and administrators who are unable to translate their problems into feasible demands upon technology'. It was an attempt to bridge technological solutions with organisational problems that started IS work. Some might say that despite the plethora of information systems development tools that have become available since 1973, little has changed in relation to bridging the gap between user's expectations of system capability and how well these expectations are met by the perceived usefulness of delivered information systems. Indeed the increasing rate of development of technology might even be fuelling higher expectations by users which information systems developers are finding increasingly difficult to meet. Such a gap between stakeholders' expectation expressed in some ideal or standard and the perception of the delivered system is defined as an IS failure [3].

2 A Gap Analysis of IS Failure

The expectation-perception gap or IS failure can be assessed by a comparison of
- an IS user's expectation of his/her requirements - stated or unstated, conscious or merely sensed, technically operational or entirely subjective, and may be a

moving target in a dynamic organisational environment, and
- the IS user's perception of the performance of the delivered system (based on conscious and unconscious judgment) after he/she has some experience of using the system.

An expectation-perception discrepancy related to a single transaction leads to user dissatisfaction. Incidences of dissatisfaction over time results in users' negative feeling and eventual rejection of the delivered information system. A delivered information system may mismatch users' expectations in one or more important aspects [4]: it may fail to provide sufficient functionality, its performance may be inadequate; or it may not provide a good fit with the organisation's practices and procedures. It may fail in all these respects, yet still conform to the functional, performance and design specifications formally agreed between users and developers at the outset. Information systems, as a bridge between technological solutions and organisational problems, must be crossed from the side of organisational users. A systems project, no matter how expensive and elaborately designed, is still of little value if it does not perform as its users expect.

The expectation-perception failure of IS development can be understood and analysed by a gap model [5] as illustrated in Figure 1. The model features discrepancies or gaps that need to be closed in order to achieve success in IS development projects. Here, IS failure is defined as a gap between user's expectation and perception of the performance of a delivered system. The expectation-perception gap (Gap 6) is in turn caused by five interrelated gaps (Gap 1 to Gap 5) throughout the process of Information system development (ISD).

2.1 The cognition gap (Gap 1)

The cognition gap (gap 1) is a difference between 'what the users need' and 'what the users think they need'. User expectations, are the de facto requirements against which the success of a delivered system will be judged. However, most IS professionals have a myth about user expectations. As the saying goes: 'Users don't know what they want. Users keep changing their minds.' System developers just wish users could have worked out ahead of time what they want and communicate the requirements to them in unambiguous writing. The identified requirements, should then be signed and sealed once and for all time. Unfortunately, such a positivistic view of requirements analysis is deemed to be too simplistic. Factors contributing to the cognition gap include:
- **Requirements analysis is not based on positivism**. User needs which shape user expectations, do not 'exist out there' and ready for the 'picking'. Users initiate an IS project when they experience a felt need for information, a holistic sense of something missing in the current system, an awareness that technologies have the kind of capability which might help. It is legitimate for users to have only a very fuzzy idea of their requirements. User requirements are not easily articulated as they are just mental models in users' minds.

- **Users requirements are constantly changing**. Systems users are embedded in a constantly changing organisational environment and situation which are often unpredictable, apparently illogical and incomprehensible. In order to deal with the uncertainly, most successful organisations have very flexible and responsive informal systems which grow and decay as required. Under such circumstances, it is virtually impossible for the users to produce a set of unalterable requirements specification.

- **Users have limitation and bias in information processing**. Due to the availability bias, users may elucidate only those organisational requirements related to problems that are current, frequent and easier to recall from. After initial requirements are stated, users, because of the confirmatory bias, may selectively detect only information to support the original statement. The idea of representative bias suggests that users tend to believe a small sample of transactions as being typical of the population from which it came.

    Helping users to set their expectations of the new system at an appropriate level is the first and possibly most crucial step in achieving project success. IS developers must be aware of the cognition gap of users, and take measures to aid users to articulate what they want based on what they need now and possibly in the future.

2.2 The comprehension gap (Gap 2)

The comprehension gap (Gap 2) is a discrepancy between 'what the users need/want' and 'what the developers think the users need/want'. Information systems professionals, as pointed out by [6], 'have expanded their roles from product developers and operations managers to become service providers' Providing services that users perceive as excellent requires that the service providers know what users need and want. There are various obstacles that may inhibit IS professionals from gaining a comprehensive picture of users expectations:

- **Requirements analysis should be inside-looking-out**. Despite a genuine interest in providing effective services to users, many IS professionals miss the mark by thinking outside-in - they know what the users should need and deliver that - rather than inside-out. Systems developers, very often, overestimate their own capabilities, authority and power in relation to the users. They simply do not seek inputs from users to define their professional services.

- **Conflicting users requirements**. The information systems developers' task in understanding users requirements is made more difficult by the fact that most IS projects have a surprising diversity of users (referred by some authors as stakeholders), each with different expectations. So, even if users are able to articulate their needs, it may still be the case that the identified requirements are mutually contradictory or jointly define a much larger system than can be budgeted.

- **Users requirements are culture bound**. No one can understand a culture unless he/she is inside it, and once a person is inside a culture, he/she will be unaware of it. If a systems analyst remains as an outsider of users' culture, he/she is unlikely to be able to interpret the culture bound requirements as insider members do, and so is likely to get the interpretation rejected. If a systems analyst acts as an insider, he/she will then take the culture bound requirements for granted without self-reflective questioning.

- **Communication barriers between users and analysts**. The importance of user-analyst relationships in systems development has been widely recognized. However, it is not always possible to maintain a continuous line of communication between users and developers due to various barriers (e.g., background, concerns & languages) between the two parties. Due to the lack of communication, developers have difficulties in comprehending users' information requirements.

Not knowing what the users expect is a serious concern of information systems developers. Being a bit wrong about users requirements can mean expending money, time and other resources on things that do not count to users. Being a bit wrong can even not surviving in a fiercely competitive market.

2.3 The expression gap (Gap 3)

The expression gap (Gap 3) is a difference between 'the developers' understanding of users' needs/wants' and 'the translation of developers' understanding into a requirements specification'. Understanding users' expectations is an essential step in delivering a successful information system, but once system analysts know what users expect, they face another critical challenge: using the understanding to elaborate the understanding into a formal requirements specification for subsequent systems development. The process of translating requirements in minds to requirements on paper is by no means straightforward because of the following reasons:

- **The process of structuring needs is problematic**. An IS developer's mental constructs (e.g., perceptual processes, values, ethics, motives, prejudices, intellectual ability, experience, etc.) have an effect on the understanding he/she gained of the situation. It is, very often, those mental constructs rather than the expertise of a developer that determine the relevance and importance of elicited users' requirements. The task of determining feasibility, prioritizing identified users requirements, depends, among other things, on the personal characteristics of the systems developers.

- **Modeling reality is problematic**. When IS developers translate their understanding of business tasks into technical functions, they map human activities, objects, events into 'processes', 'data format' and 'data structures'. While this reduction is useful and inevitable, it should be noted that no model or modeling technique is capable of capturing the degree of complexity of an organisation's requirements. Systems developers should not be so enthralled by today's graphic, narrative, and representational modeling aids that they lose sight of their mission and forget that the map is not the territory.

Systems analysts can be compared to translators. Translators convert documents written in one language into another while systems analysts convert users requirements into systems requirements. Yet, no matter how good is a translation, it can never be perfect. There are always errors that occur in translations.

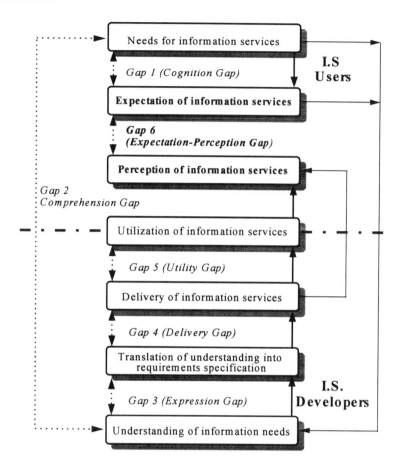

Figure 1: An expectation-perception gap analysis of IS failure

2.4 The delivery gap (Gap 4)

The delivery gap (Gap 4) is a difference between 'what is specified' and 'what is delivered'. In some cases, IS professionals do have a fair understanding of users' expectations and do set appropriate specifications and still the delivered system falls short of what users expect. In order to deliver an information system that meets users' expectation, IS developers need to analyse the requirements specifications, detail the physical and logical design of the systems, and provide the software required and other technical services. Issues related to the systems construction process have long been a focus of IS research and studied exclusively under two disciplines - IS project management and software engineering.

- **IS project management**. IS project management is about the planning, organizing, directing and controlling of resources to maintain several necessary conditions of IS development so that the target systems can be delivered successfully. Three conditions that are generally used to evaluate the effectiveness of project management are 'performance, time and cost' [7]. It is not possible to achieve project success in IS development if any one of the three dimensions fail.

- **IS software engineering**. Software engineering [8] refers to the application of formal and rigorous methods to ensure the quality of the software deliverables of an IS are kept within specified standards. IS software quality is a combination of desired attributes such as conformity, usability, reliability, efficiency, security, auditability, maintainability, reusability, flexibility and portability. Software quality can be maintained by ensuring that a whole range of technical and organisational issues are adequately addressed by IS developers.

The delivery gap indicates discrepancies in the ability of systems specialists to transform users' requirements specification into tangible IS product and service deliverables. IS professionals can narrow this gap by applying good project management and taking an engineering approach to software development.

2.5 The utility gap (Gap 5)

The utility gap (Gap 5) is a difference between 'what is delivered' and 'what is being used'. An information technology system is physically constructed by actors working in a given social context, it is also socially constructed by actors through the meanings they attach to it. The social and physical construction of a technology do not stop at the point of systems delivery, but also occurs at the post-implementation phase. The utility gap measures the extent to which the utilization of an operation system is consistent with the original design intent of its systems developers. This gap is a result of several phenomena:

- **Technologies are socially reconstructed**. A technology can be appropriated in diverse ways and have different meanings and effects for different users. Users could mediate technological effects, adapt systems to their needs, resist them or choose not to use them at all. The flexibility in use of a technology, according to [9], is influenced by characteristics of the material artifact (e.g., the specific hardware and software comprising the technology), characteristics of the human agents (e.g., experience, motivation) and characteristics of the use context (e.g., social relations, task assignment, resource allocations).

- **Time-space discontinuity between the design & use of an IS**. With many IS projects, the activities that constitute the technology are often separated in time and space from the activities that are constituted by the technology, with the former typically occurring in developer organisations, and the latter occurring in user sites. Due to the time-space discontinuity between the design & use of an information system, it is not surprising that IS users and developers often have very different interpretations of the role and utility of the underlying technology.

- **Lack of proper training**. Users' perceptions of the performance of an information system are not based on the delivered functions, but on the functions that they can use. As [10] says: people don't pay for technology; they pay for what they get from technology. In this way, IS success do not build on how a technology is constructed, but rest on how much users use a new technology and how differently they use it. Inadequate and improper training is a key reason users reject and resist the implementation of new systems.

The existence of the utility gap suggests the effectiveness of an information system can be diminished by users' inability to grasp the larger purpose and significance of the underlying technology. A 'technically successful' system can result in organisation chaos if its implementation phase is ineffectual and fail to meet user expectations.

3   Use of the gap model by IS practitioners

Figure 2 exhibits the various problematic issues and their relationships with the gaps that lead to failures in information systems development. In this extended model, as in the basic gap model (Figure 1), the gap between users' expectations and perceptions of an information system (Gap 6) results from five gaps (Gaps 1 through 5) during the process of IS project development. Each of the five gaps is in turn caused by various factors that are itemised in the left-hand column of Figure 2. In this way, we may argue that information systems failure (or users' expectation mismatch) results from one or more of the following reasons:

- users' inability to cogitate their information needs;
- developers' inability to comprehend users' information needs;
- developers' inability to translate their perceived information needs of users into requirement specifications;
- developers' inability to transform specified needs for information provision into systems deliverables;
- users' inability to utilize the delivered systems to satisfy their information needs

The expectation-perception gap (Gap 6) is a function of gaps 1, 2, 3, 4 and 5. Thus, the key to achieving success in information systems development is to keep Gap 6 closed by closing Gaps 1 through 5. IS practitioners need to monitor all the contributing factors and determine, perhaps through structured analysis, which factors are critical for achieving success in a particular project setting. Figure 3 depicts a logical process which IS practitioners can employ to enhance the chance of project success. The sequence of questions of the six boxes on the left side of the figure corresponds to the six gaps illustrated in Figures 1 and 2. Specifically, the process can begins with an understanding of the extent of Gap 6 and then successively searching for evidence of Gap 1 through 5, taking corrective measures wherever and whenever necessary.

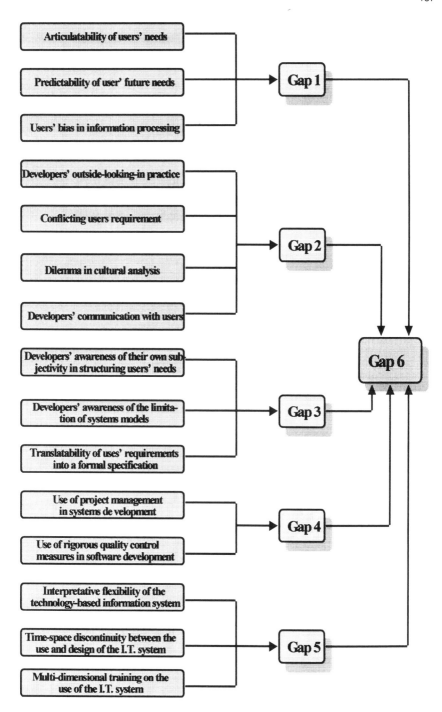

Figure 2: An extended model of the expectation-perception gap

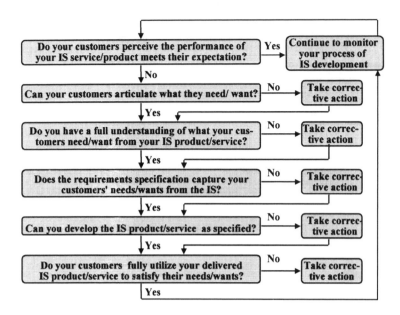

Figure 3: A logical process to analyse the expectation-perceptation gap

4 Implications of the gap model for ISD process

The expectation failure (or mismatch) leads to resources being spent on refining systems or worse delivering systems, which are simply not used by their host organisation. The most common explanation of this discrepancy is the reliance of IS developers on a product centred perspective for systems development which assumes that user needs can be defined and that solutions to these needs can be engineered using an appropriate systems development methodology. However as organisations increasingly question their purpose and processes and as boundaries between organisations become increasingly fuzzy and vague, it is no longer possible to start with the notion that it is necessary to create or computerise an information system. IS development thus has to be seen as a continuous process which is led by the human activity system in the organisation which the information system will serve [11], [12]. Any and every information system can always be thought about as entailing a pair of system, one a system which is served (the organisational activity system), the other a system which does the serving (the information technology system) as shown in Figure 4 [13].

Whenever one system serves or supports another, it is a very basic principle that the necessary features of the system which serves can be worked out only on the basis of a prior account of the system served. This must be so because the nature of the system served will dictate what counts as 'service' and hence what functions the system which provides that service must contain. It follows that any method or methodology that seek to guide individual in making effective IS development must meet the following criteria:

- It should provide mechanisms to make sense and understand the behaviour of human activities which an information system is developed to serve;
- It should render a seamless transition between its resulting information requirements model and the process to design a technology-based system to satisfy those requirements.

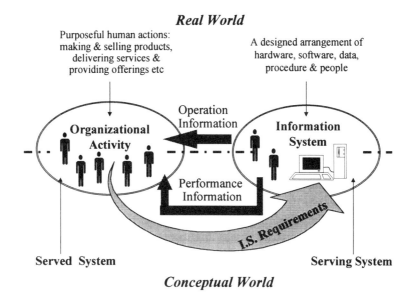

Figure 4: The served-server concept [13]

5 Conclusion

The notion of expectation-perception failure, as argued by [14], is comprehensive enough to encompass other systems failure concepts such as correspondence failure [15], process failure [16], interaction failure [17], etc. in the IS literature. It has significant implications on the development and management of technology-based information systems.

Several factors have been identified by the expectation-perception gap analysis for IS failure, with many factors relating to organisational and human aspects of IS development. Information systems development concerns 'an interplay of human, organisation and technical factors which cannot be easily separated' [18]. The main role of an information system is that of a support function, such systems do not exist for their own sake. Thus, the correct place to start an ISD project is not the information system but the organisation activities that an information system is to serve.

Bridging the expectation-perception gap also requires that IS professionals take a radical shift from being the proprietor of information systems and products to being service providers to end-users. [19] suggests that IS departments should be viewed as a service enterprise responsible for providing business solutions rather than solely technical support, and individuals served by IS should be regarded as customers rather than users. In order to deliver systems and services that IS customers (users) perceive valuable, IS managers must become expert in determining and assessing users' expectations and perceptions.

The contribution of the expectation-perception gap model lies in providing a fresh look at the role of IS professionals and the current approaches to IS development.

References

1. Jayaratna N. Understanding and Evaluating Methodologies, NIMSAD - a systemic framework. McGraw-Hill, Maidenhead, 1994
2. Stamper RK. Information in business and administrative systems. Batsford, London, 1973
3. Lyytinen K. Expectation failure concept and systems analysts' view of information system failures: results of an exploratory study. Information & Management 1988; 14: 45-56
4. Shand RM. User manuals as project management tools: part I - theoretical background. IEEE Transactions on Professional Communication 1994; 37(2): 75-80
5. Zeithaml VA, Parasuraman A, Berry LL. Delivering Quality Service: Balancing Customer Perception and Expectation. The Free Press, NY, 1990
6. Pitt LF, Watson RT, Kavan CB. Service Quality: a measure of information systems effectiveness. MIS Quarterly 1995; 19(2): 173-187
7. Cleland DI, King WR. Systems Analysis and Project Management. McGraw-Hill, NY, 1983
8. Boehm BW. Software Engineering Economics. Prentice Hall, Englewood Cliffs, NJ, 1981
9. Orlikowski WJ. The duality of technology: rethinking the concept of technology in organisation. *Orghanization Science* 1992; 3(3): 398-427
10. Drucker P. Innovation and entrepreneurship: practice and principles. Harper & Row, NY, 1985
11. Checkland PB. Systems Thinking, Systems Practice. John Wiley & Sons, Chichester, 1981
12. Walsham G. Interpreting Information Systems in Organisations. John Wiley & Sons, Chichester, 1993
13. Winter MC, Brown DH, Checkland PB. A role for Soft Systems Methodology in information systems development. European Journal of Information Systems 1995; 1(4): 130-142
14. Lyytinen K, Hirschheim R. Information systems failures – A survey and classification of the empirical literature. Oxford Survey of Information Technology 1987; 4: 257-309
15. Alter S, Ginzberg MJ. Managing uncertainty in MIS implementation. Sloan Management Review 1978; 19: 23-31
16. Brooks FP. The Mythical Man-Month. Addison-Wesley, Reading, Mass, 1975

17.   Lucas HC. Implementation: the key to successful information systems, Columbia University Press, NY, 1981

18.   Walsham G, Symons V, Waema T. Information systms as social systems: implications for developing countries. Information Technology for Development 1988; 3(3): 189-204

19.   Kettinger WJ, Lee CC. Exploring a 'gap' model of information services quality. Information Resources Management Journal 1995; 8: 5-16

Applying Semiotic Methods To Requirements Recovery

K. Liu, A. Alderson, H. Shah, B. Sharp and A. Dix
School of Computing, Staffordshire University
PO Box 334, Beaconside, Stafford, ST18 0DG, UK
(K.Liu, A.Alderson, H.Shah, B.Sharp, A.J.Dix}@soc.staffs.ac.uk

Abstract

One of the most difficult, yet crucial, tasks in any project of re-engineering or extension of a legacy system is to understand the system and to recover the original requirements. To develop an effective method of requirements recovery for legacy information systems, the AMBOLS project proposes a semiotic framework. In complement to other conventional methods of systems engineering, two semiotic methods, Semantic Analysis and Norm Analysis, have been adopted for elicitation, derivation and representation of users' requirements. The AMBOLS method recovers the requirements by analysing the normative behaviour of the legacy system in its context, and observing and modelling the interactions of its users.

Key Words: Information Systems, Legacy Systems Re-engineering, Requirements Recovery, Semiotics, Semantic Analysis, Norm Analysis.

1 Introduction

There has been an increasing awareness of the issues surrounding legacy systems driven particularly by attempts to employ business process re-engineering techniques. To remain competitive, businesses must continually change their processes, sometimes radically, though more often incrementally, to cope with their changing environment. As a result, IT systems become inadequate in reflecting business needs, either operationally or economically, and so become legacy systems.

Legacy systems remain supportive to core business functions and are 'indispensable' to the business. Frequently, complete replacement of such systems is viable neither operationally nor economically, so re-engineering or extension is inevitable. Unfortunately lack of accurate system documents or, even worse, complete unavailability of documents, has made system re-engineering costly and difficult.

The AMBOLS project [3,4] addresses the recovery of requirements by using a semiotic approach to analyse and model the behaviour of the system. The focus is on observation of the system in operation. The approach complements to other conventional methods of systems re-engineering, and will contribute particularly requirements engineering in information systems development. The project approaches recovery of the requirements for a system from analysis of the behaviour it exhibits. The research adopts the methods of organisational semiotics [7] to develop a method for studying and modelling the behaviour of legacy systems. Semantic Analysis and Norm Analysis is used for modelling the system's behaviour and capturing the business rules implemented as operational constraints in the system. The AMBOLS approach allows system analysts and engineers to understand a legacy system in the absence of source code.

2 User Requirements

Specification of requirements and validation of their satisfaction is the essence of successful systems engineering. User requirements are key to forward engineering. We differentiate between user requirements, which are elicited from the system's stakeholders and expressed in user terms, and system requirements, which are derived from the user requirements and expressed in technical terms. The user requirements express the problem, while the system requirements express the solution. When dealing with business change, knowing what the system was required to do is vital to keeping the system in step with business needs. Successful re-engineering of legacy systems requires that we understand the requirements for the re-engineered system and that we recover the requirements of the legacy system, so that we may specify changes to the legacy system on the basis of changes in requirements. Further, if a system is to be modified it is essential to understand the original design intention. Without this knowledge we may inadvertently damage required functionality. Recovering the requirements of legacy systems is the first essential step for any re-engineering activities.

Reverse engineering has generally been considered as an approach to re-engineering. An extensive and extending body of research has addressed the reverse engineering of legacy systems. Chikovsky and Cross [1] give a taxonomy of such approaches. Many successful translations from code to code, and from code to design including from code to data structure, have been made. However, in forward engineering, each stage of development transforms the expression of the requirements into a new representation introducing detailed peculiarities of meaning (semantics) which are the results of creativity of systems engineers, of the particularities of the representation, and of the demands of the available implementation platform, both hardware and software. Recovery of original requirements from code by reverse engineering techniques is very difficult.

Various classes of user requirements generally apply to a system:

- functional requirements - what is the system required to do.
- non-functional requirements - the technical constraints under which the functions must be delivered, such as performance, reliability, size and environmental factors.

- business requirements - constraints relating to the business such as cost, schedule, quality and policy. The business requirements express the operational policy of the organisation as business rules. There may also be business policies enforcing use of particular hardware and software. The policy itself will have been influenced by technology available to the business at the time.
- discipline requirements - standards applying to the development disciplines employed, imposed by the business or externally, extant at the time of creation.

The importance of recovery varies for these classes of requirements. Their accessibility from design information also varies, as we discuss here. Their accessibility to observation also varies as we discuss later.

Functional requirements are of high importance. They may appear the easiest to reconstruct from the design, but the user requirements may be obscured. The functionality provided in the design does not have a one-to-one mapping to functional user requirements. The design functionality may bring together different user requirements in one design element - such economy is generally considered to be the essence of effective design. The design functionality will frequently be 'distorted' to meet non-functional constraints, such as performance and size. It may even be distorted by the available software and hardware. As an example, ponder whether knowledge of the designs of the systems relating to the Gemini and Apollo missions would lead very easily to the user requirement to "land a man on the Moon and return him to Earth alive".

Non-functional requirements are also of high importance. They are likely to be even more difficult to retrieve from design. Generally technical constraints have no direct representation in the design and so are very difficult to deduce from the design.

Clearly business requirements constraining the original legacy system development, such as resource and delivery date constraints, are no longer of interest. However the business rules are of high importance. They exhibit the same difficulties of extraction as the functional requirements. One clear difficulty is that we have no access to the business as it was when the system was created. The system becomes a legacy system because the business has moved on. As things stand with the current low uptake of business process modelling, we are unlikely to have a representation of the 'legacy business' to analyse.

Discipline requirements, such as applicable standards, are unlikely to be derivable from the design or code. However they are of little current importance as they change with time.

3 Organisational Semiotics Methods

The project has adopted semiotics, the study of signs established by Peirce [2], as one of the theoretical foundations for developing its methods and techniques for requirement recovery. Signs enable the description of the state of affairs of organisational and computer systems. They provide us access to the past and future, beyond our direct experience. Semiotics offers a systematic way of studying all the aspects of signs used in human communication. These aspects include the media, structure and organisation (or syntax), meaning (or semantics), functions and effects in relation to the (proper) use of signs. These activities of creating and using signs, symbols, analysis reports and design documents are the central part of information systems work.

Organisational semiotics and the analytical methods [7] offer a theory of understanding business organisations as systems where signs are created and communications take place for business purposes. An IT system, forming an integral part of the business organisation, is governed by business rules. Two semiotic methods, Semantic Analysis and Norm Analysis, can help in studying the organisation and the IT systems. A key foundation for these two methods is the logic of norms and affordances, NORMA, which was proposed by Stamper [6] and detailed more recently [7]. Semantic Analysis offers a rigorous process and a set of concise notations for requirements capture. It enables one to focus on capturing generic patterns of behaviour and the interrelationships of the system's operations, and hence their meaning. Norm Analysis provides a formula for representing business knowledge imposed on the business and IT system.

Method engineers are seldom explicit about their philosophical positions but these have far-reaching effects. For example, the classical methods of systems analysis and design recognise only the existence of signs (messages and records) in their formal structures. NORMA is radically different in adopting a subjectivist stance and an agent-in-action ontology.

This philosophical position states that, for all practical purposes, nothing exists without a perceiving agent nor without the agent engaging in actions. That is to say, each thing depends for its existence upon the existence of its antecedents. Words and expressions we use are names for invariant patterns in the flux of actions and events which agents experience. The classical distinction between entity, attribute and relationship disappears to be replaced by the concepts of agents, affordances (the actions or attributes of agents) and norms (for the socially defined patterns of behaviour) related to their antecedents to indicate the ontological dependency.

Figure 1 shows an Ontology Chart for an insurance company dealing with a claim on a policy. Agents (in ellipses) have affordances (plain text). The antecedent relationships are shown by lines, with antecedents shown to the left.

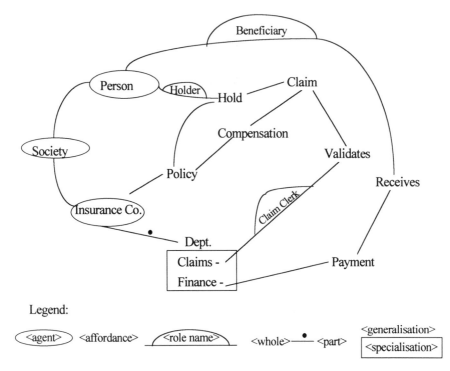

Figure 1: Ontology Chart for Insurance Company

The agent-in-action ontology has important implications for requirements engineering [5]. In particular, it requires the relevant agent to be specified in every component of the requirements definition. The benefits of this constraint are: (a) we know the originators responsible for production of requirements are the users of information; (b) we can handle differential meanings for the same term; (c) we know exactly whom to consult over details of design; (d) we can organise norms (system functionality) according to the various agents involved. These will help us in the recovery of requirements of legacy systems. Clearly a philosophical position is not a side issue but of fundamental practical relevance.

Our philosophical arguments lead directly to the observation that an agent in a situation where it experiences certain invariants (or affordances) becomes a modified agent, such as:

    (person, policy)hold

where a person acquires an ability of holding a policy. Both the *person* and *policy* are the joint antecedents of the invariant *hold*, which means that holding of a policy is only possible when both the person and the policy exist. A modified agent with the additional affordance can behave in ways that are not possible otherwise. So we may have

    (person, policy)hold claim

which is not a direct affordance of

    person.

Norms exist in a community and govern how members behave, think, make judgements and perceive the world. The shared norms define a culture or subculture. A subculture may be a team who know how to work effectively together, and their norms include a solution to their organisational problems. Once we know the norms of an organisation, we can deduce its information requirements. Every norm has the general form:

Whenever <condition>
if <state>
then <agent>
is <deontic operator>
to perform <action>

The condition part determines what information the norm-subject (an individual person or a group) needs to be able to obey the norm; while the consequent leads, sooner or later, to the generation of information for others either directly through sending messages or indirectly through the influence of the norm upon actions. If we know the various norm-subjects who are the agents in the organisation and we know the specific norms they should obey, then we can deduce what information individual or group agencies in the organisation will need and what they produce for others to use.

Norms govern the behaviour of business organisations and are embedded in their supporting computer systems as conditions and in their work practices as rules for using the computer systems. The computer system records and provides the information required by the agents, acting as a memory for data, transforming and communicating it as required.

NORMA expresses knowledge about a situation using very few concepts. To describe a system in technical terms we must discuss, as a minimum, functionality (function, data flow, control flow), behaviour (state, transition, event, action, condition) and data (entity, attribute, relationship), together with the processes it is embedded in (role, state, action, condition). NORMA describes the system using agent, role and affordance, together with norms (subject, event, action, and deontic attitude) as shown by the entity-relationship diagram in figure 2. The use of many different concepts in technically oriented representations requires fine distinction in categorisation of information, creating difficulties for non-technical contributors to requirements capture.

We can map the semiotic concepts to the technical concepts. From preceding examples, we can quickly recognise correspondences. Part of our ongoing work is to isolate these relationships, giving a firm link from the representations of organisational semiotics to those of requirements modelling.

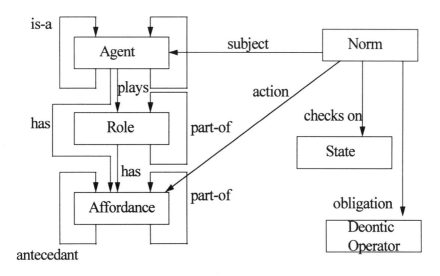

Figure 2: The Concepts of Semantic and Norm Analysis

4 Using Semiotic Methods for Requirements Recovery

An IT system can be analysed at three levels. The *structure* refers to the components and their interconnections. The structure will determine the *behaviour,* which is realised at the level of the integrated components, and is regarded as the potential capability of the system. Finally, *functions* are exhibited behaviour that has been permitted by the rules and constraints (Figure 3). We can also observe that the system operates within one or more processes of the business. The functions employed, and the way in which they are used, are determined by those business processes. Users interact with the system only through the functions. For systems re-engineering in this project, functions are behaviour that is governed by and conforms with business knowledge and rules (or *norms*, because they make the system behave in a normative manner). These functions should support business operations. Other parts of the potential behaviour (or system capability) may not give benefits to the business organisation and hence may be inhibited by business rules.

We can relate the kinds of requirements - functional, non-functional, business and discipline - to our three levels.

At the functionality level, we see the functional requirements of the system satisfied. We can observe these functions in the context of the effects of the business requirements (business rules). The business rules may be imposed by the actions of users or they may be embedded in the implementation of the system. We can also observe the effects of the non-functional requirements.

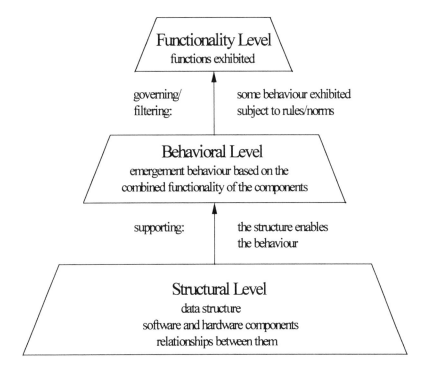

Figure 3: A Three-Tier Systems Model

At the behavioural level, the emergent behaviour of the combined components is expressed. The functional and non-functional requirements, and possibly some business rules are expressed here. The system is not observable at the behavioural level; we always see result of filtering through business rules at the functionality level.

At the structural level, components are created (or obtained) whose combination will satisfy the functional and non-functional requirement. Some business rules may be implemented within individual components (for example, as triggers in a database) or by the combination of components. Business requirements relating to the development process, such as schedule and cost, apply at the structural level. Business requirements such as hardware and software policy may be obvious from the components used. Discipline requirements relate to the engineering disciplines used to create the components of the system and so apply at this level. At the structural level we observe only the physical components of the system. We assume that internal detail of components is not available to us. Exceptions occur were the physical components themselves offer facilities for investigating their internal detail (for example, viewing a database schema).

Any recovery of requirements we make must be by observation of the structural and the functionality levels. We can make deductions about these observations, a process which can be assisted by knowledge of the business processes in which the system is operated. Many methods of reasoning, including abductive reasoning which is rooted in semiotics, can be used. The process of analysis is iterative with continuing, substantial involvement from the users.

Non-functional requirements are difficult to recover. However, size requirements might be retrieved by assuming that the delivered system met its requirements. Then the observed size can be assumed to be the required size. We may be able to make similar assumptions to determine performance or reliability requirements. If we observe physical replication of components, we may be able to deduce requirements for system availability, and so on. Creating techniques for recovering different kinds of requirements is a major element of the ongoing work of the project.

In this method of studying legacy systems at the three levels, techniques are drawn from various sources and disciplines. At the functionality level, Semantic Analysis and Norm Analysis can be applied. Data requirements can be derived from observed inputs and outputs. At the structural level, reverse engineering can recover data structures, some software components and relationships between data and components. These are generally implementation issues, but they relate to the requirements, and therefore are helpful to the recovery of requirements.

Using organisation semiotics, we can capture the ontological dependencies of actions performed by the IT system and users. The method guides the analysts to elicit and capture the requirements through an iterative process with the help of the stakeholders of the IT system.

Norm Analysis is applied in conjunction with Semantic Analysis and usually utilises the results of Semantic Analysis. Norms, which may be business rules, organisational procedures, company policies and workflow processes, govern the behaviour of the IT systems and the users. Norm Analysis, offering techniques such as *responsibility definition*, *proto-norm analysis*, *trigger analysis* and *detailed norm specification*, will guide the analysts in acquiring business knowledge (the norms).

5 Summary

In this paper we have described our approach to the legacy systems and proposed to address the problem of legacy system from the semiotic perspective. Whilst a number of researchers have taken the reverse engineering approach to legacy systems we argue that the central issue of the legacy problem resides in the difficulties in accessing the requirements and applicable business rules for the original system. As a result we have proposed to use the Semantic Analysis method combined with NORMA to analyse and model the system's behaviour. Semantic Analysis will allow us to derive the ontological dependencies of actions performed by the legacy systems and its users while Norm Analysis will help us model the business rules. We believe that the AMBOLS approach can provide the basis for re-engineering or modification of IT systems. It can assist reverse engineering by revealing the user requirements and will provide a powerful means of verification for any re-engineering projects.

Our requirements recovery is organised into a process with clear objectives of developing a semantic model and eliciting norms. It relies heavily on observations of the behaviour of the IT system and the interactions with the users, with the support of any original systems documentation available. It can be expected that hypotheses must be made of the system's internal structure which enables it to perform certain functions and to display certain behaviour. These hypotheses can then be verified in further analysis. Therefore, the investigation is characterised by an extensive use of abductive reasoning.

As a means of capturing, presenting and discussing information gathered from users, the organisational semiotics techniques provide the conceptual simplicity which assists the interaction of users and analysts. Comparison with requirements engineering techniques and experience shows an ontology chart is normally much simpler and more succinct in presentation and richer in semantics, compared to the equivalent presentation of other systems analysis methods. This aids validation of the requirements model by the analysts and the users and owner of the system - in many cases, the stakeholders' approval and their confidence in the analysis is crucial.

Our semiotic based approach is currently focused on a system's behaviour, relating principally to its functional user requirements. Clearly Norm Analysis should be useful in extracting business rules. In future work we will consider how we may address the other kinds of user requirement identified earlier in this paper.

Acknowledgements

This research project is supported by The British Research Council EPSRC (Grant No. GR/L43473). The case study in Figure 1 is based on an internal paper by A.D. Jaffar.

References

1. Chikovsky EJ, Cross II JH. Reverse Engineering and Design Recovery: A Taxonomy. IEEE Software 1990; 7(7):13-17

2. Hartshorne C, Weiss P (Eds.). Collected Papers of Ch. S. Peirce (1931 - 1935). Cambridge, Massachusetts, 1960

3. Liu K, Alderson A, Shah H, Dix A, Sharp B. The AMBOLS Project, http://www.soc.staffs.ac.uk/~cmtkl/ambols/summary.html, 1997 [Accessed 30/4/1998]

4. Liu K, Alderson A, Sharp B, Shah H, Dix A. Using Semiotic Techniques to Derive Requirements from Legacy Systems. SOCTR/98/03, School of Computing, Staffordshire University, 1998

5. Liu K, Ades Y, Stamper RK. Simplicity, Uniformity and Quality: the role of Semantic Analysis in systems development. In: Ross M, Brebbia CA, Staples G, Stapleton J (Eds.) Software Quality Management, Vol 2, Building Quality into Software. Computational Mechanics Publications, 1994, pp219-235

6. Stamper RK. Knowledge as Action: A Logic of Social Norms and Individual Affordances. In: Gilbert GN, Heath C (Eds) Social Action and Artificial Intelligence. Gower Press, Aldershot, 1985

7. Stamper RK. Signs, Information, Norms and Systems. In: Holmqvist P, Anderson PB, Klein H, Posner R. (Eds) Signs of Work: Semiotics & Information Processing in Organisations. Walter de Gruyter, NY, 1996, pp349-397

'Can Intranet Development be a Valuable Means of Organisational Learning?'

Christine Schweighart
Department of Computing
University of Central Lancashire
PRESTON PR1 2HE, UK.

Marie Reynard
Alva Conseil
5 Rue d'Alger
75001 PARIS
France

e-mail:christine@moya.demon.co.uk

e-mail: reynardm@aol.com

Abstract

The following paper sets out an exploration of the contribution that intranet development and use can bring, not only as an e-mail and publishing medium, but also for its use as a communication medium to facilitate organisational learning. Changes due to new technology and education needs are introduced, then current project management is considered. The paper ends concluding that methods following a traditional life-cycle approach to application development do not support the educational process required, and that an explicit management of learning outcomes is needed within intranet development projects.

Keywords: intranet development; organizational learning; learning outcomes; participative design; CSCW.

Introduction

As companies use internet technology to publish information internally in networks or intranets, a pool of information is made available to employees. Management of this information goes beyond the limits encountered in the development of databases in organisations. Organisations are aware of the strategic advantages that can be obtained from this form of information, and have begun to exploit this resource through intranet developments.

There are different contributing factors to the development of intranet information management.

1. The innovation in technology for the improvement of access to data and the processing by search engines.
2. The increasing sophistication of the product developed to kindle cognitive interaction between individuals using intranets.
3. The process of development itself.

These three elements are interrelated.

1.Technical Aspects (what can be done?)

When someone refers to 'the Web', the connotation is a mass of graphical data. How can we apply this technology to benefit people trying to find useful information in complex and dynamic environments?

1.1 Establishing Standards

Programming languages to prepare Web documents do not offer such facilities as can be found in desktop publishing applications, for positioning and manipulating contents.

The language generally used to display documents on the Web, HTML (Hypertext Markup Language), allows authors to define the contents structure by enforcing a set of attributes or tags. The set of attributes used is insufficient to provide complex document structures (for example, with a wide range of database fields...) and the database structures cannot be achieved in web use. To overcome this, the World Wide Web Consortium (W3C) is developing a Document Object Model, which treats the content of the Web page as a collection of objects. This allows a standardisation, and adds a level of 'what is represented' i.e. at a meta level.

1.2 Extensibility

The World Wide Web Consortium (W3C) has developed an Extensible Markup Language (XML) to help make the data independent from the authoring tools and delivery engines. It also allows information providers to define new tag and attribute names; and in combination with a standardised document object model, indexing searching and other automated processes that require more structure than may be present in the data itself can be achieved. Instead of using HTML tags to define the presentation qualities of the page content, this may be done using Cascading Style Sheets (CSS's), leaving the use of tags for the definition of content structure. CSS mechanisms are outside XML, but developing a stylesheet programming language is part of the W3C focus (Bosak, 1997).

Search Engines

Search engines are programmes that collect data from the 'net' and provide it to the person making the query in a useful way - either to provide direct access to the source, or some description of how to obtain it.

Table 1. Types of Indexing for Data Used in Search Engines.

Statistical	Permutation	Citation	Association
Words that appear often are therefore significant for the text	The title is more informative than any other sentence in the text, and is used as a basis for the search.	The references in a document are used for the query.	Based on the co-occurrence of words.

No one method is best for general searching. Different interpretations may occur in a search: there may be a semantic gap between what the author of the query intends in the use of key words, and what is referenced by the search engine. The search engine may scan material and detect words that have been written in a different context producing many 'matches' which are really unwanted noise, it can be difficult to refine the search to eliminate these unwanted sources.

The demand for more precise search processing is enormous. To increase the efficiency and capability of search engines, information on the web can be described with meta-data via a Resource Description Framework (RDF) based on the semantic context. The RDF and XML are complementary.

1.3 Performance

Intranet systems can also be linked to external networks offering a large range of possibilities to use information. People can access either from inside the network of workstations or from another geographical location, at different times.

An end user can access a central database and information can be displayed in a web page. The data can be updated or manipulated locally to redraw the page. They can be linked to tables or 'form' elements, with viewing and updating possibilities. New data can be entered via these 'forms', and sent back to the server, updating the database globally (Heinle, 1997). An intranet based process offers a two-way communication with enormous potential for exchange and use of information in companies.

The appeal of intranet implementation is in the vision that corporate decision making processes can be made in a more fully informed environment by a larger number of people and within a much shorter time scale. However, there are conflicting views as to whether collective decision making is or is not facilitated by this informal communication (Brennan & Rubenstein 1995). Also, there is further debate as to the appropriateness of using a model of rational bureaucracy as a means of understanding corporate decision-making (Reed & Hughes 1992, Du Gay 1996).

1.4 Cognitive Aspects (Value Added - what the use of this media brings)

We can use these new technologies to help a search engine collect sources containing, for example, 'jaguar' - we can use a meta-tag to refine this label and make a distinction between the jaguar car or the jaguar animal. It is not a miracle answer, however, because the super-ordinate category to jaguar the animal could also be 'feline'. This changes a keyword search through the volume of pages for statistical indexing, into a search much reduced in volume through the filter of meta-tag use, increasing the speed and selectivity of the search.

Categorisation of the semantic content of the Web page at a higher level requires a dynamic provision of the labels by the authors. There is a tendency to use one level of terms at a basic level of categorisation in a language community. Studying the development of early language use, Nolan observes that if one is shown a picture of a collie-dog and is asked to say what it is, 'dog' is the most likely answer, and not 'animal' or 'collie' (Nolan 1994)..

This latter point is worthwhile giving consideration, because if material in a page could be of value to many different communities, there are inherent barriers stemming from the differences in perception of semantic meaning and also realisation of the categorisation of the content, i.e. to use the above analogy a shepherd might see collie -dog and ask for collie, a Polynesian might see collie-dog and say animal. Thus one can start to perceive a situation where classification systems start to become a language-tool in their own right.

It is almost impossible to classify data on the web automatically because of the differences in categorisation built upon different communities perceptions. An individual cannot be sure that others will interpret his 'categorisation' in the same way. To be able to overcome this, some improvement can be made if a page author can specify the page content. Many people, however, do not have the understanding of the topic, or perceive the need to do this yet.

Certainly raising awareness that there may well be semantic differences between different groups is needed in information systems development. However, a move towards uniform categorisation, as defined above, for an intranet development throughout a global organisation, would be more a process of re-conception for individuals in order to generate a meaningful language for the collective members of an organisation.

2. Organisational Learning

The use of new intranet technology therefore brings a variety of learning issues. Firstly that learning must occur in order to apply the technology e.g new skills to use the search facilities which also entails fostering collective meanings; secondly that the use of web technology allows new possibilities to further the organisation's aims; and that achieving the combination of these two requires an organisational learning experience.

Organisational learning is a complex concept, here the authors wish to focus on the learning from an individual's experience that could be shared by others in an organisation more widely than at the 'first hand' or individual level. It is the capacity in an organisation to have a collective 'know-how' about carrying out the activities of the group.

When the capacity is not present outsiders are often called upon to structure and bring about the communication processes and to stimulate innovative thinking. In the case of using web technology, the consultancy work that is contracted is symptomatic of the absence of these skills in-house. Schein (1995) sees it as a special ability, and one cannot assume that this ability is well developed in an organisation.

> 'The ability to create new organizational forms and processes, to innovate both in the technical and organizational arenas, is crucial to remaining competitive in an increasingly turbulent world. But this kind of organizational learning requires not only the invention of new forms, but their adoption and their diffusion to the other relevant parts of the organization and to other organizations in a given industry. *Organizations still have not learned how to manage that process. The examples of successful organizational learning we have seen either tend to be short-run adaptive learning, doing better at what we are already doing, or, if they are genuine innovations, they tend to be isolated and eventually subverted and abandoned.'* Schein 1995 (Present authors' italics).

If Schein is correct to say that the adoption and diffusion of new processes and organisational forms to enable innovation is not managed well, and it is indeed necessary for the introduction and maintenance of an intranet, what is it that needs to be done?

2.1 Can Groupware and New Technologies Assist in the Adoption and Diffusion of Organisational Learning?

Unlike database development, there is an opportunity to enable organisational learning inside the process of introducing intranet technology into an organisation due to its very nature. Evolutionary development of groupware applications can be used to initiate reflection upon the interrelation of action and events, leading to the full implementation which is intended to facilitate computer aided learning (CAL). However groupware often has a narrow focus on software packages for groups, and not as a supporting technology for collaborative work forms (Bannon 1998).

Research into the effectiveness of CAL has tended to focus on measurement of message exchanges and not on improvements made due to organisational learning (Goodman and Darr 1996). According to Goodman and Darr (1996) there are three areas which could be monitored

a) problem-solution exchanges occurring and being communicated to organisation members,

b) storing these exchanges, and

c) shared interpretation by members about the exchanges and updating of organisational 'memory' of their experiences.

The latter point is particularly absent from CAL monitoring. Groupware can be described as "computer software geared to group collaboration" (Haavind 1990). It should provide efficient multiple communication, the capability for storing data on problem situations and the problem-solving process. Therefore, groupware can support learning communities, however, evaluation of its contribution to stimulate organisational learning has not been adequately researched.

Communities need diffusion of learning from the individual level to and between groups. In certain environments diffusion may not be not acheivable (Goodman & Darr 1996). In others, to enable the diffusion it may be necessary for each part of the community to initiate its own learning processes which then needs to be communicated and exchanged in a wider arena. The co-ordinators of the intranet development may need to become facilitative 'teachers' who use appropriate methods of structuring both the individual learning of technological skills and the collective reflection, or adaptive response, across the organisation .

2.2 Learning Outcomes

As a 'teacher' the co-ordinator may wish to structure team exercises. Here it is essential to define the intended learning outcomes of any team-building exercises that are planned. Exercises consume effort and resources, the measurement of their performance requires that the intended purpose must be made very clear.

Monitoring the success of these exercises could be a valuable way of qualifying the contribution of the 'learning' aspects and consequent events, and provide a research base to ameliorate the quality of the product (see fig.1) . In addition to the main purpose, many *actual* learning outcomes of team-building are personal and

conscious engineering of these raises ethical issues. Some examination of the
ethical issues would be needed in further research

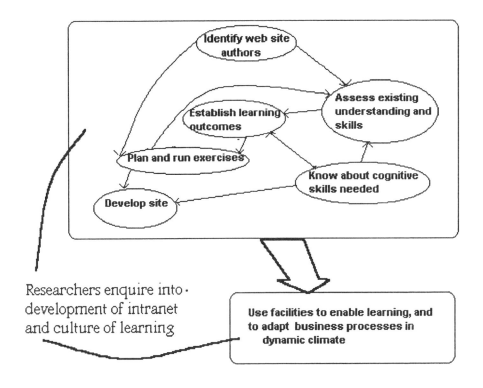

Figure 1. Model of Learning Management in
Development Process.

2.3 Stimuli for Learning

The desire to use the technology for the sake of it, can be a source of valuable
learning. 'Playful searches for knowledge are important activities in a learning
organisation (Senge 1990)' (Goodman & Darr 1996). Curiosity can stimulate
involvement in more directed learning exercises. Some people will be attracted to
the technology, others may be attracted if the objectives of the development match
their own, accepting the technology as a means.

Individuals must have the skills to use the technology, and, when able to apply it to
further collective aims, they must be able to represent their problems in a way that
connects with the contributions of others. An individual's technical competence
facilitates contribution and adoption, even in a context where social norms could
hinder organisational learning (Constant et al 1995) - the technology can help to
overcome some of the social barriers.

Different groups of people can take a topic and produce document material from their perspective, these documents can be shared and discussed. The explicit presentation of viewpoints can provide insight into other communities' value sets and a more informal cohesion can result (Gerstein & Shaw 1992). The involvement of many individuals in the authoring process could provide many unexpected benefits, from the socialisation that occurs preparing a site.

Multi-media use provides a different induction than normal 'training', the network of people that have had on-line induction seem to continue to share experiences and learning. A wider network of communication can be established using this technology and groupware in the organisation.

'Case study' material from others, made available through an intranet, can stimulate the application of the new ideas throughout the organisation. It may be difficult to recognise a similar problem in someone else's case study. But if it does happen and useful strategies are shared, it stimulates trying new ideas out.

2.4 Creating New Understandings: The Process of Concept Building

Improving the quality of information use, by enriching the interpretation of categorisations discussed in 1.4, requires a process of re-conception. This is a significant activity which demands some exploration.

Concept learning is probably the most important of all learned behaviour (Davis 1966). Gagne describes concept learning, as a process where the learner becomes conscious of similarities among known concepts, as a learned ability to discriminate essential features of things or events and group them systematically into cohesive categories (Curzon 1990). Learning how to develop a new concept , and not only understand an already defined concept, needs careful attention to be engineered.

Historically, society has viewed concept learning as the concern of the University or other educational institutions. In our current environment, the provision of learning is not solely in these institutions, but is also seen to belong in industry (NAGCELL 1997). Is an intranet project an appropriate space to teach and learn? 'Life-long learning', if it is to be universal, should be integrated into the working environment. An introduction of change is a good time to seek to structure situations for learning and learning to learn.

It would beneficial for organisation members who are co-ordinating the intranet development to foster concept building and to stimulate positive values towards a learning culture. These individuals need teaching skills to structure group learning in the development and maintenance, to improve the communication in operational processes of the organisation.

3. The Process of Development: How Projects Are Currently Managed

This third section explores current Information Systems development in a web-based context. It is based upon one of the authors' experience in actual projects.

3.1 Definition of Objectives for the Project

Before starting a project, it is imperative to have a clear view to be sure that the media being chosen is suitable to the aims of the project. This can be done through a "needs" analysis. The following represents a typical series of questions reflecting what should be addressed. Going through this basic checking procedure will help make sure that the project is mature enough and that the appropriate people are involved.

Table 2. Needs Analysis.

Context	Aims	Sponsorship
What is the project context ?	What are the aims of the project ?	Which people in the company can help the project ?
Which event has triggered the idea of the project?	What are the end results desired of the project ?	Are there key people outside the company who are able to help ?
Are there parallel experiences that can be drawn from other situations or circumstances?		Who is the contact ?
		Who influences decision-making?

3.2 Team Building as a Social Technique

Developing an intranet project is not like a database project. The information being stored is related to the organisation strategy and business needs and is more of an organic entity than a statistical database, it is essential to establish an ongoing relationship between the senior management (who can identify their business needs, or have the power to drive perceived needs forward) and the organisation members that implement the application. A senior management steering committee should be put in place. Intermediate management would be concerned too and teamed with information systems people.

A symbiotic way of working together should be allowed to develop, to achieve a multi-disciplinary team. It is interesting for those who are participating, due to the richness and breadth of interaction they encounter, and for the support that can be accessed. It helps bring a positive attitude towards the project.

Choosing the team members is part of the process. These people would typically be involved in the success of the company and be sensitive to roles of end users of the company. It is important that they can put themselves in the place of others, to select the right information to put in and to be able to advise on the information presentation. They should be computer literate but not 'computer-freaks'- the focus must not be on the technology *per se*. Their ability to talk in an informed manner with a large range of people would be essential. Members of the team would also need to be capable of taking responsibility and have the confidence to implement decisions that emerge.

3.3 Ergonomics

Particular attention should be given to the ergonomics of the application, this requires the adoption of basic skills to have occurred. Information structure, access mode and presentation should respect a proper standard, an understanding of the concepts detailed in section 1 of this paper is needed in order to establish and observe standards. Language should be oriented to the stakeholder groups, who must be able to find relevant information easily and be confident that they have covered all the fields they are looking for. Search tools and facilities have to be present to facilitate the use of the application. The development team has to empower the organisation members, facilitate access and ease usage, in short, create ideal situations for interaction, learning from collectively reflecting upon experiences and enabling creativity.

3.4 Methods

The application development process experienced by the authors has usually followed quite traditional phases of analysis and design, consisting of a study of the project opportunity and inception; analysis, design and software choice; application development, testing and implementation; and maintenance /evolution.

The use of a traditional model, as such, is appropriate at one level to address the technical issues seen in section 1 of the paper, but not at a second level to aid the learning issues brought out in section 2. What is also needed is a kind of development and 'maintenance' of the people side. The equivalent of this can be seen in education, in course development where a sequence of topics are planned in working sessions and guidance is given. It is highly dependent upon what the people in a particular situation need to learn and therefore a synthesis of method needs to happen at the level of the unique project.

3.5 Prototyping

Prototypes are essential to make sure that the development is working in accordance to people's needs in the analysis and design phase. This will confirm the appropriateness and the ergonomics of the project's creation. In addition, it enables development costs to fully reflect the development time, and avoids expensive down-time whilst 'bugs' are ironed out. It is an opportunity for reflection, to be able to capture the lessons in a form accessible to others, a structure is needed to clarify the interrelated events in this reflective learning process. The use of learning outcomes can be used as a framework for comparison of the expectations and results of the prototyping work.

3.6 Stimulation and Facilitating Use

The development of the technology itself will not necessarily enable a successful change process. But, to ensure that the technology does not introduce a constraining element its application must be transparent. Application display alone is not enough to allow people to use it. The project should be explained at all the stages : from the *inception* to the *implementation* and during its life time. Launching is important, but so too is the post-launch. The implementation team should monitor the use of the application: Which pages are consulted? Is the application responding to the original needs or do these needs change? What do people like about the application? Are they aware of all the possibilities? The communication and accompanying actions have to be planned at the beginning because they take time and have budget implications.

3.7 Maintaining the Application

As the information stored in an intranet is very often strategic and business oriented, it is dynamic. The web site has to be evaluated and updated to evolve constantly and sustain the interest of the users. It is reasonable to expect that evaluation would be more effective in an organisational context where it has been initiated in the development process. The application should be a competitive tool for the company, therefore in the development process there is a need to focus upon the broader issues, to enable this ethos to be sustained afterwards.

Very often in companies, web applications are developed by the relevant managers who are specialists in the content area. They have a good understanding of all the content needed for the application i.e. objectives, business aims etc... The trouble is that they have also to become a sort of 'webmaster' as well as carrying out their normal managerial role. Where before perhaps two or three secretaries or assistants could update information, intranet developments need differently qualified people to adapt the application to changing needs. The level of expertise is really based in three areas: Web development technology; business knowledge; and marketing of the web product. Maintenance at the level of business knowledge can be done by a number of employees, managing the context locally with a central co-ordinator.

3.8 Control (of cost, time, and satisfaction) of all the Proceeding Things

Charges, costs, delays and return on investment have to be evaluated. In intranet projects it may be difficult to know the return on investment. Some results are more qualitative than quantitative. We need to be able to evaluate qualitative values as well as quantitative ones.

Conclusions

The teaching of cognitive skills (such as the ability to classify and develop hierarchies) should be given a place in project management. This kind of education is not well supported in traditional structured methods, where only training for implementation or prototyping to elicit user needs is considered. Paying some attention to more generic education by introducing a method to structure the reflective process is worthwhile because application maintenance requires individuals with special skills. Valuable human resources can be diverted from operations management if it is the only area where these skills and reflective abilities can be found.

To achieve competitive advantage it would be wise to invest in the development of a learning resource. The intranet is a practical framework for interactive multi-directional development to enable continuous learning and adaptation to occur, with the aim of increasing synergy in corporate groups. To stimulate organisational learning through use of intranet technology, the development process must foster different kinds of learning processes. Traditional methods focus mainly upon the technical dimension, however specific tools to enable discussion about the learning content at various levels are also needed.

Exchange of learning of different kinds is by its nature precarious. There are obviously many factors in everyday organisational realities which would affect the communication of the process. A supportive environment can be fostered by beginning to develop this learning process in the intranet development. Perhaps the question is not only 'Can intranet development be a valuable means of organisational learning?' but also 'How does organisational learning aid intranet development?'

References

Bannon (1998) 'Computer Supported Collaborative Working: Challenging Perspectives on Working and Technology' *Information Technology and Organizational Transformation* Eds. Galliers, R.D. & Baets, W.R.J. **Chap. 2.** Wiley.

Bosak, J (1997) 'XML, Java and the furture of the web.'
Http://sunsite.unc.edu/pub/sun-info/standards/xml/why/xmlapps.htm

Brennan. L,L. and Rubenstein. A.H. (1995) 'Applications of Groupware In Organizational Learning' *Trends in Organizational Behavior* Vol **2,** Chap. 2. Wiley.

Constant, D., Sproul, L & Keisler,S. (1995) 'The Kindness of Strangers: On the usefulness of weak ties for technical advice' *Organization Science*

Curzon,L.B. (1990) *'Teaching In Further Education: An Outline of Principles and Practice'* (**4th Ed.**, Chapter 8) Cassell Educational Ltd., London.

Davis, G.. (1966). "A note on two basic forms of concepts and concept learning." *Journal of Psychology* **62**.

Du Gay, P. (1996) 'Making Up Managers: Enterprise and the Ethos of Bureaucracy' in Clegg & Palmer Eds. Chap. 1 (1996) *The Politics of Management Knowledge*, Sage Publications, London.

Goodman, P. S., and Darr, E. D. (1996) 'Computer-Aided Systems for Organizational Learning' *Trends In Organizational Behaviour*, Vol **3**, Chap.5 pp81-97 Wiley Chichester.

Haavind, R. (1990) Groupware: Addressing a need for improving productivity.' *Electronic Business* **16** (18), pp 69-72.

Heinle, N. (1997) 'Creating Multimedia With Dynamic HTML: An overview.' Http://www.dhtmlzone.com/articles/dhtmloverview.html

National Advisory Group for Continuing Education and Lifelong Learning (Nov 1997) First Report 'Learning For The Twenty-first Century'

Nolan, R. (1994*) 'Cognitive Practices Human Language & Human Knowledge'* pp122-123 Blackwell, Oxford.

Orlikowski, W.J. (1993) 'Learning from notes: Organisational issues in groupware implementation' *The Information Society*, **9**, pp 237-250.

Reed, M. and Hughes, M. (1992) *'Rethinking Organisation'* pp6-7 Sage Publications, London

Schein, E.H.,1995, Three Cultures of Management: The key to Organisational Learning in the 21st Century. Available online at: http://learning.mit.edu/res/wp/10011.html2p

Combining Methodologies: Issues Arising, and Lessons Learned, from Developing a Knowledge Management System

Cameron Leask
Arthur Andersen Business Consulting
199 St Vincent Street
Glasgow G2 5QD
0141 248 7941
Cameron.W.Leask@ArthurAnderson.com

Royston Seaward
Arthur Andersen Business Consulting
1 Surrey Street
London WC2R 2PS
0171 438 2992
Royston.Seaward@ArthurAnderson.com

Charles McLachlan
Arthur Andersen Business Consulting
1 Surrey Street
London WC2R 2PS
0171 438 2992
Charles.McLachlan@ArthurAnderson.com

Abstract

This paper examines how more than one methodology can be used in an industrial setting to achieve a desirable outcome, and critically evaluates the degree to which the methodologies and methodology users can be effectively combined. It is written in the context of projects that analyse and design a system to facilitate effective knowledge sharing.

Keywords

Combining Methodologies, Knowledge Sharing, Knowledge Management, Soft Systems Methodology, Communities of Practice, KnowledgeSpace^{SM}, Mental Construct Confusion

Introducing the Situation of Concern: knowledge management

As large enterprises strive to remain successful in increasingly competitive and intangible markets, we are discovering that the need to utilise the knowledge of the enterprise effectively is fundamental. The success of the enterprise depends on its ability to apply the collected knowledge of its experienced people in situations where those individuals might not otherwise have been involved. The problem is finding an approach to turn the "tacit" personal knowledge of individual members of the organisation into "explicit" corporate knowledge that can be disseminated throughout that organisation.

Traditionally many of these enterprises have applied their knowledge resource in an *ad-hoc* fashion, finding a form of informal knowledge sharing (typically defined by geographical proximity and management responsibility structures) to be adequate, in most cases, for the purpose of conducting their operations profitably.

While the informal application of knowledge has clearly served these organisations adequately to date, we note that many now find that *ad-hoc* approaches become unsustainable as the organisations grow and expand. As a consultancy practice, we have recognised this trend in our own operations, as we have become more adaptive to our customers' demands. In other industries too, enterprises now recognise the power of systematic sharing and application of organisational knowledge resources.

This paper reviews the application of methodologies in projects to develop systems that foster and support effective knowledge sharing. This is done using the NIMSAD framework (Jayaratna 1994), of problem situation, problem solving process, problem solver and evaluation.

Methodology Context – the problem situation

The situation of concern described above for organisations can be characterised as the recognition of an organisational desire to move to a situation where

- Everyone in the organisation performs at their optimum level;
- Best Practices are consistently applied in all areas of operation;
- Collaborative behaviours are supported and rewarded;
- Innovation is rapidly and effectively embraced; and
- Skills and capabilities within the organisation are applied to the appropriate tasks and problems

These objectives are supported by the strategic belief that it is vital to share and apply the collective knowledge of the organisation effectively, in every applicable situation.

In generic terms, the problem situation can therefore be defined as

- the need to build organisational processes which generate shared knowledge
- the need to build systems which allow the organisational participants to find, learn and apply shared knowledge for use in problem-solving within the organisation

Culture is the final, vital, component of the organisational infrastructure, and this must encourage and reward the contribution and utilisation of knowledge across the organisation.

Project Components

Consequently we can identify two basic components of a knowledge management project.

- The **first** considers the organisation as a *human activity system* (Checkland 1981) and relates to organisational culture, its strategy and the motivations of its people. At the core of learning and sharing knowledge is the need to build meaning into the workplace.
- The **second** component is the *supporting information systems*, which enable and support human activities. Although an information technology component is not mandatory to share knowledge, the use of IT can be easily demonstrated as being essential to the success of the project in many circumstances. Without technology, the desire to share knowledge is difficult to crystallise into effective and efficient work practices. The knowledge repositories and networks become powerful enablers and tools for increasing the value and creation of knowledge.

The first component of the problem situation – which regards the organisation as a human activity system – points to developing the organisational culture and the motivations of its participants. The methodology chosen to address this component of the project must address a number of critical organisational issues. These typically include the strategy, culture and leadership of the organisation, and also encompass many of the "interpersonal" and political aspects of organisational processes. We have found the methodologies for "soft" or ill-defined situations work best for this component.

The second component – which provides supporting technologies to help sustain the change suggested by the first – requires a rather different approach, and must take the outputs of the first component as a starting point for creating a technological "solution" to support any action taken as a result. It will hopefully be clear to the reader that a methodology that works best in "hard" or well-defined situations will be best here.

Methodology choice: the problem-solving process

Figure 1 shows how the knowledge management project can be perceived as three distinct tracks within a simple framework. It is important to recognise that this framework applies equally as well to the organisational process and culture ("soft" systems) aspects as it does to the systems development ("hard" systems) aspects of the project.

Figure 1: High-level project framework

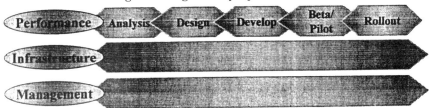

- **Performance**. This track of the framework includes the analysis and design stages where we consider the problem situation and design a solution. It then moves forward to the use of tools and techniques for solution delivery.
- **Infrastructure**. This track contains all the tasks required to ensure that the architecture to support the project is in place. This includes IT architectures and standards, and crucially also includes many of the ongoing "soft" initiatives such as Change Management, communication strategies and performance measures.
- **Management**. This track identifies the tasks required to keep the project under control and ensure quality. This includes project planning, leadership and co-ordination.

(Our primary interest in this paper is the methodologies used in the analysis and design phases of the performance track, although readers should note how the activities described impact other tracks of the project.)

Methodology Choice 1 – Human Activity System

The methodology we use to approach the first component is a proprietary one developed by our firm. It has very clear roots in the "Soft" Systems Methodology (Checkland 1981), and also has similarities to the ETHICS methodology (Mumford 1983a, 1983b).

The methodology assumes a start with the unstructured problem situation, as outlined previously, and begins by creating insights of the organisation, its strategic aims and the perceived situation of concern. The incorporation of organisational strategy helps to widen the perspective of the problem solvers, to ensure that they...

> "...build up the richest possible picture ... of the situation in which there is perceived to be a problem" (Checkland 1981)

Within a business model ("rich picture") of the organisation as it relates to knowledge management, it is usually possible to categorise the "relevant systems" in four broad categories:

- Knowledge content and structure
- Processes for learning, creating, organising and sharing knowledge
- Roles and tasks of people in the knowledge process
- Technology base

This abstraction of relevant systems corresponds to Checkland's "Root Definitions" stage. Once this stage has been reached it is possible to then move on to create conceptual models of the relevant systems and the ways in which they interact.

Checkland's "comparison" stage typically occurs during facilitated workshop sessions when the consultants and clients gather to review the findings of their (collective) work. The result of these sessions is what Checkland describes as "Feasible, desirable changes" (i.e. design) for the organisation. These changes will include

- knowledge management plans (strategic plans for knowledge management within the enterprise);
- identified *Communities of Practice* (key groups of participants in the knowledge organisation);
- a prioritised list of potential knowledge initiatives; and
- a list of hypothesised infrastructure requirements for technology, people, processes and content.

We conduct workshop sessions throughout the project and we have found that the *design act* of "comparison" takes place during every such session. There is typically a smooth transition during the project lifetime from analysis to design in these areas, and it is often difficult or impossible to determine the point at which analysis ends and design begins.

These outputs from the workshop sessions can be effectively used as the basis for further investigation. They provide a framework within which we continue the analysis – this time at the Communities of Practice level – using a very similar methodology.

Methodology Choice 2 – Supporting Information Systems

The methodology used to approach the second component of the project is also a proprietary one. This is called the *Arthur Andersen KnowledgeSpace*^{SM} methodology. The methodology is most suited to developing knowledge solutions in "hard" or structured situations.

Much of the analysis work on the situation of concern has been undertaken by this stage (as part of the "soft" systems work), and this methodology concentrates on the analysis and design of the technology tools which will support the "desirable/feasible systems" (Checkland 1981) which have been identified. These technology tools may include convergent (moderated) best practice repositories, divergent (unmoderated) knowledge sharing tools, distance learning materials, support models, tools to support virtual teaming, diagnostics and many others.

The methodology addresses the identified "soft" requirements as shown in Table 1.

Table 1: Mapping between "soft" and "hard" requirements

Identified Requirement "Soft"	Supporting implementation "Hard"
Technology	IT Solutions
People	User- and community-specific implementations
Processes	Workflow, navigation, search flows
Content	Organisation, classification, search width and depth

The approach taken is largely object-oriented and uses design tools such as the UML (Unified Modelling Language) (Booch *et al* 1997). It follows the broad "macro" approach established by Booch (1994) of establishing core requirements, modelling desired behaviour, designing an architecture and implementing a solution. At a more detailed level, an approach akin to the "micro" approach that Booch discusses is also followed.

An early step is to categorise content by knowledge area and subdivide by class. A *knowledge class* is the collective term for knowledge objects which share common, defining characteristics. This defines categories of knowledge. (For example, "best practices" and "tools and techniques".) A *knowledge object* is a complete, discrete package of information that has stand-alone meaning. They are instances of content within knowledge classes. (For example, best practice descriptions for a business process.)

Knowledge Attributes are the defining characteristics of a class of knowledge objects. Consequently they differentiate knowledge classes. This can be seen as the pieces of information that when brought together, become the knowledge object. Some examples of attributes for the class of 'best practice' would be the process definition, experts in the process, description of approaches, tools to apply, case studies, or performance measures related to the process.

There will often be an iterative cycle while the relationships of inheritance and aggregation, the attributes of each knowledge class and the appropriate abstractions are generated.

The classification scheme that results from this approach allows search flows to be determined. These partially define the routes by which users of the system will access the knowledge content and they also provide some of the initial input to the design of the object repository.

The work done in the "soft" components of the project work allows us to design workflow and system navigation, and linked to the classification scheme, this generates a different set of repository requirements.

The output from this work is a design for systems that directly support the knowledge management strategies identified in the earlier stages of the project. The design covers the object repository, classification schemes, navigation, search flows and overall system workflow. This design is platform-independent, and is entirely focused on the knowledge management needs of each community.

Further Methodology Choices

It is important to recognise that the two methodologies outlined above are *only two* of the methodologies used on a project such as this. A number of other methodologies are required to address problem situations within the project, for example:

- Build, beta, rollout methodology for IT systems development (performance track: hard systems)
- Build, pilot, rollout methodology for process and cultural development (performance track: soft systems)
- Infrastructure development methodology to generate the cultural, leadership and procedural shifts which will support the pilot and organisational rollout of effective knowledge sharing (infrastructure track: soft systems)
- … and so on

We have chosen to exclude these from the body of discussion in this paper but their choice and use remain fundamentally connected to the analysis and design methodologies that we have briefly described above.

Multiple Methodologies, Multiple Users – the Mental Construct Confusion between problem solvers

Typically we have found that many methodologies fail to recognise the importance of the *team* aspects of the "methodology user" or "intended problem solver". It is our experience that in the majority of cases there are *multiple* problem solvers, and it is our preference as consultants to ensure that the problem solvers are from *both* sides of the client – consultant divide.

As previously described, we are (within the context of a knowledge management project) operating with *at least* two methodologies. Because of the nature of teams, it is possible (and, arguably, desirable) that each participant in the project team may have to work within any or all of the methodologies at various times throughout the project lifetime.

Consequently the issues of mental models, *Weltanschaung* and "mental construct" (all of which are typically recognised by few methodologies) are complicated by the interactions of multiple mental constructs, using multiple methodologies within the same situation of concern. In this paper we refer to this complication as *Mental Construct Confusion*.

Mental Construct Confusion arises because of the differences in mental construct between each participant in the problem-solving process. The human quality of uniqueness is shared by all "intended problem solvers" and each one brings a different perspective to every situation.

There are three dimensions of Mental Construct Confusion. The first dimension is a straightforward one concerning the differences between clients and consultants. This difference is usually clearest at the start of a project, when the consultants' thinking processes are furthest from those of the client staff. For each participant, a move along the axis can be considered to be a process of building *depth* of knowledge in the area of concern.

The second dimension of mental construct confusion within the team is the difference between the people with strong skills derived from "hard" (structured) situations, and those with strong skills derived from "soft" (unstructured) situations. The understanding of both is vital to the project: those with hard skills need to understand methods of determining the requirements for any system that they may build. Those with soft skills must understand the information needs of those who will build the systems to support the knowledge management plans they create. A move along this axis can be considered to be a process of building *breadth* of knowledge for each participant in the area of concern.

The third dimension is "mental construct" itself. Jayaratna's (1994) list of "mental construct" elements has been used in Table 2 to illustrate some of the elements of this dimension.

We can illustrate any one of the elements in the third dimension. This is demonstrated in Figure 2, which shows the client – consultant dimension mapped against the hard skills – soft skills dimension, when considered from a "models and frameworks" perspective for a "clients A and D" and "consultants B and C". Every participant on the project team can be mapped on such a graph. Theoretically, if we were to draw a line (a *line of confusion*) between any two individuals on such a graph, the gradient and length of the line would be indicative of their ability to communicate effectively, relative to any other pair on the same graph.

Table 2: Third Dimension of Mental Construct Confusion

Mental Construct element	Client	Consultant	"Hard" Skill user	"Soft" Skill user
Perceptual Process	"Internal" to situation of concern	"External" to situation of concern	Systematic	Systemic
Values & Ethics	Unique	Unique	Consistency, order	Consensus, accommodation
Motives and Prejudices	Unique	Unique	Unique	Unique
Reasoning ability	Pragmatic; based on previous experience of "what works" in the enterprise. Political aspects dominate	Pragmatic; based on experience in variety of client situations. Intellectual aspects dominate	Best in structured situations with clearly defined issues	Best in unstructured situations with poorly defined issues
Explicit Experience	Enterprise and/or process specific	Process-specific; many enterprises	Structured situations	Unstructured Situations
Implicit Experience	"Domain expert"	"Process expert"	Unstructured situations	structured situations
Skills and knowledge sets	Enterprise-and/or process specific	Process-specific; based on wide experience of similar situations	Technological or task-specific	Interpersonal or process-specific
Structuring process	Decomposition, divide and conquer	Generalise, specialise	Decomposition, divide and conquer	Cause and Effect
Roles	Consumer, Enquirer, Acquirer	Adviser, expert	Technologist	Process specialist, communicator or facilitator
Models and frameworks	Organisationally bound	Conceptual	Technology-bound; specific	Intuition-driven

It is important to realise the importance of the lines of confusion: they illustrate the differences in perspective for any two individuals. They are also indicative of a creative tension that will exist between the members of the group as they each work towards a shared problem solution.

Figure 2: Models and frameworks dimension of mental construct confusion

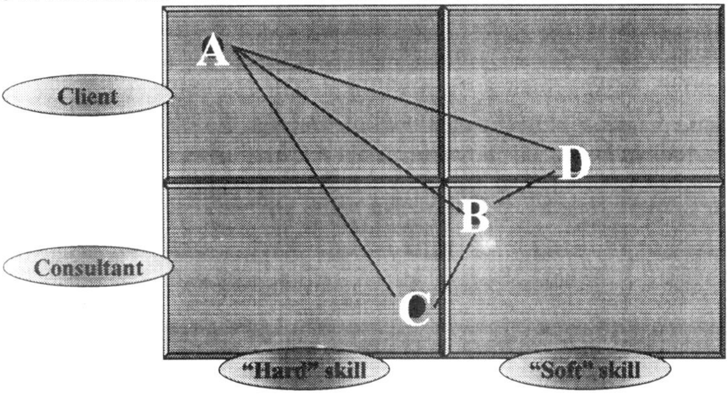

Managing the impact of Mental Construct Confusion

We suspect there may be an "optimal length" for lines of confusion. When the lines are too short, the problem solvers have similar perspectives: they can communicate within their range of experiences but lack breadth of perspective to see the wider issues affecting the problem situation. Similarly, when the lines are too long, the problem solvers have many valid perspectives on the problem: the wider issues they identify will be many and varied, but the problem solvers may lack common understanding of the problem because each sees it from such a different viewpoint than the others.

The "optimal" situation occurs when the problem solvers can share enough of each individual's perspective with the group to reach a sufficiently shared understanding of the problem situation.

We manage the impact of Mental Construct Confusion in a number of ways. The most important of these are workshops - with skilled facilitators to help develop a shared vision of the situations of concern. The sessions involve clients and consultants, and serve to integrate the dimensions of "mental construct confusion", and to "optimise" the lines of confusion by helping the participants share their perspectives on each situation.

A number of tools and techniques are used in the workshop environment, including conversational tools (such as ladders of inference) and electronic voting systems (which can be used to help reach consensus among participants). We have often found that it is appropriate to establish the project team as an Action Learning Set (Revans 1971). Action learning techniques address the learning needs of teams. In the context of the methodology users on a project, they operate within the infrastructure track of project, and are outside the scope of this paper.

Team members are also encouraged to participate in reflection sessions (part of the action learning techniques) throughout the project lifetime, to maintain their shared vision of the problem and proposed solutions. This helps to ensure that experience and lessons learned are shared, and this provides useful feedback for each participant. In turn, this helps to manage the mental construct confusion within the team.

Within the framework presented in Figure 1, we find that these workshop techniques are useful throughout the project lifetime, and are applicable in both the management track and performance track (methodology use) activities. This also facilitates the infrastructure track, as team performance can be significantly improved by the constant reflection in a team environment. In addition, these skills are transferred to other team members (e.g. clients), giving them the ability to adopt these new approaches on future projects.

Evaluation

The development of an IT-based knowledge management system cannot be considered in isolation. It must be performed with regard to the strategic intent of the organisation, its participants, their culture, and knowledge requirements. We know from experience that the implementation of cultural change and fostering of a knowledge-sharing ethic are at least as important as the implementation of the systems that facilitate the knowledge sharing.

In this paper we have highlighted two principal issues:

- When more than one methodology is involved, it is vital for methodology selectors and users to identify and understand any links which may exist between the methodologies being considered for use;
- When more than one problem-solver is involved, it is vital that the issues associated with mental construct confusion are understood.

Consider the following simplistic example. Two companies wish to merge and they need to analyse their market fit and their ability to integrate their systems. These two needs have been captured in the generation of "relevant systems".

The market fit analysis will probably require a "soft" approach, while the systems integration will require a methodology for "hard" problems. Unlike the knowledge systems example in this paper, the *methodological fit* – the linkage between the most appropriate methodology for each relevant system – is likely to be very poor. Further, we can postulate that the mental constructs of typical methodology users in the market fit project are likely to be very different from those performing the integration project. This polarity in methodology fit, and the likelihood of significant mental construct confusion suggests that that it may be difficult to integrate the participants in the project team if we attempt to perform the two projects together.

These lessons learned make "sense" because we know that it would be very unusual in practice to combine a market fit project with a systems integration project. The power of this conclusion is maximised when two or more methodologies are required to address related "problem areas" within a situation of concern, and where a wide variety of candidate methodologies are applicable to the various "relevant systems" of the situation.

The importance of the links between the methodologies in the case of developing a knowledge management system is crucial. Without the integration between the various "soft" and "hard" methodology components (and, indeed, the methodology users) it would be exceptionally difficult to successfully develop and implement cultural, process and technological improvements which would be of positive lasting benefit to the organisation.

Tackling the two components individually with ill-suited or non-integrating methodologies would most likely result in an inferior final outcome. Such an approach could not provide a set of cultural, procedural and support system improvements which would address the organisational need for knowledge so fully as those generated by methodologies which integrate well and feed from each others' outputs.

Conclusion

In this paper we have discussed some of the issues encountered when addressing a problem situation with two or more methodologies and a team of methodology users.

Conclusion 1: Methodological fit is critical to overall project "success"

When combining methodologies we have identified the concept of *methodological fit*. This concept emphasises the consideration of the strengths and weaknesses of each candidate methodology for a project, and the focus that each would bring if employed. Jayaratna (1994) presents a model based on the work of Leavitt (1972) which allows us to examine the focus of the methodologies discussed in this paper. (See Figure 3)

Figure 3: Modified Leavitt model of organisation showing methodology focus

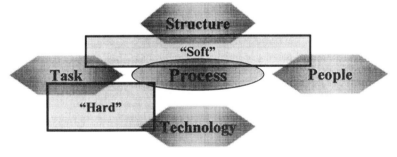

The figure shows how the "hard" (task driven) methodologies combine with the "soft" (issues driven) methodologies. The "soft" methodology in this paper generates a list of "desirable/feasible systems". Each element on this list becomes the starting point for a sub-project using the "hard" methodology.

The missing organisational dimension (process, people and technology) is addressed by further methodologies (process driven) which are employed within the infrastructure track of the project, and have not been discussed here.

The corollary of this is that methodologies *cannot effectively be chosen as independent components*. The "success" of a project is fundamentally linked to the abilities of the chosen methodologies to link successfully, both in terms of "deliverables" (i.e. methodology outputs) and methodology focus.

We believe it can be seen that *effectively* combining methodologies with a high degree of methodological fit should lead to solutions which address issues from a broader range of organisational sources than any single methodology could.

Conclusion 2: Mental Construct Confusion presents both an opportunity and a threat to overall project "success"

When considering teams of methodology users we have identified the concept of *mental construct confusion*. This concept emphasises the impact of differing mental constructs which become involved the problem-solving process. As Jayaratna (1994) points out:

> "Methodology users who become alert to these philosophical assumptions embedded in a methodology and in their own thought processes are in a much better position to benefit from the use of that methodology than those who ... remain unconscious of the philosophical assumptions they make."

The mental construct confusion model illustrates how this awareness of "embedded assumptions" can be applied to the methodology user's understanding of the philosophical assumptions (mental construct) made by their fellow methodology users (i.e. not just the assumptions of the methodology).

We believe that this model can be used, at an abstract level, to consider how teams of intended problem solvers might be structured to reach an "optimal" situation where the different perspectives of each participant are combined in an effective way with those of other participants.

Acknowledgements

We are grateful to Arthur Andersen Business Consulting for allowing us to use and refer to proprietary methodology material.

References

Booch, G. (1994) *Object-Oriented Analysis and Design with Applications (Second Edition)*, Addison-Wesley, Menlo Park, California

Booch, G., Rumbaugh, J., Jacobson, I. (1997) *Unified Modelling Language Semantics and Notation Guide 1.0*, Rational Software Corporation, San Jose, California

Checkland, P.B. (1981) *Systems Thinking, Systems Practice*, Wiley, Chichester, UK

Jayaratna, N. (1994) *Understanding and Evaluating Methodologies – NIMSAD*, McGraw-Hill, London

Leavitt, H. (1972) *The Volatile Organisation: Everything Triggers Everything Else*, Managerial Psychology, University of Chicago Press, Chicago

Mumford, E. (1983) *Designing Participatively*, Manchester Business School, Manchester

Mumford, E. (1983) *Designing Human Systems*, Manchester Business School, Manchester

Revans, R. (1971) *Developing Effective Managers*, Longman, London

Deny All Knowledge? Examining the Epistemological Assumptions of Anti-Foundationalist Information Systems Design Methodologies

Francis Wilson and Debra Howcroft
The Information Systems Research Centre,
University of Salford
Salford
England

Abstract

This paper identifies the interest of information systems theoreticians and practitioners in research and methodological design as a conceptual analytic enterprise that transcends the assumption that its principles are founded upon scientifically derived formalisms. The anti-foundationalist model of information system research and methodological design is one in which questions of validity can neither be posed nor answered in reference to a scientific, extracontextual reality but are intelligible and debatable only within the precincts of the contexts or situations in which they are derived. This paper debates whether anti-foundationalism in information system design as a model of epistemology provides practitioners and researchers with directions for achieving the epistemological state it describes and whether, if practitioners and researchers are able to learn and adhere to the principles of anti-foundationalism, this will provide an improved methodology for information system project development.

1 Introduction

In identifying information systems (IS) theory at the most general level it is possible to perceive two basic forms which conform to the foundationalist and anti-foundationalist epistemologies. The success of foundationalism in information systems design methodologies (ISDM) may be seen to rest upon the development of positivistic, `hard' ISDM over the last 30 years and its success in this project may be regarded as a microcosm of the Enlightenment legacy and its claim to emancipate humanity from the shackles of custom and dogma. The basis of the assumptions of hard ISDM development is that an increase in scientific, natural and social knowledge would enable an increase of control by men and women over their own fate. Thus the basis of positivistic foundationalism in ISDM is identifiable in the attempt to ground inquiry and communication and design in a manner which excludes any reliance upon mere belief or unexamined practice. The first twenty years of ISDM reflected this perspective in terms of the production of a number of foundationalist structured design methodologies. This approach of `hard' systems thinking embraces such methodologies as classical operational research, systems analysis and systems engineering. In the last decade however ISDM theorists and practitioners have become aware of the failure of many of the social systems to which they apply their methodologies to respond to the traditional positivist prescription: more knowledge, more control. In this regard IS designer and theoretician interest has moved towards attempts to understand the new kinds of uncertainty resulting from human development, described by Beck [1] as a `risk society', which is inherently unamenable to `the Enlightenment prescription' and may be classified into the category of anti-foundationalism. These new theoretical considerations have resulted in a change in systems theory in the discourse of the computing and managerial sciences towards a increased interest and emphasis upon the `softer', interpretivist and critical approaches to design and implementation methodology. `Soft' systems methodologies rejected the separation of fact and value in analysis and has as its central interest the study of how actors within systems interpret their worlds The emphasis in soft systems thinking is on how to cope with ill-structured problems or `messes' [2]. The interest in soft systems has increased recently with the much-promoted need for enterprises to `transform' themselves through the use of information systems. This has led to a debate upon whether the growth of technical expertise and the use of computer-based technologies results in a rationality which places too much emphasis upon technocratic modes of organizational control. The result of this has been an attention to developing theories that evaluate the effects of technology and organisational change in terms of the actions, reactions, and interactions of the interested parties. In evaluating the effects upon the development of information systems this includes assessments by managers, information system professionals and users at all stages of a system's development and operation. These developments of theory have resulted in considerable academic debate on the value of soft systems and its consequences and the interest in the question of theory continues to remain central to discussions of the teaching and practice of ISDM.

2 Foundationalist ISDM

In reviewing the approach of foundationalist systems the ideal is to establish the ground for a science of human behaviour. Having identified this ground it then becomes possible to order design activities so that they become anchored to it and are thereby rendered objective and principled. The ground so identified must have certain (related) characteristics: it must be invariant across contexts and even cultures; it must stand apart from political, partisan, and `subjective' concerns in relation to which it must act as a constraint; and it must provide a reference point or checkpoint against which claims to knowledge and success can be measured and adjudicated. In information system design the dominant paradigm for the application of `systems based' knowledge to practical human problems has evolved from classical scientific method derived from the physical sciences. As Checkland and Scholes [3:17] observe, these are all based upon `a "how oriented" activity,' the assumption of the problem analysis is `predicated on the fact that the need and hence the relevant need-meeting system, can be taken as given.' The approach relies on rationality in general and logic in particular and the belief that a neutral-observation language in the form of `scientific' thought processes can be applied equally to getting a person to the moon and to solving problems of the inner city or drought-stricken areas in Africa. Thus within organizations foundationalism becomes `an amplification of the idea that what goes on in organizations is rational decision making in pursuit of declared objectives' Checkland and Holwell [4: p.78]. The foundationalist project in ISDM can be understood to be the product of a series of converging theoretical grounded developments. Work in various disciplines; theoretical biology, computer sciences, information theory, linguistics, economic game theory, political science, communication theory, cybernetics, operational research; converged to shape a general systems theory movement [5]. It is from this assumption of the grounding of the general systems theory movement in the various scientific disciplines that its program of research in the direction of building and elaborating ISDM models has proceeded. The successful foundational IS project provides a `method,' a recipe with premeasured ingredients which when ordered and combined according to explicit instructions [the possibility of explicitness is another foundationalist assumption] will produce, all by itself, the correct result. In conceptualising a model of an organisation in which IS work is to be undertaken Checkland and Holwell [4] identify the goal-seeking model which informs much of the IS literature and describe `the model of an organization which sees it as a social unit functionally organized to achieve corporate goals, and an approach to inquiry based upon the kind of positivistic hypothesis testing which is so well established in the natural sciences' (p.78). In ISDM to support the foundationalist model the result would be the assigning of correct descriptions to entities, data flows etc and the deployment of a structured design methodology whose repeatable outcome is certain to its users. This certainty of outcome is assured by its promoters who consider that in its embodiment is the discovery of rules which are so fundamental as to be universal, rules that if correctly followed will always lead directly to coherent intelligibility in the understanding and modelling of the problem area. Thus the premise that the functionalist ISDM perspective relies upon is the availability of a set of formal constraints which have the characteristics of abstractness, generality, invariance across contexts. Once these constraints have been discovered and put in place, the resulting system takes on an independence of action that is capable of regulating complex systems.

3 Towards Anti-Foundationalism

With the ascendancy of foundationalist ISDM came the concern that the assumptions informing the work of foundationalist theorists of IS design failed to take into account that as information technology extends throughout an organisation, becoming pervasive to the extent that numerous tasks and decisions are controlled by it, the conceptualizations and meaning of technical rationality may similarly become distorted. Checkland and Holwell [4] identify that 'where conceptualization is based on the interests and agendas of individuals or sub-groups within the organization as well as the overall declared, public, 'official' account of the organization. The two will rarely map each other exactly' (p.83). To the extent that managers are dependent on, and accepting of, computer based systems to aid their actions, the technical representations and languages which underlie such systems may be overlooked. Organisational members may have little awareness of the limitations and premises inherent to the system [6].

4   Anti-Foundationalist ISDM

The emergence of the idea that humans continually create and recreate social reality through social action and the use of language in the IS field has been given considerable support since the 1980's. As Boland [7] notes, 'We all know that information is the meaning or inward-forming of a person that results from the engagement with data. Yet we continually avoid the problem of meaning in our information systems research' (p.36). As IS practitioners and theoreticians have become aware of this failure over the last two decades there has emerged a debate upon how new methodologies could recognise that 'there is no permanent "social reality" except at the broadest possible level, immune from the events and ideas which, in the normal social process, continually change it' [4: p.104]. In this investigation researchers were seeking methodologies which would circumvent the criticism made of the foundationalist project and provide 'richer' insights into the developing use of computer-based systems within organizations.

The evolution of these studies of the computer/user relationship came to focus upon the development of new methodologies to support the understanding of systems. A major influence in the development of a methodological approach came through the work of Churchman [8, 9] who suggests that 'the systems approach begins when first you see the world through the eyes of another.' The incorporation of this philosophy into systems concepts is illustrated by Churchman [8] in his attempt to change the understanding of 'objectivity' within the systems approach. In the 'hard' and 'cybernetic' systems traditions, objectivity is perceived to rest on the efficacy of some model of the system of concern. The objectivity of the model is rarely questioned. For Churchman 'systems', and whether they work or not, are as much in the mind of the observer as they are in the 'real world'. A model can only capture one possible perception of the nature of a social situation. Objectivity, therefore, can only rest upon open debate among many different perspectives. The results of systems analysis receive their guarantee from the maximum participation of different 'stakeholders' in the design process. This fundamental shift is one which is necessarily adhered to (in theory at least) in all the 'softer' systems methodologies. Under this view the prescriptions of systems modellers and methodologists remain valid only if they can produce the means of better organising open and free debate about the value or otherwise of existing and proposed systems designs. Rather than attempting to reduce the complexity of organizational situations so they can be modelled mathematically or cybernetically, developments in systems thinking sought to explore them by working with the different perceptions of them that exist in peoples' minds. From this anti-foundationalist perspective systems are seen as the mental constructs of observers rather than as entities with a real, objective existence in the world. Multiple views of reality are admitted and their implications are examined. Values are included rather than excluded (in theory) from the methodological process [10]. The privileged role of experts is questioned and an attempt made to include problem-owners and other concerned individuals in carrying out the study and finding possible ways forward. The immediate aim is to reach an `accommodation' about action to be taken. This should emerge from a debate involving all those interested in the decision and its implementation. A longer-term objective is to encourage and institutionalise a process of continual learning among the participants of the (social) system being addressed. Thus the ideas which form the basis of the soft (interpretivist) approach are those which are concerned with the notion of a specific objective, or set of objectives, held by an individual or a group concerning the behaviours of individuals of a different group in relation to some system. This is concerned with an `implementation process', i.e. a progression of organisational change whereby a significant difference in certain organisational parameters occurs and becomes permanent.

In the current developments of methodologies that support this approach Checkland and Holwell [4] present an understanding of how the interpretivist approach allows for a `sense-making process'. Thus anti-foundationalism in IS design proposes that questions of fact, truth, correctness, validity, and clarity can neither be posed nor answered in reference to some extracontextual, ahistorical, non-situational reality, or rule, or law, or value; rather, anti-foundationalism asserts, all of these matters are intelligible and debatable only within the precincts of the contexts or situations or paradigms or communities that give them their local and changeable shape. As Checkland and Holwell assert:

> `With "meaning" at the core of the concept of information and hence at the core of the IS field, work in that field has to be done outside any belief that there is the possibility of a static social world "out there", with purposeful action defined once-and-for-all and supported by "information requirements" defined only by instrumental logic' (p. 238, emphasis in the original)

Thus anti-foundationalist ISDM examines the components of the foundationalist world-view and denies those components the stability and independence and identity that are necessary if they are to be thought of as anchors for theoretical postulations. Entities like the world, the organisation, and the self can still be named; and value judgements having to do with validity, factuality, accuracy, and propriety can still be made; but in every case these entities and values, along with the procedures by which they are identified and marshalled, will be inextricable from the social and historical circumstances in which they do their work. In exploring this process Checkland and Holwell [4] state their interest `both in how ideas shape what people do and in the way in which what people do shape the ideas: in ideas and action mutually creating each other' (xiv-xv). This is the 'process in which human beings make their perceived world into a social haven comfortable enough for them to live in: the process of meaning attribution, in which perceptions are linked together and built into larger wholes' [4: p.238]. In summary, the very essentials of systems design that are in foundationalist ISDM discourse opposed to the local, the historical, the contingent, the variable, and the rhetorical, turn out to be irreducibly dependent on, and indeed to be functions of, the local, the historical, the contingent, the variable, and the rhetorical.

In the field of ISDM the anti-foundationalist argument is to be found in derivatives which include Institutional Democracy Design, Rational Argumentation Design [11], Consensual Communication Development [12], Soft Systems Methodology and Process for Organizational Meanings [4]. Recent use of actor-network theory, based upon the work of Callon [13] and Latour [14] in the field of ISDM highlights how foundationalist theory fails because it is from its initial principles implicated in everything it claims to transcend [15].

5   The Foundationalist Rejoinder

The considerable interest in this area is apparent in the number of reviews which may be identified to fall within the anti-foundationalist framework. However, it would be too much to say that the foundationalist argument lies in ruins. It is in fact remarkably resilient and resourceful in the face of attacks against it. The resistance or persistence of foundationalism usually takes the form of a counterattack in which the supposedly disastrous consequences of anti-foundationalism are paraded as a reason for rejecting it. Since the sum total of the traits of any empirical phenomenon is infinite, anybody attempting to describe it must decide (consciously or unconsciously) what to note and what to leave unrecorded, and how much attention and space to give to each mentioned item or aspect. However neither the canons of veracity and exactitude nor the distinctions of philosophical semantics, nor even a recourse to unemotional recondite words, can provide a line of escape from the necessity of making such choices. This lack of an independent platform to ground veracity is cited as a central problem of anti-foundationalism (As every journalist knows, even a picture of a simple event like an accident or a brawl can be altered out of recognition by picking on one assortment of details rather than another; just as a speech can be utterly distorted by stringing together selected, though literally correct, quotations). The consequences of the loss of foundation are usually said to extend to the loss of everything necessary to rational inquiry and successful communication.

This is a dark prophecy, a foundationalist nightmare vision in which a liberated self goes its unconstrained way believing and doing whatever it likes; but it is also a misreading of the central principle of the anti-foundationalist stance. This central principle of anti-foundationalism in ISDM is its insistence upon *situatedness*. A situated self is a self whose every operation is a function of the conventional possibilities built into environmental context. Thus in using Vickers' theory of `appreciative systems' Checkland and Holwell identify that these operations `are themselves internally generated by *the previous history of the system itself* and its interactions with its environment' (p. 47 original emphasis). In anchoring the subject to the social situation Checkland and Holwell's anti-foundationalist perspective reveals the subject to be always and already tethered by the local or community norms and standards that constitute it and enable its rational acts. In deploying Vickers' theories Checkland and Holwell propose that `we always see the world through a `filter' created by previous judgements about it. New judgements both reproduce the previous `settings' and create new ones, changing the filter in so doing: an appreciative system is always the product of the previous system itself and its interactions with its environment' (p.73). Checkland and Holwell also note that `we always *selectively* perceive parts of the world, as a result of our interests and previous history' and that `the act of attributing meaning and making judgements implies the existence of standards against which comparisons can be made, standards of good/bad, important/unimportant, etc' [4: p. 99-100]. Such a subject can be many things: certain, confused, in turmoil, at rest, perplexed, etc and that while it may not be sensible to assume that this behaviour reflects a systemic real-world actuality there remains the opportunity to develop a `process of inquiry' that `can be organized as a learning system' [4: p.78] which will allow the inquirer to understand these sets of beliefs within their situated, systemic constraints. However in its insistence upon the situatedness of the individual, anti-foundationalist ISDM cannot have the negative consequences feared by those who oppose it.

6   The Consequences of Anti-foundationalism for ISDM

The attraction of anti-foundationalism for the IS theoreticians who promote it and find in it the basis of extensive development in ISDM follows directly from the demonstration that foundationalist methodology is based upon a false picture of the human situation. Since it is not the case, as foundationalists assume, that the scene of communication includes a free and independent self facing a similarly independent world to which it can be linked by the rules of a universal language, a methodology based on these assumptions will necessarily fail of its goal. Thus Klein and Lyytinen [16:143] suggest that `the separation of information systems goal from human purpose and the identification of data with measurable facts conceals the real nature of information systems as social communication systems'; and that, `under scientism, science rather being a critical conscience and teacher of practice, becomes its myopic servant' [16: 151]. Conversely, if the correct understanding of the human situation is, as anti-foundationalist ISDM presents it, one of individuals whose acts are socially constituted and who are embedded in a world which is a function of the historical and conventional forms of thought that bring it into being, then it becomes possible to extrapolate from this understanding a better set of methods for operating in the world we are constantly restructuring and reconstructing, a better set of rationales and procedures for making judgements, and a better set of solutions to the problems of IS design. In referring to Schon's [17] ideal of a `reflective practitioner' Checkland and

Holwell [4] promote their model as a `high level tool for structuring reflection' (p.237) and suggest that their methodology provides a `process outcome, an intellectual tool which helps furnish a process of inquiry for making sense of a field, a tool available not only to reflective practitioners but to reflective researchers and reflective students as well' (p. 238). In a similar vein Hirschheim and Klein's [11] proposal for Rational Argumentation Design identifies that their `neohumanist paradigm seeks change, emancipation, and the realization of human potential and stresses the role that different social and organizational forces play in understanding change. It focuses on barriers to emancipation - in particular ideology (distorted communication), power and psychological compulsions, and social constraints - and seeks ways to overcome them' [11: 109].

In examining the development of new information systems methodologies it is possible to identify the relationship between the anti-foundationalism and the emergence of the so-called `risk society' [1] which is inherently unamenable to `the Enlightenment prescription' of found thought. From this increase in what Giddens [18] describes as manufactured uncertainty there has developed a `post-traditional order' of society where risk and uncertainty on a world scale results from `action at a distance' where single decisions [from interest rates to nuclear safety] may have dramatic and rapid effects upon the global economy. The new ISD methodologies with their promotion of change, transformation, contextual variability, social-reflexivity, etc., are seemingly suited to the new emphasis in business organisation upon process over product, the replacement of particular standards of correctness by the fluid and dynamic standards of effectiveness and continuous improvement and the growing demand that people make more and better informed decisions for themselves on a range of decisions in their own work and in their personal lives.

This shift in orientation is not new since the admonition to examine organisational processes rather than functions is now conventional practice which is reflected in the many variations of the `quality' management and `reengineering' genres. In anti-foundationalist ISDM it seems that this conventional wisdom has found a new paradigm, one that the system designer can presumably draw upon in order to operationalise their knowledge. This prospect becomes even more attractive as it allows the designer a way of explaining what is at least perceived to be the failure of many systems implementations. It now becomes possible to view implementation failures as the result of the deployment of the wrong epistemological assumptions, and now that the right ones have been discovered, success or at least dramatic improvement should follow.

The introduction by anti-foundationalism of the claims of situation, history, politics and convention in opposition to the more commonly successful claims of foundationalist ISDM provides much of interest to practitioners and researchers in the field. However, the proposition that anti-foundationalist arguments and ISDM methodology as process in some sense `go together' raises the complications of whether the first can serve as a theoretical resource for the second or that, conversely, the elaboration of the second depends on a prior understanding of and commitment to the first. Thus the central questions are whether anti-foundationalism in information system design as a model of epistemology provides practitioners and researchers with directions for achieving the epistemological state it describes and whether, if practitioners and researchers are able to learn and adhere to the principles of anti-foundationalism, this will provide an improved methodology for information system project development?

Here it is proposed that the answer to these questions is no; moreover, it is an answer dictated by anti-foundationalism itself. It is an answer implicit in one of Derrida's [19: p.9] characteristically enigmatic pronouncements: 'This situation has always already been announced.' By 'this situation' Derrida means the situation in which knowledge is always and already mediated, the situation in which language rather than being the mere medium or instrument with which we interrogate the world is itself the origin of the world, of our modes of interrogation, and of ourselves. It is the situation that Derrida comes to announce in *Of Grammatology* and elsewhere; yet he says it 'has always already been announced.' Derrida's point is that since it has always been announced, it cannot be discovered, at least not in the sense that would allow IS designers purchase upon it that they did not previously have. That is, the IS designer realization that something has always been the case does not make it more the case than it was before s/he realized that it was; the designer is still, epistemologically speaking, in the same position s/he was always in. The fundamental difficulty about being objective about IS design situation subjectivity stems from the inescapable circumstances that neither the requirement of factual correctness nor the canon of semantic neutrality tells designers anything about what to include and what to leave out when they are describing a situation. The fact that they are now able to announce that all the systems participants (including the IS designer) are situated does not make them more situated, and even when they could not announce it, being situated was always their situation.

However, the anti-foundationalist proposition suggests that this 'new' self-consciousness is something the IS designer is able to achieve in a space apart from situations and to make this reflexive knowledge a knowledge which is firmer and more 'true' than the knowledge that was previously available without reflection. Thus in 're-establishing the human agent as an actual creator of social reality through the attribution of meaning to observations and experience' the provision of a set of methodological tools allows the anti-foundationalist inquirer to 'draw upon phenomenology, hermeneutics and interpretive sociology' which will escape the strictures of 'positivism, and lead to a variety of modes of inquiry other than hypothesis testing' [4: p.78]. However in deploying these 'methodological tools' the inquirer is once again reflecting the aspirations, ideals and assumptions of liberal thought in that valid knowledge may only be achieved disinterestedly in the manner of projecting observer impartiality on a particular situation, however it is an assumption wholly at odds with anti-foundationalist principles of this form of IS research and design. The contradiction is in centre of the anti-foundationalist argument. This is the argument that begins by denying the possibility of a knowledge that is independent of our beliefs and practices and ends by claiming as one of its consequences the achieving of just such an independence. This is the claim which anti-foundationalist insight makes in its proposal of providing us with a perspective upon events which now places us in a position either to have a greater understanding of a situation or to achieve new objectives. Thus the claim in which the notion of situatedness is said to be a methodological tool which allows us to gain a purchase upon situations is finally a claim to have escaped situatedness, and is therefore nothing more or less than a reinvention of foundationalism by the very form of thought which has supposedly denied its validity.

Thus as an example of methodologies which promote the possibility of 'richer concepts of "information system" and "information systems development"' Checkland and Holwell [4] outline a series of proposals which will inform their anti-foundationalist ISDM where 'the aim is to define plausible purposes and ways in which it would be possible to pursue them..............what are sought are *accommodations* which enable energy to be enlisted in undertaking action relevant to plausible purposes' (p.112, original emphasis). In defining 'plausible purposes' Checkland and Holwell redescribe anti-foundationalism so that it becomes a new and more fashionable version of functionalist systems approach, a political vision that has at its centre the goal of disinterestedly viewing contending partisan perspectives which are then either reconciled or subsumed in some higher or more general synthesis, in a larger and larger 'accommodation' - a word Checkland and Holwell repeatedly use. In identifying this methodological sleight-of-hand it must be yet again stated that this aspiration is incompatible with anti-foundationalism because it assumes the possibility of IS designers gaining a perspective upon their own beliefs, a perspective from which those beliefs can be evaluated and compared with the similarly evaluated beliefs of others. This is the central principle of anti-foundationalism in its insistence upon the inescapability of situatedness, and if situatedness is inescapable, IS designers cannot possibly identify in non-evaluative ways their own beliefs, because as situated beings some set of beliefs of which they could not be aware would be enabling any identification they might make; and, therefore, the act of identification would from the very first be 'evaluative' throughout the design process. One could escape this logic only by saying that while the operations of the mind are always a function of context, in one operation, the identification of its own context and that of others, it is independent. Such an exemption is obviously contradictory and marks a return in Checkland and Holwell's discourse of the foundationalism they have supposedly banished.

The project of building a larger and larger consensus on the insight of anti-foundationalism can only commence if the first tenet of anti-foundationalism, the situatedness of all knowledge and of all acts of knowing, is overlooked. It is overlooked as a necessary (but not sufficient) condition for the development of a 'high level tool for structuring reflection' (p.237) and to allow the practitioner to construct IS designs which reflect the currently fashionable concerns with the goals reform and emancipation [20]. The reasoning is understandable: since the lesson of anti-foundationalism is that the world and its facts are not given but made, it follows that those who have learned the lesson will feel free to make them again. However in this reasoning the IS designer once again makes the error previously identified, the error of thinking that a conviction as to the circumstantiality of everything we know can allow them a perspective upon their circumstantial knowledge and enable them to change it. The point is that circumstantiality (another name for situatedness) is not something that the IS designer can escape by recognizing it, since the act of recognition will itself occur within circumstances that cannot be the object of self-conscious attention. Thus reform and emancipation can take no particular warrant from anti-foundationalism, and to think otherwise is once again to make the mistake of making anti-foundationalism into a foundation.

In summary the knowledge that the IS designer and participants is in a situation has no particular significance for any situation they happen to be in, because the constraints of that situation will not be relaxed by that knowledge. In the promotion of anti-foundationalism perspectives in ISD, while it may provide academics and practitioners with the possession of a new philosophical perspective, it will not equip them with a tool for operating in the world they already inhabit. Being informed that they are in a situation will not help IS designers to dwell in it more perfectly nor to develop information systems within it more successfully.

When Checkland and Holwell [4] state that `models or pictures...are never descriptive accounts of "what is the case"; rather they provide categories and language enabling us to describe what is perceived to be the case' i.e. discourse conventions which may be identified by anti-foundationalism, they are open to the same criticism that they level at foundationalist theorists who assume that what counts as information is fixable and static and where the rules formulated to describe behaviour are the same rules that produce the behaviour. This is also their assumption in as much as they believe that a description of how we come to know what we know can be turned into a set of directions for knowing (i.e. Soft Systems Methodology, Process for Organizational Meanings etc.) `in order that deliberate intentional action can be taken, including action in the name of the organization, or some part of it, as a whole' (p.113). As a searching critique of method, soft systems methodology cannot itself be made the basis of a method without losing its anti-foundationalist character.

However in countering these criticisms proposals may be made which suggest that the link between anti-foundationalism and IS can be preserved by making it weaker. It may be argued that even if anti-foundationalism cannot serve as a methodological tool with which to master situations, it can direct us to a new areas of understanding and learning about IS design. This is in effect what is urged by Checkland and Holwell [4: p.97] when they quote the example of Stamper [21] who, they say, `advocates a focus on the social process in which shared meanings are attributed to selected data, and would base IS development upon a study of the social norms which entail meaning attribution.' Thus all the IS developer requires is help in understanding the social norms themselves in all their fullness and then the staple activity of methodology instruction will be analysis of the semantic and conventions of the particular target area. As Stamper suggests that 'Meanings belong to human agents....If we can keep track of those agents and what they do, we shall devise a new semantics that can be applied successfully to business, legal and other social information systems.' [4: p. 97]. Here the advice is, if all knowledge is the result of 'social norms', then it is necessary to develop a 'new semantics' to understand these situations. The trouble with this advice is that in its strongest sense it cannot be followed, and in its weaker sense it cannot help but be followed, even when it hasn't been given. It can't be followed in the strong sense because it would amount to understanding social norms as if they were a new kind of object to which the researcher could now turn their attention, and that it is possible to achieve a distance from them such that the designer/researcher's accounts of them would be a form of 'true' knowledge. But both these moves once again reinvent foundationalism by substituting for the discredited notion of determinate facts the finally indistinguishable notion of determinate 'social norms' and by rendering unproblematic the researchers relationship to these newly determining entities. The truth is that a situation is not an entity, but a bundle of tacit or unspoken assumptions that is simultaneously organizing the world and changing in response to its own organizing work. A situation is always on the wing, and any attempt to capture it will only succeed in fixing it in a shape it no longer has. Moreover, from the recommended 'action research' attempt to capture knowledge of social norms must itself be mounted from within a situation, and therefore the knowledge afforded by such an exercise is not only out-of-date but disputable. In short, if the development of an IS theory of situations is inefficacious, the development of a 'new semantics' of situations themselves is impossible and a contradiction in terms.

In another sense, however, the weak sense, the development of 'new semantics' of situations is not only possible but also inevitable, irrespective of one's 'doctrinal' position. For if anti-foundationalism is correct and everything we know is always a function of situations, then every development IS research methodology is always the result of and the producer of further situational knowledge, whether we label it so or not. That is to say, even if a designer is being presented with a methodology as if it were independent, detached, and transferable, it is not thereby rendered independent, detached, and transferable. Therefore promoters of ISDM are always developing 'new semantics' of situations because they can do nothing else.

In conclusion the argument can be reformulated in terms that might seem paradoxical, but are not: if all knowledge is situational and we are always and already in a situation, then we can never be at any distance from the knowledge we need. Anti-foundationalist ISDM cannot present us with the knowledge we seek because its lesson is that we already have it. This is explicitly the lesson taught by Polanyi [22] in the name of 'tacit knowledge'. Tacit knowledge is knowledge already known or dwelt in; it cannot be handed over in the form of rules or maxims and theories; there is no transition from `knowing that' to `knowing how.' As Checkland and Holwell observe `the act of creating information is a *human* act, not one which a machine can accomplish... (and) no designer can *guarantee* that his or her *intended* attributions of meaning will be universally acceptable' (p. 91-92, emphasis in original). However, Checkland and Holwell [4: p.219] apparently forget this and devise their own curious epistemology which `requires a number of distinctions to be made which establish a language of: `"data" (the factual invariances); "capta" (the data selected, created, or to which attention is paid); "information" (meaningful selected data in context); and "knowledge" (larger, longer-living structures of information)' and thus provide a theoretical rationale for certain ways of IS design as opposed to others and for their `Process for Organization Meanings' methodology in `which any organization with aspirations to survive has to think about seriously' and where `some version of the process will have to be institutionalized in an appropriate form which fits the organizational culture'. But this is to turn the knowledge that knowledge is tacit into a recipe for achieving it, when of course the lesson of tacit knowledge is that it cannot be achieved by recipe, by the handing over of an explicit maxim, even when the maxim is itself. Nevertheless Checkland and Holwell [4: p.219] maintain that in organizations `it is a process which will need to be continuously managed... given its susceptibility ... "maverick" members'. As an argument that denies the possibility of IS design by rule, the theory of tacit knowledge cannot legitimate another set of rules for IS design. Neither can it rule out any. According to Checkland and Holwell "information systems development" must start by carefully defining the action to be served, in its specific context, and using that definition to decide what information is needed and how technology can help provide it' (p. 219). But this is itself a maxim and one that is difficult to distinguish from the `intelligence, design, choice' model of Herbert Simon. In any IS development the designs will be made in part because the maxims the designers are given are not explicit at all, in the sense of being detached from a tacitly known practice, but are the precipitations of a particular IS design practice, whether they are presented as such or not. The notion of tacit or situational knowledge is simply too powerful to be endangered by foundationalist `hard' methodologies that are ignorant of it and in the strongest sense foundationalist methodologies cannot be ignorant of it, no matter how much they try. The lesson of tacit knowledge, the lesson that it cannot be the object or the beneficiary of self-consciousness, must be extended to the theory of itself. Knowing that knowledge is tacit cannot put IS designers in more possession of it or enable them to possess it in a heightened way; and not knowing that knowledge is tacit cannot deprive them of it. To make the notion of tacit knowledge either into a recipe for methodological development or into a set of requirements for a `good' practice is to exempt it from its own insight.

7 Conclusion

In conclusion the promotion and success of the anti-foundationalist, interpretivist systems methodologies is a strong testimony to the need felt by many academics and practitioners to believe that what they do can be justified or explained by a set of principles that stands apart from their practice, by a theory. One cannot argue against that need, nor can one dismiss the narrative of self-discovery it often produces, the narrative in which conversion to a theory in information systems development leads directly to a revolution in practice. But this is a narrative that belongs properly to a foundationalist ISDM hero, to someone who has just discovered a truth above the situational and now returns to implement it; it cannot, without contradiction, be the narrative of an anti-foundationalist ISDM hero who can only enact his heroism by refusing to take either comfort or method from his creed. It is a hard move to make or not to make because it brings so little immediate satisfaction and leaves the would-be IS theorist with so little to do. If IS theorists renounce foundationalist epistemology there remains two alternative courses of action: either IS theorists may assume that design practice has nothing to do with theory, or they can make the opposite assumption and try to use the new developments in post-structuralist theory as the basis of a new practice in the development of IS methodology. By choosing the latter IS theorists give themselves the incalculable advantage of having something to say and something to sell. This advantage is noted in the Ambrose Bierce definition of the noumenon in his work, *The Devil's Dictionary* [23]:

Noumenon, *n.* That which exists as distinguished from that which merely seems to exist, the latter being a phenomenon. The noumenon is a bit difficult to locate; it can be apprehended only by a process of reasoning - which is a phenomenon. Nevertheless, the discovery and exposition of noumena offer a rich field for what Lewes calls "the endless variety and excitement of philosophic thought." Hurrah (therefore) for the noumenon! (p.231)

References

1   Beck, U. Risk Society: Towards a New Modernity. London: Sage, 1992.

2   Ackoff, R.L Redesigning the Future: A Systems Approach to Societal Problems. New York: Wiley, 1984.

3   Checkland, P.B. & Scholes, J Soft Systems Methodology in Action. Chichester: Wiley, 1991.

4   Checkland, P.B. and Holwell, S.   Information, Systems and Information Systems. Chichester: Wiley, 1998.

5   Lilienfield, R. The Rise of Systems Theory: An Ideological Analysis, New York: Wiley, 1978.

6   Orlikowski, W. Computer Technology in Organizations: Some Critical Notes, 4th Annual Conference on Organization and Control of the Labour Process, UMIST, 1986.

7   Boland R J. The In-formation of Information Systems. In: Boland R J and Hirschheim R A (eds) Critical issues in Information systems. John Wiley and Sons, Chichester, 1987, pp363-380.

8   Churchman, C.W. Operations Research as a Profession. In: Flood R.L. and Jackson M.C. (eds.) Critical Systems Thinking: Directed Readings. John Wiley, Chichester, 1970.

9   Churchman, C.W. The Systems Approach and Its Enemies. New York: Basic Books, 1979.

10   Wood-Harper, A.T. Research Methods in Information Systems: Using Action Research, in E. Mumford, *et al.* (eds.) Research Methods in Information Systems. Amsterdam: Elsevier, 1985.

11   Hirschheim, H. and Klein, R. Realizing Emancipatory Principles in Information Systems Development: The Case for ETHICS, MIS Quarterly, 18: 1, pp. 83-109, 1994.

12   Hirschheim, R. and Newman, M. Symbolism and Information Systems Development: Myth Metaphor and Magic, Information System Research, 2, pp. 1-34, 1991.

13   Callon, M. Some elements of a sociology of translation: domestication of the scallops and the fishermen of St Bieuc Bay, in J. Law (ed) Power, Action and Belief: A New Sociology of Knowledge? Sociological Review Monograph no. 32. London: Routledge, 1986.

14   Latour, B. Science in Action. Havard: HUP, 1987.

15   McMaster, T., Vidgen, R.T. and Wastell, D.G. Technology Transfer - Diffusion or Translation, in T. McMaster, et al., (eds.) Facilitating Technology Transfer through Partnership: Learning Through Research, Chapman and Hall: London, pp. 64-75, 1997.

16   Klein, H and Lyytinen, K. The Poverty of Scientism in Information Systems, in Mumford, et al. (eds.) Research Methods in Information Systems. Amsterdam: North Holland, 1985.

17   Schon, D. The Reflective Practitioner – How professionals Think in Action, Basic Books, New York. (1983)

18   Giddens, A. Living in a Post-Traditional Order, in U. Beck, A. Giddens and S. Lash, Reflexive Modernization, Cambridge: Polity Press, 1994.

19   Derrida, J. Of Grammatology. trans. Gayatri Spivak, Baltimore, 1976.

20   Wilson, F. (1997) The Truth is Out There: The Search for Emancipation in Information System Design, *Information Technology and People* Vol. 9.

21   Stamper, R. (1987) Semantics, in R.J. Boland and R.A. Hirschheim (eds) *Critical Issues in Information Systems*, Chichester: Wiley.

22   Polanyi, M. (1967) *The Tacit Dimension*. London: Routledge.

23   Bierce, A. (1989) *The Devil's Dictionary*. Harmondsworth: Penguin.

Emerging Technologies and Situated Requirements

Jim Hughes
Information Systems Research Centre
University of Salford
Salford. UK

Trevor Wood-Harper
Information Systems Research Centre
University of Salford
Salford. UK
and
School of Information Systems
University of South Australia
Adelaide. Australia

Abstract

The system developer is faced with the emergence of new technologies together with new ways of doing business and new ways of organising and working. Separately and together these present problems for the systems developer involved in requirements determination particularly if the developer is concerned with situated rather than solely formal requirements. This paper draws upon the learning from action case studies from traditional organisational settings which suggest that the use of Grounded Theory may be the basis for addressing some of the problems of determining situated requirements in this emerging technological environment.

1 Introduction

Given the emergence of new technologies and new ways of working problems arise for the systems developer in determining requirements for information systems (IS). This is of particular concern if the developer considers the elicitation of situated or context based requirements to be as equally important as formal requirements. The problem may be at a logistical level in terms of the practicalities of overcoming time and space issues such as how can the developer find out what X and Y want if X works 100 miles away from Y and both X and Y live 500 miles from the developer? The problem may be at a methodological level in terms of selecting appropriate methods for determining requirements. This paper considers situated requirements determination in new technology environments and as a result a changing role for IS developers.

The paper begins with an explication of situated requirements and expresses the case for their importance in the requirements determination phase of information systems development. The paper then considers a possible method - Grounded Theory - to be used for situated requirements. This will be expressed as learning from action case studies from traditional organisational structures which the authors' use as a basis for discussing the implications for new forms of organisation.

2 Situated requirements

In this section consideration will be given to the need in information systems development for situated requirements. The classical approach to requirements revolves around the role of the requirements engineer as expert and in using a term such as engineering it constrains the process to be largely technical. Indeed the main role of the requirements engineer is said to be to 'capture' requirements. The suggestion being that requirements may be difficult to find but they exist in a deterministically fixed form and indeed the implication is that there is a finite number of them to be found. The classical methods are restricted to questionnaire and interview but as Jirotka and Goguen, (p.4, 1994) note *'the analysis of the materials gathered is largely left to intuition'*. McDermid (1994) questions the formal technical approach since although global considerations of requirements may be included in the requirements specification these tend to be problematic since they deal with properties that may be considered to be emergent rather than decomposable. Typically then if the functionality and other non-functional properties can be decomposed into modules then these may be allocated to software engineers to implement whilst the emergent properties are largely ignored. Additionally since the validation of requirements is often made more problematic because of the semantics of natural language then McDermid somewhat cynically suggests that the requirement specification merely documents

"what it is that the analyst thought it was the problem owner said he thought he might want, not what he'll get!" (McDermid, p.25, 1994).

An alternative to this formal approach considers the situated nature of requirements. Goguen (1992) expresses the relationship between formal, context insensitive information, which he labels 'dry', and informal situated information which he labels 'wet'

"Formal information occurs in the syntactic representations used in computer-based systems. Informal situated information arises in social interaction, for example, between users and managers, as well as their interactions with systems analysts. Thus requirements engineering has a strong practical need to reconcile the dry and the wet" (Goguen, p.1, 1992).

Goguen's perspective is interesting since in addition to applying techniques from the social sciences to requirements elicitation, notably ethnomethodology and conversational analysis, he also demonstrates that 'dry' abstract data types occur in ordinary discourse in everyday life. He provides six characteristics which he considers to be the 'qualities of situatedness'. These are largely derived from the work of the anthropologist Lucy Suchman, (1987) and are given in Figure 1.

The qualities of situatedness

1. *Emergent*	Social events can not be understood at the level of the individual, that is, in terms of individual psychology, because they are jointly constructed as social events by the members of some group through their interaction.
2. *Local*	Actions and their interpretations are constructed in some particular context, including a particular place and time.
3. *Contingent*	The construction and interpretation of events depends upon the current situation (potentially including the current interpretation of prior events). In particular interpretations are subject to negotiation, and relevant rules are interpreted locally, and can even be modified locally.
4. *Embodied*	Actions are linked to bodies that have particular physical contexts, and that the particular way that bodies are embodied in a context may be essential to the social interpretation of some events.
5. *Open*	Theories of social events (both those constructed by participants and by analysts) cannot in general be given a final and complete form, but must remain open to revision in the light of further analyses and events.
6. *Vague*	Practical information is only elaborated to the degree that it is useful to do so; the rest is left grounded in tacit knowledge.

Figure 1 The qualities of situatedness (adapted from Goguen, p.168, 1994)

If Goguen's premise is accepted and the concern for situated requirements is as important as formal requirements then even a brief analysis of the elements in figure 1 causes concern with respect to emerging technologies and new ways of organising work. Not least among these are the issues of geographically dispersed groups and multiple and varying localities. The issues which arise are concerned with how in logistical terms, given these constraints, might a system's developer collect and analyse situated requirements? The significance of situated requirements is particularly important in these emerging organisations since for the traditional organisational structures domain knowledge may be assumed if, for example, the developer had worked in similar domains.

What is critical for the future is that no domain may be considered to be similar to the next and this challenges the underlying and often implicit assumptions that are made for traditional structures. If information systems development is to be a genuine response to organisational requirements then the authors would maintain that it is essential that methods are used which enable the developer to find out in sociological terms what is going on and to help the developer make explicit any underlying assumptions that are being made about social and organisational structures since in every new situation the technologies will be challenging these assumptions. Clearly methods themselves cannot alert developers to challenge assumptions therefore it is worth briefly considering the extent to which existing information systems *methodologies* can support the developer in firstly alerting her/him to challenge assumptions and secondly to provide methods for eliciting situated requirements.

One might intuitively expect that the human-centred and participative methodologies have a role to play in this regard and structured methodologies less so simply because of the well documented assumptions that underpin these methodologies (Jayaratna, 1994; Walsham, 1993; Hirschheim et al., 1995). However Nicholson and Hughes (1996) considered these two typical approaches to information systems development from three perspectives appropriate for understanding the emerging technologies - dynamic structures, culture and timescales. They concluded from their analysis that whilst human centred and participative methodologies present *desirable* features for new forms of organisation and working these are not features which may be *feasibly* implemented. On the other hand the structured methodologies broadly present feasible features to enable information systems development in new forms of organisation. Perversely this has little to do with the desirable features but more to do with the fact that the structured methodologies more easily deal with the technological or formal aspects of information systems development.

Together with the earlier discourse on situated requirements the future may look gloomy for those interested in situated requirements simply because the methods for addressing the problems have not been established. The following section considers a possible method - Grounded Theory - for addressing some of these feasibility issues by drawing on the lessons from the use of a method in traditional organisational structures for determining situated requirements (Hughes, 1998).

3 A way forward?

3.1 Grounded Theory

Grounded Theory or as it is more properly titled 'The Discovery of Grounded Theory' (Glaser and Strauss, 1967) is a method ostensibly used by social scientists for the analysis of qualitative data. In this method conceptual properties and categories may be 'discovered' or generated from the qualitative data by following a number of guidelines and procedures. The two critical stages of Grounded Theory identified by Glaser and Strauss (1967) are firstly that of constant comparative analysis, a procedure for the identification of conceptual categories and their properties which may be embedded in the data and secondly theoretical sampling which is both a category enriching and disconfirming procedure. The procedures associated with the analysis revolve around the coding of transcripts and the development of categories which lead to the emerging theory.

Glaser and Strauss' (1967) original work had three main purposes. To offer the rationale for empirically generated theory that was 'grounded' that is to say generated and developed through the inductive analysis of data collected during research projects. The second aim was to suggest the procedures and the reasons for them and the third aim was to propose legitimacy for careful qualitative research. Interestingly the final aim has been achieved to the extent that Grounded Theory underpins many models of qualitative research (Dey, 1993). However Grounded Theory differs from other approaches to the analysis of qualitative data because of its emphasis on theory. A major criticism however is that the definition of theory may be too austere or formal. Indeed it may be argued that the Grounded Theory procedures are positivistic and may lend themselves more to structured analysis methods than interpretive methods particularly given the emphasis placed on the reinterpreted scientific criteria, such as repeatability, that must be applied to Grounded Theory research in order to validate the research process, (Strauss and Corbin, 1990; Corbin and Strauss, 1990). In reply Strauss and Corbin (1994) note two important aspects of Grounded Theory

"First, theories are always traceable to the data that gave rise to them...Second grounded theories are very 'fluid' because they embrace the interaction of multiple actors, and because they emphasise temporality and process" (Strauss and Corbin, 1994, p.276).

They stress that grounded theories are interpretive in their nature. Denzin (1994) seeks to reconcile this problem by maintaining that Grounded Theory can be considered as post-positivist since although its proponents emphasise the 'good science' model it continues to fit itself to more interpretive styles. This paper considers Grounded Theory in this way and agrees with Miles and Huberman (1994) who consider the post-positivist perspective to place an emphasis on multiple realities and researcher interpretation. Thus the use of Grounded Theory and the results produced may be said to be contingent upon the situation or domain under study and the perspective of the Grounded Theory researcher. This is more in line with the constructivist criteria for quality of research which rely upon the richness or authenticity of the learning that is achieved and an understanding of the constructions of others, and on the ontological authenticity in terms of the development of the researcher's personal constructs (Guba and Lincoln, 1994).

Whilst this debate may be interesting when considering the use of Grounded Theory as a set of research methods it becomes particularly important when the emphasis is on the use of Grounded Theory in *practical* requirements determination projects. Hughes (1998) reports on two such action case studies in which the systems developer used a conjunction of Grounded Theory for data analysis and ethnomethodology as the paradigm of inquiry for determining situated requirements.

3.2 The role of the systems developer

The critical point to emerge from Hughes' (1998) study was the perspective of the systems developer. During the study the dilemma was always present between Grounded Theory as positivist set of procedures and the developer as interpretivist analyst. Although the studies drew on ethnomethodology as providing the epistemological basis of the methods used, the procedures themselves - coding, comparing, categorising, saturating - had a positivist feel to them. Indeed it may be said that it was the developer's personal constructs and skills that helped derive the information rather than the use of the procedures and it was the developer's perspective that maintained the interpretive style rather than Grounded Theory. More generally this raises questions for experienced Grounded Theorists. What is it in the Grounded Theory procedures that helps the researcher to abstract a rationale or philosophical perspective? There may be little attention given to how the data was generated or collected. If the data collected has already been structured by the collection process, for example through structured interviews, then no rationale can be abstracted by the use of Grounded Theory. In the studies core categories were used to focus the data collection and to shorten the time taken to analyse. This decision - a departure from ethnomethodology and from Grounded Theory procedures - almost certainly ensured that the subsequent structuring was due to the developer rather than the method.

With this emphasis on the role of the developer rather than the methods used then what assistance does this give to addressing the issues of emerging technologies and new forms of organisation? Most importantly it begins to address the limitations of the Nicholson and Hughes (1996) analysis given earlier where the human centred and participative methodologies have been, in a sense, artificially separated when considering a response to the characteristics of new forms of organisation. The authors would maintain that the most significant factor is not the features of the named methodology but rather the mental constructs and skill sets of the systems developer. This places a tremendous emphasis on the training and preparation of emerging systems developers and not just on the tools and techniques they use.

The authors would also propose that on logistical grounds Grounded Theory procedures may be used to elicit situated or indeed formal requirements using the emerging technology. For example the possibility of conducting interviews at a distance with interviewees or focus groups with teleconferencing techniques, e-mail or groupware and analysing the recorded transcripts to derive a grounded theory which expresses the situated requirements.

3.3 The use of computerised analysis tools

A major problem which came from the action case studies was the time taken to perform the Grounded Theory procedures. Wherever Grounded Theory has been used on practical projects this has always been an issue (Pidgeon, Turner and Blockley, 1991; Oliphant and Blockley, 1991). For the action cases the problems of time constraint were mitigated by the use of a software package, QSR NUDⅢIST (Richards and Richards, 1991), for coding indexing and sorting categories. The use of computers in qualitative analysis may be open to the criticism that for interpretive research the software may lead the research. Yet as Kelle (1995) points out much of this hostility has dissipated with the increased use of sophisticated software packages designed specifically to aid text structuring, indexing and storage. This would certainly need to be a feature of any method for determining situated requirements if the results are to be useful that is to say at the very least, in terms of time and the largely interpretive style of analysis.

3.4 Situated requirements

The final learning point is about situated requirements themselves. The action cases were based on traditional organisations where the account of organisational life provided by the use of the methods represents the situated requirements of the organisation. The account can be said to align closely with the characteristics of situatedness given in figure 1 above. The account generated by the analysis may be complemented by more formal requirements elicitation methods. What is important, as Goguen (1994) notes, is that

"..information that is heavily situated should come with pointers to its context ....This should help us to effect an ongoing, practical reconciliation between formal technical issues and socially situated issues in the actual practise of requirements engineering, as is needed for building systems that work successfully in their social context." (Goguen, 1994, p.194 (Goguen's emphasis)).

The action cases pointed to the interviewees in the studies who felt that it enabled them to feel ownership of the final account. The studies helped to identify further roles for the systems developer not normally associated with traditional or scientific methods of problem formulation or requirements determination. The role of the developer in determining situated requirements is to bring the interviewees into the structuring process through the validation of interim and final accounts. In stressing the importance to the interviewees of using their own words in the interim and final accounts the analyst is educating the participants and engaging them also to consider their ethical position. This may be considered burdensome for the systems developer but as Walsham (1993) and Hirschheim and Klein (1989) argue it is through the articulation of underpinning assumptions and an express statement of an ethical position that creative information systems solutions are more likely to be attained. This also returns to the earlier issue raised in the paper regarding the need for developers to make their own assumptions explicit since in new forms of organisation no domain may be considered to be similar to the next. Together with the participants (users) the developer can challenge assumptions regarding technologies and organisational forms to enable a deeper understanding of change rather than tacit acceptance.

Individual developers who facilitate learning or aim to educate participants can enable them to be economically more productive for the organisation. This learning function may be facilitated through technologies such as groupware or e-mail as it is already in some universities. One may see therefore that an aspect of the developer's role is to enable participants during the intervention and to give ownership of the problem and the problem definitions to the participants and not to claim that ownership for themselves.

There is a resonance here with the work of Ngwenyama and Lee (1997) who consider the use of critical social theory (CST) when investigating computer mediated communication and specifically electronic mail. They question the implicit positivist assumptions that the processing of data into information is mainly the job of computer hardware and software and maintain that it is performed by human beings themselves. Furthermore they assert that interpretivist assumptions based on mutual understanding pay little or no attention to the emancipation potential of communication and the human actors' 'critique of validity' of what is being communicated. Interestingly they also contend that a CST perspective suggests no a priori reason to suppose that richness in communication is dependent on face to face interaction or body language. Clearly this also helps to alleviate the geographical problems faced by developers whose requirements domain is geographically disperse. Ngwenyama and Lee also stress a distinguishing feature of the CST perspective is the emphasis on the actors in the social situations and how they act to 'contextualize' communications. Good understanding of this perspective may help developers enhance the educating potential of methods which they use.

A difficulty when applying the above in the context of new technologies and new forms of work is the extent that the qualities of situatedness can be successfully achieved as noted earlier. Of the six qualities given in figure 1 most can be arrived at through the Grounded Theory analysis and the enlightened view of the developer given above. That is to say taking as an example a geographically disperse workgroup it may be possible to derive the emergent properties of the work and to explore the social interpretation of events that these groups share. The Grounded Theory analysis also allows for the openness to rapid change and the elicitation of *some* of the tacit knowledge held by the groups. The characteristic that continues to be problematic is the concept of embodied actions which depend on the physical context. Since in domains where the physical environment is only metaphorically represented through individual screens then the idea of an embodied concept is conceptual rather than physical.

Problems and challenges remain, however the learning from the traditional organisation and the Grounded Theory procedures as a method of analysis may help to restore some confidence that the future does not necessarily have to be determined by technological change nor developed solely through structured methods. The cautionary note is that the fundamental ingredient in this is the role of an enlightened developer open to the situated requirements of information systems.

4 Summary

This section presents a summary of the arguments presented and tentatively points to possible outcomes from future action based research in this area.

- The premise is that for the development of any information system the determination of situated requirements is fundamentally important since we are moving into problem domains in which we have little or no idea what is happening nor do we have any guide from experience in traditional organisational forms. Developers therefore need a deeper sociological understanding of what is happening.
- Learning outcomes from action case studies using Grounded Theory as a method of determining situated requirements may suggest a case for optimism since
  ⇒ they suggest a new role for the systems developer in which their personal mental constructs and skill set are more important contributors to understanding methodology than are the methods being used;
  ⇒ the use of computerised qualitative data analysis tools can help speed analysis and also enable data collection across the emerging technology;
  ⇒ The qualities of situatedness can in principle mostly be established.
  ⇒

Work has already begun in this area and will concentrate on the use of these methods using action case studies in new forms of organisation with geographically disperse groups with greater consideration of Ngwenyama and Lee's (1997) work on critical social theory. Work will also proceed on the design of practical education programmes for systems developers to enable them to understand the issues and respond ethically to the challenges they face.

References

Corbin, J. and Strauss, A. (1990) 'Grounded Theory Research: Procedures, Canons, and Evaluative Criteria' Qualitative Sociology. Vol. 13(1) pp. 3-21.

Denzin, N. (1994) 'The art and politics of interpretation' in Denzin, N.K. and Lincoln, Y.S. (Eds.) Handbook of Qualitative Research. Sage. London. pp. 500-515.

Dey, I. (1993) Qualitative Data Analysis: A User-Friendly Guide for Social Scientists. Routledge. London.

Glaser, B. and Strauss, A.L. (1967) The Discovery of Grounded Theory: Strategies for Qualitative Research. Aldine. Chicago.

Goguen, J.A. (1992) 'The dry and the wet' in Falkenberg, E.D., Rolland, C. and El-Sayed Nasr-El-Dein El Sayed (Eds.) Information Systems Concepts: Improving the understanding. Elsevier Science Publishers B.V. (North-Holland) pp. 1-17.

Goguen, J.A. (1994) 'Requirements Engineering as the reconciliation of social and technical issues' in Jirotka, M. and Goguen, J.A. (Eds.) Requirements Engineering: Social and Technical issues. Academic Press. London.

Guba, E.G. and Lincoln, Y.S. (1994) 'Competing Paradigms in Qualitative Research' in Denzin, N.K. and Lincoln, Y.S. (Eds.) Handbook of Qualitative Research. Sage. London. pp. 105-117.

Hirschheim, R. and Klein, H.K. (1989) 'Four Paradigms of Information Systems Development' Communications of the ACM. Vol. 32(10) pp. 1199-1216.

Hirschheim, R., Klein, H.K. and Lyytinen, K. (1995) Information Systems Development and Data Modelling: Conceptual and Philosophical Foundations. Cambridge University Press, Cambridge, UK

Hughes, J. (1998) 'The Development of the GIST (Grounding Information SysTems) Methodology: Determining Situated Requirements in Information Systems Analysis' Ph.D. Thesis. Department of Computing, Mathematics and Statistics, University of Salford, Salford, UK.

Jayaratna, N. (1994) Understanding and Evaluating Methodologies. McGraw Hill. London.

Jirotka, M. and Goguen, J.A. (Eds.) (1994) Requirements Engineering: Social and Technical Issues. Academic Press, London.

Kelle, U. (Ed.) (1995) Computer-Aided Qualitative Data Analysis: Theory, Methods and Practice. Sage. London.

McDermid, J.A. (1994) 'Requirements Analysis:orthodoxy, fundamentalism and heresy' in Jirotka, M. and Goguen, J.A. (Eds.) Requirements Engineering: Social and technical issues. Academic Press. London. pp. 17-40.

Miles, M.B. and Huberman, A.M. (1994) Qualitative Data Analysis. Second Edition. Sage. UK.

Ngwenyama, O. and Lee, A.S. (1997) 'Communication Richness in Electronic Mail: critical social theory and the contextuality of meaning' MIS Quarterly. Vol. 21(2) pp. 145-167. (www.management.mcgill.ca/homepage/Leean/ngwlee97.htm Web version of paper with corrections, May 1998)

Nicholson, B and Hughes, J. (1996) 'An uncertain future for information systems methodology in virtual organisations' Proceedings of the Second Conference on Projectics. Bayonne/San Sebastian. pp. 163-178.

Oliphant, J. and Blockley, D.I. (1991) 'Knowledge-based system: Advisor on the Earth Retaining Structures' Computers and Structures. Vol. 40(1) pp. 173-183.

Pidgeon N.F. ; Turner, B.A. and Blockley, D. I. (1991) 'The use of Grounded Theory for conceptual analysis in knowledge elicitation' International Journal of Man-Machine Studies. Vol. 35 pp. 151-173.

Richards, T. and Richards, L. (1991) 'The NUD•IST qualitative data analysis system' Qualitative Sociology. Vol. 14(4/2 Winter).

Strauss, A.L. and Corbin, J. (1990) Basics of Qualitative Research : Grounded Theory Procedures and Techniques. Sage. Beverly Hills, California.

Strauss, A. and Corbin, J. (1994) 'Grounded Theory Methodology: An overview' in Denzin, N.K. and Lincoln, Y.S. (Eds.) Handbook of Qualitative Research. Sage. London. pp.273-285.

Suchman, L. (1987) Plans and Situated Actions: The Problem of Human-machine Communication. Cambridge University Press. Cambridge, UK.

Walsham, G. (1993) 'Ethical Issues in Information Systems Development - The Analyst as Moral Agent' in Avison, D., Kendall, J.E. and DeGross, J.I. (Eds.) Human, Organizational and Social Dimensions of Information Systems Development. North Holland. Amsterdam. pp.281-294.

Information Systems And Organisational Change: the use of 'Project Engineering' in a Hospital Emergency Service

Jean-Michel Larrasquet
Isabelle Franchisteguy
GRAPHOS-CNRS
IUT de Bayonne-UPPA
3, av. Jean Darrigrand
Tel: (+33) 5 59 52 89 56
Fax: (+33) 5 59 52 89 89
E-mail: larra@iutbay.univ-pau.fr

Nimal Jayaratna
School of Computing & Management Sciences
Sheffield Hallam University
Sheffield S1 1WB, U.K.

Keywords

Health care systems, organisations, information systems, project, project life-cycle.

Abstract

This paper presents important observations and lessons learned from being involved as system analysts in the reorganisation and the development of information systems for an emergency service in a French hospital.

The lessons reveal that if the development of information systems is separated from the specific culture of the users and their ways of working, then it will have very little chance of success. This is particularly so in organisations where services performed are 'on' people as opposed to 'for' people and the service providers are highly knowledgeable and have a strong commitment to their work. Traditional or structured methodologies that seek to treat humans as functional and rational boxes are appropriate for these environments.

1   Introduction

Health care service organisations, such as hospitals, represent an example of a complex service industry. It is a very specific domain because of the specialised complex medical knowledge and skills that are required. But at the same time it is a domain where simple notions such as patients' comfort, accommodation and friendly treatment by employees play a part in the patients' decisions on where to receive treatment.

Methods that are suitable for re-organisation of industrial organisations and the service sector (Mahe, 1997) are certainly useful for application development in hospital organisations. However, it is necessary to consider that such methods deal with humans or humans in distress. In fact, medical environments are where not only disease but also anxiety and emotions are ever present.

Life and death issues and the management of implications in emotional contexts make such environments considerably complex in cultural terms. The main features of a hospital culture seems to be the involvement of doctors and nurses in care and cure. The dismissal of any consideration that is not to do with care and cure may ignore essential aspects e.g. the assistance to people in distress. Care and cure are the most important (for doctors often it is 'cure' more than 'care'), and not bureaucratic tasks such as having to write records or fill forms. Computer applications for management use are considered a waste of time by doctors. Technical systems (computers) are considered as resource consuming activity sets that are irrelevant to patient care. However, technology that is used for direct patient monitoring and treatment are considered beneficial especially as they also contribute to the specialist's own skills development.

Many of the habits are inherited from history of care and medicine, training the medical staff have received as well as from the historical culture of the particular establishment. These characteristics make it difficult for IS solutions to be developed that will be effective in practice. Most information systems proposals are made by systems specialists/software engineers, who are not doctors or nurses. Doctors believe that the problems they face are medical problems which require medical solutions that fit within the established culture. They do not understand, at least at a patient level, the need for other viewpoints. If a patient is to be cared for in a holistic way, then multi-dimensional viewpoints need to be taken. They need to cover the different processes the patient will go through with different professionals, i.e. physiotherapists, different services and other establishments.

In the case of an emergency service, 'urgency' is a highly determining value, In these environments 'time' is a critical value as well as emotions felt by the medical specialists. There is usually shared mental representations and values linked to immediate and direct involvement or intervention of the doctors. These action oriented, highly responsive and charged environments make specialists feel that their time should not be wasted on non-medical activities such as form filling and data entry.

A methodology for such environments has to consider different ways of going about the development task, to include the users and to incorporate facilities provided by emerging technology such as the Internet and Intranet. Our experience reveals that the task emphasis should be focused more on culture change than on information systems development.

1.1   The Context of our Action-Research

Emergency Services are usually presented as the 'star service' of hospitals. They come under pressure to show good standards in their activities, performance, quality of care, comfort and image. For many people, these services are also their first step in the process of hospitalisation.

An Emergency Service is of high variety (Ashby, 1951; Beer, 1988). This means that the variety built into the service must be able to match the variety of patients as well as the variety of their requests and needs. Patients undergoing vital emergency treatment take priority over patients who have to wait for programmed hospitalisation and treatment, whose illnesses are serious but not critical and who seek treatment for social or psychiatric disorders. For each patient, the emergency service carries out a number of different activities: admissions, consultations and diagnosis, and treatment. These are carried out under time pressure and other numerous constraints e.g. non-availability of diagnostic equipment. The activities become even more complex when one considers the cultural context in which the service operates.

Emergency Services, however, depend largely on downstream (ancillary) services. The flow of patients is often slowed down because of the waiting periods attached to the downstream activities such as X-ray, laboratory testing etc. These downstream activities are managed in different ways to those of the emergency services and their activities are usually not co-ordinated. They have their own programmed activities and often do not have free space for patients who come via the emergency service. Emergency services also depend on specialists' advice who can either amplify or attenuate variety (Ashby, 1951). When a patient is gravely ill, doctors in emergency services often seek advice of specialists. In the current environment demands can be made by Emergency Services on a particular specialist for advice which interrupt the specialist's services to their own patients. Similar problems are created with all shared critical services. Usually, these services are not organised according to the priority of urgent cases, but other criteria e.g. comfort of the team (x-ray and imaging services), technology or laboratories. Doctors in the Emergency Services have to struggle with other fundamental and downstream services for advice, service and results. Conflict between the service provision and cultural practices incurs huge wastage in resources and contributes to patients' waiting times, delays and service dissatisfaction.

The sector is coming under increasing resource constraints. Managers/administrators are under pressure to demonstrate that the resources are used efficiently. However, medical and nursing professionals do not believe that the service needs to be re-organised. Within this environment, the development of information systems using methodologies that have proven their use in industry (Gane and Sarson, 1979) is possible. However, such methodologies have to be adopted to fit the cultural context. Methodologies that recognise and accommodate the role of culture will be more effective. (Checkland, 1981; Checkland and Scholes, 1981).

2 Perspective to Adopt for Improvement of Emergency Service

We have spent a considerable amount of time working with the medical staff trying to understand the functions they perform. Some of the senior medical specialists realise that there is a need to look at the service from the patient as well as from a medical point of view. Following are perspectives we explored according to SSM framework of ideas (Checkland and Scholes, 1991).

The first perspective was to look at the service from the doctors' point of view. The work with medical staff has helped us to define three categories of patients according to the condition of patients. They in turn follow three different process flows of treatments:

- Emergencies which have to be treated in a time critical way. These are of the highest priority.

- Minor emergencies, sometimes called 'fast-track', who need to be treated in a rapid way by assigned medical staff in a flow production form.

- Other patients who have to be treated in different ways involving a variety of treatments. These are not emergencies but still require individual attention.

The solution is to have a specially trained nursing staff managing the reception and involved in initial assessment of the patients. They are responsible for the categorisation of patients as well as for managing the dissemination of information to patients' relatives. This is a very critical role. This means that the emergency service requires information systems that help to support the activities of the service provision. This certainly is not the way the service is currently organised or current information systems development works.

2.1   Patient Perspective

If we are to seek holistic improvements of health care, we need an organised set of activities that also cater for the patient's needs. Observation of the Emergency Service in practice revealed that medical staff act in intuitive ways. The tasks they are supposed to perform should be based on the seriousness of the patients' state of health. However the medical staff attention to patients is usually based on the tasks that had been completed before by others. For example, when an X-ray arrives they look for the patients so that the next task in the sequence can be activated. This kind of approach to service care incurs considerable wasted effort on the part of the nurses. Most communication in this context is verbal, the practices are heavy on resource consumption and is less effective.

This form of behaviour is akin to 'job' production techniques and not 'flow' production techniques that are found in many IS applications. As Avenier (1995) discusses, people's functions are based on action-reaction mode and not on a pre-conceived flow. Any information system should respond to the high variety needs of medical staff as well as the patients' anxieties. The triggering of treatment flow should take into account the patients' emotional needs as well.

2.2   New Technologies

There are a range of new information technologies which can help to optimise scarce and critical resources as well as to help share resources. They can help improve inventory control or provide telemedicine. Deschandol (1996) discusses several possible applications.

- Data transmission (radio, image). For example, a doctor in an emergency could obtain advice from a surgeon without forcing him to abandon his/her current work.

- Transmission of patient records.

- Ability to consult medical databases.

Intranet and Internet based information networks can support the collaborative work of organisational networks. These can provide access to medical records both within and outside the hospitals.

Emerging technology can facilitate collaborative work e.g. internal and external networks, links with general practitioners, downstream services and external service providers. These technologies enable the formation of new organisational forms. This means that the service provision of emergency services needs to be re-examined in the light of the emerging technologies.

2.3   Towards news organisations?

Information systems and other organisational activities have to be integrated to help them adapt to changes in a progressive way (Franchisteguy, 1997), allowing the formation of networks and new organisational focus such as 'process based' organisations.   Organisational activities should not be adapted to match the information systems as have been done in the past in the hospital sector.

The integrated computer supported organisations have to perform in a dynamic context (Latour, 1991). Such complex changes create interactions and can generate conflicts, but also innovations by modifying practices and even creating new ones. When compared with other industries, health care systems are slow to adopt to information technology developments. Many hospitals have not yet computerised their patients' medical records and only use computers for accounting, finance and human resource management. However, building new computer supported systems and new infrastructure for information may improve the quality of care, and can contribute to cultural shifts where necessary.

As part of our work we visited several recently built emergency services. We notice that there is no ideal 'system' that we could imitate. Existing systems are not specially effective because they have been constructed with traditional methods and from a computer scientist's point of view (Berbain, 1996). Poor requirements make computerised tools ineffective.

Based on a new paradigm, health organisations can perform more effectively if they are based on process based paradigms. They should be organised around the persons providing:-

- Care for the health needs of the patient

- Attention to the patient, family e.g. cater to social, psychological humanistic needs

- On line information for the professional so that they can provide an effective service at a reasonable cost.

Ergonomic studies show that the effectiveness of an information system depends on its appropriation by the users and on how users have been initiated and trained in the use of it (Etourneau, 1997).

Even if medical professionals are increasingly conscious that their activities must be organised, training, education and assistance are necessary to overcome cultural resistance which often is very strong. Further, in the case of such a qualitatively complex activity, the development and use of information systems must be a co-operative activity.

3   Developing Information Systems in Such Environments

Traditional linear life cycle: defining the target

In traditional IS development, a target information system to support organisational activities may be abstracted based on criteria of effectiveness and efficiency, and within a given set of constraints. Such constraints can present, to some extent, similarities with classical requirements made for service and production systems (Gleick, 1993; Stacey, 1992; Larrasquet, 1997).

In effect, a traditional linear lifecycle-based approach would certainly be able to develop an information system in a hospital emergency service to help develop 'systems' for monitoring of patients. However, to be effective, they should be based on processes and persons.

- Providing holistic attention to the patient and his/her family, from cure-related aspects to social, psychological and humanistic aspects, in an organised manner.

- And providing on-line information to monitor the activities in such a way that each patient receives the best integrated service in a reasonable time period and within a reasonable level of cost.

Such an information system should also be able to provide information on capacity (in order to estimate a probable time of treatment for any patient entering the system), and information on the progress of cure and its continuation for the patient and his family. It should also support the general management systems of the hospital.

In the case of a complex service, such as the Emergency Service, it is essential that IS specialists treat the situation as a qualitative complexity (Morin, 1994; Le Mocque, 1995). Therefore, the starting point should not be a formal and consistent specification as is the case with traditional IS development, but an understanding of the characteristics that make the service systems effective. This is the reason why defining and producing information systems in such environments must be organised to deal with complexity, and facilitate the entry of systems analysts in the improvement cycle of the service. Regular work-teams, quasi-constant relationships, on-going specifications, exchanges, discussions around the approximate models are the forums where issues related to on-line usability of the tools have to be discussed and tested using prototypes, and collective evaluation. This is the way to ensure that all concerned actors are building systems in a collective sense and feeling that they are progressively producing 'their' own systems (Mumford and Beekman, 1994).

3.1 Towards an integrated-holistic project life-cycle

These reflections suggest the need for an integrated-holistic project-type organisation i.e. development of a never ending concurrent and integrated logistics engineering system (Berthelemy, 1992) but these must be developed as on-going collaborative support systems.

Successful introduction of computer systems requires work to be performed in teams, not only on requirement analysis but also on later stages of the life-cycle. This is the way to ensure acceptance and ownership of 'systems' which are necessary in this kind of 'hyper-cultural' environments. Rather than work at requirements, IS specialists should work on the 'issues', thus helping to define IS as an organisational problem. It is in this context that we have embarked on the use of SSM ideas (but not the methodology). We found that the presentation of a formal methodology without a deeper understanding of cultural resistance would be detrimental to the introduction of the methodology at a later stage.

Shared engineering and co-management lead to a new concept of 'life-cycle'. It is built from the concepts of concurrent engineering, integrated logistics cycle, prototyping and life-long (never ending) cycle. We took part in a similar project with 'SEI-Fagor software house' in France for building systems to achieve ISO 9001 (obtained in 1995). It treated the company concerned with project based management instead of treating it as a software engineering company. Namely, the company became known not for 'software engineering' but for 'project engineering' (Claveranne, Larrasquet, Jayaratna, 1997). Soft Systems Methodology (SSM) is typically the kind of methodology that can be used for understanding organisations as general processes (Checkland and Scholes, 1990). The fact that cultural groups resist organisational improvement and implementation of information systems underlines the necessity to find a way of constructing consensus in the building of systems.

4   Conclusion

In health service environments we face a qualitative and complex set of user inter-actions, decision making and service goals. This challenge may be addressed by re-organising work in order to reach a concensus around progressively useful information systems. Such a venture is fundamentally cultural. It is also about management of change. Culture change based projects take time. Changing culture and taking part in culture change process is not a technical process. This is why it is inappropriate to consider that we, IS-IT people, have the relevant concepts, tools (life-cycle, methodologies, development tools ...), and skills to manage the development of complex and evolving systems. Instead, our methodologies should accommodate and embrace cultural dimensions as essential areas for change.

References

Avenier M.J. 'Problematique du 'pilotage' des organisations sociales : une formulation stimulee et rendue operationelle par les nouvelles technologies de l'information', 2nd Congres biennal AFCET95

Berbain X. 'Apprendre l'informatique a l'hopital, une experience a partager', in Annales des Mines, Gerer et comprendre, Decembre 1996.

Checkland P.B., Scholes J., Soft Systems Methodology in action, John Wiley, 1990.

Claveranne J.P., Larrasquet J.M., Jayaratna N. Projectique a la recherche du sens perdu, Economica, 1996.

Deschandol P. 'La telemedicine a la croisee des ... soins', in Teletravail, Fevrier 1996.

Etourneau C. 'Informatique et qualite font bon menage aux urgences', in Decision Sante, 1-15 Avril 1997.

Franchisteguy I. Contribution a la modelisation et a l'optimisation des processus au sein du Centre Hospitalier de la Cote Basque. Un point de depart : ; le service des urgences. Memoire de DEA MASS, Universites Lyon1-Lyon3, Septembre 1997.

Franchisteguy I. 'L'Hopital-reseau : comment l'hopital sort de ses murs', XIV Congreso de Estudios Vascos, 'La sociedad de la Informacion', Panplona, 25-27 Novembre 1997.

Gleick J. Chaos, Abacus, 1993.

Larrasquet J.M. 'L'Entreprise a l'epreuve du complexe, Contribution a la recherche des fondations du sens, These de doctorat en sciences de gestion, 1997.

Latour B. Nous n'avons jamais ete modernes, essai d'anthropologie symetrique. L'Harmattan, 1991.

Le Moigne J.L. Les epistemologies constructivistes, Que-sais-Je? PUF, 1995.

Mahe T. 'Hopital-industrie : memes problemes, memes remedes', in Industries et Techniques, Avril 1997.

Morin E. La complexite humaine, Champs-L'essentiel, Flammarion, 1994.

Mumford E., Beeman G. Tools for change and progress, CSG Publications, 1994.

Stacey R. Managing chaos, dynamic business strategies in an unpredictable world, Kogan Page, 1992.

Information Technology Support for the Learning Organisation

Laurence Brooks and Helen Webb
Contact address: Department of Computer Science
University of York
York
YO10 5DD
+44 1904 433242
Laurence.Brooks@cs.york.ac.uk

Abstract

This paper investigates the role of information technology (IT) tools within the Learning Organisation (LO). While there is some support for the increase in popularity of LOs among researchers and within the business community, there has been little investigation into how IT tools can be used to increase the effectiveness of the LO principles. Given the size of annual investment in IT by these organisations, this is a surprising outcome. However, as the concepts of the LO are becoming more widespread and accepted, researchers are realising the importance of the links with IT tools and are beginning to examine them more closely.

Although current IT tools could support the LO principles, there are few that have been developed specifically for this purpose. This paper shows that there appears to be a lack of conclusive evidence that more developed LO's are using more IT tools to support the LO principles. However there may be some interesting trends developing.

1 Introduction

Faced with an increasingly unpredictable and dynamic business environment, many organisations have moved away from older management ideas and begun looking to new initiatives based on continuous improvement programmes. However, organisations are finding that previous similar programmes have succeeded or failed depending on human factors such as skills, attitudes and organisational culture and that an organisation cannot improve without first learning something new.

The latest continuous improvement programme is the practice of the Learning Organisation (LO). The LO concept is based on the principle that there is much underdeveloped potential within organisations, which used effectively could greatly increase performance. The LO's focus is a commitment to continuous learning. Although debated for about the last ten years, these ideas have only recently been put into more practical terms and therefore organisations have begun to introduce them. This paper details the outcomes of an investigation into the role information technology (IT) support tools in the context of the Learning Organisation.

2 The Learning Organisation

The LO was first popularised in 1990 with Senge's book 'The Fifth Discipline' [1], and followed by a range of other books and articles. Pedler, Boydell and Burgoyne [2] were the first to develop the idea in the UK and use the term 'learning company'. Although the term 'learning organisation' has only been around for about the last ten years, 'organisational learning' can be traced back much further.

2.1 Linking Organisational Learning with The Learning Organisation

Argyris and Schön [3], describe organisational learning as 'the detection and correction of error'. This can occur where an error is detected and corrected thereby permitting an organisation to carry on its present policies/achieve objectives, (known as *single-loop learning* (O-I)). Whereas *double loop-learning* (O-II) occurs when error is detected and corrected in ways that involve the modification of an organisation's underlying norms, policies and objectives. Argyris and Schön believe that organisational learning occurs independent of the individuals within it, but cannot occur without them. Therefore individual learning is a necessary, but not sufficient, condition for organisational learning.

It is impossible to reason anew in every situation so we all develop what Argyris calls 'theory-in-use', a set of rules that individuals use to design and implement their own behaviour, and understand the behaviour of others. These rules become so taken for granted that people do not realise that they are using them. The reason why we find this behaviour difficult to change is that the theory-in-use that we actually use is rarely the one that we think we use. If people were asked what rules they think they use to govern their actions, they would give what Argyris calls an espoused 'theory-of-action', which is different from the one in use.

Overall, Argyris and Schön's approach to organisational learning is to create an environment which encourages O-II learning. This will not be achieved until members learn how to change their behaviour, and therefore change their theories-in-use. This involves the process of a completely new company culture which uses failure as an opportunity to learning and encourages open discussion and risk taking.

It appears that the concepts of organisational learning and the learning organisation stem from the same root. Both the theory of O-II learning and the concept of the learning organisation are designed to overcome the organisational culture of treating failure as an embarrassment to be hidden and forgotten. They both encourage the culture of treating failures as opportunities to learn. The major difference, is that the *practice* of the learning organisation has been developed much further. Organisational learning concentrates on the loop learning models while the learning organisation, although building on the same base principles, is a much larger set of principles.

3 Principles of the Learning Organisation

The idea of a LO is intangible and difficult to measure. No one set definition exists. However the main characteristics are agreed as being: adaptive to the external environment, continually enhancing capability to change, continually probing its own basic assumptions, developing collective as well as individual learning and using the results of learning to achieve better results. It is a way of continuously improving company performance and can achieve and sustain competitive advantage. There is no end point in the 'quest' to become a LO. As the concept is one of continuous improvement, the total realisation of the LO never occurs, it is an ideal to be striven for.

3.1 Identifying 'Learning Disabilities'

Before an organisation can aspire to be a LO it must first identify its 'learning disabilities'. Senge [1] believes the first step along the path towards the LO is the identification of 'the seven learning disabilities'. Pearn and Mulrooney [4] suggest the way to get started is to perform a learning audit while Pedler *et al* [2] describe an assessment of the learning climate. Overall these approaches are all associated with assessing the company 'culture' to see what can be introduced to change it [5].

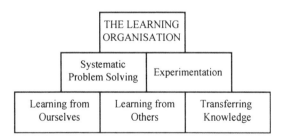

Figure 1, Activities within the Learning Organisation

Having identified the learning disabilities within an organisation, processes need to be put in place to encourage a culture which eliminates them. The majority of literature on the LO states that there is no one 'blueprint' for a LO: Garvin's framework encompasses the main ideas from each of the main approaches [6], describing LO's as skilled at five main activities (see Figure 1). The framework explains that most organisations will have some of these activities already in place but few are consistently successful because they rely on 'happenstance and isolated examples'. By creating systems and processes that support these activities and by integrating them into the daily operations, an organisations' learning can be managed more effectively.

3.2 Learning Organisation Activities

Garvin explains that to put each of the LO activities in place they must be accompanied by a mind-set, tool-kit and pattern of behaviour. The LO is more than initiating a change of processes, it is about changing the culture of the whole organisation. To change the culture, Senge [1] describes five disciplines, mastery of which will provide every employee with the new mindset required to create the LO. The five disciplines must develop together, it is not sufficient to develop them independently, which is much easier to do. Therefore systems thinking is referred to as the 'fifth discipline', an integrating action, fusing the disciplines into a coherent body of theory and practice.

- **Systems Thinking** - Systems thinking is a body of knowledge and tools which aid decision making by considering the whole system to a problem, rather than isolated parts.
- **Personal Mastery** - Personal mastery is the discipline of continually clarifying and deepening personal vision, and determining the things which matter.
- **Mental Models** - Mental models are deeply ingrained assumptions, generalisations, pictures or images that influence how people understand the world and how they take action.
- **Building Shared Vision** - This discipline concerns building a shared picture of the future the organisation seeks to create.
- **Team Learning** - As has been explained, collective learning cannot occur without individual learning, which is not merely the sum of the learning of the individuals. This discipline is concerned with helping teams to work better.

These disciplines can be used in all of Garvin's five activities to innovate learning organisations. They are bodies of theory or technique that must be studied and mastered. Senge describes them as "developmental paths for acquiring certain skills or competencies" [1]. He compares them to disciplines such as accountancy but explains that they are different because they concern "how we think and what we truly want and how we interact and learn with one another".

4 Information Technology And The Learning Organisation

4.1 IT Support Tools for the Learning Organisation

The literature review identifies five principle activities which form building blocks for the LO, with activities 3, 4 and 5 supporting activities 1 and 2 (see Figure 1). While there are IT tools to support activities 3, 4 and 5, there appear to be few IT tools available to directly support activities 1 and 2. However because activities 1 and 2 are built on the other three activities, any of the IT tools could be used within them. For example a microworld *is* an experiment with a new approach, and CBR tools could be used as part of the systematic problem solving process.

Figure 2 demonstrates the links between the LO activities and available IT support tools.

ACTIVITY	PROCESSES	SUPPORT TOOLS
Activity 3 - Learning From Own Experience And Past History	Reflecting on, reviewing past successes and failures Uses failure as opportunity to learn learning the subject and learning to learn	Microworlds Best Practice Databases CBR Tools Personal Learning Tools
Activity 4 - Learning From Experience And Best Practice Of Others	Learning from occurrences outside immediate environment	Expert Systems CBR Tools Best Practice Databases
Activity 5 - Transferring Knowledge Quickly And Efficiently Throughout The Organisation	Moving away from traditional 'training'. Providing members with multiple sources of information. Providing members with the facilities to help themselves to learning. Providing incentives for knowledge transfer	Email, conferencing Electronic Bulletin Boards, Forums Groupware Internet Intranet, Extranet Personal Learning Tools

Figure 2, Links Between the LO Activities and IT Support Tools

4.1.1 Microworlds

Microworlds are a tool used to try and overcome the problems of the complexity inherent in the business world and the usefulness of failure as a learning tool which is in itself potentially dangerous for the organisation. A microworld has come to mean any computer simulation of an environment in which people can run experiments, test different strategies, and build a better understanding of the aspects of the real world which it depicts [7]. This makes it possible to see the effects of decisions made in complex business systems without the real world constraints of time or cost.

4.1.2   Expert Systems

When an organisation has a complex decision to make or a problem to solve, it will turn to someone else with specific knowledge and experience in the area for advice - an expert. An expert system is decision-making software that can reach a level of performance comparable to a human expert in some specialised and usually narrow problem area [8]. It will be able to suggest a diagnosis when the relevant data for a specific situation are entered. The systems use artificial intelligence techniques to store the knowledge.

4.1.3   Case-Based Reasoning (CBR) Tools

The use of cased based reasoning systems (CBR) aims to overcome the problems of expert systems. While they are similar to expert systems in that they provide a suggested diagnosis to a problem or decision, they use previous situations as a knowledge base for the solution, rather than trying to store a humans' explicit knowledge [9]. Thus CBR tools use a simple program of matching the current problem against problems that have been solved successfully in the past.

4.1.4   Best Practice Databases

Some organisations have started to introduce 'best practice databases' as a means of storing information on internal or external best practices. Internal best practices might be the methodology of an outstanding project which a department conducted, or an external best practice might record processes used by an industry leader.

4.1.5   Groupware

The term groupware refers to software products that support groups of people engaged with a common task or goal. For example, Lotus Notes is a client/server platform for developing and deploying groupware applications. This 'knowledge sharing' application allows multiple users to manage compound documentation, and communicate effectively over geographically dispersed and remote locations. It integrates many of the tools already discussed. Richard Karash states that communication, co-operation and sharing are essential elements of the LO and since groupware supports these, it will contribute to organisational learning [10].

4.1.6   Personal Learning Tools

Technological advances have led to the design of many new tools available for personal learning. One area of development is *virtual reality (VR)*. The basic concept of virtual reality is that the person believes what they are doing in the computer generated environment is real, even though it has been artificially created. This environment is perfect for the learning by doing scenario and aims to increase learning in the same way as microworlds. Another area of development is interactive PC video training. Decisions made by an individual on the computer cause different video clips to be played to create an interactive environment. Although this environment is not as interactive as VR , as the video clips have to be pre-filmed it has a larger scope due to less programming required. Other personal learning tools include touch screen TVs and interactive PC tutorials.

While there are many more IT support tools that could be linked to LO concepts, it appears that very few have been specifically developed for this type of use. Further there is little evidence to support their active use in this manner. Therefore, the remainder of this paper will investigate whether, and in what ways, organisations have recognised this potential in their IT tools.

5 The Survey

The method employed was a postal questionnaire survey to establish which (if any) IT support tools identified in the literature review and are currently being used to support the LO. The questionnaire was divided into sections relating to the different types of learning which may occur in the organisation, learning from others, learning from experience and transferring knowledge.

5.1 Results

The first analysis stage involved the tabulation and documentation of the findings while the second stage focused on a trend analysis. The quantitative results were tabulated into frequency tables. A thematic analysis was applied to the qualitative open questions, which drew out common themes in answers, as documented in the results. The aim of the questionnaire was focused on discovering more information about the usage of the IT tools in the LO context. The following section details the results from the main body of the questionnaire.

5.2 Electronic Mail

While 91% of the sample had an email system, less than a third of these had a conferencing facility, and sending/receiving detailed documents was the most popular use. However while popular, email was only used for this purpose infrequently. 71% perceived email to be a more effective form of communication than others available within the organisation. It appeared that perceived effectiveness of email was strongly influenced by whether the email software had a mechanism for notifying the user upon the arrival of a new message.

5.3 Bulletin Boards and the World-Wide Web

52% of the sample had electronic bulletin boards or open forums where employees could leave messages or discuss topics. 69% of the respondents worked in organisations which had access to a network, with 62% having access to the Internet and 31% access to their Intranet. No organisation had an Extranet. Of the organisations surveyed, 33% used groupware and, over two thirds of those use Lotus Notes. The main uses given for groupware were: conferencing; special interest groups; discussion, sharing documentation; project management; sharing, developing ideas; tracking software development; best practices; managing local groups.

5.4   Learning Through Experience

The results from this section concerned the use of microworlds and reflective learning. It shows that 49% used microworlds for simulating real situations, while 15% used them for simulating fictional situations. Over 70% of the respondents appeared to use spreadsheets to produce the simulated environment, and of the remaining 20% used some form of modelling.

When projects have been completed, or important problems have been solved, only 30% of organisations had processes in place for reviewing and learning from the way they have been conducted. Of that, 9% were informal and not documented, 12% were documented on paper and stored and 9% held in a database.

5.5   Learning From Others

In the sample it appears that 35% made use of best practice databases, 20% used benchmarking databases, 20% used expert systems, 13% used CBR tools and 15% used some other knowledge sharing system.

5.6   Personal Development

While some answers in this section are quite ambiguous, the results show that the most popular personal learning tool was interactive PC video (73%). On-line Internet training and group Internet forums (13%) as well as virtual reality (8%) were mentioned as training tools, but appeared very new in this area.

5.7   IT Tools and the Learning Organisation

24% said that some IT tools had been introduced purely as a result of the introduction of the concepts and culture of the learning organisation. For example, the creation of a Learning Resource Centre containing resources such as Computer Based Training (CBT) multimedia development tools. Figure 3 shows how the organisations fell into the LO categories.

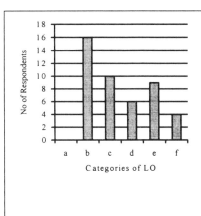

a - The organisation is completely unfamiliar with the LO and has in place none of the concepts which have been explained.

b - The organisation uses some of the systems or concepts explained but does not yet recognise itself as an aspiring LO.

c - The organisation recognises itself as an aspiring LO and has started to put some processes in place.

d - recognises itself as an aspiring LO, has started to put some processes in place and has introduced the new concepts and culture to all members.

e - The organisation is aspiring towards the LO but still needs to spread the concepts and culture further.

f - The organisation has been working towards the LO for some time and has fully implemented a programme of continuous improvement to ensure very member of the organisation is working towards the LO goals.

Figure 3, Self Categorisation of Organisations as LO

6 Analysis

The objective of the main research was to establish which IT tools were being used to support LO's. The general aim was to ascertain which organisations in the sample were aspiring to be LO's in order to establish which IT tools they were using to support these aspirations.

It is clear that all the IT tools described earlier are used in many organisations:

- The majority of organisations have an email system, but not a conferencing facility.
- The most popular use for email is communication between users internally, it is used less for communication outside the organisation.
- Most organisations believe email is a more effective form of communication than others available.
- The major use of the Internet and Intranet was for reading distributed organisational information within the organisation.
- Groupware is not a greatly used tool, this could be due to the large investment which is needed in such a venture.
- The most popular personal learning tool is interactive PC and video.
- Most IT departments are not playing an active role in organisations' aspirations to become LO's.

6.1 General Observations

While IT support tools are in widespread use in the sample organisations, most have not been introduced as a consequence of the introduction of LO concepts and culture. Of those tools directly linked to LO concepts and culture, the main finding was the introduction of Learning Resource Centres (LRC's), which contain personal learning tools for members. Therefore it appears that the most common initiative concerning IT tools to support LO concepts is to concentrate on individual, rather than collective, learning. Possibly this is due to collaborative learning tools already existing in the organisation.

Microworlds are one of very few tools which have been developed for specific use within the LO. The difficulty with the questionnaire, was trying to get across the definition of a microworld. It is likely that many of the models that the respondents had referred to as microworlds, were not 'true' microworlds. This was evident in the amount of respondents which stated that their microworlds were modelled on spreadsheets, when microworlds traditionally use modelling software (about 50% of the sample). In addition the uses given for these microworlds, were not appropriate for 'true' microworlds.

Those respondents which used microworlds, for 'business game playing', would be the organisations that may be using them in their true sense. It was evident that some of these organisations *were* using microworlds according to Senge's definition, as they were using modelling software such as Vensim and ithink. Only 15% of organisations were using this type of microworlds. This was low, taking into account that many of the organisations in the survey were in the higher LO groups, which indicated they had introduced the LO concepts for some time and microworlds are a central part of many authors' suggested steps towards the LO.

Although some microworlds were in use, few were being used as a learning tool. This could be because of the significant shift required in business culture, before time is allocated for business 'game playing'. Even though type A microworlds are differ from Senge's perspective of a microworld, any kind of modelling used is a useful learning tool and is relevant in the LO.

It is interesting that the majority of respondents believed their IT department did not take an active role in their organisations aspiration to become a LO. It is apparent that there are many useful IT tools available for use within the LO, but unless the IT department who have the knowledge and technology, fully realises the potential of the LO concepts, it will not understand the role of IT tools within the strategy. This emphasises the need for communication across functions.

6.2   Observations Concerning Categories of LO

Even though IT tools are widespread, not every tool is used in every organisation. However there should be some evidence to show that the organisations which have had LO concepts and culture in place for some time, would have more of the IT tools used to support the LO than organisations who had only just introduced the concepts. This was investigated by looking at specific tools, comparing those organisations in the higher LO groups to those in the lower ones.

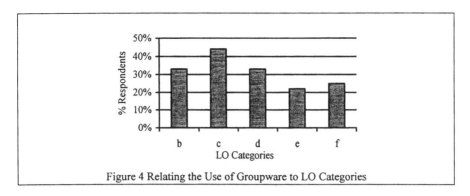

Figure 4 Relating the Use of Groupware to LO Categories

From Figure 4 (the level of groupware used by each LO group), it is evident that there is no relationship between the higher LO groups and an increased use of groupware. Looking at IT training, the LO literature stated that a principle of the LO was to move training from a 'push' to a 'pull' activity. Therefore the organisations in the higher LO groups should be providing more on-demand training than the organisations in the lower LO groups. Again the results clearly show that there is no relationship between the type of training provided and the LO groups.

There had been no conclusive evidence so far to indicate that IT tools which could support the LO principles are used more by the higher LO groups than the lower ones. Therefore, the use of the number of tools in general was investigated, and again the survey data indicates clearly that there is no relationship between the LO group and the number of tools it has in use. The results only show a sporadic distribution among all groups of LO.

6.3   Summary

The literature provides considerable evidence that there are a number of IT tools available for supporting the LO. It was thought that the organisations who had been established as aspiring LO's should have more of the tools in use. However, results from the empirical research showed that although the IT tools were in use, there was no relationship between how far along the path of aspiration towards the LO an organisation was and the number of IT tools in use.

One explanation for this lack of findings could lie with the difficulty in categorising the development of a LO. The aim of the categories used was to establish how developed each organisation was in the LO concepts, but there is little differentiation among the categories. Therefore it was difficult to make assumptions by category, as they were not completely clear cut. This was further exacerbated by the uneven distribution among the LO groups.

Another explanation of the non-correlation could be due to cost. Some of the organisations could have perceived that the use of these IT tools to support the LO were effective, but have failed to implement them due to the costs involved.

Finally the absence of a relationship between IT tools and the LO could be due to differences between those organisations who are beginning to aspire to be LO, and those who started on the path some time before. Although the literature explains that the LO embarks on a process of continuous improvement, these new initiatives do have a habit of being popular within the organisation for a while and then 'fading' away. In the survey the group with the largest number of IT tools is group C. This could be that organisations in this sector are just beginning to move towards the LO concepts, and therefore have not yet made significant investments in support tools.

7 Conclusions

The increasing pressures on organisations today have caused them to move away from traditional management ideas and look to new initiatives. One of the more popular of these has been the learning organisation (LO). This is seen as a continuous improvement process based on the principle that there is much underdeveloped potential within organisations, which if used efficiently could greatly increase performance.

This paper has presented an investigation into how information technology tools are actively used to support the learning organisation, and explored the relationship between the developmental stage of a learning organisation and the level of information technology tools in use. The results indicate that while the use of these tools is widespread throughout organisations, there is no significant evidence that this relationship holds true. If nothing else this serves to further reinforce the gap between the theories and recommendations found in the literature, and the actions and behaviours found in organisations.

Further it appears that there are a number of lessons which could be learned from the study. Firstly that for organisations to progress and develop further into learning organisations in the future, there will have to be greater communication and cooperation between the various sections of the organisation. Most notably, to make the best use of IT support tools it will increasingly become important to educate and motivate the IT department towards LO concepts and principles. Equally, the remainder of the organisation will need to be educated such that they can better appreciate the role these tools can play in their commitment towards the continuous learning process.

In addition, there is a need for senior management to recognise the benefits of IT tools for supporting the LO, and therefore to empower the individuals within, what are increasingly, technologically led organisations. As is clear from the literature and the empirical study, there is considerable scope for organisations to make much more effective use of the IT tools they currently employ, to support LO elements, such as sharing lessons learned. Finally, the significant differences between findings from the literature and the empirical research signifies a gap between theory and practice.

Given that both theory informs practice, and vice versa, it is vital that this area is re-evaluated and the potential for IT support for the LO properly unleashed.

References

1. Senge PM. The Fifth Discipline: The Art and Practice of the Learning Organisation. Century Business/Doubleday, London, 1990.
2. Pedler M; Burgoyne J; Boydell T. The Learning Company: A Strategy for Sustainable Development. McGraw Hill, London, 1991.
3. Argyris C; Schön DA. Organizational Learning: A Theory of Perspective. Addison-Wesley, 1978.
4. Pearn C; Mulrooney C. Tools for a Learning Organisation. Institute of Personnel and Development, 1995.
5. Kline P; Saunders B. Ten Steps to a Learning Organisation. Great Ocean Publishers, Virginia, 1993
6. Garvin DA. Building a Learning Organisation. Harvard Business Review 1993; July-August 78-90.
7. Senge P; Kleiner A; Roberts C; Ross RB; Smith BJ. The Fifth Discipline Fieldbook: Strategies and Tools for Building a Learning Organisation. Nicholas Brealey Publishing, London, 1994.
8. Turban E; Mclean E; Wetherbe J. Information Technology for Management: Improving Quality and Productivity. John Wiley & Sons, Canada, 1996.
9. Watson I. The Case for Case-Based Reasoning. Unpublished, 1994.
10. Karash R. Groupware and Organisational Learning. Unpublished http://world.std.com/~rkarash/GW-OL/, 1995.

Is it all in vain?
The Effect of Systems Development Education on Practice:
The Multiview - Example

Karlheinz Kautz[*], Jan Pries-Heje[*], and Lone Malmborg[+]
Karl.Kautz@cbs.dk, pries-heje@cbs.dk, lone.malmborg@mah.se
*Copenhagen Business School, Department of Informatics, Denmark
[+] Malmö University College, School of Art and Communication, Sweden

Abstract

For a number of years diffusion and adoption of system development methods has been subject to research. One important factor is education and training. However, research on the role of formal university education and the adoption of system development methodologies is quite sparse. This is the background for this study The research investigates to which degree a methodology taught for 12 years at a university has been adopted by the students and the organisations they are working for and what the role of education was in this process. Reasons for adoption and non-adoption are discussed to answer whether methodology education at universities is all in vain.

1 Introduction

Since the 70s methodologies for the development of information systems have been promoted. However, they are still not widely used. In 1986 Yourdon [1] stated that 90% of the world wide computing professionals are superficially acquainted with structured methods, but only 10% of the all IT organisations use them in an appropriate way. More recently Hiddings [2] found that methods are only used by a third of the information systems practitioners. As one reason for non-adoption Floyd [3] puts forward that structured methods only support the more technical aspects of information system development and that they are therefore inadequate for modelling major aspects of complex systems. Raghavn & Chand [4] found that practitioners experience methods as rather complex and do not see any advantage from their use. They also argued that there is a gap between how method developers understand methods and how possible adopters perceive them. They conclude that methods are either oversold or poorly communicated. Fichman & Kemerer [5] support this conclusion.

Education and training are frequently mentioned as being one of the most prominent means of communicating system development methodologies. Leonard-Barton [6] emphasises the significance of training not only for the direct users of a method, but also for their supervisors. She also refers to the timing of the training. Training should be closely connected to the actual use of a method to facilitate the adoption of the method. Kozar [7] surveyed the participants of a course about a requirements analysis method three months after the classes and found that the training itself had little influence on the adoption, but personal characteristics and organisational factors like management support seemed to be of more importance. Kautz & McMaster [8] performed a case study on the adoption of a method in a large public service organisation and found similar results. Although the developers there appreciated the training, the adoption process failed due to various other reasons.

The role of communicating system development methodologies through formal university education and its relation to other factors of adoption has however not been subject of any of these studies. This is the background for this study. We are interested in whether university education is all in vain or whether it has any influence on practice, especially on the employment of system development methodologies and methods.

Since 1986 undergraduate students in their last year at the Copenhagen Business School have been trained in the Multiview methodology [9, 10]. Multiview seems to be good starting point for investigating the influence of university education on the adoption of system development methodologies. It has been developed and tested in practice based on the insight that a merely technical perspective is not adequate for the development of information systems. It combines the technical perspective of information systems development with a systemic and a social one. From a pedagogical point of view Multiview appears to be an appropriate instance to introduce students to system development methodologies. Besides combining different perspectives, it promotes the need of choosing and adjusting method components and techniques according to the problem at hand. At the same time it provides some guidance for the transition between the individual phases and defines a holistic, yet flexible framework, which distinguishes the methodology from a totally loose 'tool kit' approach.

The research presented here aims at interrogating to which degree this particular methodology have been adopted by the students in the organisations they are working for today. We will investigate the adoption of the component methods and techniques of the methodology. In addition, we will look at the adoption of the methodology's underlying philosophy and perspective. Furthermore, we will inquire whether the idea of applying structured approaches in general as opposed to ad-hoc ways of developing information systems has been adopted by the students. Finally, we will see what the reasons are for adoption and non-adoption.

The paper is structured as follows: In the next section the Multiview methodology which is subject of this investigation and the way it is taught are presented. Then the research approach is explained. Subsequently, the results of the study are described and discussed. The paper finishes with some conclusions.

2 Teaching Systems Development

When one looks at how information systems are developed in practice one usually finds a group of people going through a number of phases, typically focusing on "what to do" before answering and implementing "how to do it".

Based on studies of practice, and also based on researchers or consultants trying to find solutions to problems experienced in actual system development, a large number of systems development methods have been published since the 70s (see f. ex. [11-17]).

Avison & Fitzgerald [18] define an information systems methodology as "a collection of procedures, techniques, tools, and documentation aids which help the systems developers in their effort to implement a new information system. A methodology will consist of phases, themselves consisting of sub-phases, which will guide the systems developers in their choice of the techniques that might be appropriate at each stage of the project and also help them plan, manage, control and evaluate information systems projects.". Avison & Fitzgerald [18] also emphasise that a methodology usually will be based on some philosophical perspective on the world.

When teaching students at a university how to carry out systems development it would be foolish just to let the students try it without any advice. Here systems development methods come in as good collections of advice. This advice can be used in university exercises. However, small exercises won't transfer the "look and feel" of real development projects. Therefor it is an obvious idea to let the students try out systems development in projects.

2.1 Teaching Systems Development at the Copenhagen Business School

In 1984 a new education programme combining computer science, information systems and business administration started at the Copenhagen Business School. The programme is organised as 3-year undergraduate study with the succeeding possibility for a master degree. For the first year of study 65 students were accepted. The purpose of the undergraduate education programme was defined in the following way [19]: "The purpose of the undergraduate programme is to give the students the necessary knowledge to be able to take part in functions related to requirements specification, development, use, operations, maintenance, marketing, and sale of information systems, based on the broadest possible general knowledge of relevant national, social and business related issues."

In 1986 when the students were in the third and last year of their undergraduate studies the focus was defined as information systems and systems development.

Existing systems development methodologies were evaluated and it was decided to use the Multiview methodology [9]). This decision was made partly because it introduced important parts of a number of popular systems methodologies, such as structured analysis and design. And partly because it emphasised the idea that multiple perspectives can be valuable when developing information systems.

In the first year Multiview was taught, all students were assigned to the same project. Multiview was only used to analyse what had been going on after the fact. However, this was not very successful and as a consequence in 1987 projects lasting for 10 weeks were established, where the students in groups of 4 or 5 were supposed to go to an existing organisation and to use the Multiview methodology to analyse and design (parts of) an information system fulfilling a real need. This project-based way of teaching systems development was evaluated as very successful by both teachers, students, and the organisations involved. Thus since 1987, all students participating in this education programme have been taught the Multiview methodology and have used it a project in a real commercial or public sector organisation outside academia. Up to 1997, exactly 572 students, in classes of 30 to 60 attendees, have successfully passed this course. The authors of this paper have all at different points in time held the course.

2.2 Teaching the Multiview Methodology

The Multiview methodology covers five different phases of system analysis and design, each with its own view of the problem and with methods and techniques for solving that aspect of a systems development problem:

1. Analyse human activity system
2. Analyse entities and functions or Analyse Information
3. Analyse and design socio-technical system/aspects
4. Design human-computer interface
5. Design technical subsystem/aspects

In the human activity system analysis phase emphasis is put on analysing a problem situation as a whole from a systemic perspective avoiding a too early decomposition of the problem in distinct areas. Techniques from Soft Systems Methodology [13, 16] are used to perform this stage. Rich pictures are a pictorial way of representing the perception of a problem situation in a graphical, but minor formal way. Root definitions are textual descriptions of relevant problems and issues on which to focus attention and conceptual models are diagrammatic representations of the activities performed in the problem situation. The output from this phase is either a "human activity system model" or a "primary task model".

The output from the analysis of the human-activity system is then used as the basis for the analysis of activities and information from a hard systems, or technical-oriented perspective. Functional decomposition and data flow diagrams as known from structured analysis [11, 14] as well as entity-relationship modelling techniques

[20] are proposed to provide a more formal specification of the aimed at information system.

In the next phase the system is (re-) designed from a socio-technical perspective taking people's need and work environment into account to find an appropriate organisational and technical solution. Techniques and survey instruments to analyse the professional setting are based on the ETHICS methodology [12,21].

Parallel to this phase the human-computer interface is designed. The methodology gives no explicit help for what techniques to use. Only general guidelines and heuristics for screen layout and man-machine interaction are provided.

General guidelines and heuristics are also what are included in the fifth phase of Multiview on the design of the technical aspects. General advice for the use of structured English as a specification language is given, but no further mention is made of techniques for the architectural and procedural design of the future system.

In the context of the education program of the Copenhagen Business School Multiview is taught in approximately 60 class hours. The students in the course on definition of information systems are introduced to the phases of the Multiview Methodology in formal lectures and small exercises based on the textbook and supplementary original literature. In parallel, in the second half of the course projects using the Multiview Methodology take place.

2.3 The Projects using the Multiview Methodology

In Denmark there is a long tradition for projects as an extremely important part of the pedagogical layout of courses in information systems and computer science. As early as 1970, Peter Naur, the first full professor in computer science in Denmark, designed a study programme in computer science. A central element in this programme were projects. Naur [22] defined projects as follows: "By a project we mean the work going into solving a partly defined, not too small, but definite problem, involving design and planning for new construction as essential parts."

What was special about projects Naur [22] described using the following the characteristics:"... first, it involves *problem solving*. Second, in addition to solving, project activity involves *problem definition*. Indeed the initial definition of the problem to be solved in a project is normally quite incomplete, or even logically inconsistent. It is an important part of the project activity to discuss the definition of the problem, to clarify it, to make it more definite, to modify it, to discover contradictions in it, and to discuss and resolve the contradictions. Third, project activity involves the *contact* and *organization* of the group of people engaged on the project. Typical projects can only be successfully tackled by having several, or many persons working in parallel."

When the combination programme in computer science and business administration started at the Copenhagen Business School in 1984 a major inspiration was the programme Naur had built at the Copenhagen University. Therefor it was natural to emphasise projects as an important part of the pedagogical layout of the programme. However, where Naur's programme in the academical environment of the university typically had smaller projects 4-6 weeks, where all students solved the same problem, it was decided to implement project work of a longer duration, namely 10 weeks to be performed in real organisations. Thus, the projects in which the students use the Multiview methodology in practice are unique for each group. The impulse for this came from other programmes at the Copenhagen Business School.

The projects are the turning point from the lecture-based teaching of the first two years to practice-based training within the education in information systems development. Each year in May the students form groups of four to five member. Over the summer the students are asked to find a company or an organisation with a need for information systems analysis and design. In the beginning of September the course starts teaching the Multiview methodology. In October the students are supposed to have defined the problem statement of their project. From October to December the groups are actually applying the Multiview methodology in the company or organisation. Based on the application and the experiences gathered they write a 70-100 pages report, documenting their analysis and their proposal for the design of an information system. Finally, in January of the next year the project report is used as basis for final examination of the students in the information systems topic.

The aim of the project-based education is to provide the students with the ability to choose, tailor, adjust and use methodologies in general and the Multiview methodology in particular to define information systems in their professional life. This is the background for our study.

3 The Research Method

To investigate the relation between formal university education and the adoption of the methodology a survey instrument was developed to reach as many of the graduates as possible. The questionnaire consisted of 5 parts. Part 1 asked for demographic information about the respondent, especially the class year and the current occupation. Part 2 and 3 were directed at those who use or have used the methodology and information about the kind of projects, where the methodology was applied, which method components were utilised and about the respondents' opinion concerning the education, was asked for. Part 4 covered the non-adopters and their reasons for non-adoption as well as their conclusions about the training, which they had received in the university. Finally part 5 dealt with the general attitude towards the methodology independent of adoption or non-adoption and gave the opportunity to comment on the survey itself.

In total the questionnaire contained 28 questions and about 70 different attributes and consisted of both multiple choice, Lickert-scale based and open-ended questions. It was first tested with three selected graduates who represented the adopter and the non-adopter group and based on the feedback the instrument was revised.

The university has a complete record of all graduates, thus 572 questionnaires were sent out; of these 54 came back as the recipients could not be reached by mail and of the remaining 518 at cut off date 142 had answered. This results in a response rate of 27.4%. From these replies, 25 stated they had used or use the methodologies after they had left the school, whereas 117 declared that they had never used the methodology after graduation. The distribution of adopters and non-adopters in percentage is 17% adopters and 83% non-adopters. However, out of the 25 who claimed to use the methodology, one had delivered the survey in the wrong category, one only used it as a lecturer, and one has only used it as a student which leaves 22 questionnaires for evaluation. All questionnaires of the non-adopters could be used. The numbers in the following presentation vary as not every respondent answered each question and as some reported experience from more than 1 project, where the methodology had been adopted.

The aim of the research was a first exploration of the relationship between university education and adoption of system development methodologies. Thus no hypothesises were pre-formulated and tested. This is also the reason why no statistical correlation of the different variables was sought.

The quantitative survey technique was however combined with a qualitative analysis of all answers to the open-ended questions using the grounded theory methodology [23]. This research methodology allows the development of a substantive theory of a problem under investigation without prior hypotheses. The chosen grounded theory approach is composed of an alternation between three different coding procedures to analyse the collected data: open, axial and selective coding.

Open coding is the process of carefully and open-mindedly breaking down, examining, comparing, conceptualising, and categorising data. The aim is to find related phenomena or common concepts and themes in the accumulated data and to group them under joint headings and thus identifying categories and sub-categories of data.

Whereas open coding fractures the data and allows the building of some categories and their common properties, axial coding puts the data back together by making connections between a category and its sub-categories.

Selective coding finally is the process of determining a core category, relating it to all other categories, validating these relationships, and elaborating those categories that need further refinement and development. The definition of only one core category is recommended to maintain clarity and precision and to achieve a tight integration of all categories.

Several alternations between the three coding procedures were necessary to find a satisfying categorisation. This categorisation could however be backed up by the quantitative analysis of the survey and will be presented in the next section.

4 Results and Discussion

The presentation of the results takes its point of departure in the two groups of adopters and non-adopters, who consist of 22, respectively 117 individuals. Various categories can be identified concerning their considerations about the methodology. The two groups hold different opinions about the methodology education and its influence on the respondents' appreciation of the basic concepts of the methodology. They have disparate perceptions about the methodology's compatibility with existing company's standards and its suitability for the company's' business and application areas. Finally, they differ in their apprehension about the support offered by the methodology to solve actual problems independently of a particular application area. Before we discuss the results in more detail, we start however with some general demographic information about the respondents.

4.1 General Demographic Information about the Respondents

The respondents of the survey work in different occupations, both in terms of industry sector and in terms of the respondents' job function in a company or organisation. Table 1 shows a broad categorisation: Most of the respondents - not very surprisingly - are employed in companies related to the software business, followed by banking and/or insurance companies, public sector and educational organisations, and finally general consulting firms.

	Software Development	Banking/ Insurance	Public Administration & Education
total	48	21	19
non-adopters	37	17	18
adopters	11	4	1

Table 1: Business sectors represented in the survey (part 1)

	General Consulting	Other	IT-related functions	Non IT-related functions	Unknown
total	12	37	107	23	9
non-adopters	11	32	93	15	9
adopters	1	5	14	8	-

Table 1: Business sectors represented in the survey (part2)

A rather large number of respondents are grouped in the 'Other' category. This does not only cover respondents in e.g. production business, but also respondents who are studying on the graduate level, and those who have not answered this question. A further look at the respondents' job functions in their current occupation reveals that most of them are engaged in IT-related functions. A classification of non-adopters and adopters according to business sector and job functions provides however no distribution, which allows a conclusion about their use or non-use of the methodology.

year	'87	'88	'89	'90	'91	'92
non-adopters	6	11	6	8	2	11
adopters	5	1	3	-	-	1

Table 2: Non-adopters' and adopters' graduation years (part 1)

year	'93	'94	'95	'96	'97	total
non-adopters	18	13	14	16	12	117
adopters	3	1	2	3	3	22

Table 2: Non-adopters' and adopters' graduation years (part 2)

The same is true if the year of their graduation is considered. No immediate relation between adoption and non-adoption, which might refer to the quality of a class in terms of the general abilities of the students or of a particular teacher and his/her style of education can be found in this data (see table 2).

With regard to methodology adoption, one respondent declared that he had totally forgotten the methodology, as he had no occupation in system development. As such he was part of the 25% - 30 individuals - who answered that they did not work within system development and had jobs where Multiview was irrelevant. Obviously for them the methodology education had no influence on adoption or non-adoption of the methodology. To which extend this was the case for the remainder of the sample will be subject of the next sections.

4.2 Methodology Education

The Multiview methodology or some of its component methods have been used or adopted by 22 respondents. They provided detailed information about 23 projects where the methodology had been applied: 7 adopters had deployed it in more than 3 projects, 12 in just 1 project and the rest in 2 or 3 projects. Thus, no absolute account of the number of performed projects can be given. This is however not relevant for this study. The same is true for the fact that no information is available whether the utilisation has stopped or not.

The adopters stated that learning about Multiview had given them an overview over the different aspects of system development and an understanding of the activities, which have to be performed in system development projects. The methodology and the training in it were considered as a good introduction into the subject field. One respondent described the methodology as an excellent pedagogical tool and another one underlined the value of the student projects in which the methodology and most of its techniques were tried out extensively and mainly as described in the textbook.

Some former students emphasised the role of good teachers in this context and reinforced the role of education to appreciate the basic concepts behind a methodological approach to system development.

Concerning the quality of the education, the majority stated that the training had either given them an understanding of the single techniques to master them completely or at least provided them with an introduction which they could develop into mastery through practice. This had enabled them to use the methodology in concrete problem solving situations.

Only few adopters thought that parts of the education had been insufficient. This was true especially for the analysis of the socio-technical aspects, the development of user interfaces and the technical design activities. They meant they had needed an extra effort to achieve mastery of the techniques in practice. Strong critique was stated with respect to the Multiview textbook. Many adopters complained that the component methods were described imprecisely and inconsistently and that the interaction between the different stages of the methodology was weakly explained. The example in the book were judged to be hard to use as guidelines as they appeared to be too straight forward for a complex real-life problem situation. Thus, several respondents concluded that learning the methodology required the use of the original texts explaining the component methods. This was especially emphasised by one adopter who stated that Multiview in particular applies the Soft Systems Methodology in a way which could be debated as it, in contrast to the original, delimits the number of possible problem solutions very early in the development process.

The overall judgement of the methodology was very positive: The assessment of the training in the individual component methods and techniques is presented in table 3. As a result, 14 adopters would recommend Multiview to other developers, but not for direct use. The methodology was suggested as a device for training and education in system development or as a resource for the selection of methods. Some adopters limited their recommendation to parts of the methodology, especially to the parts from the Soft Systems Methodology. Others advocated Multiview in general as a basis for a methodological approach to systems development or as a background for tailoring their own methodology suitable for their respective organisation or problem situation.

Of the 117 respondents, who had replied that they did not use the methodology, only 23, 20% of the non-adopters, definitely did not want to recommend Multiview to other potential adopters. In addition, 10 were insecure whether they would advise the utilisation of the methodology or not.

	mastery of the techniques	good introduction	insufficient introduction
Rich pictures	12	10	
Root definitions	9	11	1
Conceptual models	8	13	1
Function charts	4	13	1
Data-flow diagrams	6	12	1
Entity descriptions	9	12	1
Socio-technical	4	14	5
User interface	2	10	7
Technical aspects	1	15	5

Table 3: Quality of training in the methodology's techniques

Concerning the quality of the education only four non-adopters thought that the training had been so bad that a major effort by themselves would be needed to use the methodology in practice, nine others were not sure whether they mastered the methodology. In contrast 22%, 26 of the non-adopters answered that the education had given them the necessary understanding to completely master the methodology in a use situation. The majority, 74%, 87 individuals, meant that the education had given them an introduction into Multiview which they could develop into mastery through further use in practice. In addition, seven respondents stressed that the training had given them a good introduction into system development and system development methodologies in general. It had provided them with knowledge about how methods and techniques could be combined and how important social and human issues were for system development.

The textbook was however sharply criticised by the non-adopters. They characterised it as confusing and superficial, especially the part about socio-technique was felt to be very weak. The description of the methodology and its component methods was experienced as very abstract and the component methods were perceived as little connected to each other. Therefore, also some non-adopters recommended to use the original literature to provide a better understanding of the techniques used in the different stages

Finally, one responding non-adopter stated his opinion that Multiview as taught could not be applied stringently, but that the principles and ideas were very useful. Others supported this by explaining that the methodology built their basis for the selection, adjustment and use of other methodologies and that they appreciated having background knowledge about a holistic, multi-perspective approach to system development. Thus 44 individuals, 38% of the non-adopters, although not using the methodology themselves would recommend it to other developers.

Evidently, understanding and adoption the methodology was affected by the textbook which quality was partly judged as being poor. In this respect, the education can be improved either using of the original literature or by amending the textbook. Given however the overall positive evaluation of the education and the comparably low adoption rate, a thorough analysis of further factors which support or inhibit the adoption of the methodology and their relationship to the education is necessary. Starting with the respondents' appreciation of the basic concepts of methodology, these will be discussed in the remaining sections.

4.3 Appreciation of the Basic Concepts of the Methodology

Adopters declared that they considered Multiview not as a cooking book-like approach which has to be followed as in the examples in the textbook, but accentuated the adaptability of the methodology to a given problem situation as an important feature. The methodology provided them with inspiration to develop suitable approaches themselves. As a flexible framework it fostered the ability to combine methods and techniques to carry out specific projects. Its embedded multi-perspective was mentioned as allowing different views on one problem situation and supporting an understanding of social aspects and the inclusion of more human aspects. These characteristics assisted the development of appropriate problem solutions.

However, some adopters stated that Multiview as a whole seemed to be very idealistic and theoretical as opposed to the reality of commercial life and that this might impede its dissemination. Especially the socio-technical approach was brought up as not applicable in real life. System thinking was perceived as being very abstract, hard to understand, and difficult to apply outside academia. It was also said that the value of rich pictures in an area characterised by a preference for more formal techniques was not easy to understand and therefore not appreciated.

Project no./used technique	1	2	3	4	5	6	7	8	9	10	11	12
Rich pictures	x	x	x	x	x	x	x	x	x	x	x	x
Root definitions	x	x		x	x			x	x		x	
Conceptual models	x			x				x	x		x	
Function charts			x	x			x		x			
Data-flow diagrams	x		x	x			x	x	x	x		
Entity descriptions	x		x	x			x	x	x	x		
Socio-technical	x	x		x				x	x			
User interface		x		x					x			x
Technical aspects				x					x			x

Table 4: Use of the methodology's techniques (part 1)

Project no./used technique	13	14	15	16	17	18	19	20	21	22	23	tot.
Rich pictures	x	x	x	x	x		x	x	x		x	21
Root definitions					x		x	x	x		x	12
Conceptual models				x	x		x	x			x	10
Function charts				x	x							6
Data-flow diagrams				x	x		x	x	x	x		13
Entity descriptions				x	x		x	x	x	x		13
Socio-technical				x	x	x		x				9
User interface				x	x	x		x				8
Technical aspects				x	x	x		x				7

Table 4: Use of the methodology's techniques (part 2)

Thus, in accordance with the ideas of Multiview not all parts of the methodology were used to the same degree. Only in 3 projects all methodology components were applied. In the rest adjustments had been performed: in some cases only some methodology components were selected, in others the original methodologies or methods like the Soft Systems Methodology or Structured Analysis and not the Multiview interpretation were used. Furthermore, the methodology was supplemented with methods for project management, cultural analysis, stakeholder analysis, work flow analysis, prototyping or formal specification techniques.

The degree of the adjustments was judged differently, ranging from radical to very modest, but it was felt legitimate as part of the adoption of Multiview. As a result, the majority of the adopters were satisfied with the utilisation of the method components and their outcome (see table 5).

	very satisfied	satis-fied	ok	less satisfied	not satisfied	total
Rich pictures	15	4	1	1	-	21
Root definitions	6	3	2	-	1	12
Conceptual models	5	4	-	-	1	10
Function charts	1	-	2	2	1	6
Data-flow diagrams	5	1	6	-	1	13
Entity descriptions	5	2	4	1	1	13
Socio-technical	1	4	3	-	1	9
User interface	-	-	3	4	1	8
Technical aspects	-	2	1	3	1	7

Table 5: Adopters' satisfaction with the used method components

In contrast, by far the largest group of non-adopters, 36%, 42 individuals, the stated that it had never felt natural to them to use the methodology. A few respondents emphasised that Multiview was too comprehensive, complex and long-winded to be applied. Most of the component methods were seen as very traditional and Multiview was thus equated by some nearly exclusively with the Soft Systems Methodology, which deals predominantly with organisational issues. One respondent put forward that Multiview's orientation towards such problems and socio-technical aspects should not be part of the work of system developers, but should lie with the customer. Someone else claimed that the methodology gave too much influence to the users and a third one was totally disagreeing with the basic ideas of the methodology.

The main difference between adopters and non-adopters seems to be that the adopters have understood that methodologies and Multiview in particular can and have to be customised in concrete use situations. Despite a partly critical attitude towards the methodology, they had tailored and adjusted it such that it served their purposes and could be appropriately used in their projects. This had apparently an influence on their perception of the methodology's compatibility with existing company standards and its suitability for various application and problem solving areas and is discussed in the next sections.

4.4 Compatibility with Company Standards and Suitability for Business and Application Areas

Company standards represented a significant obstacle for the adoption of the methodology: 17% of the non-adopters, 20 persons, said that Multiview was incompatible with their organisation's procedures for method use and 11 respondents answered that their companies had an own methodology which they used. A few, namely 8 respondents also expressed that the methodology was opposed to their company's culture. Multiview was considered as too idealistic and too soft. Some argued that this might be a reason why more traditional, older managers in both supplier and customer organisations did not appreciate the approach. Finally, 10 former students reported that they worked in companies that do not use methodologies for system development at all. The survey, however, did not investigate whether the respondents were not in a position to introduce a new methodology or whether they did not see any benefits in a potential introduction of Multiview.

The companies' business areas also seemed to be a major constraint for the utilisation for a particular methodology: 25% of the non-adopters named this as a reason for not using Multiview. Further, 35% affirmed that the methodology had not been applicable in their company's problem areas, and 15% were not sure whether the methodology was suitable for their problem fields. As examples they mentioned the definition of IT strategies, the design of technical, 'user-less' software systems, the development and adjustment of standard packages, the development of multimedia systems and the development of workflow- oriented systems. Ignoring possible benefits of a thorough early analysis of the problem at hand, the main critique was that Multiview gave too little concrete help for the technical activities of these application areas. An interesting statement was made by one individual who put forward that Multiview dealt explicitly not only with technical development, but also with organisational change and that this might be an explanation why more technical-oriented companies and system developers did not want to apply the methodology.

In contrast, adopters did not mention any special business or application areas as being less -suitable or better suitable for Multiview with the exception of its support for organisational change in general or organisational change through the introduction of information systems. One respondent stated that to his knowledge Multiview was the only methodology providing this combination and saw this as opposed to some non-adopters as an advantage. As described in the preceeding section adopters dealt with potential deficiencies of the methodology by supplementing it with appropriate method components.

Concerning the objectives of the projects where Multiview had been used, 8 projects aimed at general problem solving, 4 explicitly at organisational change and 16 were system development projects. This shows that the methodology was applied in various problem situations.

A few adopters also mentioned that many companies have their own methodologies, which they do not want to change, but this did not seem to be a major barrier for them. In the actual projects, 15 adopters acted as project leaders and the remainder as ordinary project members. But only in 4 projects the methodology was the officially approved standard. It looks as if the adopters were in a power position to overrule company standards or had a mandate or the courage to utilise a (new) methodology. It also indicates that the use of the methodology was not deeply anchored within the organisations.

4.5 Support for Solving Actual Problems

Concerning the support for solving actual problems it was stressed that the methodology was applicable for blurred and ill-defined problem areas. Most adopters emphasised that Multiview helped elucidating the problem domain and gave an overview over the problem. A third of the methodology users stated that the methodology structured both the problem situation and the solution process. It was seen as beneficial that the methodology not just supported the development of one solution, but that it assisted the elaboration of several, alternative ways of resolving a problem. Beyond the deployment of the methodology as a device for structuring used by individuals and for the project group, the adopters listed some characteristics of Multiview, which were related to the presentation and communication of thoughts and ideas to other project members or stakeholders in the development process as an advantage.

The results produced with the techniques of the methodology were appreciated as means for the preparation of meetings and for the introduction of discussions and debates. Especially, the value of rich pictures was underlined in this context. In addition to serving as a presentation means, Multiview was considered as a good co-ordination device and communication tool. Again, rich pictures were named in particular; one respondent paraphrased a well-known saying and put forward that a rich picture tells more than 1000 words. Others saw the value of the methodology in its support for constructively dissolving conflicts. The techniques in the early stages were furthermore described as also being understandable for non-IT people. This was supplemented by nearly half of the adopters by the opinion that the methodology and the intermediate products developed by its utilisation provided a framework for a shared understanding of all people involved. In addition, the use of rich pictures was experienced as enjoyable and pleasant, which contributes to project members' motivation and a positive atmosphere in a project.

Some adopters disagreed about the appropriate problem areas. One adopter meant that Multiview was only suitable for uncomplicated systems, whereas another one postulated that the methodology presupposes the problem to be solved to be imprecise.

Several adopters criticised that Multiview does not contain any assistance for project management and saw this as a possible reason for others to reject the methodology in total. Others stated that the methodology comprises too many problems areas and thus too many methods and techniques which make it very time and resource consuming such that the customers might not pay for its use. One adopter named explicitly functional decomposition and entity analysis as requiring too much detail and effort. The demand for conscientiousness and accuracy - although requested by methodologies in general - was emphasised especially as important, but difficult to fulfil for a methodology with many component methods.

Non-adopters shared a number of these reasons, which were based on their perception of how the methodology could be used to solve actual problems. As mentioned earlier some of them had experienced Multiview as too broad and comprehending and long-winded to be applied, especially in small projects. This resulted in a situation where 15% regarded the methodology as too time-consuming and only appropriate for large projects. The close, 'prescribed' co-operation with users was also named as a problem, making the methodology not suitable for projects, which involve management or external customers. Finally, non-adopters argued that the methodology was only appropriate for ill-defined problems, one thought however that it could not be used in areas where information was varying based on the informer's perspective and where knowledge was hard to access.

For non-adopters these reasons were so serious that they at least partly contributed to their rejection of the methodology, whereas adopters were able and willing to handle these seeming insufficiencies as described in the preceding sections. Some of the reasons for non-adoption lie certainly outside the direct influence of education; on the other hand non-adopters have their entire experience of the methodology from one practical project only. With respect to the impact of education, this may indicate that one system development project might not be sufficient to pass on the message of a methodology and that more practical projects already during the education are needed.

5 Conclusions

Is it all in vain? This was the question at the start of this article. Does methodology education at universities have any effect on practice? One might conclude so as only 22 respondents of our survey had used or adopted the methodology. But is it really the task of university education to convince students to adopt one particular methodology. We do not think so and we also see that education only has limited influence on factors like power and power structures in organisations which affect the adoption of innovations like systems development methodologies.

In our sample, adopters seem to have better understood the basic concepts of the methodology, the idea of tailoring method components to fit concrete problem situations and the benefits of dealing with non-technical issues in systems development. We have not looked in detail into the impact of the lecturers on teaching, but the education could definitely be improved by a better textbook and by more practical projects as part of the training.

But, both adopters and many non-adopters evaluated the education very positively and would recommend the methodology. The education has given them important insights about the advantages and the different possibilities of defining and using methodological approaches to systems development. This has influenced their practice.

Thus, no, it is not in vain. Methodology education – at least in our case- has had a positive effect on practice.

References

1. Yourdon E. What ever happened to Structured Analysis? Datamation 1986; June: 133-138
2. Hidding G J. Reinventing Methodology: Who reads it and why? Communications of the ACM 1997; 40 (11) : 102 -109.
3. Floyd C. A Comparative Evaluation of System Development Methods. In: Olle T. W et al. (eds) Proceedings of the IFIP Conference on Information Systems Design Methodologies: Improving the Practice. North-Holland, Amsterdam, The Netherlands, 1986, pp. 19-54
4. Raghavan S. A, Chand D. R. Diffusing Software-Engineering Methods. IEEE Software 1989; July: 81-90
5. Fichman R. G, Kemerer C. F. Adoption of Software Engineering Process Innovations: The Case of Object Orientation. Sloan Management Review 1993; Winter: 7-22
6. Leonard-Barton D. Implementing Structured Software Methodologies: A Case of Innovation in Process Technology. Interfaces 1987; 17 (May/June): 6-17
7. Kozar K A. Adopting Systems Development Methods: An Exploratory Study. Journal of Management Information Systems 1989; 5 (4): 73-86
8. Kautz K, McMaster T. Introducing Structured Methods: An Undelivered Promise? A Case Study. Scandinavian Journal of Information Systems 1994; 6 (2): 59-78
9. Wood-Harper T, Antill L, Avison, D E. Information Systems Definition: The Multiview Approach. Blackwell Scientific Publications, Oxford, UK, 1985
10. Avison D E, Wood-Harper AT. Multiview - an exploration in Information Systems Development. McGraw-Hill, London Maidenhead, UK, 1990
11. DeMarco T. Structured Analysis and System Specification. Prentice Hall, Englewood Cliffs, USA, 1979
12. Mumford E, Weir M. Computer Systems in Work Design - The Ethics Method. Associated Business Press, London, UK, 1979
13. Checkland P. Systems Thinking, Systems Practice. Wiley, Chicester, UK, 1981
14. Yourdon E. Modern Structured Analysis. Prentice Hall, Englewood Cliffs, USA, 1989
15. Coad P, E Yourdon, E. Object-Oriented Analysis. Yourdon Press Computing Series, Prentice-Hall, Englewood Cliffs, NY, USA, 1990
16. Checkland P, Scholes J. Soft Systems Methodology in Action. Wiley, Chicester, UK, 1990
17. Coad P, Yourdon E. Object-Oriented Design. Yourdon Press Computing Series, Prentice-Hall, Englewood Cliffs, NY, USA, 1991

18. Avison D E, Fitzgerald G. Information Systems Development: Methodologies, Techniques and Tools. McGraw-Hill, London, Maidenhead, UK, 1995
19. Copenhagen Business School Study Board. The official curriculum requirements' document for the combination study in computer science and business administration. Copenhagen Business School, Copenhagen, Denmark, approved 8th of May 1986
20. Chen P P. The Entity-Relationship Model-Toward a unified View of Data. ACM Transactions on Database Systems 1976; 1 (1)
21. Mumford E. Effective Systems Design and requirements Analysis - The ETHICS Approach. MacMillian Press, London, UK, 1995
22. Naur P. Project Activity in Computer Science Education. In: Naur P. Computing: A Human Activity. ACM Press, Addison-Wesley, 1992
23. Strauss A, Corbin J. Basics of Qualitative Research. Grounded Theory Procedures and Techniques. Sage Publications, Beverly Hills, CA, USA, 1990

IS THERE ANY IMPLICIT KNOWLEDGE MANAGEMENT WITHIN SOFTWARE PROCESSES?

Bridget Meehan & Ita Richardson
Department of Computer Science & Information Systems &
The Small Firms Research Unit
University of Limerick
National Technological Park
Castletroy
Limerick
Ireland
Telephone: +353-61-202765
E-Mails: bridget.meehan@ul.ie
ita.richardson@ul.ie

(**Key Words**: knowledge management, software processes).

Abstract

In the near future, the success or failure of any company will be determined by how effectively and explicitly it manages its knowledge. The time has come for companies to start treating their knowledge as a corporate asset.

The processes by which software companies develop their products are the core components of their business. It is vital that the knowledge about these processes be managed effectively and explicitly. This paper presents research which is a starting point for such knowledge management. It shares findings about the kind of implicit knowledge management that exists within two software processes in a small Irish software company.

1.   Introduction

The research in this paper investigates the knowledge within software processes, to discover how it is implicitly managed, and to discover if more effective and explicit knowledge management could enhance process performance.

Section two of this paper gives some background on the research presented. Section three of this paper discusses the methodology used to conduct the research. Section four reveals the findings to date, and section five analyses these findings. Finally section six concludes on the work done so far.

2.   Background

A software process can be defined as "a set of activities, methods, practices and transformations that people use to develop and maintain software and the associated products" (Paulk et al, 1993).

There are three levels, of software processes: the organisational level, the project level, and the software development level. **Organisational level** processes include recruitment, training, reward schemes, organisational planning, project acquisition, and resource acquisition. At the **project level**, processes include how resources such as people, skills, office space, hardware, and software are planned, and how time schedules, budgets, and risks in the project itself are planned. At the **software development level**, there are processes for specifying and documenting system requirements, prioritising requirements, planning for changes in customer requirements, planning for reuse of designs and code, prototyping, emphasising readability, standardisation and simplicity in code, testing code so it meets requirements and meets quality standards, planning for software integration and software installation, and planning for maintenance.

Research coming from various sources, including the Software Engineering Institute (SEI), and the European Software Institute (ESI), suggests that improving processes during the development of software leads to improved quality in the end-product, greater customer satisfaction, greater return on investment, greater productivity, shorter time-to-market and increased competitiveness (Steinmann and Stienen, 1996; Como and Kugler, 1996; European Software Institute, 1997). Models developed to improve software processes include the Capability Maturity Model (the CMM), Bootstrap and SPICE (Paulk et al, 1993; Sanders, 1996; European Software Institute, 1997). One of the issues these models look towards is improving the effectiveness and efficiency of software processes. Effectiveness in a software process means that the steps in the process are working. Efficiency in a software process means that the steps in the process are being performed in the best way. None of these models touch on the knowledge that exists in software processes, what kind of role this knowledge might have in them, or how proper knowledge management might effect software process improvement. The research in this paper presents a first step in doing just that.

It is important at this stage to define both knowledge and knowledge management. Knowledge should not be confused with data or information. Data is made up of facts or symbols taken out of context, and has no direct meaning. Information is data placed in some context which has acquired meaning and value. Knowledge meaningfully structured information (Zack et al, 1996). So for example, "£900" is data, "the balance in my bank account is £900" is information, and "I have to pay £250 rent tomorrow, so I do not really have £900 to spend on myself" is knowledge.

There are two kinds of knowledge: explicit knowledge and tacit knowledge. Explicit knowledge is knowledge that can be expressed formally, knowledge that can be 'seen'. Tacit knowledge is knowledge that cannot be easily expressed or communicated. Tacit knowledge is about human judgement, about experience, about intervening and compensating from problems (Vasandani, 1995; Stein, 1995).

Knowledge management can be defined as the explicit and systematic management of vital knowledge and its associated processes of creating, gathering, organising, diffusion, use, and exploitation. It requires turning personal knowledge into corporate knowledge that can be widely shared or transferred throughout an organisation, and appropriately applied (Skyrme, 1997). Knowledge management programmes must manage both explicit and tacit knowledge.

Knowledge management has been predicted as a vital factor in the survival of businesses in the approaching knowledge economy. The environments in which organisations exist is full of discontinuous change and potential surprise (Malhotra, 1997). They are dynamic and unpredictable. Such environments are known as wicked environments. In this climate, the traditional approach of trying to predict very far into the future fails. Being able to anticipate changes which occur often and without warning is the key to survival. Knowledge is the vital component in anticipating these changes. By not managing knowledge consciously and explicitly, companies can expect to lose the knowledge of key employees when they leave, make poor decisions based on faulty knowledge, be unable to answer customer queries quickly or at all. Can any company afford for this to happen?

Software processes are core to the business of software companies. Therefore, effective and explicit knowledge management within software processes is crucial. There are few companies which effectively and explicitly manage the knowledge in their software processes, but all software companies manage this knowledge at least implicitly. Investigating the kind of implicit knowledge management that exists in software processes is a starting point for looking at ways to implement knowledge management explicitly. By investigating this many questions can be asked as a result. For example, does knowledge management have an effect on software process performance? Does effective knowledge management in software processes make these processes more successful? Could knowledge management be used to improve less successful software processes?

3. Methodology

To conduct investigations into the implicit knowledge management within software processes, qualitative studies have been performed on two software processes within three small Irish software development companies. The two processes chosen for the research were the software requirements process and the software design process, both from the software development level. Processes from the software development level were chosen from because software development is the core activity in any software company. The requirements and design processes occur at the initial stages of software development, and require a lot of tacit knowledge when being performed. As the research is particularly interested in tacit knowledge, these two processes were ideal candidates for investigation. The same two processes were chosen in all three companies.

In depth studies were performed by conducting three interviews with each of the three companies. At the initial interview for each company, the interview candidate was given a self-assessment questionnaire to complete. This questionnaire contained twelve multiple-choice questions about software development level processes, for example, software requirements, software design, coding, testing, and maintenance.

The questionnaire allowed the interview candidate to give an initial assessment of the success of the twelve processes for the company. A successful process in the questionnaire is defined as one that is "planned, controlled, well defined, and repeatable from project to project throughout the whole organisation". A less successful process is one that is "not well defined, changes from project to project, is not repeatable, and is not uniform throughout the whole organisation" (European Software Institute, 1997). The results of the self-assessment questionnaire were treated with caution and were used to get a rough idea of what processes are like, and as an addition to the data gathered.

In each company, two further interviews were carried out, one for each of the processes chosen. These interviews were open-ended, and used a combination of the unstructured interview technique and interview guidelines (McNiff et al, 1996). In both these interviews, questions such as the following were asked:

- In what way is the process taught or passed on?
- What public documents are available about how the process is performed?
- In what way are solutions to problems within the process recorded for future use?
- Where do you think employees keep a lot of their knowledge on the process and problem solutions?

The data gathered at the interviews was analysed using the constant comparative method (Maykut and Morehouse, 1994; Riley, 1990), which involves sorting the data into relevant categories. Data gathered at the interviews was sorted into eight categories:

- knowledge creation: when employees learn new things from other employees, from books, or by doing their own research;
- knowledge storing: when employees retain knowledge in their heads, documents, files, databases etc.; knowledge includes knowledge about past experiences about the process;
- knowledge gathering: when employees pull together stored personal and company knowledge:
- knowledge dissemination: when knowledge is distributed around the company to all employees;
- knowledge use: when employees take full advantage of company knowledge about the processes and their own personal knowledge to enhance the performance of their everyday work;
- knowledge leverage: when employees make full use of company knowledge and knowledge about competitors and markets to help the company perform better;
- knowledge sharing: when employees pass on knowledge to each other by talking, working, teaching, coaching other employees; teamwork, communication, and collaboration are important here;
- Any other interesting data about the processes for example, is the process defined?.

The first seven categories listed above correspond to typical knowledge management activities.

4. Preliminary Findings

Data from one of the three companies investigated is presented in this paper. ComTech Inc. is a small Irish software company established about four years ago, with forty-three employees. It develops software for a very specialised market, a market which demands that work be done immediately. Time plays a crucial factor in this company, over and above the normal time demands that every company experiences.

The three interviews were conducted with the same interview candidate, called Tom. Tom has been with the company for four years, and is one of the main software developers there. He has a lot of experience in software development. Most of his work involves the software development level, but he has some involvement at the project level too. Due to company constraints, it was not possible for more than one employee from the company to be interviewed.

According to the self-assessment questionnaire completed at the first interview, it was found that the company's software development processes were not particularly successful overall. The requirements and the design processes were rated as being less successful. The data gathered at the in depth interviews, reinforced the results of the questionnaire for the requirements and the design processes.

A summary of the implicit knowledge management found in the data for the requirements and the design processes in ComTech Inc. is given in table 4.1.

	Software Requirements	Software Design
Knowledge Creation	No one brought from outside the company to perform process; employees performing it have been with the company for a long time; they learn the process on-the-job; thrown in at the deep-end; no encouragement for employees to perform research.	Learn process on-the-job; thrown in at deep-end; get some support and guidance from other employees, but management cannot afford too much of the time of experienced employees to be spent supporting inexperienced employees; no encouragement for employees to perform research.
Knowledge Storing	Knowledge stored in the heads of employees, and they rely solely on memory to recall the past; very little documentation; no record of the past.	Documentation poor; management feel documentation is a waste of time; no records of past; most process knowledge stored in heads of employees who perform it.
Knowledge Gathering	None.	None.
Knowledge Dissemination	None.	None.
Knowledge Use	Poor; rely on personal knowledge only to perform process.	Poor; rely on personal knowledge only to perform process.
Knowledge Leverage	None.	None.
Knowledge Sharing	Informal sharing among employees through everyday communication and collaboration; this can be lacking at times; no formal or explicit sharing; complete dependence on two employees to perform process.	Informal sharing through everyday communication and collaboration; sharing needs to be more formal in form of meetings and documentation; no incentive or recognition from management to share; too much dependence on the few who perform the processes.
Miscellaneous	Badly defined and ad hoc; efforts for improvements ignored by management.	Badly defined; management think process gets in way of releasing products; process often rushed or omitted.

Figure 4.1 Summary of implicit knowledge management in requirements and design processes

5.   Data Analysis

Using the findings from the data gathered, the authors have identified factors that reduce the success of the requirements and design processes in ComTech Inc. and demonstrate more effective and explicit knowledge management could be implemented to lessen the adverse effects of these factors on the processes:

- The processes are not defined. As a result, they are not repeatable over the whole company, and are not explicit or visible to employees (Paulk et al, 1993). This makes it more difficult for employees to understand them. More effective and explicit knowledge management could increase the visibility of the processes and make them more explicit. The more knowledge that is made available to employees, both on how to perform the processes and on how they have been performed in the past, the better employees will understand them. Better understanding leads to increased visibility and more explicit processes.

- Only two or three employees are actually involved in performing the processes. Dependence on these employees is heavy. The dependence on them is increased further since the bulk of the knowledge about the processes is stored in the heads of these few. Little or no knowledge is stored explicitly anywhere else. These employees are not encouraged to share what they know about the processes with anyone else, nor are they given any recognition if they do so. If one of these key employees were to leave the company, their knowledge about the processes would leave with them. The company would in effect loose this knowledge. This is a common problem in companies, and there are many instances of it in the literature, for example (Nevis et al, 1995). Improved storing, dissemination and sharing of knowledge about the processes would diminish the dependence on the few employees and would save the company from loss if these employees were to leave.

- The lack of explicit knowledge storing in the processes, as mentioned above, is significant for another reason. Because knowledge is largely stored in the heads of the employees who perform the processes, it means that they are the only ones who can answer questions about how the processes were performed, and how decisions were made. If they have any queries, employees involved in later stages of software development need to constantly refer to the employees who perform the requirements and design processes. They have nothing else to refer to about the processes. What if an employee needs to learn about how either of the processes are performed? Apart from the key employees, what do they have to refer to on how the processes should be performed? Improved knowledge storing could really help this problem.

- A problem specific to the requirements process noticed during the research could be lessened by improved knowledge use and leverage. We have called it the 'bottleneck' problem. This 'bottleneck' problem arises when the employees who perform the requirements process are unsure of the feasibility or complexity of certain requirements. Such requirements need to be researched to determine if and how they can be implemented. In ComTech Inc. the employees who perform the requirements process often have a limited amount of time to agree requirements with customers. Therefore, the research needed for the unsure requirements can be omitted or inadequately performed. Without being sure of their feasibility or complexity these requirements can be agreed with the customer. The research they require is often performed during the design process. And at that stage, employees sometimes find out that particular requirements cannot be implemented. Better knowledge use could help here. If all knowledge from the requirements process, including past experiences, problems and solutions, was shared with the employees performing the process, employees would approach the process not only with their own personal knowledge, but with the accumulated knowledge of any past efforts in the company. In addition, better knowledge leverage could also help. If employees had full knowledge of the market place, and of their customers, they would be more aware of what the requirements for future projects might be. They could anticipate customer requirements to some extent, and perform research on them in advance of projects. This improved knowledge use and leverage would help reduce the 'bottleneck' problem in the requirements process, and help the company respond more quickly to customers.

- Lack of commitment and support from management hinders efforts that might be made to improve the processes. Management do not encourage employees to share their knowledge about the processes. They simply want employees to get the job done. Management believe that documentation is a waste of time, and give no encouragement to employees to explicitly store their knowledge in documents. Management believe that the design process gets in the way of releasing products, and do not worry when it is rushed or omitted. Management do nothing to reduce their dependence on the few employees who perform the processes. If management took more interest in the problems being experienced in the requirements and the design processes, improvements would be made. This lack of support and commitment from management is very common, for example (Payne, 1996).

6.   Conclusion

The findings from the data show the implicit knowledge management within the requirements and the design processes in ComTech Inc. The analysis indicates that more effective and explicit knowledge management could indeed enhance the performance of these processes.

The work presented here presents data from a single company. The entire research will present and compare data from three companies. From the full data analysis, the authors will be able present further how much implicit knowledge management actually exists in these processes, and investigate whether implicit knowledge management has any bearing on process performance.

References

Como Massimo, Kugler Hans-Jurgen, "Software Process Improvement? CMM and ISO for Small Companies. Case Study of an Italian SME: 'Sodalia'", Tri-Spin News, Newsletter No. 3, June 1996.

European Software Institute (ESI), 1997, URL http://www.esi.es/. Accessed in June, 1997.

McNiff J, Lomax P, Whitehead J, "You and Your Action Research Project", Routledge, UK, 1996.

Malhotra Yogesh, "Knowledge Management in Inquiring Organisations", 1997, URL http://www.brint.com/km/km.htm. Accessed in September, 1997.

Maykut P, Morehouse R, "Beginning Qualitative Research: A Philosophic and Practical Guide", Falmer Press, London, 1994.

Nevis Edwin C, DiBella Anthony J, Gould Janet M, "Understanding Organisations as Learning Systems", Sloan Management Review, Winter, 1995.

Paulk Mark C., Curtis Bill, Chrissis Mary Beth, Weber Charles V, "The Capability Maturity Model for Software, Version 1.1", Technical Report SEI-93-TR-24, Software Engineering Institute, Carnegie Mellon University, U.S.A., 1993.

Payne Laurie W, "Unlocking an Organisation's Ultimate Potential Through Knowledge Management", 1996, URL http://www.apqc.org/prodserv.inpractice.cfm. Accessed in November, 1997.

Riley J, "Getting the Most from Your Data", Technical & Educational Services Ltd. UK, 1990.

Sanders Joc, ed., "Assessing Your Software Process", Tri-Spin News, Newsletter No. 1, January, 1996.

Skyrme David, "Management Insight No.1, The Global Knowledge Economy: And its Implications for Business", Second Series, 1997, URL http://www.skyrme.com/. Accessed in November, 1997.

Stein, Eric W, "Social and Individual Characteristics of Organisational Experts", International Journal of Expert Systems, Vol. 8, No. 2, 1995.

Steinmann Christian, Stienen Hans, "SynQuest - Tool Support for Software Self-Assessments", Software Process - Improvement and Practice, Vol. 2, 1996.

Vasandani Vijay, "Knowledge Organisations in Intelligent Tutoring Systems for Diagnostic Problem Solving in Complex Dynamic Domains", IEEE Transactions on Systems, Man, and Cybernetics, Vol. 25, No 7, July 1995.

Zack MH, Reisman JG, Serino M, "Knowledge Management and Collaboration Technologies", 1996, URL http://www.lotus.com. Accessed in September, 1997.

Acknowledgement

This research was funded by AMT Ireland, University of Limerick, Ireland.

Not Another Methodology
What Ant Tells Us About Systems Development

Jim Underwood
University of Technology, Sydney
AUSTRALIA

This paper proposes an interpretive technique for understanding IS development which uses complementary features of actor-network (ANT) theory and Foucault's theory of discourse. The technique is being applied to a loosely structured project which is working towards the construction of a flexible teaching and learning environment based on the internet. The paper traces the fortunes of two of the non-human actors in this setting. The combination of ANT/discourse theory is found to be an effective descriptive tool for IS development but it is not clear how it could contribute to a methodology. Some possible directions are suggested and balanced against possible organisational and psychological barriers to using such a methodology.

Introduction

The search for a theory on which to base the development of information systems continues. The majority of IS development projects still follow, albeit loosely [1], methodologies derived from the systems approach to problem solving popularised by the RAND corporation in the 1950s [2]. This approach takes us through the steps of problem definition, search for solutions, selection of the best alternative, implementation and evaluation. As with many methodologies what starts as a description of how particular projects were done soon becomes a normative or prescriptive theory which promises future success. This may be a reasonable transformation if the original projects were successful, but Schon [3, pp 203-212] has pointed out the difficulties of trying to use lessons from the past in current projects. After 40 years of IS development several factors encourage IS researchers to look for different theoretical bases for methodologies.

Firstly, a large percentage of computer based information systems are generally acknowledged to provide less than satisfactory service to end-users and to fall short of their original objectives. While some authors have attributed these failures to developers not following accepted theories, there is always the suspicion that the theories themselves may be at fault [4]. Also, researchers concerned with the "impact of IT" have seen the choice of development method as a political choice, with different methods carrying their assumptions about appropriate alignments of organisational and social power [5]. And new information technology may require new development methods. Interactive systems are often developed through prototyping, and the growth of the internet will see cooperative systems developed with data and processing widely distributed and with no one clearly in charge of the system. We need a theory of IS development which gives a better account of what is actually going on both politically and technically.

In this paper I consider an adaptation of actor-network theory (ANT) as a candidate for such a theory. In the next section I give a brief description of the basic elements of ANT, while the following section discusses previous applications of ANT to IT development and the relation of ANT to Foucault's theory of discourse. In the following three sections I show how extended ANT was applied to describe the development process in a loosely structured project for the cooperative use of IT. Finally I discuss whether this descriptive method could be used as a basis for an IS development methodology.

Actors, Networks and Scripts

Actor-network theory developed from studies in two related but distinct fields: the social practice of science and the introduction of new technologies. An early paper by Latour and Woolgar [6] looks at struggles over scientific truth in a laboratory, while one of Callon's early studies [7] considers fishermen and scallops as some of the stakeholders in a changing fishing industry. These examples already exhibit some of the main features of ANT. The actors (sometimes called actants) may be humans, organisations, cultures, ideas, animals, plants or inanimate objects, and these are treated symmetrically irrespective of their ontology. These actors have interests which are represented (in both the semiotic and political senses) by themselves and other actors. The actor-network is a shifting system of alliances and exchanges among the actors.

Latour [8] claims several advantages for this approach. It is symmetrical with respect to type of actor: it treats humans and machines equally; it is symmetrical with respect to outcome: failures have the same types of explanation as successes; and it is symmetrical with respect to causality: each actor influences and is influenced by other actors and the network as a whole. The equal treatment of people and machines has been criticised but it may be realistic in terms of power relations and it prevents issues from becoming invisible when their representation is transferred (translated) to an actor of a different type. If, for example, some data collection functions are transferred from police informers to computer programs it is still important to be able to talk about the power relations and motives of the collectors and their allies.

The interests of the actors are represented by scripts, usually imperative statements such as "shut the door", "pay your taxes" or "calculate the gross pay". Akrich and Latour [9] give a comprehensive set of definitions of script-related processes (such as inscription, conscription). These processes describe (amongst other things) the translation of scripts among actors, often involving a change of medium, for example from conditioned response in a human to lines of code in a computer program. Of particular interest is the idea of description (de-scription), the discovery of the words behind the things or actions. This discovery is only possible in contrived, exotic or crisis situations, such as reengineering, consultancy or system failure; in a time such as IS development when nothing is taken for granted.

Scripts are imperative but don't have intentions; actors do. An actor can develop a "program of action" [9] perhaps with the intention of maximising the number of actors following a particular script. Some actors may avoid this by following an anti-program. A program of action can include the creation of new actors suitably inscribed. The inscription is most effective if it becomes irreversible, if the actor is, with respect to that script, a "black box" and the script becomes inaccessible to other actors. My e-mail system may, for instance, be carrying a script "always archive a copy for the authorities" which will be more effective because I am unaware of it (or used to it).

ANT, Information Systems and Discourse

Actor-network theory helps us to understand the course of a project or enterprise. We can asks questions such as "How did it come to turn out this way?" (through the changing alliances of actors), "Who is influencing it?" (who has been doing what scripting?) or "Why are some actors acting this way? " (what scripts are they carrying?). These are not questions with deterministic answers but they allow a rich interpretation of the situation.

Some of the more spectacular applications of ANT have been to the genealogy of now well established scientific theories [10], the meaning of simple technical devices [8] or the acceptance of a new product [11]. More recently ANT has been applied to the development of information systems. Monteiro and Hanseth [12] claim that ANT allows a finer grained analysis of information systems than some other interpretive approaches which can treat all information systems as essentially similar. Walsham [13] worries that ANT studies are too local, ignoring the wider social environment, and that ANT is amoral and could encourage a devaluation of humans. Grint et al [14], although optimistic about the promise of ANT, point out difficulties in identifying the interests of various actants and in particular an ambiguity as to whether scripts are intrinsic to or imposed upon nonhuman actants. While it is clear that the groom says "close the door" [8] the message of the data warehouse is not so obvious.

Generalising Grint's concerns, I would say ANT fails to discuss the meanings of scripts, and gives little guidance on how the nature of particular kinds of actors affects their propensity to subscribe to particular scripts. It may be sensible to treat machines and people equally, but they are not identical. ANT may go too far in the direction of flexibility [15]. One way of dealing with this problem is to consider "external" networks. To avoid trying to understand everything at once we normally consider the actor-network for a particular setting or situation, such as the "discovery" of oxygen [16] or the development of a computer-based information system. We surround the situation with a boundary and imagine that actors outside don't matter, or can be classified as "constraints". But there are networks extending (and folding back) to infinity. We can make the "constraints" a little more realistic by acknowledging their generative networks but restricting these networks to particular issues, "political networks" or "economic networks" for instance. In my work at present I am concentrating on "conceptual networks". I could perhaps call them "semantic networks" although I suspect that term is seriously overloaded; in fact what I mean is "discourse" in the sense developed by Foucault [17]. A script carried by some actors in the current setting finds its meaning in another network which we call a discourse. In an IS development project some scripts may refer to the discourse of accounting, others to the discourse of electronics. The same words may be used but the meanings may be incommensurable. This is a major difficulty in trying to formulate "system requirements" [18]. Combining the insights of ANT and Foucault promises a two-way benefit: discourse theory allows us to see where the scripts are "coming from"; and ANT adds substance to the genealogy of the discourse [19], giving some structure to individual power/knowledge encounters. Some related work on such encounters can be found in Bloomfield and Vurdubakis [20].

The Flexible Delivery Pilot Project

This "discourse biased" version of ANT was used to investigate a project at an Australian university (the Flexible Delivery Pilot Project). Like many university projects, the Pilot Project was supported by a grant (internal in this case), had a limited life (calendar year 1997) but was actually a bureaucratic "time-slice" in an ongoing process, and had an ambiguous management structure - perhaps not unlike many other IS development projects. The idea of this project was to develop and disseminate expertise in the use of networked IT to allow students of the university greater choice in when, where and how they learnt [21]. The project was to develop (among other things) "electronically mediated structured teaching and learning environments (hereafter called electronic workspaces)" [22] by drawing together components and experience from previous separate projects. At least that is my idea of the project. From the point of view of ANT the project may or may not be defined by the various actors in various ways and will have to struggle for its own existence [23]. In another article [24] I have discussed whether the project was successful in this sense. In this article I will use the programs of one or two non-human actors to illustrate the descriptive power of the extended ANT, then discuss whether the theory could be used normatively rather than descriptively.

To apply ANT to this case I studied documents generated before and during the Pilot Project and interviewed most of the key participants. The study was commenced in early 1997 and is still in progress. From documents I extracted (intuitively) a number of key issues and concepts. I used these as a basis for the interviews, but found that each interviewee added their own concerns. All interviewees were, however, comfortable with discussing the case at the "correct" level - they discussed concepts as they related to this case rather than in general, they depersonalised any political issues and they did not introduce low level technical or bureaucratic detail. My position was that of an almost outside observer introduced to the interviewees through a primary informant who was one of the key leaders of the project. "Almost outsider" because I have previously worked at the university in question, knew many of the interviewees personally and was working with my primary informant on a grant application for a related project for 1998. While this casts severe doubts on my objectivity (not a plausible concept in ANT) it gave me the advantage of a wealth of background information.

The actors whose programs I will discuss in this paper are "Lotus Notes" and "team learning". Lotus Notes is data based group support software which is widely used in industry. Although it can be used to implement work flow systems most applications emphasise the database functions, particularly data sharing and synchronisation for remote users. Work flow features are often confined to electronic mail and discussion groups. It is regarded as the leading software of its type and for many years had a monopoly on this market. It is now owned by IBM and its overall program is to maintain its share of the market against threats from Microsoft Exchange and Netscape Communicator. It is not in general use at the university but has been used for several years by information systems students designing a new department for a simulated organisation. Lotus Notes requires a fair amount of technical support.

The organisation simulation (which is essentially a role playing exercise) has evolved from the original Reliable Motor Company by the NCC [25]. The aims were to understand the workings of an organisation and to practice interpersonal skills particularly when working in a team. To keep up with organisational reality IT tools have been introduced into the game, first electronic mail, then Lotus Notes. This allows students to experiment with different uses of IT in organisational communication. The overhead of learning Lotus Notes is justified because organisations in this town are heavy users of Notes, so IS students appreciate having this skill. I have identified the second actor in this paper as "team learning" which represents the behavioural skills that are learned in this exercise, independent of the software used. Team learning also needs to survive, though it is expensive in staff and supported by only some academics. At the start of the Pilot Project team learning was a strong ally of Lotus Notes.

This organisation simulation exercise was one of four strands which were "brought together" in the Pilot Project. The others were an initiative by the IS department to make all their course material available remotely (to their existing students) as well as face-to-face, improvement of a subject on the use of internet resources (for non-IT students, using Netscape Navigator) and the development of a new course which would have students attending the university intensively for 4 weeks then completing project work from their (remote) home locations. The latter two courses were offered by a second department, so the Pilot Project brought together four projects from two departments reporting to a central university education committee. None of these other strands seemed natural allies of Lotus Notes or team learning.

A Variety of Discourses

While Notes and team learning had been allies for a long time they have very different "home" discourses. Lotus Notes is linked to the discourse of computing: "Lotus Notes is a client-server platform for developing and deploying groupware applications. Lotus Notes allows people to access, track, share and organize information in ways never before possible, even if they are only occasionally connected to a network."; and "Collaborate - Notes makes it easier for individuals to work together with information. Documents can be passed along from one person to the next, with each adding to or refining information in the document." [26]   Here the work of the team means "working together with information". The first step in building a team is to set up a database.

Team learning, at least at this university, seems to relate more to a discourse of business processes.   "We have designed electronic workspaces to support the development and performance of flexible work groups in Information Systems units. We have designed electronic spaces for informal discussions (an electronic café), group product development, work product sharing (an electronic repository), private conversations, communication with staff, electronic submission of assessable work (and return) and electronic access to lecture, reference and other unit materials." [27]. Here the emphasis is on types of team activity. Although some of these activities are people oriented rather than task oriented they still tend to be related to information and structure - it is as if the "people" or team building activities were seen as just another task. The electronic spaces themselves start as unstructured because part of the design task of the students is to structure these spaces. Team building has often been related to another discourse, the psychoanalytical.   Freud emphasised the development of relationships between team members and the leader, while Bion traced the difficult paths a team may follow before (hopefully) settling into a cooperative work mode [28]. This discourse is not seriously discussed in any of the documents relating to the team learning project, or the subsequent Pilot Project. Another discourse which is not fully linked to this particular discussion of team learning is the educational. While many references are made to individuals gaining skills in teams (including team building skills), there are no specific references made to learning from each other.

Some of the academics involved in the team learning project are quite knowledgeable in psychology and education theory so they are not unaware of these issues. Before electronic communication was introduced to the simulated organisation another information technology was used, but only in the "real" world, not within the simulated organisation. This was video recording. Some student activities (e.g. interviewing) were recorded and played back at debriefings. These debriefings had a considerable psychological slant. It is interesting to speculate whether the alliance with Lotus Notes crowded out these psychological scripts. In any case it is difficult now for staff to follow the group formation activities, since they do not access the students' café discussions.

The issue of scripts having different interpretations in different discourses is apparent with a major script in the project: "develop electronically mediated structured teaching and learning environments". In the discourse of computing this could easily be synonymous with "build electronic workspaces"; in psychoanalysis we would talk about trust, authority and archetypes (is the workspace the home of the sage or the joker?). In educational discourse we might concentrate on how the student (or team?) constructs their own knowledge in this environment.

Changing Alliances

Towards the end of 1996 there were two events which affected the dynamics of the actor network. The Pilot Project was approved and Lotus Domino became readily available. One of the main aims of the Pilot Project was to promote a campus-wide culture of flexible delivery. The component projects should be somewhat compatible and, as we have seen, only one used Lotus Notes or team learning. The others used mainly Netscape. The program "let them use Lotus" had relied on the educational benefits for IS students and making available (through licensing agreements) free copies of Notes for the students' home computers. Students in the other courses involved in the Pilot Project would not be learning Notes because it was too difficult. The release of Domino may have saved things for Notes. Domino connects Notes data bases, mail and discussion groups to other widely used software. The "clients" (students) only need a web browser and a mail reader (any brand). A certain amount of database management can also be achieved via a browser. This development probably advantaged Notes (and its ally team learning) in the short term, but other actors became more noticeable. The Domino model turned the Notes problem around. Rather than there being a server looking for cheap and easy client software, there was now a standard and independent client interface able to link to any suitable server. This meant there were now a number of competing products such as Caucus and Top Class.

These competing server products need to form an alliance with another actor, the university computer centre. The Pilot Project is meant to consider campus wide issues, and since the IS department has neither the resources nor desire to provide servers for the whole university, and since many other departments will not wish to manage such a service, the computer centre becomes a key (if currently quiet) player. A computer centre representative said that, while they have not been funded to provide flexible delivery at present, they are investigating server software so the "necessary infrastructure" will be available. It seems likely that the computer centre will take a "middleware role" linking the students to materials on appropriate library or departmental servers.

This means that team learning (separately from Lotus Notes) also needs to make an alliance with the computer centre, or at least inscribe "students can belong to several teams" into future middleware. The program to achieve this so far has seen the inscription of "project" and "cohort" into a diagram of "Flexible Delivery Workspaces" in the Pilot Project final report [29], and the acceptance of this report as providing university wide guidelines. The report also states that "This means that each group must have a work area on a server that they can use in their own way, and must be able to set up their own discussions, bulletin boards, etc., as and when they need to." This describes what has been done with Notes but there is no reference to specific software here. Team learning is declaring its willingness to change partners, or at least making contingency plans.

Tracing through the story, I think we can see that the alliance between team learning and Notes, although quite fruitful for a time, was always at risk (all alliances are) because there was no common "home discourse" and neither party was able to irreversibly conscript the other.

Could this be a Methodology?

The example taken from the Pilot Project shows how ANT can trace the development of (some aspects of) an IS project. It also suggests that scripts are not self explanatory and that different actors may find the meaning of what is apparently the same script in different discourses. Can these techniques be used to "help" project development.

For some time [30] I have been advocating that we should try to preserve ambiguity and contradiction throughout the development process (and in the "completed" system). To engage in (say) data cleansing, which is the latest fashion in reverse engineered consistency, is to remove data which may be important to many stakeholders and to the survival of the system. An ANT/discourse based methodology might be able to preserve a realistic level of ambiguity.

The first possibility is to concentrate on the construction of a local language. Various human and organisational actors might come to use mutually understood language. Marketing, accountants and programmers might become comfortable about what "efficient" means for a particular project. In the Pilot Project case the majority of the university may accept that the Pilot Project report gives a fair enough definition of "flexible learning" for the time being. The local language can probably preserve ambiguity because it is dynamic and underdeveloped and because the actors still maintain an underlying allegiance to their home discourses. The development of the local language can be encouraged or tested by consensus or "unreality" checks: when describing do actors refer to the project network or to their home discourse? Whether such a local language will be sufficiently fluid or whether it degenerates into "groupthink" requires further investigation. In any case this approach may only preserve a subconscious or secret ambiguity under a veneer of consistency.

The second possibility is to follow ANT and keep describing. We never allow pieces of our design to become black boxes, we never accept inscriptions as irreversible. Frequent description sessions will reveal which scripts are progressing happily through the system design and which have been de-inscribed. Perhaps we need something like a script audit, where each actor (or program) registers their key scripts at the beginning. These are frequently checked for progress making the ambiguity and politics publicly visible. An actor may acknowledge a script as having lost importance (use Lotus Notes) or may object to a script which is in danger of becoming irreversible (no non-student access to web pages). From my interviews I don't believe the human actors would have any trouble identifying relevant scripts - they are all quite aware of the "politics", it just isn't part of the "methodology". What is really being advocated here is openness [31]; but ANT is a French invention, and French writers have not always been sanguine about openness in organisations [32]. Whether any network can operate with complete openness is an undecided question.

ANT does have a normative face, but only for a single actor or program. Grint & Woolgar [33] summarise how allies are enrolled.

> First the 'problematization' stage identifies key actors who are then persuaded that the solution to their own problems lies with the enrollers. Second, *intéressement* involves the gradual dissolution of existing networks and their replacement by a new network created by the enrollers. Third, the stage of 'enrolment' proper occurs, in which, through coercion, seduction, or consent, the new network achieves a solid identity. Finally, the alliance is 'mobilised' to represent an even larger network of absent entities.

This is how each program proceeds (with luck). But there are also anti-programs operating at the same time. What is the position of the analyst? They are just another actor with another program. ANT does not countenance that one actor might follow a program for "the common good" or that one program can dominate from the start. As with evolution, we can only tell who was "fittest" after the event. So this normative method (which was probably known long before Machiavelli) only operates for individual goals. This is easily conceptualised if the analyst is trying to sell something or is the clear representative of another powerful actor, but what if they are representing objectivity, ambiguity, job satisfaction or progress? Are they prepared to have their scripts open for description? In the end, as Hedberg [34] says, the analysts must disappear and each actor must be their own analyst. Perhaps we still have roles as trainers or facilitators although these roles seem to be going out of favour at present.

Conclusion

The study of the Flexible Delivery Pilot Project showed that a combination of actor-network theory and discourse theory provided a powerful interpretive tool. This experience suggests two possible ways to proceed towards a methodology, one based on encouraging a fluid local language, the other on frequently de-scribing scripts from partially built IS artifacts (hardware, software, procedures, people). Unfortunately, for either of these approaches to work, we need potential project managers and project owners to embrace the view that every IS development has a life of its own and that no single actor or alliance of actors can be assured of the outcome. And if we could get them to accept that, a methodology just becomes a useful communication tool rather than a fetish [35].

References

1. Fitzgerald B. "The Use of Systems Development Methodologies in Practice: a field study" *Inf Sys J* 1997; 7,3: 201-212
2. Optner S.L. *Systems Analysis* Penguin, Harmondsworth, 1973
3. Schon D.A. *Beyond the Stable State* Pelican, Harmondsworth, 1973
4. Beath C.M., Orlikowski W.J. (1994) "The Contradictory Structure of Systems Development Methodologies" *Inf Sys Res* 1994; 5,4: 350-377
5. Probert S. *A Critical Study of the National Computing Centre's Systems Analysis and Design Methodology, and Soft Systems Methodology* MSc thesis, Newcastle Business School, Newcastle Upon Tyne, 1991
6. Latour B., Woolgar S. *Laboratory Life: the Social Construction of Scientific Facts* Sage, Beverly Hills and London, 1979
7. Callon M. "Some Elements of a Sociology of Translation: Domestication of the Scallops and the Fishermen of Saint Brieuc Bay". In: Law J. (Ed) *Power, Action and Belief: a new Sociology of Knowledge?*. Routledge and Kegan Paul, London, 1986, pp 196-233 (Sociological Review Monograph)
8. Latour B. "Where Are the Missing Masses? The Sociology of a Few Mundane Artifacts" In: Bijker, W.E., Law J. (eds) *Shaping Technology / Building Society* MIT Press, Cambridge Ma, 1992
9. Akrich M., Latour B. (1992) "A Summary of a Convenient Vocabulary for the Semiotics of Human and Nonhuman Assemblies" in Bijker, W.E., Law J. (Eds) *Shaping Technology / Building Society* MIT Press, Cambridge Ma, 1992
10. Latour B. *Science in Action* Harvard University Press, Cambridge Ma, 1987
11. Bijker W.E. "The Social Construction of Flourescent Lighting, or How an Artifact Was Invented in Its Diffusion Stage" in Bijker W.E., Law J. (Eds) *Shaping Technology / Building Society* MIT Press, Cambridge Ma, 1992
12. Monteiro E., Hanseth O. "Social shaping of Information Infrastructure: On Being Specific about the Technology" In: Orlikowski W.J., Walsham G., Jones M.R., DeGross J.I. (Eds) *Information Technology and Changes in Organizational Work* Chapman & Hall, London, 1996, pp 325-343
13. Walsham G. "Actor-Network Theory and IS Research: Current Status and Future Prospects" In: Lee A.S, Liebenau J., DeGross J.I. *Information Systems and Qualitative Research* Chapman & Hall, London, 1997
14. Grint K., Case P., Willcocks L. (1996) "Business Process Reengineering Reappraised: The Politics and Technology of Forgetting" In Orlikowski, W.J., Walsham G., Jones M.R., DeGross J.I. (Eds) *Information Technology and Changes in Organizational Work* Chapman & Hall, London, 1996, pp 39-61
15. Latour B. "Social Theory and the Study of Computerized Work Sites" in Orlikowski W.J., Walsham G., Jones M.R., DeGross J.I. (Eds) *Information Technology and Changes in Organizational Work* Chapman & Hall, London, 1996, pp 295-307
16. Kuhn T.S. *The Structure of Scientific Revolutions (2nd edn)* University of Chicago Press, Chicago, 1970

17. Foucault, Michel *The Archaeology of Knowledge* Tavistock, London. 1972
18. Gause D.C., Weinberg G.M. *Exploring requirements : quality before design* Dorset House, New York, 1989
19. Foucault M. *Power/Knowledge* Pantheon Books, New York, 1980
20. Bloomfield B.P., Vurdubakis, T. "Boundary Disputes: Negotiating the Boundary between the Technical and the Social in the Development of IT Systems" *Inf Technology & People* 1994: 7,1: 9-24
21. "Towards a Policy on Flexible Learning at the University ... ". July 1997. (Discussion paper for senior staff) - case study organisation
22. "Teaching Grant Application", October 1996. (application from IS department for Pilot Project) - case study organisation
23. Latour, Bruno *ARAMIS or The Love of Technology* Harvard University Press, Cambridge Ma, 1996
24. Underwood J. " Using Ambiguity in Information Systems Evolution: Keeping the System Soft?" submitted.January 1998.
25. *Systems Training - Presenter's Case Study* National Computing Centre, Manchester, 1984
26. *Lotus Notes 3.3 - A Quick Tour of Lotus Notes* Lotus Development Corporation, Cambridge Ma, 1995
27. Collings P., Kleeman D., Richards-Smith A., Walker D. (1997) "Developing New Group Work Practices: An Evaluation of the Design and Use of Groupware-based Systems for a Graduate Course in Information Systems In: *PACIS '97* Queensland University of Technology, Brisbane, 1997, pp 185-192
28. deBoard R. *The Psychoanalysis of Organizations* Tavistock, London, 1978
29. "Flexible Delivery: A Guide for Teaching Staff", December 1997. (this is the final report for the project) - case study organisation
30. Underwood J. (1992) "Information Systems Work: Contradictions in Practice and Theory" In: MacGregor R. (Ed) *Proceedings: Third Australian Conference on Information Systems* Department of Business Systems, Wollongong, 1992, pp 267-274
31. Argyris C. "The Executive Mind and Double-Loop Learning" In: Bemelmans Th.M.A. (ed) *Beyond Productivity* North-Holland, Amsterdam, 1984, pp 255-275
32. Crozier M., Friedberg E. *Actors & Systems* University of Chicago Press, Chicago, 1980
33. Grint K., Woolgar S. *The Machine at Work* Polity Press, Cambridge, 1997
34. Hedberg B. "Using Computerized Information Systems to Design Better Organizations and Jobs" In: Bjorn-Andersen N. (ed) *The Human Side of Information Processing* North-Holland, Amsterdam, 1980, pp 19-37
35. Wastell D.G. "The Fetish of Technique: Methodology as a Social Defence" *Inf Sys J* 1996; 6,1: 25-40.

Participation in Information Systems Research

Briony J Oates

School of Computing & Maths, University of Teesside,
Middlesbrough, UK

Abstract

This paper summarises the arguments given in the IS research
literature in favour of participation in IS development, and
suggests that similar arguments can be made for the
participation of all the stakeholders in IS research. It invites
readers to consider how much involvement they 'allow'
stakeholders to have in their IS research. The paper
concentrates on action research, and discusses the difficulties
of evaluating action research and achieving authentic
collaboration. It summarises the nature of 'co-operative
inquiry' and proposes that the research literature of co-
operative inquiry can help us 1) to examine critically the
extent of participation achieved in IS research and 2) to
develop further and understand the nature of action research.

1. Introduction

This paper seeks to encourage researchers in Information Systems (IS) and IS
methodologies to compare their rhetoric about IS development with their own
practice as IS researchers. In particular it discusses the notion of participation and
suggests the literature of 'co-operative inquiry' can contribute to an understanding
and improvement of IS research, especially action research.

2. User Participation in IS Development

User participation in the development of an information system is a major theme in
the IS methodologies literature [1-11]. Arguments for a participative approach
include:
- The users have more expertise than the developers in the application area.
- There will be reduced risks of misunderstandings between the users and the
  systems developers.
- The users will know how the system works when it is implemented.

- The users are more likely to be satisfied with the implemented system, and committed to it.

In addition, and probably most importantly, there is the ethical argument that "people have a moral right to control their own destinies and this applies as much in the work situation as elsewhere" [7].

ETHICS [8-10] is a well-known example of a methodology which has been designed around the principles of user participation. Other examples include Joint Requirements Planning and Joint Application Design [12], Client-Led Design [13] and User-Centred Design [14]. Indeed, many IS methodologies claim a commitment to user participation, although these claims should be examined critically. Jayaratna [15] suggests there are four levels of user involvement:

- Two-way communication. Management make decisions and communicate information about them to their employees. Employees can communicate their views to management.
- Consultation. Management deliberately sets out to solicit the views of employees before taking decisions. However, the decisions still remain with the management.
- Participation. Employees participate in the discussions and decision making as a joint activity with management. Management take the responsibility for the outcome of any decisions.
- Co-determination. Employees and management participate jointly in the decision making process. Both groups are equal partners, sharing responsibility both for their decisions and their outcomes.

Jayaratna notes that co-determination is very rare because of the political nature of current organisational decision making. User participation can also be perceived to be slow and costly, and not a practical use of resources. Mumford [11] suggests that few companies will introduce participative design purely on the ethical grounds that it is beneficial to employees, rather participative design will only be accepted by industry if it can be shown to contribute to reduced risk, greater efficiency and more satisfied and productive employees. However, the difficulties in achieving user participation in IS development do not disprove the arguments for it which were summarised above. This paper now asks readers to consider what level of involvement the various stakeholders have in IS research, and whether the arguments for participation in IS development also apply to IS *research*.

3. Participation in IS Research

Researchers are invited to reflect upon how much involvement they 'allow' their 'subjects' in their research. Are stakeholders in the research and its outcomes active and equal partners, or is there a more traditional professional-client differentiation? For those proposing IS methodologies, what opportunity have IS developers had to be involved in the development of the methodology? Brechin [16] states:

> "Research tends to be owned and controlled by researchers, or by those who, in turn, own and control the researchers. Those who remain powerless to influence the processes of information gathering, the identification of truth, and the dissemination of findings are usually the subjects of the

research, those very people whose interests the research may purport to serve." (p. 73)

Brechin also suggests that control over the formulation of the research questions themselves is a key factor in determining who really owned the research.

Referring back to the previous section's arguments for a participative approach in IS development, we can re-write them for the context of IS research instead:

- The subjects have more expertise than the researchers in their own experiences.
- There will be reduced risks of misunderstandings between subjects and researchers.
- The subjects will know how the research outcomes were derived.
- The subjects are more likely to be satisfied with the research outcomes.

And again there is the ethical argument about "the all-pervasive right of persons to participate in any decision making that affects the fulfillment of their needs and interests, the expression of their preferences and values." [17, p. 16]

As involvement in research moves along the scale from two-way communication to co-determination [15], so the 'subjects' become more 'co-researchers'. Experiments, observation and questionnaires give the subjects no opportunities to decide upon the data collected and interpretations made. Interviews allow a form of two-way communication, but generally the researcher decides on the questions, interprets the responses and decides whether or not to discuss the findings with the subjects. Participant observation does mean that the researcher experiences the same as her subjects, but again her constructs and interpretations might not be shared with those she is observing, who might not even know that a participant observer is amongst them. This paper concentrates on action research, a research method used by a number of researchers into IS methodologies, as discussed in the next section.

4. Action Research

For research into IS methodologies action research has been used by a number of authors (see, for example, [18-23]). Checkland [23] provides a useful summary of the nature of action research. The researcher does not develop a hypothesis (as in positivist science) but declares a framework of ideas (F) and the methodology (M) within which they are embodied. The researcher then acts in a real world problem situation or "area of application" (A), aiming to help the people in that situation to bring about changes which they agree to be improvements. While doing this, the researcher reflects upon the declared F and M, modifying them as necessary. There is an iterative cycle of action and reflection.

Outcomes from the action research can be changes in the situation and learning by the participants about F and M. The need for participation in action research is recognised:

> "A major theme of action research is that the practitioners should participate in the analysis, design and implementation processes and contribute at least as much as researchers in any decision making."[21]

But do those practitioners take part in decisions about the methodology (M) and framework (F), or is their involvement limited to the area of application (A)? Where IS researchers conclude that their F and M are to be recommended for use by

IS developers, have IS developers had the opportunity to be involved in the development of the methodology? In many cases there is an additional group of stakeholders involved in the action research project: students, who carry out action research projects as part of their undergraduate or postgraduate studies supervised by academic members of staff. To what extent do the students participate in decisions about F, M and A? And does their status as students mitigate against authentic collaboration?

Stowell et al [22] state that so far most of the action research literature appears to focus on the arguments in favour of action research rather than positivist research methods, and to describe what comprises action research as distinct from, for example, consultancy. They suggest that more attention now needs to be paid to how an action research study can be undertaken, particularly in terms of how the rigour of the research can be maintained. Stowell et al highlight some of the practical difficulties of undertaking action research under six headings: choice of a suitable domain, engaging collaborators, planning and implementing the study, the rigour of action research, false expectations and identifying useful lessons and knowing when to bring the study to a close. These same six headings are used by Oates [24] to structure the description of the method of a pilot action research study which was recently undertaken. One conclusion of the work described by Oates was that the IS research community should develop ideas about how we should evaluate the *process* of action research studies, and their findings. To give a full, reflexive description of the process, as recommended by Stowell et al [22] is a starting point, but how should others then judge the process described? For example, was the appropriate data collected, and in an appropriate way? And how should others assess the reliability of the claimed learning outcomes?

Interpretive research such as that described by Oates [24] requires that researchers are reflexive about their own impact on the study and the people involved. A particular problem area described by Oates was the conflict of roles, relationships and needs between the academic supervisor and the MSc student who were both also co-researchers in the action research study. The author and academic supervisor wanted to learn about the use of metaphors to understand a situation during IS development. She also wanted to practise and learn about action research. The student co-researcher was also interested in learning about the use of metaphors. She also wanted to analyse, design and implement a computer-based information system for her client organisation, and, probably most importantly, she wanted to gain her MSc. There was thus a potential conflict between the needs of the author and the needs of the student co-researcher: investigating the use of metaphors versus constructing a computer-based artefact versus writing a satisfactory dissertation. (Other stakeholders in the action research, with different needs, were the client and the end users of the implemented computer system, see [24]).

For Oates there was a conflict of roles: academic supervisor of an MSc student versus a co-researcher. This was experienced as an inner dialogue about whether to encourage the MSc student to 'do her own thing' within the University constraints of an MSc project, or whether to suggest to the co-researcher to follow up a particular line of enquiry regarding the use of the metaphors. Professionally and ethically the author felt she must let the academic supervisor role take precedence: an important aspect of an MSc project is that the student decides upon her own approach at all stages. The author had recognised this conflict of roles before the action research project started. However, she notes in [24] that she now feels that it would have been (at times) less frustrating and anxiety-inducing for her if this conflict, and how they might handle it, had been more fully explored with the student co-researcher at the outset.

There was further potential for false expectations and conflict regarding the assessment of the MSc dissertation. The author, as academic supervisor, would mark the dissertation. Would the student receive a fair mark regardless of her own findings about the use of metaphors, or would she feel 'obliged' to report a favourable outcome?

In developing SSM Checkland worked in collaboration with postgraduates at Lancaster to carry out action research projects in organisations. Outcomes included changes in the organisation as well as learning about, and subsequent modification of, SSM [18, 25]. Informal discussions with other IS methodology researchers indicate that they too have carried out action research in conjunction with students, although this is not always made explicit in the literature. No description has to date been found of how such researchers addressed the political problems of being in a position of power over their student co-researchers. How did Checkland and his staff colleagues mitigate against the possibility of students reporting outcomes favourable to SSM in the hope of gaining approval and better assessment grades? Also, as staff and students at Lancaster developed their expertise in SSM, how did they deal with the possibility of 'group think' or 'self- delusion', that is, stating something to be true simply because they wanted to believe it to be so? Checkland and Jenkins [25] do say that there are some disadvantages with action research projects:

> "They have a high cost in staff time; this and their excitement tend to act against sober reflection on the lessons learned; and the action research project manager has an exacting role, simultaneously *manager*, student *supervisor* and *researcher*." (p.49, their italics)

However the paper gives no further discussion of how these problems were addressed. How did the Lancaster researchers move from excitement to sober reflection? The action research project manager did not just have several roles, there was also the potential for those roles to conflict with one another -- how was that handled? The multiple roles of the students as project *participants*, postgraduate *students* and novice *researchers*, and the consequent possibility of students not being free to voice their true views is not mentioned by Checkland and Jenkins [25].

It was the struggle with issues such as these, together with the need for guidance on how to evaluate an action research project as mentioned earlier, which led to an examination of the literature of co-operative inquiry and 'new paradigm research' [26], where the emphasis is on doing research *with* people, not *on* or *about* people.

5. The Nature of Co-operative Inquiry

Co-operative inquiry is a way of doing research where all those involved contribute to the decisions about what is to be looked at, the inquiry methods to be used, the interpretation of what is discovered and the action which is the subject of the research. In its fullest form the researcher-subject distinction disappears and all participants are both co-researchers and co-subjects [17, 27-29]. Co-operative inquiry rejects quantitative research *on* people in the positivist paradigm because [17]:

- Politically it ignores the human right of persons to participate in decisions that seek to gain knowledge about them.
- Epistemologically it produces knowledge that is not experientially grounded in the sense that the researchers are not involved in the experience examined by the research, and the subjects are not involved in the selection of the constructs which are used to make sense of their experience.

Qualitative research is also criticised where the projects are designed unilaterally by the researcher. However, qualitative researchers do seek to validate their account of the subjects' perspectives by checking with the subjects themselves. Qualitative researchers do also engage in fieldwork and become participant observers in the activities of the situation under research. Hence qualitative research *about* people is seen as a half-way house between exclusive, controlling research *on* people and fully participatory research *with* people [17]. In IS there has been some movement away from the positivist paradigm towards the interpretivist paradigm [30]. This paper encourages IS researchers to consider whether they might be able to move towards fully participatory research *with* people.

Heron [17] states that the defining features of co-operative inquiry are (pp 19-20):

- All subjects are as fully involved as possible as co-researchers in all decisions about both content and method.
- There is intentional interplay between reflection and action.
- There is explicit attention to the validity of the inquiry and its findings.
- There is a radical epistemology for a wide-ranging inquiry method.
- There is a range of special skills suited to such all-purpose experiential inquiry.
- The full range of human sensibilities is available as an instrument of inquiry.

Heron [17] suggests that there are two complementary kinds of participation involved in co-operative inquiry: epistemic participation (concerned with the relation between the knower and the known) and political participation (concerned with the relation between people in the inquiry and the decisions that affect them). He suggests the reasons for epistemic participation are (p.20):

- Propositions about human experience are of questionable validity if they are not grounded in the researchers' experience.
- The most rigorous way to do this is for the researchers to ground the statements directly in their own experience as co-subjects.
- The researchers cannot get outside, or try to get outside, the human condition in order to study it. They can only study it through their own embodiment in a relation of joint participation and dialogue with others who are similarly engaged. Such an inquiry is an experiential, inter-subjective culture, using language.
- This enables the researchers to come to know both the external forms of worlds and people and also the inner comprehension, affect and modes of awareness of these forms.

The reasons for political participation are [17, p.21]:

- People have a right to participate in decisions about research design and conclusions which seek to formulate knowledge about them.
- This gives them the opportunity to express their own preferences and values in the design.
- It empowers them to flourish fully as humans in the study and be represented as such in its conclusions.
- It avoids their being disempowered, oppressed and misrepresented by the researcher's values which are implicit in any unilateral research design.

Shakespeare et al [31] suggest that the focus on participatory research is related to debates about feminism, empowerment and post-modernism. Feminist researchers have debated the relationship of the researcher with her research subjects and questioned the ability of the feminist researcher to be a 'knower' without its attendant implications of power over her research subjects. The empowerment debate relates to the political implications of research and questions of autonomy, justice and equity in research, with the researchers aiming to help people grasp the role of knowledge as an instrument of power and control. The post-modern or post-positivism debate questions notions of knowledge, truth and validity. Heron [17] also recognises these related debates, and additionally links co-operative inquiry to a wide range of philosophies and theories including holistic thinking, learner autonomy, Aristotle, Dewey, Lewin, Taoism and Buddhism.

6. Co-operative Inquiry in Practice

Co-operative inquiry is seen as an iterative cycling between and around phases of reflection and action [17, 27, 29]:

- Stage 1: A reflection phase. A group of co-researchers come together to explore an agreed area of human activity. They agree the research focus, develop research questions or propositions for exploration, agree to undertake some action which will contribute to the exploration and decide upon a method for recording their experiences.
- Stage 2: An action phase. The co-researchers now become co-subjects, engaging in the actions agreed and observing and recording the process and outcomes of their own and each other's experiences.
- Stage 3: An action phase. The co-subjects become fully immersed in and engaged with their experience. They may break through into new awareness and creative insights, or become so involved that they lose their awareness of being part of an inquiry group and metaphorically 'fall asleep', reverting to ordinary rather than heightened consciousness.
- Stage 4: A reflection phase. The co-researchers meet again to re-consider their original questions and propositions in the light of their experiences. As a result they might modify, develop or re-frame them, reject them or pose new questions. The cycle is then repeated.

The cycling of action and reflection clearly has similarities with action research as practised in the IS field. This paper however suggests that the co-operative inquiry literature has gone further than the IS action research literature in its examination and evaluation of the process, the outcomes and the extent of participation by all affected.

Heron [17] provides an extensive exploration of the theoretical background and detailed practical guidance on the methods involved. He describes three ideal types of inquiry: full-form co-operative inquiry (where everyone alternates between the roles of co-researcher and subject), partial form co-operative inquiry (where everyone is involved as co-researchers in the reflection phases but one or two initiating researchers are involved only partially in the action phases because they are not members of the profession or organisation in which the research action is focused), and supported action inquiry (where person A proposes action inquiry to person B, educates B in the use of it, B is then the primary researcher of his/her own behaviour and A has a secondary supportive role).

Partial form co-operative inquiry seems to describe Checkland's action research [18, 19] where he used SSM co-operatively with organisational members and he himself was not a member of the organisation. We could ask, however, whether the organisational participants themselves decided they wanted to include SSM as part of the action research, or whether the use of SSM was inevitable if they asked Professor Checkland to help them. Similarly, did the organisational members contribute to the reflection upon, and modification of, SSM and the framework of ideas, or was that the territory of the academic researchers?

Supported action inquiry seems close to the action research of projects carried out by postgraduate students at Lancaster where staff were not directly involved, and the action research described by Oates [24]. Where Checkland and Oates report on their students' work in the client organisations their studies can be criticised for failing to include the epistemic aspects of participation as described in Section 5 above. Where they joined with the students in reflecting upon their work and F, M and A they achieved more participation in the epistemic sense, but their work could be criticised if they did not consider how to ensure authentic collaboration with their students i.e. the political aspects of participation. Oates and Checkland also had greater political power than their co-researchers in that they proposed and therefore in a sense 'owned' the framework of ideas and the methodology.

Heron [17] explores in detail many aspects of co-operative inquiry and the skills and methods required. Space limitations prevent their discussion here, but Figure 1 summarises the broad range of topics he covers. Clearly, as he himself cautions, Heron's description of the nature of co-operative inquiry is only one person's view of the subject; we have to develop our own accounts. Additional literature on co-operative inquiry can be found in [26-29] and issues of *Collaborative Inquiry*. As noted earlier, similar themes are also covered in the literature on feminist research methods, empowerment and post-modernism or post-positivism.

Types of inquiry
informative
transformative

Sorts of inquiry

Types of knowing
experiential
presentational
propositional
practical

internally or externally initiated
full, partial form
same, reciprocal, counter-partal or
mixed role
inside or outside
closed or open boundary
Apollonian or Dionysian
informative or transformative

Data generation methods
standard
presentational
radical memory

Kinds of outcomes
presence
pattern
propositional
practical
meta-outcomes

Inquiry skills needed
being present
imaginal openness
bracketing
reframing
dynamic congruence
emotional competence
non-attachment
self-transcending intentionality

Validity procedures
research cycling
divergence and convergence
balancing
challenging uncritical subjectivity
allowing chaos
managing unaware projections
authentic collaboration

Figure 1: Indication of range of co-operative inquiry topics covered by Heron [17]

7. Conclusion

This paper does not seek to insist that IS research can only be carried out by those directly affected. Just as in IS development, there may be resource limitations or political reasons which prevent full participation. Individual researchers might find it difficult to achieve, as a graduate student wrote in 'an iconoclast's view':

> "If, like me, you find yourself passionately attracted to the idea of a form of research which is participatory, that doesn't do damage to the world, or those upon whom or with whom it seeks to research, then don't imagine it will be easy. It's much easier to be fascist about research, to decide what you want to know, to design the methods, recruit the subjects, run the experiments, draw your own conclusions and write up your own results ... I have a horrible feeling that it is all too difficult." (quoted in Reason [29, p.3])

But this paper does seek to encourage IS and IS methodologies researchers to examine how far they *can* enable participation by others in IS research (as in IS development), to recognise the limitations of their research and claimed outcomes where full participation was not achieved, and to be open about the motives, power and involvement of all the stakeholders. IS researchers are encouraged to be reflexive in their accounts, recognising to what extent they owned and controlled the research process. The literature of co-operative inquiry and its associated themes of feminism, emancipation and post-modernism can help us in this. In addition, the literature of co-operative inquiry on the process, the skills and methods and the validity of the learning outcomes can help us further develop and understand the nature of action research.

References

1. Avison DE and Fitzgerald G. Information systems development: Methodologies, techniques and tools. McGraw Hill, Maidenhead, 1995
2. Barki H and Hartwick J. Measuring user participation, user involvement, and user attitude. MIS Quarterly 1994; 18,1: 59-82
3. Bjerknes G, Ehn P, Kyng M (eds). Computers and democracy. Avebury, Aldershot, 1987
4. Cavaye ALM. User participation in system development revisited. Information and Management 1995; 28:311-323
5. Greenbaum J and Kyng M (eds). Design at work. Lawrence Erlbaum Associates, Hillsdale, N.J., 1991
6. Macaulay L. Requirements engineering. Springer Verlag, London, 1996
7. Mumford E. Participative systems design: Structure and method. Systems, Objectives, Solutions 1981; 1:1
8. Mumford E. Designing human systems. Manchester Business School, Manchester, 1983
9. Mumford E. Designing participatively. Manchester Business School, Manchester, 1983
10. Mumford E. Effective requirements analysis and systems design: The ETHICS method. Macmillan, Basingstoke, 1985
11. Mumford E. The reality of participative systems design: contributing to stability in a rocking boat. Information Systems Journal 1997; 7,4: 309-322
12. Martin J. Rapid application development. Macmillan, Basingstoke, 1991
13. Stowell F and West D. Client-led design: A systemic approach to information systems definition. McGraw Hill, Maidenhead, 1994
14. Eason K. Information technology and organisational change. Taylor and Francis, London, 1988
15. Jayaratna N. Understanding and evaluating methodologies. NIMSAD: A systemic framework. McGraw-Hill, Maidenhead 1994
16. Brechin A. Sharing. In: Shakespeare P, Atkinson D, French S (eds) Reflecting on research practice. Issues in health and social welfare. Open University Press, Buckingham, UK, 1993, pp 70-82
17. Heron J. Co-operative inquiry. Research into the human condition. Sage, London, 1996
18. Checkland PB. Systems thinking. Systems practice. John Wiley, Chichester, 1981
19. Checkland PB and Scholes J. Soft Systems Methodology in action. John Wiley, Chichester, 1990
20. Wood-Harper T. Research methods in information systems: Using action research. In: Mumford E, Hirschheim R, Fitzgerald G and Wood-Harper T,

(eds) Research methods in information systems. North-Holland, Amsterdam, 1985, pp 169-191

21. Avison DE and Wood-Harper AT. Multiview: An exploration in information systems development. McGraw-Hill, Maidenhead, 1990

22. Stowell F, West D, Stansfield M. Action research as a framework for IS research. In: Mingers J and Stowell F (eds) Information systems: An emerging discipline? McGraw-Hill, Maidenhead, 1997, pp 159-200

23. Checkland P. From framework through experience to learning: The essential nature of action research. In: Nissen HE, Klein HK, Hirschheim P (eds) Information systems research: Contemporary approaches and emergent traditions. North-Holland, Amsterdam, 1991, pp 397-403

24. Oates BJ. Using metaphors to understand organisations: A pilot action research study. In: Avison D, Edgar-Nevill D (eds) Matching technology with organisational needs. McGraw Hill, Maidenhead, 1998, pp 370-380

25. Checkland PB and Jenkins GM. Learning by doing: Systems education at Lancaster University. Journal of Systems Engineering 1974; 4,1:40-51

26. Reason P and Rowan J (eds).Human inquiry: A sourcebook of new paradigm research. Wiley, Chichester, UK, 1981

27. Reason P (ed). Human inquiry in action. Developments in new paradigm research. Sage, London, 1988

28. Reason P. Three approaches to participative inquiry. In: Denzin NK and Lincoln YS (eds) Handbook of qualitative research. Sage, Thousand Oaks, CA., 1994, pp 324-339

29. Reason P (ed). Participation in human inquiry, Sage, London, 1994

30. Walsham G. The emergence of interpretivism in IS research. Information Systems Research 1995; 6, 4: 376-394

31. Shakespeare P, Atkinson D, French S (eds). Reflecting on research practice. Issues in health and social welfare. Open University Press, Buckingham, UK, 1993

Promise and Practice: I-CASE and Rapid Application Development in Telecom Eireann

Tom Butler
Telecom Eireann,
Cork, Ireland

Abstract

In dealing with the challenges posed by the ongoing problem of developing and integrating an evermore complex and diverse range of information systems in a timely manner, practitioners continue to grapple with important issues such as increasing developer productivity and bringing quality improvements to the process and product of systems development. Many organisations have adopted CASE tools with such outcomes in mind. Previous research into the phenomenon of CASE adoption and use has been survey-based in the main, and has resulted in some confusion over the benefits to be derived from the use of CASE tools within the systems development process. This paper adopts an interpretive, case-based research strategy to examine the adoption and use of I-CASE in one organisation in order to facilitate an enhanced understanding of its impact on the process and product of systems development. That said, the findings of this study lend support to the view that CASE does indeed have the potential to exert a positive impact on the development process and its product.

1 Introduction

Practitioners within the field of information systems are facing the dawn of the third millennium with the discipline in crisis. True, certain aspects of this predicament are traceable to the 'software crisis' of the 1960's and 70's—the year 2000 problem is one hangover from this era, for example—however, the bulk of today's problems present their own unique challenges for organisations endeavoring to develop new and evermore complex information systems. Radical improvements in the productivity and quality of the systems development process are deemed necessary to meet these challenges and, in the face of an increasing scarcity of developers, computer aided systems engineering (CASE) is considered by many to be to be the *"silver bullet"* that will help resolve the new *"software crisis."*

Over the past two decades researchers have argued that information systems development methodologies help practitioners improve both the process and product of systems development [1]; however, doubt has been raised as to whether the methodology movement has achieved these goals (see [2], for example). CASE tools provide automated support for systems development methodologies [3]. As with the methods they automate, arguments have been made that CASE tools increase developer productivity and bring efficiency and quality improvements to the development process and its product [4, 5]. Nevertheless, these claims have not been entirely vindicated and questions have been raised as to the benefits that accrue from the adoption of CASE in organisations [6, 7].

Researchers argue that the development process is not well understood [8, 9]: it therefore follows that the same could be said of CASE-enabled systems development [10]. Certainly, the mixed findings of extant research on CASE adoption and use support this argument. Much of this research has been survey-based and falls prey to criticisms such as those leveled at similar research conducted on other aspects of systems development (see, [11] for example). Qualitative, interpretive research approaches are, therefore, indicated as survey-based field studies fail to capture the 'rich picture' of the content and context of systems development [8, 12] (cf. [13, 11]). Accordingly, this study adopts an interpretive, case-based research strategy and employs Orlikowski's [14] model and framework of CASE adoption and use to guide both the research endeavour and the presentation of its findings. This approach facilitates the attainment of the research objective which is to enable the phenomenon to be understood within the context in which it occurs; it therefore allows a contribution to be made to the cumulative body of research in the area.

Following the brief literature review in the following section, an interpretive research strategy is described that operationalises the aforementioned qualitative research approach. The case report is then presented using Orlikowski's framework, and extended narratives are used to provide in-depth descriptions of salient issues related to CASE adoption and use in the organisation studied. The penultimate section discusses the impact and outcome of CASE adoption in this organisation since the original study was conducted. The final section then offers conclusions based on the research findings.

2   A Review of Research on the Introduction of CASE for Information Systems Development

The present range of problems that confront practitioners in the development of organisational information systems has prompted many to seek means to improve the productivity of and introduce quality and rigour to the systems development process and its product. CASE tools have long been considered to be a potential vehicle for easing systems development-related problems and bottlenecks [4, 14]. A recent IFIP (WG 8.1) working conference on the systems development process emphasised the importance of CASE tools and delineated the contribution they can make to the development process [15]. Accordingly, it was pointed out that the development process has become strongly influenced by the use of CASE [16]. Are these claims for the importance and utility of CASE in the development process valid? The following brief review of research on CASE offers mixed results and suggests that such claims have little basis in fact.

Designing large-scale, complex, information systems that are free of problems demands a systematic approach [17]. Wood-Harper *et al.* [18] argue that the systematic analysis and design of an information system requires a systems development methodology. The role of CASE is to give automated support to a methodology [3]. According to Jayaratna [19], over a 1000 brand-name methodologies are in use all over the world. Correspondingly, since the introduction of CASE in the mid-eighties, the number of CASE tools has proliferated: in 1990, for example, Parkinson [5] estimated that there were in excess of 1,000 in existence. As with claims for the methodologies which they automate, Aaen *et al.* [20] report that improved standardisation, more efficient systems development procedures, and improved systems quality resulted from CASE use. Banker and Kauffman [4] found that CASE tools increase developer productivity (see, also, [21, 22, 23]). In addition, CASE use is reported to have a positive influence on both the development function within organisations—by providing productivity and quality enhancements to the development process—and on individual developers—by increasing their effectiveness and engendering the development of positive attitudes [22]. Other touted benefits of CASE include its ability to facilitate software reengineering and reuse, and in its provision of an adaptable and consistent development platform for developers [23, 24].

While CASE has promised much, research has shown that it has failed to deliver on its promises. Folkes and Stubenvoll [3], for example, indicate that the reported benefits of CASE are not being realised: they cite the Butler Cox Report to support an argument that the introduction of CASE in organisations has led to a reduction in the quality of systems produced. Recent research also lends support to the view that practitioners are disillusioned with CASE viz. Kemerer [7] reports that 70% of CASE tools are not used one year after their introduction, and only 5% are widely used, but not to their full capacity. However, more recent studies indicate that the situation may not be as bad as Kemerer suggests; nevertheless, this body of research indicates that about one third of all organisations who adopt CASE abandon its use within two years of acquiring it [25, 26]. Possible reasons for this are indicated by Sumner and Ryan [6] who, on the basis of a survey of CASE users, argue that development activities such as logical modelling, prototyping, generating design documentation, creating modular program design specifications, and design training are not made easier by the use of CASE tools. These findings led Sumner and Ryan [6; p. 19] to suggest that *"CASE is simply another technology which automates a series of isolated systems design tasks, without addressing the underlying need for 'improving the systems design process."* Obviously, these conflicting conclusions in research on the topic do not indicate whether CASE has had an overall beneficial or detrimental effect on the structure and quality of the development process and its product. Guinan *et al.* [10] provide some insights as to why this may be so. They argue that the use of CASE in itself makes very little difference, related factors such as training, project size, design quality, and the integrated use of CASE tools, all contribute to the success of CASE adoption and use.

It is clear, then, that in order to resolve the contradictory findings of extant research, a comprehensive and unequivocal description of the issues that lead to the successful implementation and use of CASE needs to be obtained. The objective of the present study is, therefore, to interpret, describe, and discuss the content, context, and process by which CASE is adopted, implemented, and used in one organisation (cf. [27]). A constructivist research approach was employed, in conjunction with Orlikowski's research framework, in the achievement of this objective.

3 Research Strategy and Method

The fundamental perspective of constructivist philosophy posits that reality is socially constructed [28, 29]; therefore, research into social phenomena should be interpretivist in orientation so that contextualised meaning can be revealed in order to enable socially-based phenomena to be understood [30]. Systems development is, in essence, a multi-dimensional change process that presents itself simultaneously within several related social environments or contexts—as a reality, it is socially constructed [31] (cf. [14]). Furthermore, these environments give rise to a complex web of social conditions and factors that shape and influence the process and its product [32]. Orlikowski's [14] model of the process and context of CASE adoption and use in organisations suitably captures the complex socially constructed nature of the phenomenon. Walsham [28] argues strongly for the use of such approaches in conducting interpretivist research. Hence, in order to contribute to a cumulative body of interpretivist research on CASE, the findings of this study are reported using Orlikowski's model.

This interpretivist study on the adoption and use of CASE in Telecom Eireann is informed by Guba and Lincoln's [33] constructivist research paradigm and employs the hermeneutic method, in conjunction with the qualitative research techniques advocated by the constructivist paradigm, in the execution of the research strategy. It is outside the scope of this paper to provide a detailed account of either the constructivist paradigm or the hermeneutic method employed: the reader is, therefore, referred to the works of Lincoln and Guba [31], Erlandson *et al.* [34], and Butler [12] for a detailed description of these issues. In keeping with the tenets of the constructivist paradigm, a qualitative, case-based research strategy was adopted: this approach involved an exploratory, single instrumental case study [35]. Purposeful sampling was employed throughout [36, 37]. The case design used has been described by Yin [38] as 'post-hoc longitudinal research'. Research into the selected case was conducted through the use of individual interview and documentary sources over an initial period of one month, with a subsequent follow-up study of the company-wide implementation of the I-CASE workbench some two years later. The general interview guide approach was chosen as being the most appropriate for this particular study—a semi-structured interview strategy was chosen [36]. Additional data collection methods employed included documentary evidence, and informal participant observation and discussion. Conventional data analysis, and techniques of reduction and display were used viz. content and constant comparative data analysis techniques, meta-analysis of qualitative data etc. [36, 39, 40]. Finally, the case report approach was used to write up the research findings.

4 A Case Study of the Introduction of CASE for Rapid Application Development in Telecom Eireann

As previously outlined, this study employ's Orlikowski's [14] *Process Model of Organisational Change Around CASE Tools* to provide insights into and report on the present interpretivist study on the introduction, adoption and use of CASE in Telecom Eireann. Orlikowski's model describes the complex web of influences between process and context in CASE adoption and use, and captures the effect that such factors have on the various participants in the adoption and use process. For example, the external environmental, organisational and IS contexts all influence IS managers' attitude and expectations of CASE. These managers in turn formulate IS function policy on the adoption and use of CASE with reference to the aforementioned contexts; this is argued to lead to significant process and context change. The outcomes of CASE adoption and use are, in turn, dependent on the preceding actions, policies and practices and, consequently, exert a considerable influence on the social contexts mentioned. Table 1 arrays the model's descriptive categories into a framework that provides a synopsis of the research findings under each of the categories indicated by the model. Because Olikowski's existing framework fails to capture all the dimensions found to be of significance in explicating the phenomenon within the context of the present study, Table 2 describes concepts and associated research findings that provide additional descriptive dimensions; extended narratives are also utilised to describe particular aspects of the introduction of I-CASE referenced in the tables and found to be relevant in this organisation. The extended framework thus attempts to paint a 'rich picture' of the process and context of CASE adoption and use. In so doing, it offers descriptions of important cultural influences that help shape the psychological 'intentional states' of social actors. These 'intentional states' include, for example, social actors' attitudes and commitments. Such 'intentional states' are considered to be instrumental in guiding the actions of social actors in the construction of their realities [41,42]: CASE adoption and use in systems development is one such reality.

4.1 An Overview of the Development Product: The Generic Appointment System

The Generic Appointment System (GAS) grew out of a business need in one key area of the Telecom Eireann's operations—its telephone repair service. Business managers across the organisation recognised the need to introduce efficiencies into the manner in which repair service workloads were managed, and associated service appointments made with customers. It was hoped that the introduction of this information system would eliminate the occurrence of unproductive visits by operational staff to customer premises when customers were absent. The GAS would also assist supervisors in their task of allocating workloads to their repair teams, which consist of operational staff. Both groups therefore had a keen interest in the development and implementation of this system as it impacted on some of their basic functions. The GAS also supports the operation of the company's ten fault-handling and repair centres.

A development team that consisted of a development project manager, a user project manager, two analysts, the CASE vendor consultant, one programmer, a user representative, and three user groups, as well as a range of individual users, all participated in the development of the GAS. The development approach adopted was consistent with extant RAD approaches described in the literature viz. a RAD approach employs small autonomous teams in prototyping-enabled joint application development with user participation [43]. The CASE-supported RAD approach saw development take place within the three month time period set for the project: however, the implementation of the first phase of the GAS took a further six months. As a distributed IS, the GAS is client/server application using 8 Oracle® relational databases that serve up to 180 windows-based PC terminals in fault-handling centers around Ireland, and a further 400 in operational depots nationwide. The GAS project came in on time and budget.

4.2   The Stimulus for the GAS Development

Although the business management within the company had articulated a need for a customer appointments system, the chief stimulus for the development of the GAS arose out of an internal need within the IS function. Senior IS managers recognised that development teams needed to produce modular, maintainable, systems in a rapid manner. IS managers also wanted to maximize the productivity of a fixed developer resource and skillset, and maintain product quality. Although the IS function had a brief, but unproductive, experience with SSADM, the return to ad-hoc development practices was equally unsatisfactory. That said, the GAS project manager reported that, due to a range of development–related issues, support grew for the acquisition and use of a *"common/generic development environment that we could use, cradle to grave, to give a total life cycle coverage."* Subsequent to a rigorous vetting procedure by the IS function's quality team, a computer aided systems engineering (CASE) workbench called Information Engineering Facility (IEF) was acquired from Texas Instruments to meet this requirement. IEF is an integrated CASE (I-CASE) workbench that operationalises and automates the associated information engineering methodology [44] using a set of tightly integrated tools; essentially, it provides architectural (planning), conceptual (structured design modeling), external (prototyping), implementation (procedure writing, code generation and hardware) and execution (integration of the product

Table 1 Organisational Change Around CASE Tools in Telecom Eireann (adaped from Orlikowski, 1993)

Categories	Concepts	Research Data
Environmental Context	*Customers*	Residential customers, small and medium-sized businesses and corporate customers. Focus is on product quality, price, product portfolio, and quality issues related to service delivery, fault handling and product repair times.
	Competitors	Market deregulation has led to national and international competition in corporate and medium sized business segments. Widespread competition in all market segments of the core business, e.g. telephony, customer premises equipment, ISDN, data, switched data, satellite, telemarketing, and mobile phone equipment. Some competition in ISP market.
	Technologies	Requirement for system integration across all existing 26+ IT platforms: the existing legacy systems, e.g. TPS, MIS, DSS, FIS and data warehouse system etc., are currently being redeveloped and integrated into an overarching superstructure of an operational support system (OSS) which will include network, business, administrative, customer financial and marketing support systems. 12 major new sub-systems undergoing evolutionary development: this expanding portfolio of new IS including 50 new systems and inter- and intranet platforms. The upper, lower and I-CASE vendor products have evolved into application development environments (ADE).

Organisational Context	Corporate Strategies	The major strategy goals are to transform corporate structure and key business process to meet customer demands and competitive pressures. Reduce cost base and streamline operations. Grow market share and penetration of customer base. Leverage IT to support organisational strategies. The strategic alliance with Dutch and Swedish PTT operators brings much needed business expertise and international infrastructure linkages.
	Structure and Culture	Company structured into strategic business units to reflect business process and customer/market segment orientation. Each SBU possesses its own IT sub-function. Joint management/staff partnership within an industrial democratic framework, participative policy with employee share ownership of up to 15% of the company.
IS Context	Role of IS	Move from traditional style systems development to systems integrators (using application packages etc.) and infrastructural developers using a process driven approach.
	IS Structure and Operations	Centralized IS business unit (IT Directorate) and decentralized sub-units in each of the company's other business units. Internal recruitment drive in the face of external developer resource shortages. Standard mainframe, minicomputer, distributed systems and network development, operation, maintenance and support. End-user support and technical support. Inter- and intranet development and support.

IS Policies and Practices	Apply corporate participative development strategies: a mixture of participative design (PD) and joint application design (JAD). 'Buy versus build' systems. TQM and process improvement strategies. Recruit internally—technical and suitably qualified administrative staff—and externally—college graduates and IT professionals.
IS Staff	240+ fill-time staff include two layers of senior management, development project mangers, business analysts, systems analysts (multi-skilled), programmers, technical and network specialists.
Conditions for Adopting and Using CASE Tools *Articulating IS Problems*	Poor integration of legacy and new systems. Broad range of technologies, ongoing convergence on standard systems and interfaces. Large portfolio of existing and planned development projects. Shortage of skilled staff. Year 2000, data quality and redundancy problems with poorly documented legacy systems. Ad-hoc use of development methods and tools.
Formulating CASE Intentions	Increase developer productivity and improve development process and product quality. Standardize development process and practice across IS function. Adopt an industry standard integrated CASE workbench after screening vendor offerings

Adopting and Using CASE Tools	*Acquiring CASE Tools*	Subsequent to a rigorous selection process, IT professionals from the quality unit selected Texas Instruments' Information Engineering Facility. Although developers were trained in the Information Engineering Methodology, it was not formally adopted; implicit or informal use in CASE environment was deemed to be suffice. Emphasis on automated support of development activities rather than enforcement of methodology.
	Changing IS Policies and Practices	Incremental introduction of IEF CASE workbench. IS management decided to rapidly develop a project from its existing portfolio using a small, tightly knit development team. The I-CASE environment would be subsequently rolled-out across IS function. Policy to select software vendors for new systems based on IEF use. Focus on development-related aspects of IEF.
	Changing the IS Structure and Operations	All developers and user representatives to be trained in IEF use to maximize productivity, knowledge transfer, and return on investment. Maximize recruitment from internal labour market. Facilitate reskilling of existing and new IS function staff.
	Changing the IS Role vis-à-vis Clients	Speedy response to and implementation of customer requests for functional modifications. More active role for clients/users in development and implementation process.
Consequences for Adopting and Using CASE Tools	*Systems Developers' Reactions*	Extremely favourable response by analysts and programmers to IEF. While the traditional barriers that separated both groups became blurred due to the code generation tool, analysts felt that they had more control over the end-product, while programmers took on an analyst role.

	IS Managers' Reactions	Managers felt that their CASE adoption strategy had been vindicated by the increase in developer productivity and product quality.
	Clients' Reactions	Clients felt that they had more input into the specification and design of the development product. Impressed by the speed at which a request for change could be processed.

Table 2 An Extension of the CASE Framework: Additional Descriptive Concepts to the Adoption and Use Proces

Categories	Concepts	Research Data
I-CASE Adoption and Use Process	*Team Selection and Makeup*	The development team was selected on the basis of previous experience, skills and attitudes toward working in a cooperative manner with fellow developers and participating users.
	Training	Training was conducted in-house at the development site. It consisted of three weeks intensive instruction in the relevant areas of the IE methodology and in the IEF tool set. The user representative was also trained along with the developers in anticipation of his active participation in the development process. A consultant from Texas Instruments was to stay on-site for three months to continue training on a hands-on basis along with providing technical support and troubleshooting expertise.
	Development Approach	A rapid application approach was employed within a three-month deadline. This centered on the prototyping (external layer) facilities of IEF. The sequenced, structured SDLC approach implicit in IE and IEF was dropped in favour of a prototype-driven approach to development.
	I-CASE Tools employed	Data and process modelling, prototyping, procedure writing and code generator and testing.

Project Management	The project was very tightly controlled and monitored; however, the project manager found it difficult to time-box prototyping activities due to the creative nature of this aspect of the development process.
Requirements Analysis	Individual and group sessions for requirements analysis involving both participatory and joint application design. User representative and programmer participated in the analysis process.

Vendor Support	Vendor support proved to be vital in the use of I-CASE during development: in supporting developers get to grips and understand its features; and in solving unforeseen technical problems in the implementation and execution layers viz. application program use of network layer protocol (DECnet) to communicate with Oracle over the local area network. Vendor response time to queries was of the order of 1-2 hours turnaround, so little time was wasted in unproductive problem-solving activities.
Testing	The bug-trace facility helped developer understand the functionality of IEF as well as locate bugs in the application under development.

Miscellaneous Problems and Issues	Developers found that translating the analysis findings to CASE modelling conventions problematic and would have preferred more CASE support in this area. The prototyping tools were considered to be "the jewel in the crown" of IEF: this allowed all the benefits associated with prototyping (improved user/developer communication etc.) to be realised. Simultaneous development of application subsets or modules was afforded by IEF—this was deemed to be one of its major strengths; however, it proved to be a complex activity and developers felt that more experience was required to take full advantage of this feature. Retrofitting of design features into the GAS application was made easy due to the tight integration of each of the tools or layers; several major changes were effected rapidly leading to increased developer and customer satisfaction with IEF.

into hardware, target databases, existing applications and data networks) layers that map onto the IE methodology [45]. Besides the productivity improvements promised by IEF, IS function management also viewed the introduction of IEF as a means to improve the quality of the development process and product, and to quickly reengineer and maintain development applications. Although initial tests of IEF were favourable, IS managers were mindful of the function's previous experience with SSADM; a rigorous test of IEF's capabilities and suitability to purpose was deemed necessary in order to fully assess its potential. Therefore, a decision was made to employ IEF to rapidly develop an information system from the existing backlog of projects. A senior IS manager, who was responsible for the bulk of systems development at the time, and who championed CASE use, selected *"a small, non-critical project"*, the Generic Appointments System, to fully test the systems development capabilities of IEF (from conceptual to execution layers) within a real development environment. A three month deadline was set for the development of the project's core requirements within one operational area; full corporate-wide implementation would then be effected at a later date.

4.3   Selection of the Rapid Application Development Team

A development project team was chosen with the special needs of this development endeavour in mind: that is, team members were selected on the basis of perceived disposition toward issues of demarcation and previously observed commitment to conflict avoidance. As the GAS was to be integrated with the existing Fault Handling System (FHS), two experienced analysts with prior experience in development of the FHS were chosen, along with a programmer who had worked on a related project. Both analysts possessed experience and skills in such diverse areas as traditional systems analysis and design, programming, computer hardware and technical aspects of network communications. As with all IS development within the organisation, a user project manager and a user representative were appointed to participate in the development of this IS; these individuals had a wide range of experience in the operational areas encompassed by the proposed system. User groups provided pools of experienced users, from the operational areas of interest, to participate with the development team to generate, refine, and validate the user requirements and system prototypes. The impact of this participative approach to development, which involved a combination of both JAD and PD, was commented on by the development project manager who stated that *"the appointments system development was really driven by the user group."*

4.4   On the RAD Approach Employed

The IEF development environment supports a structured approach to development built around the SDLC approach. However, the GAS project team adopted a customized rapid application development approach (RAD) for the development of the appointments system. Basically, prototyping was the primary mechanism used to refine user requirements and to design system functionality; developers omitted certain design procedures embodied within IEF deemed not to be relevant. This prototyping approach worked well with IEF, and was approved of by the IEF consultant who was a member of the project team. However, the project manager experienced some difficulties with the project management of the RAD approach: he found it difficult to estimate and manage development activities that were evolutionary and creative in nature—here, the difficulty centred on the use of user-led prototyping. As indicated, a consultant from Texas Instruments was on-site during the initial stages (data and process modeling etc.) to assist with the CASE enabled element of the development—subsequently, this individual operated in a support capacity for the development team.

4.5   The Development of a Consensus Approach to CASE Use

The project was well managed, coordinated, and controlled; a strong positive relationship was in evidence between the development project manager and the development team. The project manager realised that because existing development-related roles were heavily demarcated within the IS function, there was the potential for intra-team conflict to develop between analysts and programmers on the one hand, and between the participating user and developers on the other. Prior to commencement of training on IEF, the project manager met with the proposed team to develop a consensus approach to CASE use. Whereas the analysts and programmers had their own areas of specialty, and were expected to contribute accordingly, there was to be no specialisation in development-related activities associated with the use of IEF—this applied to the user representative also, as he was a highly experienced technician and was, therefore, expected to participate fully with the developers in almost all aspects of systems development. In fact, it was he who was responsible for the technical implementation of the GAS. It was clear that the consensus approach adopted by the development project manager and his team created a development climate that effectively mitigated any problems that may have arisen due to 'demarcation' issues between analysts and programmers when using IEF.

5   Discussion on the Impact and Outcome of I-CASE Adoption and Use

The forgoing analysis of the introduction and use of CASE illustrates that the IEF I-CASE environment delivered on its promise of increased developer productivity and process and product improvements within the context of a RAD-based development project. Some two years after the initial study, a follow-up investigation revealed that IEF had been adopted as the IS function's application development environment (ADE) of choice for in-house 'bespoke' systems development within the organisation. Thus, the initial management goal of introducing a function-wide development environment was realised. IS managers stated that the subsequent roll-out across the IS function was facilitated by the lessons learned from the adoption and use IEF on the GAS project. This allowed potential problem areas, particularly in developer training and project management, to be addressed, and enabled the benefits associated with CASE use to be achieved in other development projects. It must be noted, however, that only the conceptual, external, implementation, and execution layers of IEF were employed: that is, the design (data and process modeling, prototyping), detailed design and implementation aspects of the systems development process.

According to IS function management, IT vendors no longer refer to their products as CASE; instead, the term application development environment (ADE) is employed. Vendors, it is reported, are of the opinion that the benefits of CASE were never fully realised and, as such, it has not been universally successful or popular with practitioners. Accordingly, they have focused on providing an integrated solution, a so-called development environment, which is basically a well-integrated set of CASE tools. This approach, it is argued, places emphasis on the strengths of CASE, and underlines the contribution it can make to the development process and its product.

6   Conclusions

Previous research has cast doubt on the benefits of CASE use. The present interpretivist investigation joins several recent studies—both quantitative and qualitative—in arguing that CASE has the potential to improve developer productivity and the quality of both the process and product of systems development. It was seen that a multitude of contextual factors exerts both positive and negative influences on the ability of developers to realise these benefits. In accordance with Bruner's (1991) observations on the formation and influence of social actors' subjective 'intentional states', it was observed that developer attitudes toward and commitment to the use of I-CASE were shaped by cultural influences emanating from the immediate development environment (e.g. the project management style that incorporated a consensus approach to I-CASE use by analysts, programmer and user representative), from the organisational environment (e.g. the participative policy on decision making and the use of JAD and PD approaches), and from the external environment (e.g. the support and advice obtained from the I-CASE vendor). Nevertheless, because the development team was specially selected to participate in, what was in essence, a pilot study on I-CASE adoption and use, it is difficult to predict the impact that other less-well disposed or skilled developers would have had in a project such as this. However, it is not unreasonable to surmise that developer attitude and cultural influences within an organisation would be significant determinants in achieving the benefits associated with CASE use. This proved to be the case as IEF was formally adopted by the IS function for use in all 'bespoke' in-house development; it was clear that the CASE implementation process benefited from the lessons learned in the pilot project as IS managers used them to mitigate potential negative contextual influences.

Although Orlikowski's (1993) model provides an adequate framework from which to conceptualise CASE adoption and use, this research illustrates that it requires extension in order to explicitly describe important characteristics of the phenomenon. The extended narratives highlighted several salient issues that required explication in regard to this. It was seen, for example, that the prototyping tools were central to the successful use of the I-CASE workbench within the context of the RAD development approach adopted. Team selection and makeup were also important. Developers found that the tools provided to implement the IE-based data and process modeling were easy to use and well-integrated with the other CASE tools in the workbench. The flexibility and ease of use of the scripting tool and code generator drew special praise from developers and end-users alike: so too did the testing and trace tool. However, on the down side, developers found that translating the analysis findings to CASE modeling conventions problematic, and would have preferred CASE support in this area also. Finally, there were several technical issues with the CASE-developed end-product that required significant problem-solving on behalf of both analysts and CASE vendor alike. All in all, the web of relationships that relates context to process, and which are mapped by Orlikowski's model, were very much in evidence. As the preceding discussion and narratives reveal, significant reciprocal influences existed between the external, organisational and IS contexts and social actors involved in the process of CASE adoption and use. Nevertheless, further empirical research is required in order to modify and validate the model and to indicate areas where alteration is required when it is applied to specific research contexts.

In conclusion, then, the 'rich picture' offered in the forgoing sections of this paper provides insights into the complex network of contextual influences at work in the adoption and use of CASE for systems development. Simplistic models of CASE adoption and use have not, in the past, fully captured the phenomenon in all its richness. The extended CASE research framework, as presented herein, provides an appropriate point of departure for future studies, and helps contribute toward a cumulative body of knowledge on the phenomenon.

References

1. Blum BI. A Taxonomy of Software Development Methods. Communications of the ACM, 1994; 37(11):82-94
2. Fitzgerald B. The Systems Development Dilemma: Whether to Adopt Formalised Systems Development Methodologies or Not? In: WRJ Baets (ed), Proceedings of the Second European Conference on Information Systems, Part IV, Nijenrode University Press, Breukelen, 1994, pp 691-706
3. Folkes S and Stubenvoll S. Accelerated Systems Development. Prentice Hall, 1994
4. Banker RD and Kauffman RJ. Reuse and Productivity in Integrated Computer-Aided Software Engineering: An Empirical Study. MIS Quarterly, 1991, 15 (3): 375-401
5. Parkinson J. Making CASE Work. In K Spur and P Layzell (eds), Case on Trial, John Wiley and Sons, Chichester, UK, 1991, pp 213-242

6. Sumner, M and Ryan T. The Impact of CASE: Can it Achieve Critical Success Factors. Journal of Systems Management, 1994; June: 16-21

7. Kemerer CF. How the Learning Curve Affects CASE Tool Adoption. IEEE Software, 1992; May: 23-2

8. Butler T and Fitzgerald B. An Empirical Model of the Information Systems Development Process. In: N Jayaratna T Wood-Harper B Fitzgerald and J-M Larrasquet (eds), Training and Education of Methodology Practitioners and Researchers, Springer-Verlag, London, 1997, pp 53-63

9. Lewis PJ. Information-Systems Development Pitman Publishing, 1994

10. Guinan PJ Cooprider J and Sawyer S. The Effective Use of Automated Application Development Tools. IBM Systems Journal, 1997; 36(1): 124-139

11. Cavaye ALM. User participation in system development revisited. Information and Management, 1995; 28: 311-323

12. Butler T. Philosophy and Method: An Application of Hermeneutic Theory for Interpretive Research in the Social Sciences. ESRC Working Paper No 09/98, National University of Ireland at Cork (UCC), 1998

13. Myers MD. Dialectical hermeneutics: a theoretical framework for the implementation of information systems. Information Systems Journal, 1995; 5: pp 51-70

14. Orlikowski WJ. CASE Tools as Organizational Change: Investigating Incremental and Radical Changes in Systems Development. MIS Quarterly, 1993; 17(3): 309-340

15. Prakash N Rolland C and Pernici B (eds). Information System Development Process; Proceedings of the IFIP WG 8.1 Working Conference on the Information Systems Development Process, Elsevier Science Publications, North-Holland, 1993

16. Györkös J and Rozman I. Assessment and control of the requirements elicitation process in an CASE environment. In: N Prakash C Rolland and B Pernici (eds), Information System Development Process; Proceedings of the IFIP WG8.1 Working Conference on the Information Systems Development Process, Elsevier Science Publications, North-Holland, 1993, pp 135-227

17. Song X and Osterweil LJ. Experience with an Approach to Comparing Software Design Methodologies. IEEE Transactions on Software Engineering, 1994; 20(5): 364-384

18. Wood-Harper AT Antill L Avison DE. Information Systems Definition: The Multiview Approach, Blackwell Scientific Publications, Oxford, 1985

19. Jayaratna N. Understanding and Evaluating Methodologies, NIMSAD: A Systematic Framework. McGraw-Hill, London, 1994

20. Aaen I Siltanen A Sørensen C and Tahvanainen VP. A Tale of Two Countries: CASE Experiences and Expectations. In K. Kendall, K. Lyytinen and J. I. De Gross (Eds.), The Impact of Computer Supported Technologies on Information Systems Development, North Holland, Amsterdam, 1992, pp 61-91

21. Dahanayake ANW Sol HG and Dietz JLG. Automated Tool Design to Imporve the Practice of Methods Use. In N Jayaratna and B Fitzgerald (eds), Proceedings of the 4th BCS Conference on Information Systems

Methodologies: Lesson Learned from the Use of Methodologies, University College Cork, Ireland, 1996, pp 117-128

22. Finlay PN and Mitchell AC. Perceptions of the Benefits From the Introduction of CASE: An Empirical Study. MIS Quarterly, 1994; 18(4): 353-369

23. Norman RJ and Nunamaker Jr. JF. CASE Productivity Perceptions of Software Engineering Professionals. Communications of the ACM, 1989; 32(9): 1102-1108

24. Iivari J. Why are CASE tools not used? Communications of the ACM, 1996; 35 (4): 94-103

25. Rader J Brown AW and Morris EJ. Operational use of CASE integration: An investigation of the state of practice. Journal of Systems Software, 1995; 28: 58-68

26. Isoda S Yamamoto S Kuroki H and Oka A. Evaluation and introduction of the structured methodology and a CASE tool. Journal of Systems Software, 1994; 28: 49-58

27. Walsham G. Interpreting Information Systems in Organizations, John Wiley and Sons, Chichester, UK, 1993

28. Connolly JM and Keutner T. Introduction. In JM Conolly and T Keutner, (eds.) Hermeneutics Versus Science? Three German Views, University of Notre Dame Press, IN, 1988, pp 1-67

29. Berger P and Luckmann T. The Social Construction Of Reality—A Treatise in the Sociology of Knowledge, Doubleday and Company, Inc., Garden City, NY, 1966

30. Lincoln YS and Guba E G. Naturalistic Inquiry. Sage, Beverly Hills, CA, 1985

31. Visala S. Broadening the Empirical Framework of Information Systems Research. In: Nissen HK Klein and R Hirschheim (eds), Information Systems Research: Contemporary Approaches and Emergent Traditions, Proceedings of the IFIP TC8/WG 8.2 Working Conference, Elsevier Science Publishers B.V. North-Holland, 1991, pp 347-364

32. Kling R and Scacchi W. The Web of Computing: Computing Technology as Social Organisation. Advances in Computers, vol 21, New York: Academic Press, 1982, pp 1-90

33. Guba EG and Lincoln YS. Competing Paradigms in Qualitative Research. In: NK Denzin and YS Lincoln (eds), Handbook of Qualitative Research, Sage Publications, CA, 1994, pp 105-117

34. Erlandson DA Harris EL Skipper BL and Allen SD. Doing Naturalistic Inquiry: A Guide to Methods, Sage Publications Inc, London, 1993

35. Stake RE. Case Studies. In: N. K. Denzin and YS Lincoln (eds), Handbook of Qualitative Research, Sage Publications, CA, 1994, pp. 236-247

36. Patton MQ Qualitative Evaluation and Research Methods, Sage Publications Ltd., London, 1990

37. Marshall C and Rossman GB. Designing Qualitative Research, Sage Publications, CA, 1989

38. Yin RK. Research Design Issues in Using the Case Study Method to Study Management Information Systems. In J. I. Cash and P. R. Lawrence (eds), The

Information System Research Challenge: Qualitative Research Methods, vol 1, Harvard Business School, Boston, MA, 1989, pp 1-6

39. Miles MB and Huberman AM. Qualitative Data Analysis: An Expanded Sourcebook, Second Edition, Sage Publications, CA, 1994

40. Calloway LJ and Ariv G. Developing and Using a Qualitative Methodology to Study Relationships among Designers and Tools. In H Nissen H K Klein and R Hirschheim (eds), Information Systems Research: Contemporary Approaches and Emergent Traditions, Proceedings of the IFIP TC8/WG 8.2 Working Conference, Elsevier Science Publishers B.V., North-Holland, 1991, pp 175-193

41. Bruner J. Acts of Meaning. Harvard Business Press, Cambridge, MA, 1991

42. Selznick P. TVA and the Grass Roots. University of California Press: Berkley and Los Angeles, CA, 1949

43. Subramanian GH and Zarnich GE. An Examination of Some Software Development Effort and Productivity Determinants in ICASE Tool Projects. Journal of Management Information Systems, 1996; 12(4): 43-160

44. Martin J. Information Engineering: Books I, II and III, Prentice Hall, Englewood Cliffs, NJ, 1990

45. Texas Instruments. IEF Technical Description—Methodology and Technical Overview. Technical Report, Dallas, TX, 1992

Requirements Engineering for Rapid Development

Malcolm Eva
School of Information Systems
Nene University College
Northampton
Malcolm.Eva@nene.ac.uk

Abstract

There is a growing trend in business to develop systems using rapid development tools and methods rather than using traditional systems analysis and specification methods. Some writers have warned of a return to the early "fag-packet" style of systems development. This paper uses the discipline of requirements engineering to validate the use of RAD techniques in identifying and responding to users' requirements for new systems. It argues that traditional systems analysis depended on identifying explicit requirements that could be verbalised; many new information systems, however, depend on identifying different forms of knowledge and requirements. Techniques employed by RAD and DSDM are eminently suited to eliciting these requirements.

Keywords:

RAD; Requirements Engineering; Tacit Knowledge; JAD; Prototyping; ACRE

Requirements Engineering

The phases of Requirements Engineering(RE) have been expressed as Elicitation, Expression and Validation (e.g. Siddiqi and Shekaran[1], Loucopoulos and Karakostas [2]). Both the title Requirements Engineering and its emphasis on correction and completeness (implied in the term "validation") suggest a positivistic view of a requirement as a nailable entity. If this were so, then the systems analyst's job would indeed be straightforward and sloppiness be the likeliest reason for new systems failing to meet the user's needs. This does not seem to be the case in practice, however, and requirements are regarded as more elusive. Goguen[3] describes requirements as emerging from the social interactions between the analyst and user, rather than being "out there", waiting to be netted by a lepidopterist engineer. This attribute of requirements is more in keeping with the holistic, systems paradigm of systems development, as exemplified in Soft Systems Methodology[4]. This view demonstrates that the elicitation and validation of requirements is a more heuristic, indeed, a dialectical, activity than the traditional "fact-finding" exercise.

Structured methodologies and traditional systems analysis have used a fixed range of techniques to elicit requirements, such as interviewing, questionnaire surveys and document searching. In Versions 1 to 3 of SSADM(Ashworth and Goodland[5]), requirements were captured by means of a Problems and Requirements List, which was completed during the interviews and other fact finding activities conducted by the analyst. These proved a staple means of identifying current activities to be carried forward to a new, automated, system.

This approach presupposes a tidy and unambiguous definition of requirements, which incorporates problems with the operations of the current system. SSADM Version 4 (e.g. Eva[6]), while introducing a more detailed Requirements Catalogue, which recorded more information *about* the requirements, (e.g. owner, source, claimed benefits, solution, service level targets) did not make any progress on the clarifying of requirements, or how to identify them. The softening of SSADM with Version 4+ was the first move on the part of the structured methodology community towards recognising that requirements analysis (or elicitation) was a more complex cognitive activity than hitherto acknowledged (NCC/Blackwell [7]). This introduced a new set of investigation techniques into the methodology, such as prototyping, Business Activity Modelling and Soft Systems approaches.

In this movement, SSADM has tried to keep up with developments in the broader world of RE. The Business Activity Model(BAM), for example, encourages a two-pronged approach to the question of requirements: identifying the business activities that require information support (What) and understanding the various business perpectives (Why). These perspectives may be seen from a number of different viewpoints, and so the possibility of exploring the weltanschauungen of a variety of stakeholders in the system is now opened up. Vidgen[8] and Darke & Shanks[9] also recognise that early acknowledgement of a plurality of viewpoints is a valuable means of identifying unexpected requirements, and provides a basis for prioritisation and negotiation.

ACRE

This paper aims to focus on one RE model, the ACRE framework, (Maiden and Rugg[10]) in order to examine the validity of a particular systems development approach, Rapid Application Development. This framework identifies and describe various requirements elicitation techniques and maps them onto specific development circumstances. ACRE draws on the theory and practice of Knowledge Elicitation as well as traditional fact finding techniques of systems analysis.

ACRE is best described as a framework rather than a methodology. It suggests a basis for analysis, but does not identify stages, steps or sets of procedures to follow. A number of methodologies for requirements analysis do exist in the marketplace, e.g. RESPECT

McGuire[11], which identifies different elicitation techniques and maps them onto situations, in a contingent approach. RESPECT also identifies a series of stages for the analyst to proceed through, identifying techniques and documentation for each. This distinction between frameworks and methodologies is described in Jayaratna[12] among other places.

ACRE is concerned purely with requirements acquisition activities, not the other phases of the RE process. The framework offers 12 acquisition methods:

Observation	Brainstorming
Unstructured Interviews	Rapid Prototyping
Structured Interviews	Scenario Analysis
Protocol Analysis	RAD Workshops (ie JAD)
Card Sorting	Ethnographic Methods
Laddering	Repertory Grids

Most of these techniques are described and discussed in Cordingley [13]. This is not an exhaustive list of course, and neither do the authors claim it to be. Other methods, such as document searching or special record keeping, as practised in traditional systems analysis, can certainly find a place in ACRE, as can Task Analysis, CSF analysis or Wizard of Oz prototyping[11].

ACRE's special contribution to this field is in mapping these acquisition techniques onto circumstances such as package evaluation and requirements procurement, identifying management constraints for each and also mapping them onto cases based on the various forms of knowledge representation.

Knowledge Types

Drawing on work in the field of knowledge acquisition for Expert Systems, ACRE recognises the following internal representations of knowledge:

Future systems Knowledge

Tacit Knowledge, which incorporates:

Compiled Knowledge
Implicit Knowledge

Semi-tacit Knowledge, which incorporates:

> Recognised Knowledge
> Working memory Knowledge
> Taken-for-granted Knowledge

Non-tacit Knowledge

These knowledge forms all present their own challenge to the requirements engineer: Future systems knowledge is, by its nature, likely to be imperfect and incomplete, particularly if it is a greenfield system rather than a replacement. In such cases especially, the authors of ACRE point out, the engineer will need to look for the three pillars of process, data and behaviour [6] that will form the core of the system. Much information will be readily available from the baseline requirements, but there will probably be hidden data to bring out at a finer grained level. In such a case many of the final requirements will not yet be known, and must wait to be identified through a process of discovery and discussion.

Tacit knowledge poses a particular challenge, as it is simply not susceptible to explication in the same way that recognised knowledge is. Tacit knowledge is a term that comes from the work of Polanyi[14], who recognised it as a piece of knowledge or a skill that a person possesses, but cannot make explicit. Another form of tacit knowledge is the making of judgements, such as used in, say, tea blending, or a manager assembling the ideal project team, who can explain choices based on skills, but has trouble justifying how a sound choice was made based on personality traits and compatibility, or perhaps sexing day old chicks as described in Lunn[15].

A systems analyst required to specify a task based on tacit knowledge, is faced with a significant problem - talking through the task, or answering structured questions on the task are inappropriate ways of describing it. Another acquisition method must be found for drawing out tacit knowledge. Observation is one way; ethnographic studies allow opportunity for this observation, but in the context of RAD are impractical. However, the workshop context enables a number of possible methods to be tried, such as scenario analysis and task analysis. Kyng[16] recognises the value of presenting the user with a prototype as soon as possible when attempting to design tasks that use tacit knowledge.

Semi-tacit knowledge, especially Taken-for-granted knowledge, poses the problem of recognising what question has not been asked because, from the information holder's view, it is too obvious to be worth a mention. An example may be a the case programmer/analyst, promoted through a career path that started from trainee programmer, who has been tasked with building an accounting package. With no background in accounting s/he may not realise that a trial balance is a necessary facility for such a package, while the accountant did not even consider such a basic facility worth mentioning. As a result, key information can be missed with neither holder nor seeker of that information being aware(Grice[17]). This is another area where interviewing or description are unlikely to be fruitful; scenario analysis and task analysis may uncover the missing knowledge, but the expert/user may still make the assumption about its obviousness. Prototyping is a surer way of plugging that particular hole, the second or third iteration being the moment when omissions or misunderstandings are likely to be identified. (Three seems to be generally regarded as the optimum number of iterations in RAD and DSDM cycles[18])

Non-tacit, or explicit, knowledge is easier to draw out of a subject than semi-tacit or tacit knowledge, which is simply not susceptible to introspection, and therefore explication (Anderson [19]). This form of knowledge needs, therefore, to be mined for in a greater variety of ways than simply interviewing the expert or user.

This paper will now examine the use and practice of Rapid Application Development in the light of the ACRE framework.

Background to Rapid Application Development

A series of surveys conducted through the latter half of the 1990s indicate that a growing number of companies are using a variety of rapid development approaches to the development of their information systems (e.g. Wetherbe et al[20], Wynekoop and Russo [21], Eva and Guilford[22].

These surveys identified that user organisations used an approach that was called severally, "Rapid Application Development", "Rapid Prototyping", "Prototyping" and "Evolutionary Development". Another approach was identified which is widely recognised and rightly deplored, "JDI" (Just Do It) [22]

Rapid Application Development(RAD) is not a new phenomenon, unique to this time. In its original guise as Rapid Iterative Production Prototyping, developed by the Du Pont organisation, or later as an aspect of Information Engineering, RAD was intended to be a disciplined and effective approach [23]. With the growth of prototyping and development tools such as Microsoft Access, Visual Basic, and Powerbuilder, the surveys show that this approach has gained in popularity in UK and the US.

The variety of terms used by respondents in the above surveys to describe their development approach raised questions as to what was being described, especially with the appearance of JDI among the responses. To clarify the issue, respondents from seven organisations were interviewed in a follow-up study [18], to establish what commonality there was in the terms as used. The interviewees were all IS developers, or IS managers in medium to large organisations.

One company was an engineering firm; one was a manufacturer; one was a major insurance company; one was a local council; two were major retailers and the seventh was a manufacturing company, preparing to expand into a European market. The engineering firm's use of prototyping proved to be JDI based, but the others all showed disciplined rigour in their procedures. They had also adopted RAD (or Evolutionary Prototyping, or Prototyping) as an organisational strategy for their new systems development and accordingly had published in-house procedures and standards. As a result of these and other interviews, the following umbrella definition is proposed, which is intended to capture the discipline of a true RAD approach.

"A method of developing information systems that involves: a development team incorporating end-user clients and IS specialists, the use of rapid development software tools, and the staged delivery of a working system by means of iterative prototyping of solutions to business requirements. A RAD project will also involve the use of high level workshops such as Joint Applications Development(JAD), and the use of timeboxing for each delivery in the project."[18]

The elements identified in this working definition, especially the membership of end-users in the design team and the use of high level workshops, are those which differentiate RAD from JDI.

JDI (and a number of synonyms), was cited as a favoured approach to the author by a number of systems developers in SMEs during an informal survey conducted among practitioner developers during 1997 in the Midlands region of the UK. The inference of JDI, consistent with the responses to the survey in [22] is that analysis and design of the problem situation are superfluous, and the time is better spent in the production of data files and the code to maintain them. The significance lay not in the fact that the companies concerned omitted the use of any named analysis methodology (in common with 31% of respondents to the survey by Wynekoop and Russo [21]), but that the *activity* of analysis was held to be a barrier to timely production of the system.

There has been a suspicion among some more sceptical parts of the practitioner community that RAD is no more than a form of JDI e.g. Herzlich[24]. This paper is concerned with forms of RAD that disclaim any association with the philosophy behind JDI.

While RAD is being taken up with increasing enthusiasm by companies, as shown by the surveys and interviews cited above, there are concerns in the community about its efficacy in terms of meeting requirements, especially non-functional requirements. Vidgen, Spedding and Wood-Harper[25] for example, warn that the need to get to market can over-ride the need for disciplined, accurate requirements specification, quality control and thorough testing.

A de facto standard for such developments in the UK is Dynamic Systems Development Method(DSDM,[26] Stapleton[27]). This framework makes explicit attempts to address the above reservations by building testing cycles and validation of business requirements into its structure.

Notwithstanding the work of DSDM and the growing adoption of RAD approaches, there is still scepticism as to its efficacy, especially in meeting requirements eg.

Daniels[28]. If RAD is to be regarded as a valid, disciplined approach to developing systems, rather than as a cowboy's tool, it must meet certain criteria: it must significantly reduce production time [29]; it must deliver systems of quality; it should deliver systems that are maintainable and it must be able to capture and meet the user's requirements. Empirical evidence gives conflicting views as to the first(Gordon and Bieman[30]); there is more work to be done in this field to give more precise data as to its success in shortening delivery time.

The interviewees cited above all identified maintainability as a problem that was to be overcome[18]. The same study showed, however, that the systems delivered were of acceptable quality. This suggests that as a means of requirements capture these RAD projects, at least, met their objectives.

Such evidence may be regarded as anecdotal, however, and may give only a limited view as to RAD's validity regarding requirements acquisition. DSDM, for example, acknowledges the importance of negotiation between stakeholders when identifying project objectives, and the iterative cycles allow regular revisiting of the requirements for re-appraisal. After three such iterations, what surety do the sponsors have that the final requirements to be implemented bear a close resemblance to the original proposed requirements? DSDM includes a validation against original business objectives as a part of its testing cycle, but this is not a prescriptive method; it is quite feasible that with time pressures on the project testing may stop at the technical acceptance of the development.

To validate RAD's rigour as a means of capturing requirements, it is proposed to identify what methods of requirements elicitation are commonly proposed for RAD projects, and see how well they map onto the appropriate knowledge representations as described in [10].

James Martin [31] identified a lifecycle for RAD projects that took them from Requirements Planning to Cutover. The cycle as he described it is misleading in that it appears to be a sequential, waterfall approach rather than iterative. However, within the identified stages it explicitly identifies Joint Requirements Planning (JRP), Joint Applications Development (JAD) and Iterative Prototyping as the requirements elicitation methods. Both JRP and JAD involve intensive and expensive workshops, each with its own level of user participation, and each with its own deliverables. The Requirements Engineer would be expected to be more concerned with JRP than JAD, yet each has its own techniques for both eliciting and validating requirements.

All companies interviewed for the study into RAD practice [18] agreed with the importance of these techniques. Iterative prototyping was generally felt to be the RAD driver for both validation of requirements and production of working systems, but the workshop, by whatever name, was the principal method for eliciting functional requirements in the first instance.

While the workshops were the forum for this elicitation, the actual techniques utilized varied. Interviews, both structured and unstructured, did not feature. The sorts of techniques actually employed included brainstorming, task analysis, scenario analysis and critical success factor analysis. The levels of granularity of the requirements extracted by these methods were markedly different: task analysis and scenario analysis yielded precise requirements for information systems, while brainstorming provided signposts only. Prototyping, an activity sometimes carried out in the workshops and sometimes outside, between meetings, provided very fine grained requirements, and tended to act as the "mopper up" of what had been omitted and overlooked - particularly the Taken-for-Granted requirements.

This finding corresponds with ACRE:

"ACRE suggests that scenario analysis, prototyping and RAD are more effective for acquiring new systems."[10]

This is explained in that both scenarios and prototypes are simulations, or projections, of the new system and its transactions with the environment. (It should be noted that the authors of ACRE use the term RAD to mean a JRP or JAD Workshop, rather than the entire repertory of development activities. For the rest of this paper the term RAD will be used in the broader sense already discussed.)

A discordant note, however, has been struck by Purvis and Sambamurthy[32], who report that designers and end-users were not convinced by the effectiveness of JAD workshops as a design forum, and reported that the interaction between the two groups was less smooth than expected. They present a number of possible reasons for this, including the scepticism of some designers who are more used to traditional methods of user-interaction and requirements elicitation. Another, significant reason suggested is that many designers are not very skilled or experienced at facilitating such workshops; DSDM proposes that it is not the designer's place to be the facilitator. A disinterested third party, with specialist facilitating skills should take that role, partly in order to help manage the conflicts and negotiations that are likely to arise[26].

Table 1 shows the mapping of the techniques employed by RAD with the types of knowledge described in the ACRE framework.

Elicitation Method	Tacit	Semi-Tacit	Non-Tacit	TFG
Prototyping	YY	Y	YY	YY
JRP	N	N	YY	N
JAD	Y	N	N	Y
Task Analysis	YY	YY	YY	YY
Scenario Analysis	YY	YY	YY	YY
CSF	N	Y	Y	N

Key: YY - Strong Fit; Y - Fit; N - No fit, or weak fit

Table 1

It may be argued that JAD and JRP, being the fora for employing other techniques, do not themselves belong on this table. Their inclusion is justified by the nature of the workshops, both being dedicated to identifying and refining requirements in this particular context in place of the more traditional fora for requirements elicitation. As mentioned above, ACRE grouped both under the portmanteau term RAD.

The traditional texts on systems analysis (e.g. Skidmore,[33] Clifton[34]) all enumerate a different repertoire of techniques for fact-finding: Interviews, Questionnaires, Observation, Record-searching, Special Purpose Records and, sometimes, Sampling. For the automation of data processing tasks, which all involve non-tacit knowledge, these generally proved satisfactory; for providing IS support for organisations, where tacit and semi-tacit knowledge is involved, they are less helpful. Where a completely new system is in development, they are, again, less appropriate.

Table 2 shows the corresponding mapping of the traditional fact-finding techniques onto the different knowledge types.

Elicitation Methods	TACIT	SEMI-TACIT	NON-TACIT	TFG
1-1 INTERVIEWS	N	N	YY	Y
QUESTIONNAIRE	N	N	Y	N
OBSERVATION	YY	Y	Y	YY
RECORD SEARCHES	N	Y	Y	YY
SAMPLING	N	N	Y	N
SPECIAL PURPOSE RECORDS	N	Y	Y	Y

Table 2

This repertoire is clearly very strong for explicit requirements, and simple automation of existing known tasks, which generally rely on non-tacit knowledge; tacit knowledge is untouched by most. The entry for observation suggests that it will uncover both types of knowledge. In fact, according to Polanyi[14], this is not so; the observation will make the observer/analyst aware that such knowledge exists to be captured, but that alone is not sufficient to impart the knowledge - tacit knowledge requires an "indwelling". In such a case, Observation would be supplemented by a technique such as laddering, which would help clarify the rationalising process of the knowledge holder. For future systems knowledge, most of the traditional techniques would not apply (by "Future System" is meant a new system rather than an upgraded current system). It would seem, therefore, that requirements that depended on tacit and semi-tacit knowledge would be less susceptible to a traditional systems analysis.

The last area to be studied in the context of ACRE is that of the constraints applied to RAD developments and the corresponding constraints in the use of the requirements elicitation techniques. ACRE identifies eight constraints, of which six are recorded in Table 3, below. The elements omitted are time for acquisition session and time to obtain requirements. They have been omitted from this table because it is felt that these constraints are implied in constraint b. An additional constraint to be analysed is level of intrusion, referring to the extent to which users are likely to be discomfited rather than the amount of their time demanded.(Each entry carries an alpha identifier, for the sake of the table which succeeds the list).

a   Meeting is needed
b   time to prepare session
c   number of requirements engineers
d   number of stake-holders
e   friendliness to stake-holders
f   technological overheads
g   Level of intrusion

Pre-requisite conditions for method use per session

Constraints	obs	Int(S)	Int(U)	proto-p	scen	JAD	card-sort	ladder	brainst	ethno	rep
a	Y	Y	Y	Y	Y	Y	Y	Y	Y	Y	Y
b	N	YY	Y	YY	Y	YY	Y	Y	N	Y	YY
c	1	1	1	2	1	3	1	1	1	1	1
d	M	1	1	M	1	M	1	1	1	1	1
e	H	M	H	H	H	H	H	H	H	H	H
f	N	N	N	YY	Y	YY	N	N	N	N	N
g	H	H	M	L	L	H	M	M	L	M	L

Table 3 (a)

1

The heaviest commitment to technology overheads lies with RAD-based techniques. One of the heaviest levels of intrusion lie with RAD too in the time needed for the JAD workshop. In other respects, though, it does not appear that the pre-requisites, or support levels, for RAD-based techniques are significantly different from other techniques. Although rapid development has, by definition, the greatest urgency, only the one requirements elicitation event, the JAD, reflects the extra trauma in the process that might have been expected.

Conclusions

The different knowledge representations with which the AI and Requirements Engineering communities work highlight the difficulty that requirements analysis can encounter. Traditional systems analysis which focused on automating data processing

---

[1]   *Key; Obs   -Observation; Int(S)-Structured Interview; Int(U)-Unstructured Interview; Proto - prototyping; scen-scenario; JAD-JRP/JAD workshop; Card-sort - Card sort; Ladder -Laddering; ethno-ethnographic study; brainst-Brainstorming; rep-repertory grid analysis* **staff resource constraints indicate the number of people needed to use the method (M=MANY); e and g are marked as: Low, Medium, High.**
[1]

looked mostly at non-tacit or semi-tacit knowledge, and in these cases a fixed set of nailable requirements were identifiable. The positivistic view implicit in the title Requirements Engineering is appropriate for such case. However, if a proposed system is to provide information support rather than to automate, the requirements may start out as being more coarse-grained and a more heuristic repertoire of elicitation and validation techniques be necessary before the requirements can be agreed. These may well involve a level of negotiation between stakeholders.

Most RAD projects fall into this latter category. As a result, the knowledge types that RAD has to address are those more susceptible to heuristic, iterative approaches than to traditional systems analysis techniques. The JRP/JAD workshop, as well as providing a forum for identifying the stakeholders' viewpoints and negotiating priorities, helps to pull out tacit and semi-tacit knowledge factors behind certain of the requirements as a necessary pre-requisite for the prototyping. This is the aspect of RAD that separates it from JDI: while the finest grained aspects are left to the prototyping to establish, the shape of the system, the weltanschauung adopted and the otherwise hidden requirements are already laid down.

This conclusion would seem to validate Rapid Application Development as an approach to systems development in these particular circumstances.

To what extent RAD can and does meet the other criteria mentioned above (shortening development time and producing maintainable systems) needs further research to clarify, but in terms of capturing elusive user requirements it can be seen that it is a considerably richer means than simply JDI.

References

[1]   Siddiqi, J and Shekaran, M. Requirements Engineering, The Emerging Wisdom, IEEE Software, March 1996, pp 15-19

[2]   Loucopoulos, P., and Karakostas, "Application Requirements Engineering", Pub McGraw-Hill, Maidenhead, 1995

[3]   Goguen, J. Formality and Informality in Requirements Engineering; Techniques for Requirements Elicitation, In Proceedings of IEEE Intl Conference , IEEE CS Press California 1996

[4]   Checkland, P, "Systems thinking, Systems Practice", Wiley, Chichester, 1981

[5]   Ashworth, C. and Goodland, M., Practical SSADM, Pub McGraw-Hill, Maidenhead 1990

[6]   Eva, M. SSADM Version 4, A User's Guide, 2/E, Pub McGraw-Hill, Maidenhead 1994

[7]   NCC/Blackwell, SSADM Version 4.2 Manual, Oxford, 1995

[8]   Vidgen, R. Stakeholder Analysis, Soft Systems and Eliciting Requirements, Information Systems Journal 1997, Vol 7 No pp 27-46

[9]   Darke, P. and Shanks, G. User Viewpoint Modelling: Understanding and Representing User Viewpoints During Requirements Definition, Information Systems journal 7, pp 213-239

[10]   Maiden, N.A.M. and Rugg, G. ACRE: Selecting Methods for Requirements Acquisition Software Engineering Journal, May 1996, pp183-192

[11]   McGuire, M, RESPECT User Requirements Framework Handbook, 1997

[12]   Jayaratna, N. Understanding and Evaluating Methodologies, McGraw-Hill, Maidenhead 1994 pp 42

[13]   Cordingley, E.   Knowledge Elicitation techniques for knowledge-based systems", in Diaper,   (Ed): In Advances in the psychology of Human Intelligence" Ellis Horwood, 1989 pp 89-175

[14]   Polanyi, M. "Tacit Knowledge in Managerial Success", The University of Chicago Press, Chicago, 1966

[15]   Lunn, JH, Chick Sexing, American Scientist, 36 1948, 280-281

[16]   Kyng M. (1991). Designing for Cooperation: Cooperation in Design. CACM. 1991, 34(12). 65-73

[17]   Grice, HP. "Logic and Conversation" In Cole, P. and Morgan, J. (Eds), 'Syntax and Semantics 3', Academic Press, New York, 1975

[18]   Eva, M (1997); Strategic Rapid Development, In Proceedings of 5th conference of Czech Systems Integration Society, Prague, Ed J. Vorisek, J Pour, 1997 pp 47-58

[19]   Anderson, J."The Adaptive Nature of Thought", Erlbaum, Hillsdale, New Jersey, 1990

[20]   Wetherbe, J., Vitalari, N. & Milner, A , "Key Trends in systems development in Europe and North America",   Journal of Global Information Management 1994, Vol 2

[21]   Wynekoop, J. and Russo, N.   Systems Development Methodologies: Unanswered Questions: Journal of Information Technology 1995 Vol 10 No 2

314

[22]   Eva, M. and Guilford S; Committed to a RADical Solution, In Proceedings of 4th BCS ISM Conference, Cork, Ed B Fitzgerald, N Jayaratna 1996, pp87-96

[23]   Martin, J "Rapid Application Development" Pub Macmillan, New York, 1981

[24]   Herzlich, P., "A Quick Win For Testing", SQM 1995, Issue 25.

[25]   Vidgen, R., Spedding, and Wood-Harper, T., The Limitations of Software Quality: Toward a Model of Information Systems Quality Assurance; In Proceedings of the 4th BCS ISM Conference, Cork, Ed B. FitzGerald and N. Jayaratna 1996, pp415-426

[26]   DSDM Manual, DSDM Consortium, Farnham, 1995

[27]   Stapleton, J. DSDM Dynamic Systems Development Method, Pub: ADDISON-WESLEY, 1997

[28]   Daniels, J. "Why RAD is BAD", Presentation at meeting of RESG. Imperial College, London, July 1996

[29]   Card,D. "Is Timing Really Everything?", IEEE Software, September 1995 pp 19-22

[30]   Gordon, V., and Bieman, J. "Rapid Prototyping: Lessons Learned", IEEE Software, January 1995 pp85-95

[31]   Martin, J. Information Engineering, Pub Prentice Hall, Englewood Cliffs, New Jersey, 1989

[32]   Purvis, R and Sambamurthy, V. An Examination of Designer and User Perceptions of JAD and the Traditional IS Design Methodology, Information and Management, 1997, 32 pp 124-134

[33]   Skidmore, S. "Introducing   Systems   Analysis" Pub NCC/Blackwell Manchester, 1994, pp 74-85

[34]   Clifton, H.D. "Business Data Systems", Pub. Prentice Hall, Hemel Hempstead, 1990, pp 261-269

Seeking Alignment of Organisation Development in Information Systems Research

J.P.Kawalek
Sheffield Business School,
Sheffield, UK

Abstract

It has been of some concern that Systems thinking has been limited in its contribution to the growing debates on evaluation of and strategy in Information Systems. The strategy debates have been dominated by economics based frameworks or social theory. So far each have differing limitations for analysis, and for the construction or realisation of practical policy initiatives to achieve organisation development. This paper explores those limitations, and argues that construction of policy initiatives involving change can only be derived by the investigation and changes in the weltanshaungen (w) of the subjects and researcher.

This 'foundation of knowledge' construction, consistent with hermeneutic traditions, has been central to soft systems. However, this notion has not been applied with specific reference to the i. Strategic Information Systems (IS) policy change by referring to changes in the 'w's' of stakeholders, with the ultimate objective of development or innovation; or to ii. the constraints on action in everyday affairs, reflected in the 'w's' and actions of the subjects. This notion has been of some importance to the field of Organisation Development for some time, which (in part) explores the psycho-dynamics of the various 'w's'. By focusing on the 'w's' with specific reference to these two points, linkage can then be made to the issues of change, and more specifically the evaluation and process of that change. The paper applies these principles specifically to Information Systems change, and by doing so argues that it provides a linkage between systems analysis and strategic initiatives. The paper argues this point, and then gives a short synopsis of a case where the ideas were put to practical application.

Introduction: the trend towards the management and strategic focus in Information Systems

The discipline of information systems consists of the conceptualisation and development of understanding around some key functional areas. These are eloquently expressed in Jayaratna 1994, p.9, and consist of five different functions (figure 1). Recently there has been much interest in the Information Strategic function as there has been a realisation of the importance for organisations to consider future direction and environment as the basis for guiding their investments and activities. The strategic issues have had an impact as the need for design of information systems to support organisation strategies. Consequently, Information Systems literature has begun to focus on planning, competitive advantage and the 'strategic' nature of Information Technology investments, with the ultimate objective of reducing cost, risk and failure (see for example the 'evaluation' debates in Willcocks, 1994, Willcocks & Margetts 1994 and the risk analysis of Dhillon & Backhouse 1995). Alternatively, analysis tends to focus on the social dynamics of the change implied in the strategic initiatives (Walsham 1993), and the constraints on achieving strategic advantage (Kawalek & Hackney 1998).

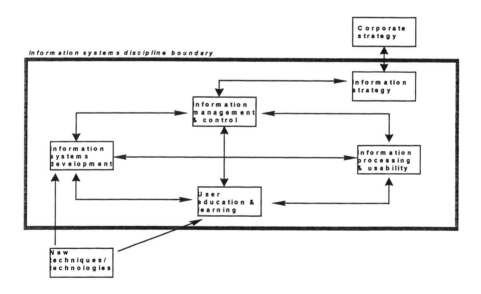

Figure 1: the five functions of the discipline of Information Systems (adapted from Jayaratna 1994, pp. 9)

The 'strategic' nature of Information Technology is based in part on the natural transcendence of the use of such technology beyond that of the 'efficiency' savings: rather technology should be seen as increasing the 'effectiveness' of organisations (see the definitions of Checkland and Scholes 1990, p. 39). Most literature on information systems strategy take 'effectiveness' of information systems to mean its contribution profit maximisation and competitive advantage, thus emphasising the 'rationality' of models used and the purposeful and linear strategies in planning. However, they discuss very few ways of how 'effectiveness' can be achieved or measured in practice, and at the point of impact, and usually do not refer explicitly to the 'transformation' as in systems thinking. By not referencing systems thinking 'efficiency' and 'effectiveness' often tends to be couched in the language of economics: it is said that the information systems can add substantial value if the change agent is aware of the contribution made in fitting or enhancing economic criteria. Certain literature extend the notion of 'fit' beyond the economic (Marcus & Robey 1983), though much of the literature tends to be based around frameworks of traditional corporate strategy and information systems specific frameworks: 'strategic' frameworks in information systems are commonly applied using (or derived from) the 'strategic grid' (McFarlan 1984), the 'stages of growth' framework (Nolan 1979), or value chain analysis (Porter & Millar 1985). See Ward & Griffiths 1996.

Problems with traditional Information Systems strategy

In the over-simplistic application of models and frameworks which direct strategy, there tends to be a number of basic assertion and assumptions made, which conveniently fit the assumptions of the dominant thinking of the Information Systems discipline. These are guided by systems concepts using ontological boundaries 'as given', and largely assume that large and stable teams are engaged in the delivery of database applications. Such developments are supported by mainly structured approaches which focus on rationalisation of data resources across organisational unit or function, and the role of the systems analyst whose role it is to 'discover' and construct the data model of the organisation (see Eva 1991 pp 116; Ashworth & Goodland 1990 pp 10; Cutts 1987 pp 23; Weaver 1993 pp 134). Ould 1992, 1993a, 1993b, 1995, Ould & Roberts 1987 articulate the principles of 'process' tools and techniques, and yet there is little that links these to ephemeral nature of boundary construction. Object orientated systems development as discussed by Booch (1994), Yourdon (1989) still feature the same dominant thinking of large stable units and departments for application development. In the late 1990's, there has seen the development of the popularity of products such as SAP R/3, which promise to help standardise routine and formal practices across seemingly traditional or assumed boundaries. However, all of these development efforts are still characterised by the following:

- a regularity of task in the use of the end product data base;
- their fundamental objective is that of efficient data organisation;
- development is achieved by Information Systems specialists;
- the tools and techniques used are project based with a focus on efficient resource management;

318

- approaches and techniques are most appropriate in large organisations where disparate data sources are rationalised and consolidated;
- it assumes to operate within the security of large organisations with stable organisation structures.

The awareness of the importance of organisational strategies may have directed the prioritisation of information systems construction or refinement, but still remain within the 'ontological' systems paradigm. The result is that the information systems specialist still continues to have a predominant view of building rationalised data systems with efficiencies in mind. This points to a failure in the traditional view of Systems, as a set of concepts to guide the activities of the information systems specialist in the dynamics of radical re-organisation and change.

These types of analysis are seen as 'classical' in their assumptions. They complement the assumptions (as articulated in the above section) and ignore the ephemeral and changing characteristics of everyday planning (for a complementary discussion see Whittington 1993), and see the user as somebody with whom interaction is a necessity *en route* to a rationalised data design, and in order to gain acceptance of the application with the implied assumptions as described above. See figure 2.

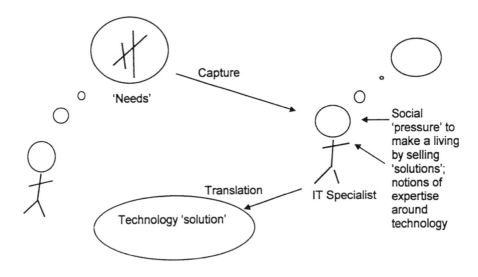

Figure 2: Traditional role for the IT Specialist. A recipe for a technology push?

Strategic frameworks of organisation in fact do not question the ontological assumptions and often make assumptions about the role as described. Ironically perhaps such analyses exist at a time when much managerial literature have emphasised a very different set of environmental circumstances. It is said to be a 'post-fordist' era, where customer expectations drive organisational form. Shorter lead times, flexibility, high aspirations of employees (Gladstone & Kawalek 1998) have been cited to result in new organisational forms which are seen as more responsive to environmental change (see Johnson & Scholes 1996). Older 'bureaucratic' organisation, based on formal hierarchy (Anthony 1965) is seen as increasingly less appropriate, and is reflected in aspects of the Business Process Re-engineering literature (see for example Harrington, HJ (1991), Davenport 1993, Hammer 1990; Hammer & Champy 1993). Outsourcing also reflects new debates regarding organisational form (see Ward, 1995). New organisational structures and forms are seen as attributable to a number of new environmental and economic pressures, and are rationalised against such pressures. Indeed, the well defined and highly demarcated roles and responsibilities, that were once a key assumption within the hierarchic and bureaucratic form, it has been claimed, has been somewhat eroded by new flexibility, flattened organisation structure as well as the 'empowered' workforce (see also Ezzamel *et al*) and 'process oriented' teams. Key roles of technology as a method of 'automation' have been replaced by its 'informating' role (Zuboff 1988) and by change which is constant, in method and structure of work practices and systems, both within and across traditional organisation boundaries.

The above represent some of the key dimensions and thrusts of Information Systems research but, whilst exploring the role of technology, many analyses fail to question some of the key assumptions being made in the field. In 'ontological' mode, application of strategic frameworks only serve to re-enforce certain assumptions such as those described. Indeed it is this failure that lead certain writers to criticise traditional approaches. For instance Ciborra 1997, pp. 1554.

> *Strategic alignment is defined as the inherently dynamic fit between external and internal business domains, such as the product/market, strategy, administrative structures, business processes and IT. Economic performance is enhanced by finding the right fit between externals postioning and internal arrangement. Research on strategic alignment has drawn a badly needed line between strategy, IT master plans and business processes and structures.*
> *Despite the wide diffusion of strategic alignment as a buzzword, elsewhere I claim that the research program that pursues this concept is lacking, if not bankrupt.*

Alternative approaches in the discipline of Information Systems

The realisation of the failure of 'systems' as a philosophy by the field of Information Systems has invited a number of researchers from other disciplines to bring to the discipline, alternative philosophical paradigms, as a way of bridging the gap. Walsham (1993) uses the principle dichotomy of formal 'structural' forms in information utilisation within organisation, and the informal everyday behaviour.

This type of analysis aligns the structuralist school in sociology and that of the 'subjective' hermeneutic tradition, and is built around Structuration Theory (Giddens 1984). Structuration is based on the dichotomy between structuralist perspectives which emphasise the bureaucratic and formal aspects of human affairs, and the interactionist approach which focuses on the informal structures and dimensions arising from human action. This theory has been playing a significant role in management theory for some years now, and has been central to much of the managerial agency and strategic choice thinking (see for example Reed 1988; Armstrong 1991). 'Structure' is used to define demarcation and hierarchy in organisation (bureaucratic) or societal form; rules, cultural norms, bureaucracy, formal procedures. Given the dynamics of organisation structural form (see Harrington, J. (1991)), there seems to be increasing debate regarding the epistemological sources of structure. Walsham (1993) has attempted to influence the thinking of Information Systems using Structuration Theory. The use of Giddens's Structuration Theory, however, has been used somewhat selectively both in current Information Systems research and in the wider management literature (see also Whittington 1992, 1993, Kawalek 1997) and, whilst being influential in academic circles, by itself has not been sufficient to influence the practice of the Information Systems field. This is because: (i) Giddens's work tends to be somewhat ambiguous in terms of how research is actually undertaken: is it from an analysis on the one hand of mental constructs (and 'boundaries') of the observed or is it, on the other hand, developed from the study of the economic and social context of the traditional historical-materialist tradition? The latter follows Giddens's own progression of thought (Giddens 1971, 1973, 1974, 1976, 1977, 1979, 1981, 1984, 1985a, 1985b, 1990, 1991, 1994). The danger with the latter is that structural form might be accused of being a construction of the observer, not of the observed. (ii) Walsham's (1993) work has failed to provide any *practical* way of construction into policy, based on Structuration theory, despite its obvious explanatory power. Therefore, whilst the philosophical issues could be argued to be relevant, a practical information systems specialist has not been able to translate the ideas into usable forms. Yet using social theory is not new to the discipline. Others have used bring Critical Social Theory (see (Flood & Jackson p.49) as a philosophy for instance. They too have not provided practical alternatives for guiding information systems practice. Whilst there is an appreciation by many Information Systems specialists that they need a different set of paradigms to guide their activities, in the absence of practical help, they have resorted to use traditional development methods and 'common sense' adjustments. Therefore, if any philosophy is to be useful to the field of Information Systems, those who are advocating new approaches, methods or paradigms, must also demonstrate their relevance to understanding and to deliver changes in practice that are in tune with the changing forms of organisation and their interactions.

'Systems' in 'epistemological' mode

'Systems' that have been used in traditional mode, which has guided Information Systems specialists for decades, have been based on 'ontological mode', ie taken as given knowledge. Such a mode makes the information systems specialist operate as if there are systems are to be found in the world. In this sense, when a system is taken 'as given', the concentration of the information systems specialist is the 'content' of that system. The effort then is directed to the improvement, re-design or construction of the components of that system. This explains the continuing pre-occupation of the desire to build and maintain 'efficiency' as a primary goal, but to also incorporate all information systems activities within this whole - hence efforts at centralisation. The dominant mindset cannot comprehend information processing or storage activities beyond their control having any value.

'Systems' in an epistemological mode, provides a fundamentally different way of design and construction. In this mode, 'systems' are taken as a set of concepts to guide the construction of boundaries. Of course there are no systems to be found in the world. 'Systems' become constructs to structure one's thinking about the world. Therefore concentration of the Information Systems specialist is on 'content' of boundaries that are created. Instead of the concentration on the content improvement, the shift enables the information systems specialist to consider the most appropriate point to draw the boundary, and to consider the rationale, objectives and implications of drawing the boundaries in the first place. For example, in the ontological mode of systems, users are often 'outside' interacting with the system, whereas in epistemological mode, users can be considered as part of a system to be designed. This means that the information systems specialist will automatically consider the mind-set of the user (or even customers!) when considering design or measuring effectiveness. See Nissen (1997). Larrasquet (1996) discusses how this form of thinking can be used for developing object oriented databases, not on traditional lines, but as dynamic and atomic information systems cells, which can join or disperse in tune with changing organisation forms. This point is particularly important in Information Systems strategy, where the change can have significant consequences on work method. It is important to be able to construct the boundaries conceptually and appropriately. However, traditional Information Systems Strategy does not in fact do this, as the stakeholders (including users) are often seen as an inconvenience to the process of strategy formulation or implementation (Kawalek & Hackney 1998).

The Case of Institute of Low Pay and Economics Research UK, (ILPER)[i]

The discipline and practice of Organisation Development has long used the 'subjective' ('w's') as a key approach in aiding policy 'interventions'. The case synopsis that follows, is one which operationalised the approach as described in figure 3. Rather than using systems or strategic concept in 'ontological' mode, it delved deep into the minds of a number of stakeholder groups in order to develop insight *and* practical policy. It recognised the difficulty in constructing practical policy from the 'w's' of the stakeholders, but tackled the problem by being open with the recognition that :

- there was no one best approach;
- learning was a central element for the stakeholders, as well as the information Systems specialist;
- the information systems specialist acted as facilitator, rather than expert;
- learning about conceptual boundaries was central to understanding the anxieties of the stakeholders;
- it was the stakeholders who played a central role in policy initiatives (not a privileged set of managers or Information Systems groups);
- anxieties were expressed in the psycho-dynamics of everyday attitudes and assertions;
- what was expressed by the stakeholders was not 'reality' only an expressed form of their version of it;
- working notes and ideas were opened up for discussion at all times, and finally used on a 'strategy day' to operationalise and prioritise policy, and to understand the consequences of any action or inaction.

Organisations face strategic challenges when changes complicate its ability to accomplish its inherited key or 'primary' task. This simple case demonstrates that the changes in the primary task has made some of the technology initiatives more complex, in that they become an organisation development problem, as well as one of information Systems strategy, or development.

Since organisation environments change in an evolutionary manner, an organisation can postpone making changes in its primary task, and this can impact on the conceptualisation of the appropriateness of a set of strategic objectives. As a result, it appears to 'drift' and certain managers tend to take up bits or parts of the primary task independently - rather subconsciously at times. Sometimes there is a gap between what the organisation believes to be its primary task, based on its history, and what in fact people are increasingly *doing* as part of their human activity systems. In this gap we can experience the organisational psycho-dynamics, often expressed in a number of ways, particularly as anxieties or anger, frustration and the like. The following case is one where the organisation were developing their web page, and the author was lucky enough to have been asked for some technical help. This technical help developed into a research exercise, because the format and the content of the web profile, became a bone of some contention and difficulty.

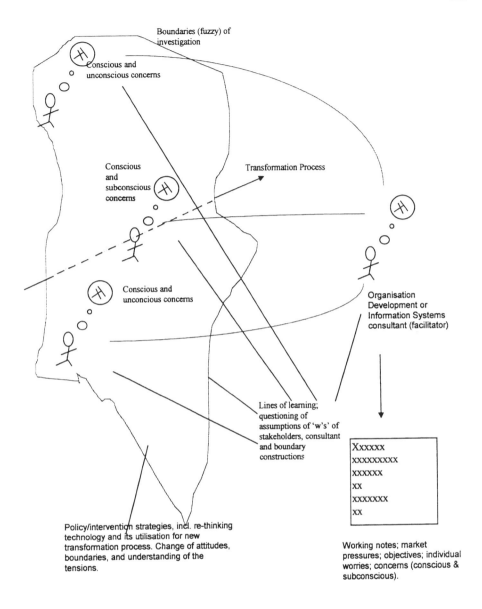

Boundaries (fuzzy) of investigation

Conscious and unconscious concerns

Conscious and subconscious concerns

Transformation Process

Conscious and unconcious concerns

Organisation Development or Information Systems consultant (facilitator)

Lines of learning; questioning of assumptions of 'w's' of stakeholders, consultant and boundary constructions

Xxxxxx
xxxxxxxxx
xxxxxx
xx
xxxxxxx
xx

Policy/intervention strategies, incl. re-thinking technology and its utilisation for new transformation process. Change of attitudes, boundaries, and understanding of the tensions.

Working notes; market pressures; objectives; individual worries; concerns (conscious & subconscious).

Figure 3: Lines of learning. The approach and assumptions taken in action research at ILPER

A policy research Institute called the *Institute of Low Pay and Economics Research* (ILPER) was committed to funding and disseminating research on or around poverty, homelessness, low pay, unemployment. It had been successful in attracting funds over the years and producing well-regarded research reports. The senior staff had produced a strategic plan a few years before the consultation, but major difficulties remained. Most important, fund-raising was falling off, while other Institutes around the UK were competing successfully for the money and visibility: the world wide web formed part of a strategic plan to develop the ILPER marketing effort. The executive director, Josef, a man in his early sixties, with charisma and connections to the rich and powerful, could still command attention and raise money from his personal network. Lately he seemed to be working harder than ever and was clearly near the end of his career. His was a common story: *"... to be honest, I've had enough. If I did not have a daughter at university, I would have gone a while ago."*

Another feature that was striking at the outset was the chronic conflict between the fund-raising and research divisions. The latter felt that the former tried to dictate research priorities based on their reading of donor interests; *"...they tend to be a bit bureaucratic..."*. The friction came out in a variety of ways. The following are direct quotations of the fund-raising department commenting on the researchers: *"...they are not the most organised bunch..."*; *"...research can be a lonely exercise, and I think they suffer a bit from their isolation..."*; *"They ignore us completely most of the time .... until we get the business...."*. It seemed that the fund-raising department felt in turn that the research division was unreliable, did not meet promised deadlines, and sometimes embarrassed the Institute with incomplete work.

There are many ways of interpreting the situation. The classic strategic view would be to interpret the situation in terms of 'fit' with the environment, and the conclusion would have been to develop strategies that would have developed this "fit", without reference to the 'w's' of the stakeholder groups. Thus new market opportunities would be analysed, new business, and new applications to meet the changed circumstances. Indeed this is exactly what happened in this case. New database applications were set up for 'strategic' purposes, which detailed over 20,000 small to medium sized companies (seen as potential partners for funding, and a potential new market). A front end Geographical Information System was developed and the Institute had employed a small team of technical support staff and two programmers. Furthermore, a WWW profile was being developed in order to help the marketing effort. A new costings application was developed which costed each research project very precisely, with rigorous budgeting and control mechanisms. These initiatives were taken in 1996, and were the result of a consultation exercise which, on investigation, had focused on the 'strategic' objectives of the Institute, with a view to discovering and prioritising of application developments. This was seen as 'classic' in its approach to Information Systems strategy.

None of the personnel were Information Systems practitioners, though many had good technical and computing skills. Indeed they were recruited as such because the Information Systems exercise had been done (or so it was said), during the previous consultation exercise. It was perceived that once the Information Systems strategy was formulated, then implementation was to be done by technical personnel.

During the first contacts with the organisation, a loosely framed set of interviews took place, and the above two paragraphs are the summary of some of the niggling issues that seemed to be apparent. Of course interpreting and prioritising of the key issues was not the focus of involvement, and could have been interpreted in many different ways. For instance the personnel may have been seen to be anxious about the relatively imminent departure of Josef: they perhaps may have worried that Institute would collapse if he were not its director. We could interpret this as presenting issues and dilemmas of systems and of organisational design: for instance we might inquire as to the nature of the boundary between the research and fund-raising divisions. How did they collaborate in planning the portfolio of research. Perhaps the research unit would be better outsourced, and the demand for research 'pulled' by demand, and in competition with other research Institutes? Alternatively it may have been better organised so that the research group were better embedded into the everyday difficulties of fund-raising. This is a question of boundary construction in epistemological mode. Yet the senior group had produced a reasonable strategic plan, based on the notions of strategic management, but they seemed unable to trust one another sufficiently nor were very skilled to steer the process of organisational change. They displayed an inability to develop learning and understanding of particular 'w's', or in dealing with issues of consensus. The strategy had left old wounds apparently un-touched.

Taking a 'rational' scientific view, of an objective reality, as in traditional science, the approach was to develop a marketing plan, to create new research products, to create a web site, software applications and so on. In this case however, the approach did not pay attention in sufficient detail over the issues of 'primary task'. It would be reasonable to assume that an organisation such as the ILPER were capable of devising the practical plans. However it must be said that the strategic plan displayed considerable technical merit in using modern management concepts such as market share, demographic analysis, market segmentation and distribution channels. However they found difficulty in making this work to make significant long term impact because of the unacknowledged experiences ('w's'), related to the primary task. It obstructed their thinking to such an extent that the WWW designs contained information about professional excellence, qualifications of the researchers and past 'success stories'. Little marketing was undertaken by discovering what clients and potential buyers might need. Yet these are outcomes, not the cause. To explore hypotheses about the ambiguities of primary task it is sometimes worth examining its history. ILPER was founded in the late sixties when a strong Labour dominated trades union movement helped develop a consensus that a modern western society could no longer tolerate the extremes of poverty among its citizens. There was considerable faith that government programmes could help poor people, and that cities could develop and renew their communities. In addition, scholars were creating a new "policy science" based on methods of evaluating social programs and assessing how social programs were and could be implemented. ILPER was a creature of its time. Under these conditions, its research program emerged from its environment. ILPER managers did not have to invent it nor convince donors of its legitimacy. It seemed that at the point where the organisation was studied as action research, the organisation dependent on donors faces a fundamental choice: do they raise money by doing what potential donors are interested in, or do they decide what they want to do and then find potential donors. In the first option, the primary task is to satisfy donors, in the second, to satisfy themselves or to follow their own value set (v). Organisations with deep roots in a donor community, such as a religious organisation or a hospital, often face no risk since the values that link the organisation and the donors are held sacred by both, and the 'v's' are shared. Because of the liberal consensus, in its earlier years ILPER could decide what research to do and then find money to support the research. It managed the uncertainty this choice imposed by relying on Josef to raise money from his own network of shared ILPER contacts' 'v's'. Increasingly, ILPER had to create its own research categories, its markets and its profile, in order to stimulate funds. Potential donors became customers and ILPER fund-raising began to express the 'v's' of the customers rather than their own. However, this shift was not acknowledged, and was in fact denied by Josef, by assuring its staff that the Institute was a "...*research Institute which fought for the abolition of poverty...*"

Since ILPER had begun to act like a service institution, it could only develop by taking on its new primary task, and had undertaken consultancy projects, and the fund-raising section had become so dominant that completing a research project had become less important than securing its funding. The tensions expressed by some of the earlier quotes was explained by this. Some apparently talented researchers had recently left. Thus by drifting from one primary task to another ILPER appeared to losing its vitality, and staff were uncommitted and seemed to be pre-occupied with over work and overtime rates.

The strategic directives document was also quite revealing. Quoted in the document was one consultant reporting of Josef's insistence that the Institute would not specialise in particular areas. This statement in the document can be usefully interpreted in a particular manner. In stressing the Institute's uniqueness it helps deny its growing dependence on donor tastes and preferences; in resisting specialisation it masks the inevitable opportunism associated with chasing money by cloaking it in principles and clouding the 'fantasy' that the ILPER can fund its own 'v's'. The tone of the document was resolutely technical, referring to audiences and segments. It conveyed a message of mastery, science, quality and efficacy. Further, there was a quotation from the head of research who noted that she did not require her professionals to write proposals. Fund-raising was in charge of this "lower" function.

These issues were discussed at length on a strategy day and practical proposals were formulated by the participating stakeholders, and lists of consequences of each were drawn up. It is too early to be able to comment on the outcome, but there was positive feedback "...*I did not want to come today, but I'm glad that I did now. I have never enjoyed a strategy day before…".*

Conclusions: the need for a discourse on the methods in Information Systems Strategy

The nature of the discipline of Information Systems implies that it has a direct effect on practical issues. Indeed the approach taken in the case described was highly practical, in that the working notes provided a discussion forum which moved beyond the 'hard' application of managerial consulting practice. The real issues of organisation was opened up to debate, and it was the ability of the subjects (stakeholders) to articulate the key issues that meant that the organisation was able to move and direct policy. The early installation of new technologies in fact hid the key issues which were seen in this case as a hedging of the central issue. In the opening of the debate, the 'w's' of the subjects were investigated and challenged. However, the process was discursive, and resulted in the subjects being able to discover and develop their own 'w's'. This notion has been explored in the social sciences. For example Freire (1972a, 1972b, 1973, 1974) suggests that the process of learning should be 'liberating' and that the necessary prerequisites for developing a 'critical consciousness' by a liberating and authentic dialogue of on-going learning and reflection. It means that the traditional education processes are overly 'passive' and assume that the learner absorbs concepts and constructions of the teacher, often alienating the learner by assuming the learner absorbs 'factual' knowledge, which is a form of social hegemony (see also Blauner 1964). This, argues Friere (1972a), tends not to *question* the social assumptions (such as the key constraints on action - 'structures' and 'boundaries') and associated vested interests. Rather, he proposes, that the educators role is "…*to propose problems about the codified existential situations in order to help the learners arrive at an increasingly critical view of their [own] reality.*" (Freire 1972b, p. 36). The dialogue for education is therefore based not on factual knowledge, but on reflexivity on the learners own experiences: "…*Such a programme is an educative and therapeutic catalyst because the intent is to engender, through reflection, new (theory-laden) self-understanding*" (Johnson 1995, p. 501). It represents an agenda where the Information Systems specialist "expert" may take on the role of facilitator to achieve self reflective learning in the subjects (which includes the Information Systems specialist), to develop new strategies and develop knowledge that is practical and adequate for resolving perceived problems, and by doing so, act as a catalyst of transformative dynamics. Reflection on the structural and bureaucratic 'constraints' is seen as part of that liberation, and epistemology returns to focus on the individual 'w's' of the subject. Methods in Information Systems strategy can usefully embrace such thinking, and this enables the underpinning of the function to move beyond the 'elitist' or 'managerialist' imposition of strategic frameworks, which may impose poor 'solutions' in the organisation transformative dynamic which are embedded within its people.

References

Anthony, R. N. (1965), *Planning and control systems : a framework for analysis*, Harvard University Graduate School of Business Administration.

Ashworth, C. & Goodland, M., (1990), *SSADM: A practical approach*, McGraw-Hill, Maidenhead.

Booch, G., (1994), 'Object oriented analysis and design with applications', Benjamin/Cummings Publishing Company, California

Checkland, P. & Scholes, J., (1990) *Soft systems methodology in action*, Wiley, Chichester.

Yourdon,E., (1994), Object oriented systems design, Prentice Hall, Englewood Cliffs.

Cutts, G., (1991), *Structured systems and design methodology*, second edition, Blackwell Scientific, London.

Davenport, T.H. (1993) *Process innovation: re-engineering work through information technology*, Harvard Business Press, Boston.

Dhillon, G. & Backhouse, J., (1996), Risks in the use of information technology within organisations, *International Journal of Information Management*, **16,** 1, 65-74.

Eva, M., (1991), *SSADM version 4: A user's guide*, McGraw-Hill, London.

Ezzamel, M., Lilley, S., Willmott., (1994), The 'new organisation' and the 'new managerial work', *European Management Journal*, **12**, 4, 454-461.

Flood, R.I. & Jackson., M.C., (1991), Creative problem solving, total systems intervention, Wiley, Chichester.

Freire, P., (1972a), Pedagogy of the oppressed, Penguin, Harmondsworth.

Freire, P., (1972b), Cultural Action for freedom, Penguin, Harmondsworth.

Giddens, A., (1971), *Capitalism and modern social theory*, University Press, Cambridge

Giddens, A., (1973), *The class structure of advanced societies*, Hutchinson, London
Giddens, A., (1974), *Positivism and sociology*, Heinemann, London

Giddens, A., (1976), *New rules of sociological method*, Hutchinson, London

Giddens, A., (1977), *Studies in social and political theory*, Hutchinson, London

Giddens, A., (1979), *Central problems in social theory: action, structure and contraditions in social analysis*, Macmillan, London

Giddens, A., (1981), *A contemporary critique of Historical Materialism*, Macmillan, London.

Giddens, A., (1984), *The consitution of society*, Polity Press, Cambridge

Giddens, A., (1985a) *The nation state and violence*, Polity Press, Cambridge

Giddens, A., (1985b) Marx's correct views on everything, *Theory and society*, **14**, pp. 67-74

Giddens, A., (1990) *The consequences of modernity*, Polity Press, Cambridge

Giddens, A., (1991) *Modernity and self-identity*, Polity Press, Cambridge

Giddens, A., (1994), *Living in a post traditional society*, in Beck, U., Giddens, A. & Lash, S., (eds), *Reflexive modernization*, Polity Press, Cambridge.

Hammer, M. (1990) Re-engineering work: Don't automate, obliterate, *Harvard Business Review*, July-August, 104-112.

Hammer, M. and Champy, J. (1993) *Re-engineering the corporation: A Manifesto for business revolution*, Harper business, New York.

Harrington, H.J. (1991) *Business process improvement: the breakthrough strategy for total quality, productivity and effectiveness*, MacGraw-Hill, New York.

Johnson, P., (1995*), Towards and epistemology for radical accounting: beyond objectivism and relativism*, Critical perspectives on Accounting, **6**, 485-509.

Johnson G., & Scholes K. (1989), 'Exploring Corporate Strategy', Prentice Hall.

Larrasquet, JM., (1995), Proceedings of the Projectics Conference, Bayonne, France.

McFarlan, W., (1984), Information technology changes the way you compete', *Harvard Business Review*, May-June, pp. 98-103.

Nissen, Hans-Erik, Two questions methodology users better learn to ask, in Jayaratna, N., Wood-Harper, T., Fizgerald, B., Larrasquet, JM., (eds), Proceedings of the 5th BCS Conference on ISD Methodology, (in print).

Nolan, R., (1979), Managing the crises in data processing, *Harvard Business Review*, March-April, pp. 115- 126.

Ould, M.A. & Roberts, C., (1987), *Defining formal models of the software development process*,
in Brereton, P. (ed), Software Engineering Environments, Ellis Horwood.

Ould, M.A., (1992), Process Modelling with RADs. Part 1: The modeller's needs and the basic concepts of process modelling, *Iopener*, Volume 1, Number 5.

Ould, M.A., (1993a), Process Modelling with RADs. Part 2: The modelling method and its notation, *Iopener*, Volume 1, Number 5.

Ould, M.A., (1993b), Process Modelling with RADs. Part 3: Handling large and complex models, *Iopener*, Volume 1, Number 5.

Ould, M.A., (1995), *Business Processes - Modelling and Analysis For Re-engineering and Improvement*, Wiley, Chichester.

Porter, M.E., Millar, V.E., (1985), How Information gives you competitive advantage, *Harvard Business Review*, pp. 149-160.

Walsham, G., (1993), *Interpreting information systems in organisations*, Wiley, Chichester.

Whittington, R., (1993), *What is strategy and does it matter?*, Routledge

Whittington, R., (1992), Putting Giddens into action: social systems and managerial agency, *Journal of Management Studies*, 29(6), p. 693-712

Willcocks, L., (1994), *Managing Information Technology Evaluation*, in Galliers, R.D. & Baker, B.S.H., (1994), *Strategic Informaiton Management*, Butterworth-Heinnemann, Oxford, pp. 362-381.

Willcocks, L. & Margetts, H., (1994), Risk assessment and information systems, *European Journal of Information Systems*, **3**(2), 127-138.

Yourdon, E. (1989), *Modern structured analysis*, Prentice Hall, Englewood Cliffs, NJ.

Zuboff, S., (1988), *In the age of the smart machine*, Basic Books

---

[i] For the purposes of confidentiality, a *nom de plume* is used

Supporting the End User Computing Process

M J Taylor, E P Moynihan, O J Akomode
School of Computing and Mathematical Sciences,
Liverpool John Moores University,
Liverpool, England

Abstract

End user computing is a growing aspect of the IT activity within UK organisations. The number and size of end user developed applications is steadily increasing, yet little attention is paid to the processes by which such applications are developed and maintained. In this paper we examine how end user computing activities are supported within UK organisations. This paper is the result of a research programme involving case studies in thirty four UK organisations aimed at improving business systems.

1 Introduction

End user computing is found in both business and technical computing, although in this paper we are focusing on its use in business administration. It is where the user of a business application computer system is responsible for the development and maintenance of the application computer system, e.g. by writing software in a fourth generation language to produce statistical reports. As an example the business application computer system developed could be used to analyse sales and marketing data. The business application computer system user is also responsible for operating the application computer system e.g. by keyboard work and taking regular security copies of data. Typical end users might have titles like accounts clerk, production planner, or marketing executive. End user computing is contrasted with the role of a traditional computer department which develops and maintains business application computer systems, for instance by writing COBOL software. The computer department is also responsible for a substantial part of the computer operations, especially where these are based on a central mainframe. Needless to say hybrid situations exist where, for example, the users develop only the simpler software and leave the more advanced programming to IT specialists. The various approaches to dividing systems work between users and IT specialists is a contemporary management issue which is discussed in books such as Laudon and Laudon [1].

within organisations [3], [4]. The proliferation of personal computers within organisations has meant that an increasing number of end users are now capable of potentially developing their own applications [5], [6]. Overall there has seen a dramatic increase in the percentage of organisational data that is held by, and manipulated by end users [7].

The process we are examining here is the support provided within UK organisations for the development and maintenance of business computer applications by end users. Taylor *et al.* [8] had noted that research is required into the management and support of end user computing activities in order to reduce the potential for harm to organisations from uncontrolled end user developments.

2 Previous research

The discussion below describes some of the conclusions and suggestions of previous research workers and authors concerning the development and maintenance of business application computer systems by end users.

2.1 The need for standards and information systems methodologies

Despite the growth in end user computing, little attention is paid to the processes by which end user applications are developed and maintained [9], [6]. The process of end user development can differ from the traditional systems development life cycle [6]. Kettlehut [10] and Sumner [11] had noted that formal systems development practices were rarely followed in the end user computing environment. Karten [12] identified establishing guidelines for end user application development as one of the ten key challenges in managing end user computing. Bento [13] confirmed that end users needed development methodologies as much as suitable software tools to ensure successful projects. Sumner and Klepper [14] in a study of 33 user-developed applications also noted that end user development activities rarely follow the same development discipline as IT department projects. Barr and Foley [15] noted that end user developed systems were evolved, rather than developed, by amendment and experimentation until the required functionality seemed to be obtained i.e. a form of prototyping.

2.2 Quality control

Barr *et al.* [16], Schultheis and Sumner [17], and Pierson *et al.* [18], suggested that there is a real need to improve the quality assurance of the end user computing process. Barr and Foley [15] stressed the need to improve the quality of end user development by applying BS5750 (now BS EN ISO 9000) and other related standards to end user software development. The quality of end user developed application computer systems can be enhanced through the use of the quality assurance mechanisms embedded in most mature information systems methodologies. For example the cross-checking that is possible through use of SSADM (Structured Systems Analysis and Design Method) due to its three views of the system in terms of processes, data, and time. See SSADM [19]. Information systems methodologies can also help to ensure that the developed application computer systems are complete in the sense that all aspects of the requirements are considered. Wilkinson [20] noted the lack of testing guidelines for end user application developers. Barr and Foley [15] and Barr et al. [16] suggested that testing of end user developed systems was superficial at best, and completely non-existent in other cases.

2.3 Training

Taylor et al. [8] noted that end user training in general appeared to be weak within UK organisations. In particular, Taylor et al. [8] found that typically end users had received little if any training in the use of the tools they were developing application computer systems with. Jenson [21] in a survey of 97 American organisations, concluded that the majority of organisations do not provide training for end users in application development methodologies. Fitzgerald and Cater-Steel [22] had however suggested that end user training is critical to the successful use of end user development tools. Karten [23] and Alavi et al. [24] hinted that end users typically have little if any formal training in systems development techniques. De Thomas et al. [25] found that in the case of spreadsheet-based end user application developments, the majority of end users had to learn the spreadsheet package unaided. Chan and Storey [26] and Zinatelli et al. [27] commented upon the strong need for training for end user spreadsheet developers. Angell and Smithson [4] commented that lack of systems analysis and design skills by end users led to quality problems in the application computer systems developed by them.

Previous research [28],[[6] had hinted that the level of support provided by the IT department is crucial to the success of end user computing projects, but had not really examined the nature of such support. Kozar and Mahlum [29] and Liu [30] recommended that end user groups should be taught the information systems methodology, and then assisted in the use of the information systems methodology by a 'chief developer' in the information centre.

2.4 Management

Unless action is taken to effectively manage and control end user developments, then the integrity of organisational data affected by such systems may well deteriorate [17], [31], [32], [33]. Checkland and Holwell [34] noted the dangers of end user computing for a co-ordinated information strategy in an organisation.

Many organisations are beginning to deploy end user developed applications to support core organisational activities [35], and this is an area of deep concern. McGann [36] had noted that the majority of end user developed systems were difficult even for the original developer to maintain. End users could develop and maintain their own systems to the same standards as the IT department [37], [38].

3 Research method

Researchers have criticised the lack of empirical research on information systems in real organisational contexts (e.g. Hamilton and Ives [39]). In particular, empirically-based studies on the end user computing process have been few [40], [6]. In general more research is needed into the actual practice of information systems development and maintenance in organisations.

This research was based upon case studies in thirty four UK organisations conducted during 1994, 1995 and 1996. The organisations were from both the public and private sectors of UK industry and covered a range of industrial activities. The size of the organisations chosen ranged from seven staff to over thirty thousand staff. The case-study approach was used because the researchers and others believe that case studies allow the study to be done in a natural setting, learning about the state of the art, and generating theories about actual practice. Also, the case study approach allows the nature and complexity of a process to be more freely studied, and situations which are new and rapidly changing can be more readily handled [41]. Gummesson [42] states that an important advantage with case-study research is the opportunity for a holistic view of a process : "The detailed observations entailed in the case study method enable us to study many different aspects, examine them in relation to each other, view the process within its total environment and also utilise the researchers capacity for understanding. Consequently case-study research provides us with a greater opportunity than other available research methods to obtain a holistic view of a specific research project".

The case studies were conducted using semi-structured interviews which typically lasted between one and two hours with supporting techniques such as observing operational systems, and inspecting small samples of program code and documentation such as standards manuals, and examples of analysis and design artefacts. Details of the organisations studied are shown in Table 1.

The main questions posed by the researchers were :

- What training do end user application developers and maintainers receive ?

- What quality assurance and quality control measures are applied to end user computing activities ?

- How is end user computing supported or assisted by the IT department ?

- How are end user computing activities co-ordinated ?

- What standards are applied to end user computing activities ?

The case study material was analysed by the researchers looking through the interview notes taken and samples of documentation and code provided and identifying :

- If training was given to end user developers within a given organisation, and if so what type of training.

- If any quality assurance or quality control measures were applied to end user development and maintenance, and if so what type of measures.

- If end user computing was supported by the IT department, and if so what form the support took.

- If end user computing activities were co-ordinated, and if so what co-ordination mechanisms were used.

- If any standards were applied to end user computing activities, and if so what form the standards appeared in.

4 Research results

4.1 Training and support

This research appeared to indicate that the majority of the end users in the thirty four organisations studied received virtually no training in systems development techniques. Indeed not all the end users had even been provided with training in the use of the development tools they used. Thus end users who had been trained in how to use a particular development tool were still not aware of fundamental systems development techniques such as the need for thorough testing of developed applications. Table 1 shows details of which organisations did provide training in development tools for their end users. By development tools is meant the computer languages, utility packages, network utilities and other IT tools with which end users can develop their own applications. In the thirty four organisations researched the end user application development tools utilised were limited to spreadsheets, databases and query languages. Table 1 shows the end user application development tools used within the different organisations researched. This research found that typically end users may have at most attended a two day basic training course on any relevant software tools.

There were a number of mechanisms encountered in the thirty four organisations researched by which the IT department aimed to provide support for end user computing activities. Guimaraes [43] had commented upon the diversity of end user support services found amongst organisations. The only mechanisms for end user support encountered in the thirty four organisations studied were:

(1) *Facilitators*. A facilitator is a member of the IT department whose job it is to guide end user developers through the development process, and to assist in the maintenance of end user developed application computer systems. Facilitators were used in only two of the organisations researched.

(2) *Co-ordinators*. A co-ordinator is a member of the IT department whose role is to co-ordinate end user development activities. By this is meant that duplication of end user developed application computer systems should be avoided, and re-use of already developed application computer systems should be achieved. The main co-ordination mechanisms for end user computing activities encountered in the thirty four organisations researched included printed newsletters, computer bulletin boards and direct contact with the co-ordination staff. Co-ordinators were used in six of the organisations studied.

(3) *In-house help desk*. An in-house help desk provides telephone contact for answers to any queries that end user developers may have when developing or maintaining their application computer systems. The help available in the thirty four organisations researched ranged from support for the development tools used by the end user application developers, through to full project support. In-house help desks were used in nineteen of the organisations studied.

The number of organisations that used the different mechanisms for providing IT department support for end user computing activities is shown in Table 1.

4.2 Application of quality assurance and quality control

Review and inspection procedures in end user computing activities appeared to be informal, if they existed at all, within the thirty four organisations researched. There was practically no documentation relating to how end user developed systems were tested produced in any of the organisations researched. This research indicated that if they did any testing at all, end users tended to test their own computer applications by means of a few 'standard examples'. This meant, for instance, that the 'non-standard' transactions, or unusual combinations of data or processes would often not be adequately tested.

4.3 Application of standards and methodologies

This research indicated that none of the end users in the thirty four organisations studied followed any kind of information systems methodology for developing and maintaining their own application computer systems. However, the research suggested that the productivity of end user application development might be improved by the use of information systems methodologies, since such methodologies provide a tried and trusted framework for the stages of development. In this manner the suspect informal process typically encountered in end user application development should be reduced, and overall quality increased. Where an incremental approach is desired then a more formal prototyping or RAD (Rapid Application Development) approach could be used.

4.4 Possible risks to organisations

This research indicated that there are possible risks generated by end user computing that may have adverse effect on the business life of organisations. Such possible risks include the following:

(1) A lack of adequate knowledge and commitment to quality assurance systems on the part of the end user may result in unsuitable systems that may be detrimental to business management and operations.

(2) The end user scenario may encourage the development of 'private' information systems at the expense of shared enterprise resources and may consequently reduce the level of productivity in an organisation.

(3) End user computing may lead to an expensive duplication of information systems if organisational co-ordination is not appropriately managed.

(4) An end user may not be able to explicitly and accurately specify systems requirements due to lack of adequate knowledge in the use of suitable methodologies and their associated methods. The situation may lead to inadequate systems analysis and poorly developed applications which may increase business risks.

(5) Inadequate documentation, poor backup procedures and lack of appropriate knowledge of data security were common in end user computing activities in the organisations studied. This situation may adversely affect the competitiveness of an enterprise.

Akomode et al. [44] discuss detailed issues about the risks associated with the development of information systems, which may be useful in appreciating and averting risk issues relating to end user computing activities in order to minimise business risks in organisations.

5 Conclusions

In this paper we have discussed the support provided for end user computing activities within thirty four UK organisations. This research indicated that the support provided for end user computer application development and maintenance is an important area to address. Unless action is taken to effectively support end user developments the integrity of organisational data affected by such computer application systems may well deteriorate [17], [31], [32], [33]. As many organisations are beginning to use end user developed computer applications to support core organisational activities [35], this is an area of deep concern. Further research is required into this area to develop more detailed managerial strategies to reduce the potential for harm to organisations from uncontrolled end user developments [8].

References

1. Laudon K. C. and Laudon J. P. Management Information Systems, Prentice Hall, London, UK, 1996.
2. Hackathorn R. D. End user computing by top executives. Database 1988; 19, 1:1-9.
3. Kettelhut M. C. Supporting end user database development. Data Resource Management 1992; 3,3:29-39.
4. Angell I., Smithson S. Information Systems Management, MacMillan, London, UK, 1991.
5. Moynihan E. Business Management and Systems Analysis, Alfred Waller, Henley-on-Thames, UK, 1993.
6. Amoroso D. L. Organisational issues of end user computing. Data Base 1988; 19, 3:49-58.
7. OTR. IT skills for the 1990's, Organisation and Technology Research, London, UK, 1995.
8. Taylor M. J., Moynihan E. P., Wood-Harper A. T. End user computing and information systems methodologies. Information Systems Journal 1998; 8, 1:85-96.
9. Amoroso D. L., Cheney P. H. Testing a causal model of end user application effectiveness. Journal of Management Information Systems 1991; 8, 1:63-89.
10. Kettelhut M. C. Don't let users develop applications without systems analysis. Journal of Systems Management 1991; 42,7:23-26.
11. Sumner M. (1987) Information systems strategy and end user application development. Database 1987;18, 4:19-30.
12. Karten N. Managing end user computing when the only constant is change. Journal of Systems Management 1987; 38, 10:26-29.

13. Bento A. M. (1989) Can end users develop their own database oriented decision support systems ? Journal of Computer Information Systems 1989; 30, 1:13-21.
14. Sumner M., Klepper R. The impact of end user computing on information systems development. Computer Personnel 1986; 10, 4:16-24.
15. Barr S., Foley R. End user firsts. CA Magazine 1993; 97, 10:46-50.
16. Barr S., Foley R., McMullen M. Towards a quality management system for end user application development. In: Proceedings of Software Quality Management Conference, July 1994, Edinburgh, UK, pp 497-510.
17. Schultheis R., Sumner M. The relationship of application risks to application controls : a study of microcomputer based spreadsheet applications. Journal of End User Computing 1994;6, 2:11-18.
18. Pierson J. K. *et al.* Determining documentation requirements for user developed applications. Information and Management 1990; 19:21-31.
19. SSADM Reference Manual, version 4+, NCC Blackwell, Oxford, UK, 1995.
20. Wilkinson S. Making the most out of users who program. PC Week 1989; 5, 1:48-49.
21. Jenson R. L. End user control environments and the accounting managers perceived quality of the applications. Information and Management 1993; 25, 5:245-252.
22. Fitzgerald E., Cater-Steel A. Champagne training on a beer budget. Communications of the ACM 1995; 38, 7:49-60.
23. Karten N. Integrating IS disciplines into end user training. Journal of Information Systems Management 1991; 8, 1:75-78.
24. Alavi M., Philips J. S., Freedman S. M. An empirical investigation of two alternative approaches to control of the end user application development process. Database 1990; 20, 4:11-19.
25. De Thomas A., Ray H. N., Rowe R. The electronic spreadsheet : its use as a decision support tool in small firms. Journal of Computer Information Systems 1991; 31, 3:38-44.
26. Chan Y., Storey V. The use of spreadsheets in organisations : determinants and consequences. Information and Management 1996; 31, 3:119-34.
27. Zinatelli N., Cragg P., Cavaye A. (1996) End user computing sophistication and success in small firms. European Journal of Information Systems 1996; 5, 3: 172-81.
28. Bird J. Managing Information Technology, Micro Myopia. Management Today 1992, February.
29. Kozar A. K., Mahlum J. M. A user generated information system : an innovative approach. MIS Quarterly 1987; 11, 2:163-173.
30. Liu J. P. Utilising the trend of end user development. Journal of Systems Management 1989; 40, 1:28-30.
31. Klepper R., Sumner M. Continuity and change in user developed systems. In: Desktop Information Technology, Kaiser and Oppelland (Eds.), Elsevier Science Publishers, Amsterdam, The Netherlands, 1990.

32. Robey D., Zmud R. Research on end user computing : theoretical perspectives from organisation theory. In: Desktop Information Technology, Kaiser and Oppelland (Eds.), Elsevier Science Publishers, Amsterdam, The Netherlands, 1990.

33. Yeager J. Pitfalls of end user computing. Information Executive 1990; Autumn: 43-45.

34. Checkland P., Holwell S. Information, Systems and Information Systems : making sense of the field, John Wiley, Chichester, UK, 1998.

35. Sumner M., Klepper R. Information systems strategy and end user application development. Database 1987, Summer :13-30.

36. McGann J. A. Meeting the challenge of end user computing. Journal of Systems Management 1990; 41, 3,:13-16.

37. Evans R. Reaping the full benefits of end user computing. Computerworld 1989; 23:67-71.

38. Nantz K. S. Supporting end user application development with the information transformation analysis management model. Journal of Microcomputer Systems Management 1990; 2, 3:9-15.

39. Hamilton S., Ives B. MIS research strategies. In: Information Systems Research, issues, methods and practical guidelines, Galliers R. (ed.), Blackwell Scientific Publications, Oxford, UK, 1992.

40. Cheney P. et al. (1986) Organisational factors affecting the success of end user computing. Journal of Management Information Systems 1986; 3, 1:65-80.

41. Benbasat I., Goldstein D., Mead M. The Case Research Strategy in Studies of Information Systems. MIS Quarterly 1987; September :369-386.

42. Gummesson E. Qualitative methods in management research, Sage, New York, USA, 1991.

43. Guimaraes T. (1996) Assessing the impact of information centres on end user computing and company performance. Information Resources Management Journal 1996; 9, 10:6-15.

44. Akomode, O. J., Lees, B., Irgens, C. (1997) Applying information technology to minimise risks in satisfying organisational needs. In: Information Infrastructure Systems for Manufacturing, Goossenaerts, J, Kimura, F and Wortmann, H. (eds), Chapman & Hall, London, 1997, pp 242-253.

Type of org.	No. of employees (approx.)	No. of IT staff (approx.)	EUC tools used	Training in tool provided	Type of. EUC support	No. of IT support staff
Engineering	8000	50	QL	Y	HD	2
Comp. Serv.	90	35	SP	N	None	0
Engineering	350	7	QL	Y	HD	1
Manufact.	1600	18	QL	Y	None	0
Fin Services	4000	160	SP,QL	Y	HD,CO	9
Fin. Services	240	12	SP,QL	Y	HD,CO	1
Fin. Services	120	10	SP,QL	Y	HD,CO	1
Fin. Services	50	8	SP,QL	Y	HD,CO	1
Fin. Services	40	7	SP,QL	Y	HD,CO	1
Fin. Services	3000	110	SP,QL	Y	CO,F	5
Public Utility	7500	120	SP	Y	HD	4
Manufact.	2500	40	SP	Y	HD	1
Comp. Serv.	300	220	SP	N	None	0
Manufact.	430	6	SP	N	None	0
Fin. Services	3400	80	SP,QL	Y	F	2
Manufact.	90	2	SP	N	None	0
Distribution	15000	30	SP	Y	HD	1
Defence	7500	40	QL	Y	HD	1
Local Gov.	30000	40	SP,DB	Y	HD	2
Higher Ed.	2000	18	SP	Y	HD	1
Distribution	9000	40	SP	Y	None	0
Manufact.	2100	18	SP,DB	Y	HD	1
Civil Service	3000	320	SP	Y	HD	4
Local Gov.	80	6	SP	Y	None	0
Manufact.	6000	6	SP,DB	Y	None	0
Retail	4500	140	SP	Y	HD	3
Distribution	53	2	SP	N	None	0
Manufact.	1200	40	SP	Y	HD	1
Distribution	1500	30	SP	Y	HD	1
Manufact.	2300	15	SP	Y	None	0
Manufact.	1400	18	SP	Y	HD	1
Shipping	100	0	SP,QL	Y	N/A	N/A
Warehousing	18	0	SP	N	N/A	N/A
Distribution	7	0	SP,DB	N	N/A	N/A

Key :
EUC tools used : SP = Spreadsheet, QL = Query Language, DB = Database
IT Dept. support : HD = In house help desk, CO = Co-ordinators,
F = Facilitators

Table 1. Details of organisations studied.

The Problem of Defining Objects: A Critical Evaluation of Coad and Yourdon's Object Oriented Analysis Using the Nimsad Framework

Helen Campbell
Department of Computing
University of Central Lancashire
Preston
PR1 2HE
H.Campbell1@uclan.ac.uk

Abstract

In Object Oriented Analysis by Coad and Yourdon the concept of 'object' is considered to have identity, state, behaviour and properties and can be characterised by a set of operations that can be performed on it or by it and its possible states. It is not explained in terms of any meta-level model of human sense-making. That is objects are not defined rather they are described.

This paper critically evaluates Coad and Yourdon's Object Oriented Analysis (1990), using the NIMSAD framework, with an emphasis on the criteria used to identify objects.

1 Introduction

The aim of the current research is to determine how a number of well-known object-oriented analysis methods identify objects and whether /how they differentiate between objects and entities. The long term aim is to specify a way of identifying objects that does not rely on statements such as:- 'An object is an entity with methods' or 'An object is an entity in the real-world about which there is a need to store information'; both of which raise the question 'What is the difference between an entity and an object'?

This paper critically evaluates the first of the selected methods - Coad and Yourdon's Object Oriented Analysis (1990), using the NIMSAD framework (Jayaratna, 1994). The NIMSAD framework has been used for critically evaluating other methods and provides for critical evaluation along three dimensions; the problem situation; the problem solver; and the methodology.

2 Problem Solver or Methodology User

NIMSAD framework helps us to assess our own 'mental construct' and then whether OOA discusses the need for 'mental constructs' characteristics and their desirable levels in order to apply the methodology successfully.

The text (Coad and Yourdon, 1990) is written for a specific target audience, that is those currently employed in an analysis capacity.

> ' We have aimed this book at the practising systems analyst, the person who has to tackle the real-world systems development projects every day....... the strategy used to identify objects comes from practice and experience in the field';

Coad and Yourdon (1990) assume a fundamental understanding of computer technology and systems analysis concepts, experience of data flow diagrams and entity relationship diagrams as pre-requisites of object oriented analysis, as they say OOA constructs come from Entity Relationship Modelling, Semantic Data Modelling, Object Oriented Programming and Knowledge Based Systems. From the perspective of data analysis and database design, the underlying logic for this statement needs to be challenged. Entity Relationship diagrams are the end result of the data analysis process and the normalisation exercise and are therefore the first step in a design strategy. How can they inform an analysis method? The statement appears to indicate that the analysis method is design led. It would appear that Coad and Yourdon are attempting to shift the design principles used into analysis as there is little or no real understanding of the analysis process from the data perspective, their previous experience being from a task oriented approach.

OOA talks about the experience element of the framework and that does not alert its users to their 'mental constructs' nor does it help them to examine the high level of preparation they should have in order to use the methodology successfully. In keeping with the philosophical paradigms, it is evident that OOA assumes that the use of its techniques will yield the same results irrespective of the nature of the 'mental constructs' of its users (Jayaratna 1994).

OOA has a strong focus on techniques - in some situations it would be feasible for two technically competent OOA users to derive two different object models. It could be argued that because of the cyclic nature of the methodology objects that are missed initially <u>may</u> be uncovered at a later stage and, due to its relative immaturity, analysts may be still developing their techniques and determining which problem situations are most applicable.

Coad and Yourdon acknowledge (see anecdote) that analysts from different backgrounds are likely to produce different results although it has to be said that the anecdote is related in order to justify the development of OOA.

One team of analysts (DFD Team) started projects using data flow diagrams to develop overall functional decomposition, as a framework for further specification. A second team of analysts (Data Base Team) started by focusing on the information the system needed to do its job and then building an information model (Entity-Relationship model).

Over time the DFD Team continued to struggle with basic problem domain understanding. In contrast the Data Base Team gained a strong, in depth understanding of the problem domain. Results did not mesh together and the Data Base Team was perceived as irksome, even somewhat troublemakers.

The same pattern was repeated several years later. The DFD Team progressed rapidly, ahead in time and political power. The Data Base Team gained tremendous insight, vital to analysis but all to often ignored. Again the Data Base Team and leaders were perceived as troublemakers.'

This anecdote is used to highlight the perception that there was a need to identify a way that would help analysts gain much needed problem domain understanding and then add the behaviour (output from the processing) requirements within a framework of that understanding. From this it would appear that the DFD Team viewed the problem situation from a descriptive perspective whereas the Data Base Team viewed it from an design perspective and it is extremely difficult for the different perspectives to be appreciated in a working environment. As Jayaratna (1994) indicates it is difficult to train scientific- and engineering-based practitioners to appreciate the epistemological notion of 'systems' or to train social- and political-based practitioners to appreciate the ontological notion of 'systems'.

3 Problem Situation

Reasons for Finding Objects and Classes

The rationale and motivation behind identifying Class-&-Object are identified by Coad and Yourdon as:-

- Identifying objects and classes matches the technical representation of a system more closely to the conceptual view of the real world.

This is a solution driven and opportunity seeking approach and it raises a number of problems. As there is not one conceptual view of the world it must be asked 'Whose view of the 'real world'?' In the absence of any discussion are we to assume that the 'real world' view is the analysts view of the consensus viewpoints of all the stakeholders? What is required is not matching the technical requirements, but rather finding out what problems there are in the 'real world'. In fact this is mixing up current/desired states and the use of design concepts to derive desired states (Jayaratna, 1994).

- Emphasis on Class-&-Object is a desire to create a stable framework for analysis and specification. Class-&-Object are relatively stable over time, and provide a basis for moving over time towards reusable analysis results.

Reuse analysis is seen as a way of accommodating both families of systems / and practical trade-offs within a system. OOA organises results based on problem domain constructs, for present reuse and for future reuse. This comes from the object oriented programming context where classes and objects within the classes are defined once. The code can then be used or re-used when required. A new object within the class can be defined by adding it to the type hierarchy and specifying the attributes that characterise it.

OOA suggests that previous results in the same and similar problem domains are considered to determine whether there are any Whole-Part structures which can be directly reused. This implies that previous OOA has been carried out and that the terminology /understanding of Class-&-Objects is used consistently throughout the organisation, i.e. within a university a student may be considered as Student, Graduate, Diplomate and Graduand, for different purposes in different 'systems' within the organisation. Which object would be deemed to be correct for reuse purposes? Is the same information required for each object or does it differ?

It could be argued that if an analysis of the entire organisation has been conducted and then a sub-domain identified for design /implementation purposes, the results of the analysis exercise (object model diagrams etc.) would be stored. The object model diagrams could be considered at a later date if another sub-domain within the organisation were then identified for design /implementation purposes.

- Analysts focus on an object's state and behaviour together. Separating process analysis from data analysis is not even worth considering, consider as an intrinsic whole.

Data abstraction is the method commonly used by analysis methods that are data oriented. The underlying philosophy being that the data are stable and less subject to change than the processes. These approaches are used by database analysts to identify entities and attributes which can then be normalised and Information Engineers, where database management software is assumed but not required. (Conger, 1994)

Coad and Yourdon claim that the principle of data abstraction can be the basis for organisation of thinking and of specification of a system's responsibilities. In applying data abstraction, analysts define 'attributes', and then define 'services' that exclusively manipulate those 'attributes'. The only way to get back to the 'attributes' is via a 'service'. 'Attributes' and their 'services' may be treated as an intrinsic whole. However statements such as '....the OOA analyst focuses on Class-&-Objects, structures and attributes - and then proceeds to a fuller consideration of services' make one question how 'attributes' and 'services' are being treated as an intrinsic whole.

Inheritance is used in many data driven analysis methods, the difference here is that the attributes (expressed as data) and the 'services' (expressed as methods) are represented on the same diagram and not on separate diagrams.

- The OOA model provides a basis for an initial expression of the system context. Context is not defined by a diagram, drawn by a systems analyst making a technical decision. Rather, clients, managers, analysts, competitors, government regulators and standard bearers all affect the system context over time. System context is an indication of how much of the problem domain will be embraced by the automated system, what data will be held over time, and how much processing sophistication will be included.

Object Oriented Analysis is identified as 'the challenge of understanding the problem domain, and then the systems responsibilities in that light. Analysts must consider the problem in which they work... first they must understand the problem domain at hand.... If an analyst simply assumes s/he has the subject matter knowledge s/he is likely to indulge in thinking that will lead to fuzzy requirements.'

The implication of this is that by considering a problem in object terms rather than in data or process terms a greater understanding of the complexity of the problem domain will be understood. This must depend on the competence and expertise of the analyst, an inexperienced person is just as likely to miss the complexity of the problem domain using this method as with any other method. OO concepts will only help to focus on formal operations performed by or on data.

- The final motivation for identifying Class-&-Object is to avoid shifting the underlying representation as we move from systems analysis to design.

The way of thinking about systems analysis is influenced by preconceived ideas of how we would design a system to meet its requirements; ideas about design are influenced by preconceived ideas about how we would write code; ideas about coding are strongly influenced by the programming languages available.

Coad and Yourdon acknowledge that analysis has only been considered once a programming language has been developed, and design strategies have been developed. Although there is a claim that analysis is implementation free, design considerations and the implementation language will restrict what problems will be perceived and structured.

The same notation is used for both the analysis and the design phases of Coad and Yourdon's method. This effectively means that analysis results do not have to be interpreted in order to 'fit them' into a design method, which frequently results in a mismatch between what is being requested by the analysis phase and what is actually designed. The design therefore does not become the designer's interpretation of what the analyst thinks the client wants. This follows the same route as previous methodologies, i.e. structured system design was extended to structured systems analysis, object oriented design has been extended to object oriented analysis without any major changes.

Coad and Yourdon define 'system's responsibilities' as an arrangement of things accountable for, related together as a whole; used in this way 'system's responsibilities' are considered as the pre-specified boundaries of the problem situation with 'system' being used in an ontological sense, i.e. analysis process assumes that the world is composed of systems and sub-systems. 'Systems' and the problem situation, are taken as given without question, as is the boundary of the problem situation. This is at variance with a previous statement by Coad and Yourdon 'approaches to analysis are 'thinking tools' used to help in the formulation of requirements.' The method does not take an epistemological approach to the analysis process where 'systems' can be used to **think about** some part of the world. (Lewis 1994), However Coad and Yourdon appear to be talking not about models for understanding a 'system' but models to organise a solution.

This implies that the analyst does not question the motivations and justifications for the 'system' nor does he/she question the correctness or otherwise of the perceived boundaries. Effectively any difficulties with the final solution can be claimed to be outside the system boundaries. This creates a 'safe' problem for which there could be a desired solution already in existence.

3.1 How to identify objects:-

The initial problem situation has been identified as one of terminology and in particular the identification of 'objects'. The use of definitions from encyclopaedia's or dictionaries is used extensively by Coad and Yourdon. Definitions are stated from one source only and then applied to the terminology used in the method, in many cases the definitions are taken from the normal usage of the terms, in others they claim to be taken from the scientific perspective. This approach relies heavily on the reader's/users having a shared understanding of the semantics as well as the usage of the terms.

Coad and Yourdon use the following definition of object taken from Webster's (1977).

> Object - A person or thing to which action, thought, or feeling is directed. Anything visible or tangible; a material product or substance.

This definition of 'object' means that abstract ideas or concepts, within the problem domain, that may need to be represented cannot be considered as objects and would therefore be missed. The definition itself is too general to be helpful in determining 'objects'.

One could consider the 'definitions' of objects proposed by authors within the computing field rather than rely on a generalised definition: e.g.

> Object:- an abstraction of a data item characterised by a unique and invariant identifier, a class to which it belongs and a state represented by a simple or a structured value. (Bouzeghoub, Gardarin et al 1997)

This 'definition' however **describes** the characteristics of an object rather than giving an actual definition of the concept of object. These definitions, together with those used by other authors, appear to refer mainly to those objects that could be considered as being relevant to the data requirements of the problem situation. Object, however, should be taken in the widest sense of the word which could also include interface objects and control objects that are relevant to the problem situation.

The 'strategy (for identification of objects) comes from practice and experience in the field', this would suggest that Coad and Yourdon use approaches, that they are familiar with, without understanding exactly what principles are being applied and why. This does not help either experienced or inexperienced analysts and gives no insight as to how objects can be identified. It also assumes that analysts using this method have a shared understanding of the semantics as well as the usage of the terms.

The approach taken by OOA appears to indicate that analysts should determine what they can about the problem domain and problem situation by asking questions. Clients, users and experts should all be consulted as should any documents; invoices, receipts, reports etc. This appears to be no different to the approach taken by structured systems analysis methods.

As an initial starting point, the nouns, and by implication the subjects and objects (in a grammatical context), within the discussion transcripts and the documents are highlighted. These initial potential objects are mainly related to the data requirements of the problem situation. The problem situation is then considered, using the following criteria in order to identify further objects:- structures, other systems, devices, things or events remembered, roles played, operational procedures, sites, organisational units.

Coad and Yourdon state that criteria earlier in the list are more likely to be a source of potential objects than those lower in the list. The list of potential Class-&-Objects can then be considered against a further mechanistic set of criteria which Coad and Yourdon claim will assist in determining whether a the Class-&-Object should be included:- needed remembrance, needed behaviour, multiple Attributes, objects in class, always applicable Attributes, always applicable Services, not merely derived results. This is a mechanistic approach to validate the objects that have been identified in order to justify their inclusion as potential objects. Only 'raw data' should be considered as input to the 'system' - anything that can be calculated (derived results) should be discarded as possible Class-&-Objects.

3.2   Structures

In OOA the term 'Structure' is an overall term, describing both generalization-specialization (Gen-Spec) and Whole-Part structures.

3.3   Generalization-specialization

Gen-Spec may be viewed as part of the 'distinguishing between classes' aspect of the three basic methods of organisation that Coad and Yourdon claim pervade human thinking. This is based on classification theory. Less formally a Gen-Spec structure - from the specialisation perspective - can be thought of as an 'is a' or 'is a kind of' structure. Whole-Part structures can be thought of as a 'has a' structure. 'Has-A' and 'Is-A' are considered in Extended (Enhanced) Entity Relationship (EER) modelling as particular types of relationship which would indicate the same types of constructs as Coad and Yourdon's Gen-Spec and Whole-Part structures.

Coad and Yourdon claim that Gen-Spec and Whole-Part focus the attention of the analyst and problem domain experts on the complexity of multiple Class-&-Objects. Using Structures the analysts 'push the edges' of the system's responsibilities within a domain, uncovering additional Class-&-Objects (implicit in the requesting document that might otherwise be missed.) In addition inheritance is applied particularly in Gen-Spec, so that generalised Attributes and Services are identified and specified once, then specialised appropriately.

This appears to indicate that having determined an initial set of objects, consideration of the objects in terms of generalisations-specialisation or Whole-Part structures is likely to identify further objects. The initial system boundary is 'taken as given' by the client, however consideration of objects in structure terms may indicate that there are interface objects or control objects that were not apparent from documentation or discussion. These are the objects that are seen as 'pushing the edges of the system's responsibilities'.

Gen-Spec and Whole-Part constructs appear to be taken from EER modelling where supertype and subtype are defined. A supertype being a generalisation of an entity and a subtype being a specialisation of an entity. The same arguments are used in OOA as in EER modelling to determine which is the most appropriate way of modelling the situation. Coad and Yourdon imply that more consideration should be given to the problem domain and the usage of the Class-&-Objects within it than to the relatively mechanistic method of identifying all generalisations and specialisations based on the specified attributes.

3.4   Whole-Part

Consideration of the potential Class-&-Object in terms of Whole-Part structures asks if the object contains separately identifiable parts or whether it is a part of another Class-&-Object. Coad and Yourdon view this 'as helpful in identifying Class-&-Objects at the edges of a problem domain, and the system's responsibilities in that domain'. When considering Whole-Part structures, it is suggested that the following are considered:-

assembly-parts; container-contents; collection- members (and its varieties).

Assembly parts are those objects that could be considered as consisting of a number of different parts i.e. a car can be considered to be an assembly with engine as parts.

Container-Contents are those objects that could be considered to be a container that another object can be found inside, i.e. The car is considered as a container with a driver inside, if the problem domain and the system's responsibilities include knowing about and assigning driver(s) to specific cars then a **Driver** Class-&-Object is required.

Collection-members structures consider objects that contain or consist of a collection of another object, i.e. An organisation could be considered as having a collection of clerks. This is only a valid Class-&-Object if there is a need to keep information about clerks in this form.

3.5   Subjects

Subjects are described as mechanisms for guiding the reader (analysts, problem domain expert, manager client) through a large, complex model. Coad and Yourdon recommend that a team of senior analysts do a rapid first pass identification of Class-&-Object and 'structures' and then identify an initial set of 'subjects' which can be fine tuned later. They do not offer any insight as to how this procedure should be conducted. This strengthens the previous discussion that indicates that identification of potential Class-&-Objects is largely based on expertise and craft knowledge of the method and the problem domain. Further discussion of 'subjects' is beyond the scope of this paper.

3.6   Defining Attributes

Attributes add detail to the Class-&-Object and 'structure' abstractions. If another part of the 'system' needs to access or otherwise manipulate the values in an object, it must do so by specifying a Message Connection corresponding to a 'service' defined for that object. This is a specification discipline, with narrow, well defined interfaces between portions of the overall specification - encapsulation and data abstraction therefore come to the fore front. It is argued that over time the problem domain Class-&-Objects are likely to remain stable, however 'attributes' and attribute values are likely to change.

I would argue that this activity should be carried out earlier. It is more 'natural' to identify important attributes at the same time as the Class-&-Object. This would then help in the determination of Gen-spec or Whole-Part structures. Each Class-&-Object would need to be re-visited in order to identify other attributes that have been missed earlier.

Relevant attributes are determined by looking at each Class-&-Object in turn and deciding what information about the Class-&-Object needs to be known and remembered over time, and what states the attributes can be in. Each 'attribute' should capture an 'atomic concept' meaning a single or tightly related grouping of values, i.e. individual data element (driver's license number) or a natural grouping of data elements (legal name, or address which includes town and postcode). Having determined a list of attributes one can eliminate those that are not relevant to the problem situation.

3.7   Lessons Learned

The evaluation of OOA has indicated that design solutions determine what is required, instead of approaching the problem situation with an open mind and determining an appropriate solution. This method assumes that an object oriented solution is feasible and necessary and consciously looks for previously defined objects that can be reused. This effectively means that the anticipated object oriented solution determines the notional system (Jayaratna, 1994) and influences what is identified in the current state.

This raises a number of issues that must be addressed in order to determine the applicability of object oriented analysis to a problem situation.

- There is a need for sound methodological reasons for using Object Oriented Analysis initially.
- The question 'Do we need an Object Oriented system?' must be addressed, in order to determine whether this is the most effective system to develop for the problem situation.
- There is a need for the method to identify criteria and concepts that can be used to help structure our thinking about 'real world' attributes in Object Oriented terms without losing its complex connections.

References

Bouzeghoub, M., G. Gardarin, et al. (1997). Object Technology Concepts and Methods, International Thomson Computer Press.

Coad,P and Yourdon, E (1990) Object Oriented Analysis, Prentice Hall

Conger, S. (1994). The New software Engineering. Belmont, California, International Thomson Publishing.

DeMarco (1979). Structured Analysis, Yourdon Press.

Fichman, R G. and Kemerer, C F (1992). Object-oriented and Conventional analysis and design methodologies: comparison and critique. IEEE Computer October 1992

Jayaratna, N. (1994) Understanding and Evaluating Methodologies. McGraw-Hill

Lewis, P. (1994). Information-Systems Development, Pitman.

Yourdon, E. (1989). Modern Structured Analysis, Prentice Hall.

The Role of Object-Oriented Modelling Methods in Requirements Engineering

Linda L. Dawson and Paul A. Swatman

School of Management Information Systems, Deakin University, Burwood, Victoria, Australia

Abstract

In recent years many organisations have been moving to the use of object-oriented methods for the development of information systems. Many claims have been made about the efficacy of object-oriented methods for specifying and building software and information systems. Several studies have looked at small groups (often students) using object-oriented methods for small one-off exercises or problems. These studies lack information about how real systems are being developed in practice. There is a need to investigate the use of object-oriented methods by practising professionals in the production of requirements specifications for "real world" sized projects. In this paper firstly we outline a conceptual framework of "what might be happening" in professional object-oriented requirements engineering based on the common characteristics of published, well known object-oriented methods. Secondly, we describe a research plan for a set of case studies that are currently being undertaken.

1 Introduction

In recent years many organisations have been moving to the use of object-oriented methods for the development of information systems. Many object-oriented methods have been published, based on an underlying paradigm of objects, classes and inheritance [1], but little is understood (at least on the basis of sound empirical evidence) about how object-oriented methods are used by practising professionals.

Several studies have looked at small groups (often students) using object-oriented methods for small one-off exercises or problems. These studies lack information about how the results might be generalised to real systems which are being developed in practice. Indeed, as we argued in [2] any such generalisation would be unfounded.

Some studies [3-6] have looked at how analysts apply general problem solving and reasoning skills to the process of requirements engineering while other studies [7-10] have addressed specific aspects of using and learning object-oriented methods compared to other methods.

Various methods, both qualitative and quantitative, have been used to collect data on the behaviour of system developers. Protocol analysis [11] is one of the most frequently used methods [3, 5]. *Protocol analysis* is a data gathering technique which typically requires participants to "think aloud" while solving a problem or performing a task. Records of these thinking-aloud protocols are audio- or video-taped and are called *concurrent* protocols. *Retrospective* protocols are recorded with participants after the task has been completed and involve questioning the participants about what they were thinking while performing a specific task or sub-task.

In order to understand *what* successful professional developers do, *how* they do it, *why* they do what they do and *when* they do what they do further investigation is needed. Key areas needing further investigation and quantification include the notion of experience, problem size and work patterns [2].

This paper presents the foundations of a program of research into object-oriented requirements engineering. The conceptual framework describing what might be happening in professional practice is described in Section 5. Section 6 describes a research method based on case studies of practising professional requirements engineers. In this paper the terms "requirements engineer" and "systems analyst" will be used synonymously.

2 Background

2.1 Requirements Engineering

Requirements engineering is the first stage of information system development. Carroll and Swatman [12] have argued that the predominant literature on the requirements engineering process is fundamentally flawed - in that the process is presented as either a linear, or a cyclic process of specification evolution. Preliminary work, reported in Carroll and Swatman [13]; Carroll et al [14], extends to requirements engineering the work of Khushalani et al [15] who showed, through an extensive and detailed protocol analysis-based study, that "design" in a software context is *opportunistic* and insight-driven rather than incremental and evolutionary. Consequently, we suggest, the *professional* requirements engineering process is poorly understood and documented within the literature.

Software engineering developed as a discipline to address the need for developing large complex software systems in an organised and structured manner.

Requirements engineering [16, 17] specifically addresses the problems associated with errors in functional specifications which result in the costly maintenance or failure of software systems [18-20]. Requirements engineering has now expanded to include more than just software construction [16, 17] and is now an accepted term in information systems for defining the process and outcome of systems analysis.

Although there is no commonly accepted definition of requirements engineering [16, 17] our working definition is:

> "Requirements engineering is a process of elicitation, modelling, and validation of information system requirements which provides a specification which is the basis for the design and implementation of that information system."

This definition places the requirements engineering process early in the system development cycle, although in many projects it may not necessarily be the very first phase. It may be that the requirements engineering process is triggered by preliminary investigations [21] or questionings of users and clients of the way activities are undertaken within their organisation [22].

Pohl [23] proposes three dimensions of requirements engineering. These three dimensions can be outlined as follows:

Representational issues	involve the range of representation methods from informal, natural language specifications to formal specification.
Social domain issues	encompass the social process involved in the iterative, co-operative elicitation of information for building requirements. Of particular importance is the aspect of communication between end users and analysts in establishing and documenting system needs within the organisational context.
Cognitive domain issues	are concerned with the understanding of the problem itself within the problem domain using various conceptual models.

A useful framework of requirements engineering processes has been proposed by Loucopoulos and Karakostas[16]. In this framework the requirements engineering process can be broken down into three sub-processes, elicitation, specification and validation, which deal with two external entities, the user and the problem domain. The purpose of elicitation is to obtain as much knowledge as possible about the problem in order to build a specification for the solution to the problem. Input comes from the user and existing information about the problem domain. Like the other two sub-processes, elicitation does not end when the next process starts. Rather, each subprocess relies on feedback from the other subprocesses. The specification sub-process provides specifications and models for verification and validation by the user and against the original problem domain.

2.2 Object-oriented Methods

Many claims have been made about the object-oriented paradigm [24-27]. These claims include:

- ease of understanding object-oriented models due to a consistent underlying representation throughout the development process
- the ability to model the behaviour of objects (encapsulation of data and process)
- ease of modification and extendibility of object-oriented models.
- ease of reuse of object components from previously designed systems
- superior data abstraction facilities including inheritance and polymorphism

When we study object-oriented methods in requirements engineering, our interest is in how experienced analysts and developers actually use such methods in "real-world" system specification. We also need to consider whether the benefits of reuse, abstraction and reduction in complexity outweigh any difficulties in learning and using to object-oriented methods.

Object-oriented systems development life cycles are usually based on non-linear cycles such as the spiral model [28] or the fountain model [29]. Henderson-Sellers [29] reflects the conventional wisdom of the object-oriented community in stating that object-oriented *analysis* provides an accurate picture of real world situation, object-oriented *design* supports good software engineering design and the goal of a good object-oriented method is the "seamless" transition between the analysis and design phases.

Further, it is generally agreed within the object-oriented world that one of the strengths of object-oriented methods is that complexity is reduced because the concept of an object remains the same throughout the development process from analysis to implementation and flow of control is modelled as interactions between objects.

In this program of research we open these key assertions to question and seek persuasive empirical evidence (for or against) which is grounded in the professional use of object-orientated methods on a commercial scale and in a commercial setting.

In an object-oriented modelling process several models are usually produced. These models can be loosely categorised as either *static* models or *dynamic* models. Static models describe objects, their characteristics and the relationships between them. Some common models are class and object diagrams [24], component notation and templates [25], object models [30], class cards, hierarchies and collaborations [31], object/class models [29], object and layer models [32] and structural models [33]

Dynamic models define states of objects, state transitions, message passing and event handling. Some common dynamic models are state transition and event diagrams [24], state diagrams [25, 30], objectcharts [29], interaction diagrams [34], rules [32], object communication models [33, 35] and dynamic models using event chains and collaborative diagrams [36-38]. Sequencing is often modelled using use cases [34], task scripts [32] or scenarios [29, 30] defining typical user interaction with the system

3 A Motivating Case

Carroll and Swatman [13] describe a case study of the requirements engineering process for a relatively simple electronic commerce application. The client, who intended to market the application to users of the internet, had extensive experience in the problem domain and some knowledge of object-oriented methods. The requirements engineer was an independent consultant experienced in both object-oriented and non-object-oriented methods. Both the client and the requirements engineer had an assistant each and there was a researcher who was a participant observer.

Before the requirements engineering process began the client had already developed some object-oriented models and purchased some hardware and software. During the requirements engineering process of six sessions over two days it became apparent to the requirements engineer (and later the client) that the application was not suited to object-oriented development since there were no active or autonomous objects in the system other than, perhaps, the system itself and there was very little potential for reuse. In essence, the problem was of a simple information storage and retrieval nature. A much simpler design and implementation was eventually agreed upon based on a standard relational database with a web-based Java front-end since most of the processing involved the maintenance and retrieval of customer and product records.

During the requirements engineering process (session 3) a SWOT analysis was done by the client of the proposed non-object-oriented/database solution. This is summarised below:

Strengths:
- should beat the due date
- easier domain to work in, therefore costs are less

Weaknesses:
- moving away from the strengths of object-orientation - better engineering and reusability

the requirements engineer argued that object-orientation would not necessarily provide better engineering for this project since relational database is a tried and tested paradigm in the senses both of problem domain and technological solution

- need to scrap a lot of work

the requirements engineer argued here that previous time and effort had not been wasted since the client still needed to "know what he wants" in the system.

Opportunities:
- early delivery date to the market, leading to market opportunities, new domains and a better understanding of the market through feedback
- can spend more money on the interface which is what the users care about most.

Threats:
- such a simple model means it is easy to copy

the competition could employ the simpler architecture anyway; but the requirements engineer also suggested a threat analysis using Porter's model of competitive forces

This case study demonstrated the following characteristics which are evident in the conceptual framework outlined in section 5:

The opportunistic nature of the requirements engineering process

The case notes describe the identification of three subprocesses of elicitation, representation (modelling) and validation. There was the evidence of feedback both within and between these processes. Often the participants left a difficult area for a while and moved on with the intention of gaining a solution by approaching the problem from a different angle. So the requirements engineering process does not appear to be incrementally evolutionary from elicitation to specification and handover. The requirements engineering process emerges as a creative process that relies on opportunistic restructuring of accumulated information and feedback. Although many textbook methodologies suggest that requirements engineering, or systems analysis, should be top down and incremental we cannot be sure that system developers always "play by the rules" Khushalani et al [15] as discussed in section 2.1.

The influence of what was already available

As with most system analysis and design, the actual specification of the system is rarely done in isolation. In this case, an interest in using object-oriented methods by the client together with pre-purchased software and hardware had some bearing on the direction of some aspects of analysis and design. Also discussion of the business context in terms of available tools and the analyst's experience often gave rise to further requirements.

Not all applications are object-oriented

In this case the method (object-oriented) had been chosen before the problem had been understood or specified. Although this may quite common, especially in large software houses where there is a proprietary approach, an independent consultant (as in this case) may advise a simpler (many object-oriented adherents might argue this point) and ultimately cheaper solution.

An important element in all these issues is the concept of the analyst's experience. This is difficult (even for the analyst) to quantify. Opportunistic restructuring is often based on an analyst's experience. "What is already available" can also mean what the analyst already knows from experience - a problem already solved, a concept applied in another context or a specific tool used before that will help to solve a problem. An experienced analyst will know about and have used various methods in the past and be able to use their experience to apply the appropriate method to the problem.

In this case the analyst "kept waiting for the problem" and at some point experience dictated that the analyst's mental model "jelled". The system was seen as "a simple system - a database". The consultant analyst is quoted as commenting "A problem with OO is that no-one knows how to put things down in a structured format (presumably for the user), unlike databases".

4 Research Questions

The broad theme of this research is encompassed in the following research question:

> "How are object-oriented modelling methods being
> used by practising professionals for requirements
> engineering?"

The emphasis is on "how and now" not the change of focus or what new literature says should be being done. We are interested in the perceived and demonstrated protocols used by practising requirements engineers.

4.1 Subquestions

The broad research question above can usefully be broken down into several subquestions as outlined below:

SQ1: "How (if at all) is knowledge elicitation influenced by the use of object-oriented modelling methods?"

Do analysts think in terms of objects as they try and build their mental model of the required system? Or does the object-oriented nature manifest itself later when the models are being built? That is, is knowledge elicitation for object-oriented systems different from elicitation for non-object-oriented modelling methods?

SQ2: "When, how and for whom is object-oriented modelling undertaken?"

Are object-oriented models shown to the user? Or are object-oriented models actually "internal" models used purely by analysts, designers and implementers?

SQ3: "How is validation performed on object-oriented models?"

How are the object-oriented models communicated back to the user for validation? Do users understand object-oriented models? Or do analysts describe their models for users using simpler diagrams and tables as in non-object-oriented methods?

5 Conceptual Framework

The starting point for this research project is the formulation of a conceptual framework showing what might be happening in object-oriented requirements engineering practice. The object-oriented characteristics of the model are based on published well-known methods [24-27, 30, 32, 34]. As we developed our model we began from Loucopoulos and Karakostas's framework, [16]. Our initial work suggested that requirements specification is not, however, based on iteration but rather on feedback and the opportunistic restructuring of information gathered and developed in three autonomous processes. This insight has led to the development of the conceptual framework (Figure 1) which underlies the remainder of the work discussed here.

Information and artefacts (eg model diagrams, documentation etc) produced in one subprocess are often fed back into other subprocesses for clarification or refinement. This model explicitly shows this feedback using arrows. In order to emphasise the fact that we do not believe that requirements engineering relies on evolutionary or incremental cycles, we shall consider the subprocesses depicted in the conceptual framework to be a set of co-operating "machines" that interact autonomously and opportunistically.

The process starts with the Knowledge Acquisition subprocess. This subprocess is initially based on knowledge contained in ill-defined user requirements and an ill-defined problem domain. Predetermined and available resources such as hardware and software already available to the client or methods and tools already familiar to the client and the analyst may also influence the starting point for elicitation. An iterative process between the analyst and the user progressively clarifies the knowledge about the user requirements and the problem domain.

The clarified knowledge about the user requirements and the problem domain are then used as the basis of the Object-Oriented Requirements Modelling subprocess. The modelling subprocess produces several models which can be categorised as static or dynamic models as described in section 2.2.

The Validation subprocess takes these models and validates them against the user's original requirements based on the knowledge about the problem domain. The process of refining the models based on validation is itself iterative.

The thin arrows in the diagram indicate interaction between the analyst and users or other actors or knowledge and artefacts gained from users or other actors. The thick arrows in the diagram indicate that the artefacts and information that go into and come out of the processes comes only from the modeller(s) or analysts.

Using Pohl's three dimensional categorisation [23] the representational dimension is defined in the Object-oriented Requirements Modelling Process and the static and dynamic Domain Models produced; the social dimension is defined in the thin arrows and the cognitive dimension is defined in the thick arrows.

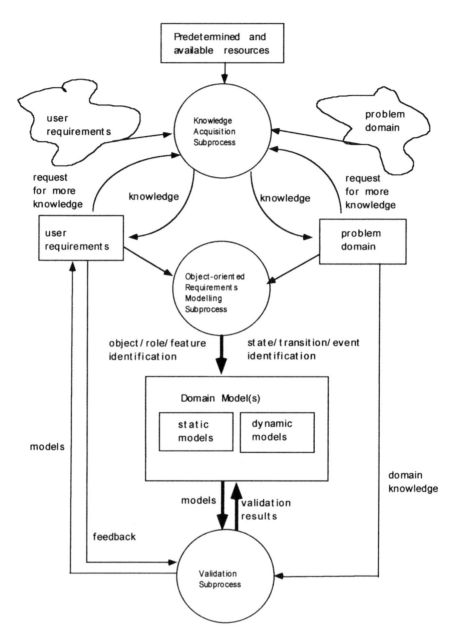

Figure 1 - A conceptual framework of object-oriented requirements engineering

6 Research Method

Miles and Huberman [39] suggest that knowing what you want to find out (as described in the conceptual framework and research questions) " ... leads inexorably to the question of how you will get that information". It might involve interviews, collecting documents, observations, recording activities on tape etc. Our research program is based on case studies of professional systems analysts who are undertaking or have undertaken requirements specification for a systems development project.

An initial pilot study will first be undertaken to refine the research questions and the research instrument.

This project does not involve action research although there will be some intervention where the researcher may need to ask leading questions. The researcher will not be working on any of the observed projects or directly with any of the participants. Data collection will involve interviewing and observing participants as they go about their work. Cases will be observed using a series of "snapshots" or meetings for interview or observation at specific intervals over the life of the project. Data will be collected in the field using various quantitative and qualitative methods based on:

- protocol analysis in the field, or "prompted" protocol analysis where subjects are not just asked to think aloud while performing tasks but are asked or prompted to say what they are doing and why.
- interviews incorporating structured/unstructured, open/closed questions
- observation incorporating prompted protocol analysis
- reflection and follow-up questions based on accumulated data so far

Each case will have a cycle with a minimum of three stages:

Stage 1: preliminary interview setting context, gathering quantitative data about the project and the requirements engineer participating (unit of analysis - see more detail in section 6.1)

Stage 2: structured and unstructured interviews using open and closed questions for gathering data about perceived activities and protocols undertaken in object-oriented requirements engineering. ie "When/what/why analysts believe they do what they do" There should be several snapshots in stage 2 based on reflection and follow-up.

Stage 3: interviews and prompted protocol analysis observations gathering data about actual or demonstrated activities and protocols undertaken in object-oriented requirements engineering. ie "When/what/why analysts actually do what they do". There should be several snapshots in stage 3 based on reflection and follow-up.

The instrumentation proposed for this project ranges from well structured in the early stages to open ended in the later observational stages allowing for collecting of data in context and for the following up of new threads discovered in the data gathering process. Detailed instrumentation is only proposed for stages 1 and 2 since the instrumentation required for stage 3 may only become apparent after some time in the field and will differ from participant to participant.

6.1 Unit of Analysis - The Analyst in Context

In order to understand the use of object-oriented models by practising professionals we must set the bounds of the research and data collection by determining the unit of analysis - the entity about which we want to gather data and the context of that entity within each case study. Yin [40] suggests that the unit of analysis defines the "case" in a case study. He suggests five possible units of analysis:

- individuals
- decisions
- programs
- implementation processes
- organisational change

The choice of the unit of analysis in a study is related to the way the questions and propositions are defined. In one sense, this project is concerned with all of the above units of analysis but the main unit of analysis is the individual experienced requirements engineer or analyst, although within the context of four other elements derived from Yin's elements [40](see Figure 2).

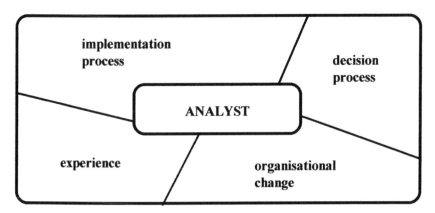

Figure 2 - unit of analysis - the analyst/requirements engineer in context

- The analyst is working in an organisation which has adopted object-oriented methods for system development. The analyst will be influenced by how the organisation has gone about implementing that change. The analyst may be one of many within the organisation who has been coopted into the object-oriented program or he/she may be part of a pilot program within the organisation.

- The analyst may have been consulted, or may not, about the decision to adopt object-oriented methods and may have been through an organisation sponsored training course.

- The adoption of object-oriented methods may have affected some aspects of the organisation's operation or may have affected the analyst's function or place within the organisation.

- An individual analyst may have had specific training in object-oriented and non object-oriented requirements engineering methods and will have specific experience with one or more methods for commercial system specification and modelling.

All these aspects will affect the gathering of data from the practising professionals that will be the participants in this study and the proposed model need to take these issues into account when formulating the first cut of questions that will go to the participants in the pilot study.

6.2 Identifying Perceived and Demonstrated Activities and Protocols

We are interested in the perceived and demonstrated activities and protocols used by professional analysts when specifying systems using object-oriented models and methods. By "protocols" we mean the sequence of tasks performed, when they are initiated, when they are deemed to be complete and in which order the analyst performs tasks and how critical that order is (or is believed to be by the analyst). By "perceived" we mean the activities and protocols the analyst *believes* he/she is undertaking and by "demonstrated" we mean the activities that the analyst can be *observed to be actually* undertaking.

7 Conclusion

In this paper we have postulated that requirements engineering, paticularly object-oriented requirements engineering may not be incrementally evolutionary or "seamless". We have proposed a model based on opportunistic restructuring and feedback from the various subprocesses, or machines, that are involved in the specification process. We have also proposed a research plan based on case studies of practising professional requirements engineers that will provide a better understanding the role object-oriented modelling methods play in this interaction between the co-operating machines.

References

1. Wegner, P.: Dimensions of object-based language design. In: OOPSLA. ACM, New York, 1987.
2. Dawson, L.L. and P.A. Swatman: Object-Oriented Requirements Engineering in Practice. In: Fifth European Conference on Information SystemsCork, Ireland, 1997.
3. Chaiyasut, P. and G. Shanks: Conceptual Data Modelling Process: A Study of Novice and Expert Data Modellers. In: First International Conference on Object Role ModellingMagnetic Island, Australia, 1994.
4. Guindon, R., Knowledge exploited by experts during software system design. International Journal of Man-Machine Studies, 1990; **33**:: p. 279-304.
5. Sutcliffe, A.G. and N.A.M. Maiden, Analysing the novice analyst: cognitive models in software engineering. International Journal of Man-Machine Studies, 1992; **36**:: p. 719-740.
6. Vitalari, N.P. and G.W. Dickson, Problem Solving for effective systems analysis: an experimental exploration. Communications of the ACM, 1983; **26**:(11).
7. Boehm-Davis, D. and L. Ross, Program design methodologies and the software development process. International Journal of Man-Machine Studies, 1992; **36**:: p. 1-19.
8. Lee, Y. and N. Pennington, The effects of paradigm on cognitive activities in design. International Journal of Human-Computer Studies, 1994; **40**:: p. 577-601.
9. Morris, M., C. Speier, and J. Hoffer: The impact of experience on individual performance and workload differences using object-oriented and process-oriented systems analysis techniques. In: 29th Hawaii International Conference on System SciencesMaui, Hawaii, 1996.
10. Vessey, I. and S. Conger, Requirements specification: Learning object, process, and data methodologies. Communications of the ACM, 1994; **37**:(5).
11. Ericsson, K.A. and H.A. Simon, Verbal Reports as Data. Psychological Review, 1980(87): p. 215-251.
12. Carroll, J. and P. Swatman: How Can the Requirements Engineering Process be Improved? In: Eighth Australasian Conference on Information SystemsUniversity of South Australia, Adelaide, South Australia, 1997.
13. Carroll, J. and P.A. Swatman, Case Notes, . 1997.
14. Carroll, J., B. Hunt, and P. Swatman, Producing quality applications for Web-enabled Electronic Commerce, . 1998: submitted to 11th International Bled Electronic Commerce Conference.
15. Khushalani, A., R. Smith, and S. Howard, What happens when designers don't play by the rules: Towards a model of opportunistic behaviour and design. Australian Journal of Information Systems, 1994: p. 13-31.

16. Loucopoulos, P. and V. Karakostas, Systems Requirements Engineering. . McGraw-Hill. London, UK, 1995.
17. Macaulay, L., Requirements Engineering. . Springer-Verlag. London, 1996.
18. Boehm, B.W., Software Engineering. IEEE Transactions on Computers, 1976; 25:(12): p. 1226-1241.
19. Jackson, M.C.: Critical Systems Thinking and Information Systems Development. In: Eighth Australasian Conference on Information SystemsUniversity of South Australia, Adelaide, South Australia, 1997.
20. OASIG, Why do IT Projects so often Fail?", in OR Newsletter. 1996. p. 12-16.
21. Avison, D.E. and G. Fitzgerald, Information Systems Development: Methodologies, Techniques and Tools. 2 ed. McGraw Hill. , 1995.
22. Checkland, P. and J. Scholes, Soft Systems Methodology in Practice. . Wiley. Chichester, 1990.
23. Pohl, K.: The three dimensions of requirements engineering. In: Fifth International Conference on Advanced Information Systems Engineering (CAiSE'93). Springer-Verlag, Paris, 1993.
24. Booch, G., Object-Oriented Analysis and Design with Applications. . Benjamin/Cummings. Redwood City, 1994.
25. Coad, P. and E. Yourdon, Object-Oriented Analysis. 2 ed. Yourdon Press/Prentice-Hall. Englewood Cliffs, NJ, 1991.
26. Henderson-Sellers, B. and J. Edwards, BOOKTWO of Object-Oriented Knowledge: The Working Object. . Prentice Hall. Englewood Cliffs, NJ, 1994.
27. Meyer, B., Object-Oriented Software Construction. . Prentice-Hall. Englewood Cliffs, NJ, 1988.
28. Boehm, B.W., A spiral model of software development and enhancement. IEEE Computer, 1988; 25:(5): p. 61-72.
29. Henderson-Sellers, B., A Book of Object-Oriented Knowledge. 2 ed. Prentice-Hall. Upper Saddle River, NJ, 1997.
30. Rumbaugh, J., et al., Object-Oriented Modeling and Design. . Prentice-Hall. Englewood Cliffs, NJ, 1991.
31. Wirfs-Brock, R.J., B. Wilkerson, and L. Wiener, Designing Object-Oriented Software. . Prentice Hall. New York, USA, 1990.
32. Graham, I., Object Oriented Methods. . Addison-Wesley. , 1994.
33. Swatman, P.A., Formal object-oriented method - FOOM, in Specification of Behavioural Semantics in Object-Oriented Information Systems, W. Harvey, Editor. 1996, Kluwer Academic Publishers: Norwell, Massachucetts.
34. Jacobson, I., et al., Object-Oriented Software Engineering: A Use Case Driven Approach. . Addison-Wesley/ACM. New York, 1992.
35. Shlaer, S. and S.J. Mellor, Modelling the World in States. . Yourdon Press. Englewood Cliffs, NJ, 1991.
36. Fowler, D., P.A. Swatman, and E.N. Wafula, Formal methods in the IS domain:Introducing a notation for presenting Object-Z specifications. Object Oriented Systems, 1995; 2:(2).

37. Fowler, D., Formal Methods in a commercial information systems setting: the FOOM methodology, in Department of Information Systems. 1996, Swinburne University of Technology: Melbourne.

38. Wafula, E.N. and P.A. Swatman, FOOM: a diagrammatic illustration of Object-Z specifications. Object Oriented Systems, 1996; 3:(4): p. 215-243.

39. Miles, M.B. and A.M. Huberman, Qualitative Data Analysis: A Sourcebook of New Methods. . Sage Publications Inc. Newbury Park, CA, 1984.

40. Yin, R.K., Case Study Research: Design and Methods. Vol. 5. 2 ed. Applied Social Research Methods Series. Sage Publications Inc. Thousand Oaks, CA, 1994.

Theory in Information Systems

Nahed Stokes

Department of Computer Science, King's College London,
Strand, London, WC2R 2LS, UK
nahed@dcs.kcl.ac.uk

Abstract

Many papers have discussed the nature of information systems (IS) as a field of study, its contents, boundaries and relationship to other disciplines. Relatively few have, however, focused on the nature of the theory per se. This paper examines IS theory as it appears in IS'97, the U.S. definition of an IS body of knowledge, and, in the U.K., in the work of Checkland and Holwell, Mingers and Stowell, and others. This paper examines also some of the current thinking about theory in the humanities and draws a parallel between current debates taking place in IS and those taking place in the humanities regarding the "Age of Theory". In particular, the paper suggests that the arguments made about feminism and other cross-disciplinary subjects could equally apply to IS.

1 Introduction

Many debates have focused on the issue of what is IS and what kind of discipline it is. IS is alternatively viewed as a multi-discipline (Mingers and Stowell, 1997, p. 12), an inter-discipline (Jayaratna, 1994, p. 21; Avison, 1997, p. 124), a sort of "crypto-science" (Probert, 1997, p. 47), a pseudo-science practised not by scientists but by alchemists (Angell, p.1997, p. 381), a social science (Land, 1985, Cornford and Smithson, 1996), a fragmented adhocracy (Banville and Landry, 1989), an essentially pluralistic field (Banville and Landry, 1989), and a set of liberal arts as opposed to a specialist discipline (Work, 1997, p. 350). For Checkland and Holwell, IS is certainly not a "discipline". They are even dubious about it being a "field" though they are prepared to concede that it may be a "primitive one" (Chekland and Holwell, 1998, p. 52). For Angell, it is an indiscipline (Angell, 1997, p. 381).

Notwithstanding this variety of views, there is "a general agreement that IS is something that is practised" (Mingers and Stowell, 1997, p. 10) and comparisons with law and medicine are often made. As pointed out by Avison, "what is practised is what is taught" (Avison, 1997, p. 128). This leaves open issues such as what is the theory in IS, how could it be defined and, more generally, what understanding a body of knowledge as "theoretical" means.

The issue of what is theory is, of course, not specific to IS. It has been discussed and continues to be discussed in the context of many disciplines. It is a particularly topical subject in the humanities at the moment. "Theory is in" is how Diane Elam starts her paper on the subject of feminism and deconstruction (Elam, 1995). Her paper was one of a collection of papers presented at a conference on "The Human Sciences in the Age of Theory" hosted by the Centre for the Study of Theory and Criticism at the University of Western Ontario (Kreiswirth and Carmichael, 1995).

This paper starts by looking at theory and its relationship to concepts and disciplines. It then examines IS theory as defined in IS'97 and reviews some of the thoughts about IS theory that have appeared in the recent work of Checkland and Howell and in the edited papers by Mingers and Stowell. The paper then examines a view of theory based on the work of Diane Elam on feminism and deconstruction. The paper highlights the fact that much of her discourse could easily be applied to the field of IS and that there are strong parallels between her arguments and those put forward by some IS researchers.

2 Theory, Concept, and Discipline

The word "theory" derives from the lexicon of ancient Greek - the word "thea" meaning "sight". Today, it denotes a systematic and speculative approach to anything. Theorising about IS and IS development has no lengthy genealogy. It is a recent development which has yet to be fully recognised as a serious intellectual discipline.

Before examining IS theory, it is worth considering the general issue of the relationship between theory and concept and between concept and discipline. Both relationships have been the subject of much philosophical debate. As summarised by Gutting (1994) "the standard Anglo-American view [shared by both positivists such as Hempel and their critics such as Kuhn] is that theories and concepts are the same. Theories are interpretations of data and therefore define the concepts in terms of which data are understood." By contrast, the French view, as exemplified by Canguilhem and later Foucault, is that theories are separate from concepts since the same concept can function in quite different theoretical contexts. For Canguilhem, "concepts give us a preliminary understanding of data that allows us to formulate scientifically fruitful questions about how to explain the data as conceptualized. Theories then provide different - and often conflicting - answers to these questions" (Gutting, 1994). For example, the concept of the motion of falling bodies introduced by Galileo (in opposition to Aristotle's) can be explained by the competing theories of Galileo, Descartes, and Newton.

Opinions are similarly divided as to the relationship between concepts and disciplines. For Canguilhem, "concepts correspond to disciplines, and the history of a concept is written within the confines of the relevant discipline. But Foucault links apparently very different disciplines by showing similarities in their basic concepts. He argues, for example, that the Classical empirical sciences of general grammar, natural history, and the analysis of wealth share a common conceptual structure that makes them much more similar to one another than any one of them is to its modern successor (respectively: philology, biology, and economics)" (Gutting, 1994).

The above discussion of the relationship between theories, concepts, and disciplines is particularly relevant to IS since it is generally accepted that IS is a hybrid or multi-disciplinary field of study which has its roots in computer science and management, with a host of supporting disciplines, e.g. psychology, sociology, statistics, political science, economics, philosophy, and mathematics (Boland and Hirschhein, 1985). Indeed, the list of disciplines that are considered to be relevant to IS seems to be growing continually. A more up-to-date list of relevant disciplines would also include cultural studies, ergonomics, ethics, linguistics, and semiology (Avison, 1997), together with anthropology and theology (Angell, 1997, p. 381). As discussed below, it is often difficult to separate the theories, concepts, and fundamentals of IS from those of other disciplines. Some IS researchers have even claimed that very little material is unique to IS (Work, 1997, p. 342).The recurring questions of how, where, and even whether there are any internal or external boundaries to be drawn within or around the world of IS are reminiscent of the questions that have occupied philosophers attempting to define, for example, contemporary French philosophy (Montefiore, 1983).

3 IS Theory - "Hard" and "Soft" Perspectives

To analyse the theory in IS, this paper will first examine and contrast two publications. The first, IS'97, is a 91-page model curriculum for undergraduate degree programmes in information systems (Davis *et al.*, 1997). The model curriculum was produced in the U.S. following an extensive and lengthy collaborative effort involving 1000 individuals from industry and academia. It describes in considerable detail the body of knowledge in IS and shows how the various elements of that body may be combined into "learning units", which in turn may be packaged into undergraduate courses. Written with the aim of helping IS academics to secure better funding for IS programmes, it provides the most up-to-date and comprehensive definition of this field of study. The second publication is a more personal effort produced, on this side of the Atlantic, by Checkland and Holwell (1998) with the aim of making sense of a field of study which they claim to be in great need of "conceptual cleansing". Their examination of the underlying concepts in IS offers a "soft" or interpretative perspective on this field which is in marked contrast to the "hard" or positivist view offered by IS'97.

The IS'97 model curriculum identifies three main subject areas making up the body of knowledge in IS. The first is IT. The second knowledge area is "Organizational and Management concepts" and the third is "Theory and Development of Systems". The knowledge areas contain major topics, which in turn contain sub-topics. The lowest level of the hierarchy is made up of some 506 knowledge elements. The IT subject area makes up by far the largest part of the IS body of knowledge. The description of the IT elements takes nearly as many pages as the description of the elements from the other two knowledge areas combined. This in a way explains why, for many outsiders, and for some insiders also, IS remains synonymous with IT. It also seems to confirm the view often held on this side of the Atlantic that the American curriculum is conceivably too computer-oriented.

It should be noted that none of the three major areas of knowledge is specific to IS. All three share elements with other subjects, such as computer science, software engineering, management, and mathematics. By contrast, Checkland and Holwell view IS as a distinctly separate area of thinking and activity. In their model, IS is one of four streams, with IT, organisation theory, and systems thinking being the other three.

Significantly, in IS'97, theory seldom appears on its own. When it does it is associated with knowledge elements such as "historical and social context of computing" and "properties of information systems" (IS'97, p. 71). Both these elements are associated with the goal to "introduce, discuss, and describe fundamental concepts of IS theory and its importance to practitioners" and its matching objective "identify and explain underlying concepts of IS discipline". More often than not, however, theory is linked to the practice or to systems development as in the curriculum area "IS theory and practice" or the knowledge area "Theory and development of Systems" previously mentioned. Many of the theories that appear in the body of knowledge are those associated with other disciplines. The curriculum area, "IS theory and practice", which purports to introduce the students to "concepts and theories that explain or motivate methods and practices in the development and use of information systems", has a wide range of topics, including decision theory (taken from mathematics), TQM and re-engineering, IS strategies, IS planning, and HCI.

This seems to give credence to the views expressed by Checkland and Holwell (1998) about IS theory. For these authors, IS theory is a practice-led theory, an account of "what works in practice". Many of the theories listed by these authors echo the theories listed in IS'97. But, despite this broad agreement as to the topics making up IS theory, the views of the IS field as conveyed by these two publications could not have been more different.

The order, coherence, and structure conveyed by IS'97's body of knowledge, with its 506 knowledge elements organised in a four-level hierarchy, is at odds with much of Checkland and Holwell's critical analysis of the field. For them, IS "does not have the kind of well-defined shape which quantum theory brings to nuclear physics". They argue that basic concepts, such as those of information and organisation, are far from coherent and that, as an intellectual field, IS "is in a fragmented state, with much of the work done within it seeming to be ad hoc rather than part of larger structures of thinking and debates such as one finds in mature fields like physics, chemistry or geography". In their analysis of the field, they state that "practically everything about it is problematical: its focus, methods, norms, language, and standards". They are particularly scathing with regard to IS theory, describing it as simply "yesterday's theory always trying to catch up with and make sense of the practice which has meanwhile moved on".

Others have also echoed these views. The lack of a theoretical clarity was recognized by Backhouse, Liebenau, and Land (1991). Avison mentions the "lack of theory in the field" (Avison, 1997, p. 128). Avgerou and Cornford (1998) also state that there is no "theory", although they identify "a few widely influential *reference* theories". They view IS theory in terms of concepts, abstract models, actual approaches, and methodologies. Angell, in his "futurologist" discussion of IS, talks about the uncertain future and expresses doubt about today's "backward looking methods of science and statistics that map yesterday onto tomorrow" (Angell, 1997, p. 380). The lack of a solid theoretical basis may explain the move away from prescriptive systems development methodologies to "contingent" frameworks such as Multiview, where the techniques and tools are chosen and adjusted according to the particular problem situation (Avison and Wood-Harper, 1990).

The need to define the theory and the need for better "theories" has been recognised by many IS researchers and academics as a necessary step for improving the funding of IS programmes within universities and IS research. Avison, for example, states that "the lack of an agreed and consistent theory is potentially disabling" (Avison, 1997, p. 128), noting that "unlike information systems most respected disciplines are built firmly on the rock of established theory" (Avison, 1997, p. 129). He argues that "it is important that most researchers work in areas that may establish the theoretical underpinnings of information systems" (Avison, 1997, p. 130) and that "the inter-disciplinary nature of the subject is no excuse for a lack of rigour" (p. 130).

Theory in inter-disciplinary subjects, argues Jayaratna, is often used as a basis for interlinking and integrating the different subject areas. He maintains that systems theory in IS is one major theory that can provide this integration as it "is very much focused on teasing out the integrative and holistic properties of a situation" (Jayaratna, 1994, p. 27). Cornford and Smithson (1996) make a similar point. For them, developing a theoretical perspective on the overall discipline of information systems "is of critical importance, for without it the subject will always be in danger of fragmenting into isolated islands of partial insight and empty technique". Their research in this area has led them, together with many other U.K. researchers, to the conclusion that information systems are essentially social systems. Indeed, many of the qualitative research methods used in IS have their origin in the social sciences. Baskerville and Wood-Harper (1998), for example, draw parallel between IS action research and action research in social science literature.

The similarities with the social sciences and the fragmentation of the field are also highlighted by Iivari, Hirschhein, and Klein (1998). Examining the concept of paradigm, which in the social sciences "captures the basic assumptions of *coexistent* theories, whereas in the natural sciences, it captures the basic assumptions of *historically successive* theories," they argue that the "paradigmatic status (of IS) as an academic discipline is like the social sciences rather than the natural sciences." Their paradigmatic analysis of five different information systems development approaches (ISDAs), where an approach represents a whole class of information systems development methods (ISDMs) which share fundamental concepts and principles for ISD, highlights the contrasting features of these approaches and, more generally, the fragmentation of the field of IS.

The link between IS and the social sciences - especially sociology - may perhaps be even more enlightening than many who support such links appreciate. For, between the 1920s and the 1940s, sociology became dominated by "grand theory" which, to some of its practitioners, seemed increasingly restrictive, out-of-touch, and sterile. Merton (1949) argued that it was time to turn away from grand theory and instead to concentrate on what he termed "middle-level theory", which could be justified in terms of actual practice. The proliferation of action research methods in information systems (Baskerville and Wood-Harper, 1998) may be symptomatic of such a move in IS.

4 Theory and the Humanities

The previous investigation of the theoretical status of IS has highlighted several viewpoints: the theory-indistinguishable-from-the-practice position, the theory-bashing position, and the purify-the-theory or keep-the-theory-theoretical position. The question of what is theory in IS remains unclear.

In an attempt to find an answer to this question, this paper will turn next to other disciplinary subjects in the humanities that have addressed this very question. In particular, it will examine some of the thinking about feminism and its theoretical status. Comparing a technology-free subject such as feminism to a technology-laden subject such as information systems seems at first far-fetched if not totally bizarre. There are, however, many similarities between these two subjects. The first and most obvious is that they are both of the same age. Modern feminism dates from the publication of Betty Friedan's book in 1963, while IS "as a field of academic study began in the 1960s, a few years after the first use of computers for information processing by organisations (IS'97, p. 6). Comparing two subjects of the same period could be viewed as one way of testing Foucault's theory that disciplines of the same intellectual era share strong similarities and are part of the same system of concepts or episteme.

Both feminism and information systems share a disciplinary uncertainty and ambiguity despite much evidence of academic activity. They are both not entirely academic. Neither subject is entirely within or completely outside the disciplinary structure of today's university.

In an essay entitled "Getting into Theory", Diane Elam argues that, although feminism cannot be considered a theory in the scientific and philosophical sense, it is nevertheless one in so far as it is said "to describe observable practices and experiences from a metadiscursive position and, as such, proffer knowledge on the basis of which further practices can be elaborated". For her, "the age of theory begins when theories fail, when no single theoretical discourse is possible any longer" (Elam, 1995, p. 89).

The above argument could equally be applied to IS. Much of IS theory is, indeed, an observation of practices and experiences. It could be argued that the proliferation of IS methods and of new ways of thinking mark the start of theory for IS, albeit of a "weaker" theory where no single theoretical discourse is possible.

Another point made by Elam is that "theory can actually be fossilized as a methodology that, in the long run, contracts rather than expands the field of knowledge and the possibility for political action". This could be an effective argument in IS against searching for a single all-embracing, overarching methodology. A similar point is made by Probert when he states that in IS "not only the search for a core of method or procedure likely to be futile, the demand for one is also" (Probert, 1997, p. 26).

It is possible, indeed, to view this drive toward an all-embracing methodology as foundationalism, the search for an end that many of the most crucial philosophers of the twentieth century, including Quine and Wittgenstein, have dismissed as futile. Many more recent thinkers, including Rorty (1979) and Bernstein (1983), have also questioned the idea of foundations, insisting not only that knowledge is mutable and perpetually subject to change, but that any adequate form of analysis must also take account of the norms and practices involved in defining that knowledge at any particular moment - norms and practices that themselves should constantly be subjected to critique and reinterpretation.

Elam further elaborates on the relationship between theory and politics:

> Theory is no longer theoretical when it loses sight of its own conditional nature, takes no risks in speculation, and circulates as a form of administrative inquisition. Theory oppresses, when it wills or perpetuates existing power relations, when it presents itself as a means to exert authority" (Elam, 1995, p. 92)

This echoes Probert's views on the relationship between IS and politics. He states, for example, that "It is important to note the political nature of information systems as a discipline. One's work can either be motivated by a desire to liberate or to enslave" (Probert, 1997, p. 57).

It is possible to view any attempt at imposing a particular IS method on the market place as a desire to enslave and the wholesale adoption of a method as the death of theory. Recognising this fact could have important implications for IS education. Angell, for example, accuses the education system of actively promoting methods, or "sanctifying lies" as he puts it, rather than studying them in a balanced way (Angell, 1997, p. 366).

Elam addresses also the issue of inter-discipline versus cross-discipline. She argues that inter-discipline and inter-disciplinary

> leave too much of a sense that old disciplinary boundaries still hold up, even if special interdisciplines are allowed to cross over them, or particular scholars are allowed to do work in more than one discipline. So, for instance, with an interdisciplinary model in place, feminism may be spotted in philosophy, biology, sociology, and literature, but no radical change need occur within each of these separate disciplines simply because they have allowed for a little inter-disciplinarity ... to think mainly in terms of disciplines and interdisciplines presupposes that the work being done is entirely academic and institutional, something that would be very difficult for feminism, for one, to accept ... By contrast, cross-disciplines, as a way of calling into question the very boundaries of disciplines, can potentially expose the impossibility of containing thought-action within the walls of the ivory tower. (Elam, 1995, p. 95)

Following the above arguments IS, too, could be thought of as a cross-discipline, although this would mean acknowledging that IS is not in itself a discipline, something that many IS researchers have forcefully contested (Probert, 1997). IS work is, after all, not entirely academic and institutional. Some disciplines have had an impact on IS. Changes, for example, in technology and organisations have forced radical changes in IS methods, even if they have not yet permeated the practice. But the same cannot be said of the majority of disciplines that are considered relevant to IS. More importantly, few, if any, of these disciplines have been affected by IS. This could, however, change in the future as applications and use of technology expand to every domain. After all, as pointed out by Angell, IS is about brokerage, and about coping with the complexities that emerge out of consequences of applying technology (Angell, 1997, p. 381).

Elam emphasises that theory can never be a set of theories or rules but is an endless *search* for rules (Elam, 1995, p. 97). This is similar to the point made by Probert when he states that "the identity of a discipline does not need to be established by some static definition. It can be founded in some evolving tradition of inquiry" (Probert, 1997, p. 26). It is this continuous search for new theories that make up the theory in IS. More graphically, theory is "both a distance travelled and the trajectory of the journey." (Kreiswirth and Carmichael, 1995, p. 4)

5 Conclusion

IS is in transition. There are many signs of tremendous academic activity. Yet it is still perceived within the more established disciplines as a matter for missionaries and their devoted disciples. There is also much scepticism about the theory in IS both within and outside academe. If an agreed curriculum provides the central underpinning of a discipline, then there is no doubt that the 91-page curriculum defined in IS'97 should give IS the status of a discipline. This paper has attempted to draw a parallel between the current philosophical debates about IS and similar debates raging in some parts of the humanities. For these, as for IS, it is still unclear whether the subjects concerned should really be viewed as essentially a collaboration among individuals working from within existing academic disciplines but attempting to widen the boundaries imposed by conventional methods of inquiry or whether they have a separate identity worthy of separate assessment and funding. The paper has also emphasised the importance of theory in inter-disciplinary work and the need to look at it as a means for continuous search rather than as a fixed set of rules and methods.

References

Angell, I.O. (1997), Welcome to the "Brave New World", in Mingers and Stowell (Eds.), pp. 363 - 384.

Avgerou, C. and Cornford, T. (1998), Developing Information Systems: Concepts, Issues and Practice, Second Edition, Macmillan.

Avison, D. (1997), The "Discipline" of Information Systems: Teaching, Research, and Practice, in Mingers and Stowell (Eds.) pp. 113 - 136.

Avison, D.E. and Wood-harper, A.T. (1990), Multiview: An Exploration in Information Systems development, McGraw-Hill.

Backhouse, J., Liebenau, J. and Land, F. (1991), The discipline of information systems, Journal of Information Systems, Vol. 1, No. 1.

Banville, C. and Landry, M. (1989), Can the field of MIS be disciplined? CACM Vol. 32, No. 1.

Baskerville, R. and Wood-Harper, A.T. (1998), Diversity in information systems action research methods, European Journal of Information Systems, Vol. 7, No. 2, pp. 90-107.

Bernstein, Richard J. (1983), Beyond Objectivism and Relativism: Science, Hermeneutics, and Praxis, University of Pennsylvania Press.

Boland, R.J. and Hirschhein, R.A. (1985), Series Introduction to the first volume of the Wiley series on Information Systems.

Checkland, P. and Holwell, S. (1998), Information, Systems and Information Systems, Wiley.

Churchman, C.W. (1971), The Design of Inquiry Systems: basic concepts of systems and organisation, Basic Books, New York.

Cornford, T. and Smithson, S. (1996), Project Research in Information Systems, Macmillan.

Davis, G.B., Gorgone, J.T., Couger, J.D., Feinstein, D. L., and Longenecker, H.E. (1997), IS'97 model curriculum and guidelines for undergraduate degree programs in information systems, The DATA BASE for Advances in Information Systems, Vol. 28, No. 1, pp. 1-94.

Elam, D. (1995), Getting into Theory, in Kreiswirth and Carmichael (Eds.), Constructive Criticism: The Human Sciences in the Age of Theory, University of Toronto Press, pp. 88 - 100.

Galliers, R.D. (Ed.) (1992), Information Systems Research: Issues, Methods and Practical Guidelines, Blackwell Scientific.

Gorgone, J.T., Couger, J.D., Davis, G., Feinstein, D., Kasper, G., and Longenecker, H.E., (1994), information systems `95 curriculum model - a collaborative effort, The DATA BASE for Advances in Information Systems, Vol. 25, No. 4, pp. 5-8.

Gutting, G. (ed.) (1994), The Cambridge Companion to Foucault, Cambridge University Press.

Iivari, J., Hirschheim, R., and Klein, H.K., (1998), A paradigmatic analysis contrasting information systems development approaches and methodologies, Information Systems Research, Vol. 9, No. 2, pp. 164-193.

Jayaratna, N. (1994), Understanding and Evaluating Methodologies, McGraw-Hill.

Kreiswirth, M. and Carmichael, T. (Eds.) (1995), Constructive Criticism: The Human Sciences in the Age of Theory, University of Toronto Press.

Land, F. (1985), Is an information theory enough?, The Computer Journal, Vol. 28, No. 3, pp. 211-215.

Merton, Robert K. (1949), Social Theory and Social Structure, Free Press.

Mingers, J.C. (1995), Information and meaning: foundations for an intersubjective account, Information Systems Journal, October, Vol. 5, No. 4, pp. 285-306.

Mingers, J. and Stowell, F. (1997), Information Systems: An Emerging Discipline?, Mc Graw Hill.

Montefiore, A. (ed.) (1983), Philosophy in France Today, Cambridge University Press.

Nissen, H.E., Klein, H.K., and Hirschheim, R. (Eds.) (1991), Information Systems research: Contemporary Approaches and Emergent Traditions, North-Holland.

Probert, S. (1997), The Actuality of Information Systems, in Mingers and Stowell (Eds.), pp. 21-62.

Rorty, R. (1979), Philosophy and the Mirror of Nature, Princeton University Press.

Work, B. (1997), Some Reflections on Information Systems Curricula, in Mingers and Stowell (Eds.), pp. 329 - 360.

Towards a Technique for Formulating Information Flows within a Human Purposeful Activity

Jun-Kang Feng

Department of Computing and Information Systems, University of Paisley, Paisley, UK

Abstract

When constructing an information system, it is important to be able to ascertain the information that the system is constructed to bear, which requires exactitude. And yet the literature of information systems development (ISD) does not seem to have provided a mechanism with such exactitude. This paper suggests integrating the framework of Mingers, the situation theory of Barwise, the information flow theory of Devlin and predicate calculus to develop a technique for formulating information flows within human purposeful activities. The idea is to capture information flows within a human purposeful activity from the point of view of the 'actor' by means of a set of formal constructs. The result shows that the use of the formal means sheds light on and injects mathematical rigour into the revelation of the information aspect of the activities, which helps the formulation of information requirements for ISD.

1 Introduction

A formalised computer-based information system, as opposed to the 'grapevine', is for the storage and provision of information on a regular basis and in a pre-defined manner [1]. A methodology for the development of such a system should be able to guarantee that the system when constructed has the capability of bearing the information that the system is constructed to bear.

And yet, well known and widely used methodologies such as SSADM [2], YSM [3], and OOA [4] include neither a formal (mathematical) semantic information formulation technique nor stage. Multiview [5] has an information analysis stage by using DFD and Entity model. In general, it seems that mathematical modelling of information at semantic level such as the work of Barwise [6] and Devlin [7] is not widely known within the community of information systems development. Little has been reported on the use of their work or the like in information systems development. This seems responsible, at least, for the lack of rigorous mechanism for determining and examining the information-bearing capacity of an information system.

To decide the information-bearing capacity of an information system, the first step should be to reveal and formulate the information that is required by the user of the system in their activities. This paper presents a set of constructs and a technique for the modelling of the information aspect of human activities. This work is based upon Mingers' [8] framework for information, Barwise's [6], [9] situation theory and Devlin's [7] information flow theory and makes use of predicate calculus.

This paper is organised as follows. First, we will show that semantic data modelling as the main means of information requirements analysis should be complemented by looking at information. Then we will describe the foundations of our approach to formulating semantic information flows. Then we will present a set of constructs for modelling information. Then we will show that an elementary human purposeful activity can be elaborated with a view to revealing information flows within it. And finally, we will discuss some possible implications of our approach to information systems methodologies.

2 Looking at Information to Complement Semantic Data Modelling

Semantic modelling by using semantic models such as the Entity-relationship model [10], the Functional Data Model [11] and the Semantic Data Model [12], is a conventional means of capturing the information and data requirements for an information system [2], [13], [14], [15].

The research on semantic models was initiated in the early 1970s. Late 1980s and early 1990s witnessed some profound reviews and criticisms of semantic modelling [16], [17], [18], [19]. It was realised that data modelling is a process of inquiry, therefore the paradigms, i.e., the ontology and epistemology of, and approaches to data modelling should be examined. Conventional data modelling is taken to be scientific [20] and realist–positivist [16], [18]. Conventional semantic modelling can only be used and has been used successfully at the hard, technically-oriented side of information systems development, that is, when data requirements are well defined and the implementation of an information systems is concerned. However the role of semantic modelling has been expanded to cover early stages of information systems development, which must deal with ill-defined problem situations. Data modelling has become a data-oriented approach to information systems development. 'Modelling the world in data' was taken as a slogan for object-oriented systems analysis [15]. Therefore, data modelling requires being re-interpreted [18] and further development, and a crucial issue here is the social paradigm of data modelling and analysis. It was argued [17], [18] that data analysis leads to a model of a particular group's knowledge and perceptions of a problem situation, rather than a model of a slice of the real world, thus a new interpretative approach, in particular a sense-making mechanism, is called for. The concept of appreciation of Checkland's soft systems methodology (SSM) [21] was taken as a model of human sense-making, as SSM is a means of inquiry that is sensitive to the complex social and political nature of organisations. Lewis [17], [18] also suggests that a higher interpretative level data model be introduced into data modelling, which is complementary to the existing forms of data models. This level is based upon the 'cognitive categories' used in SSM's systems definitions.

So a model or a mechanism of human-sense making is a crucial point for information and data requirements analysis. Mingers [8] calls this sense-making mechanism a 'meaning system', which humans are always already in. In fact, Mingers took this issue a step further by clarifying the concepts sign (including data), information and meaning, which underlie the discipline of information systems and providing a conceptual framework for semantic information.

Looking at information, not just data, seems necessary, as interpretative paradigm should determine that the actors in the domain be the centre of consideration and analysis, that is, requirements should be looked at from their perspectives. This requires looking at sign, information and meaning. Information requirements are the meaning that is required for activities.

3 Foundations for Formulating Semantic Information Flows

Among the theories about semantic information that we have looked at, Mingers' [8] analysis of sign, information and meaning seems the most convincing one. His conceptualisation was arrived at by integrating the theoretical work of Maturana and Habermas into a framework provided by Dretske's [22] theory of semantic information. Mingers' view points most relevant to this paper can be summarised as follows.
• The physical world is essentially analogue and is a continuum of differences transforming and being transformed, rich in information. Objective information is converted into inter-subjective and subjective meaning through a process of digitalisation. The receiver's knowledge, intention, attention, and context determine what particular aspects of the available analogue information are digitalised into meaning.
• Data is a collection of signs brought together because they are considered relevant to some purposeful activity. Each data carries some information.
• Information is literally untouchable as humans are always already in a world of interpreted digitalised meaning, they can never interact with information in an unmediated way.

Using Mingers' ideas, information requirements can be viewed as the meaning that is required for activities. Information systems design is the construction of a 'sign system' that carries the information from which the meaning can be generated. So Mingers work provides a unconventional perspective for information systems design. However, as Mingers says in his paper, this framework, for information systems, is of a general and conceptual nature. It does not promise new methods or techniques for immediate use by practitioners, which require exactitude and concrete forms. A key issue here seems to enhance some levels of interest within Stamper's [23], [24] framework for information and the above Mingers' mechanism by some formal means. That is, to develop a concrete and mathematically rigorous mechanism that models the process that meaning is arrived at from information carried by data or a sign.

To develop a technique for modelling information, it is useful to use the 'situation theory' [6], [7]. In situation theory, an agent's world divides up into a collection of situations: situations encountered, situations referred to, situations about which information is received, and so on. The behaviour of people varies systematically according to the kind of situation they are faced with. Situations are agent-relative. The individuation of a situation by an agent does not necessarily entail the agent being able to provide an exact description of everything that is and is not going on in that situation. The most significant point of situation as far as information modelling is concerned is that an item of information is made true by a situation. For example, in a lecture situation, John is lecturing and Carol is not listening to him. The latter two are items of information. A situation is a structured part of the perceived reality that an agent discriminates by their behaviour or possibly individuates. For example, a football match is a situation, an international conference is a situation too. We will call a real world situation a *real situation*. A *real situation* is more general than *set* in that you cannot unambiguously specify the content of the situation, you can only individuate it intuitively. To alleviate the difficulties caused by this, we use the concept 'abstract situation'. The 'abstract situation' is an abstract object in the set of abstract objects with which to reason. An abstract situation is an abstract analogy of the real situations. It is a mathematical construct built out of relation, individuals and locations organised in *infons*, where an infon is a tuple of objects having or not having a certain relation or property at a point of time and space.

The situation theory provides a basis for Devlin [7] to have developed his theory of information flow. The issue of *information flow* is concerned with how information is created and one piece of information gives rise to another piece of information. Intuitively it is about how we get to know something about a situation through perception and cognition or through knowing something about another situation or knowing something else about the same situation. To capture and express these with exactitude Devlin [7] provides a mechanism. The mechanism for modelling information flow is made up of *situation types* and *constraints*. A constraint is a directed connection between two situation types. Information occurs and flows through 'pattern match'. That is, an agent is ware of and ready to use a constraint, and when an individual situation matches the situation type in the 1st position then will an individual situation of the situation type in the 2nd position be concluded.

To provide a mathematical mechanism for modelling semantic information flow, we will use the predicate logic. Predicate logic has been used for representing knowledge [25] and for data modelling [26], [27]. It is claimed that predicate calculus can be considered as a complete, integrated, and all-encompassing framework for data modelling, which mixes data and knowledge about the data. As a matter of fact, most data models revert to it to encode knowledge they did not anticipate handling [27].

4 A Set of Constructs for Formulating Information Flows

Based upon Mingers' framework, the theories of Barwise and Devlin and predicate logic, in this section, we shall describe a set of concepts for modelling semantic information, which can then be used to tackle the information aspect of human purposeful activities.

We will define **information** as what an agent extracts about a situation from the perceived world, which is what Mingers calls 'meaning'. It is a result of the interaction between part of the real world (denoted with a 'W') that an agent perceives and the readiness (denoted with an 'R') of the agent for perceiving and interpreting the part of the real world. We shall denote the result as a combination (W, R). It is taken as true by the agent. Different combinations such as (W, R) and (W', R') may give rise to the some piece of information. That is to say, we have $(W, R) = (W', R')$. The fact that these two pairs are equal means that **there is something in people's mind that the two pairs both denote**. This is to say, information does seem to exist, independent of individual agents. Obviously there can be unlimited number of such pairs that give the same information. We use $[(W, R)]$ to represent all the 'equivalent relations' of (W, R) including the above (W', R'), to mean 'the same item of information'. To give information a concrete form, we will use a number of terms, which will be explained in the following paragraphs.

The content of (W, R), which is information, is taken in this paper to consist of **items of information**. An item of information is an alleged fact that several individuals either have or do not have a certain property or a certain relationship in a context. Information, meaning, and all the other elements that may play a role in the process of the derivation of meaning from information, such as information receiver's knowledge, intention, attention, context, personal experiences, feelings and motivations can be seen as made up from items of information. This is because they can be seen as possibly complex formations of some primitives: objects and their inter-rations and properties.

We will use the term **infon** (after Devlin [7]) (often short for '*parameter free infon*') as a formal model of items of information. It is an intentional and abstract construct as a formal model of a statement of some alleged fact that several individuals have or do not have a property or relation r. An *infon* is represented by a *predicate calculus expression* with no free variables. For example, $\sigma = \text{Individual}(a_1, ..., a_n) \wedge$

TemporalLocation(t) ∧SpatialLocation(l) ∧Polarity(1)∧ r(a₁, ..., aₙ, t, l, 1) is an *infon*, and when the types of the 'terms' of the predicates are obvious, the *infon* can be simplified to be σ = r(a₁, ..., aₙ, t, l, 1). Note that the data type of 'polarity' is Boolean, the only valid values of which are 'true' or '1', and 'false' or '0'. In the above infon, a₁, ..., aₙ, t, l are certain individuals, but not named. They are not variables. We can use named individuals in an infon, such as those in scores(>=70%, Overall mark, Jane Smith, ISD, CIS, 3/7/97, 1). An infon that has no free variables is a proposition in mathematical terms. A proposition is either true or false, i.e., it is truth valued within the tacit context – the world.

When an *infon* contains at least one *free variable* (also called 'parameter'), we have a **parametric infon**. A parametric infon is an *infon* template. It is represented by a *predicate calculus expression* that is not truth valued. That is, it is not a proposition. When all its free variables *are anchored to* certain individuals, a parametric *infon* becomes a parameter free *infon*, which is a truth-valued proposition.

An *infon* is true only in a certain context, which we call **situation**. A situation can also be the context within which a parametric *infon* is instantiated, i.e., all its free parameters are anchored to individuals. A situation may be the context for only one *infon*, or a number of *infon*s.

So when talking about information, both infons and contexts are needed. We will use the term **info unit** to refer to the combination of *infon*(s) and a situation within which the *infon*(s) are believed to be true by an agent. An *info unit* is informational as far as the agent is concerned. An *info unit* can be denoted with (*s*, σ), where *s* is a situation, σ is a simple *infon*, or a compound *infon*, such as σ1∧σ2. If at least one free occurrence of parameter is involved in it, the *info unit* is called *parametric info unit*.

Using these concepts our basic idea of information modelling is this: *infons* are made true by *situation*s, and situations are distinguished by the *infons* that they make true. Situations can be generalised into *situation types* through abstraction. Situation types have *parameters* of types in their structures. Situation types are connected by **info connections**. Let us denote it using, say, C = (S₁ ⟹ S₂). S₁ is termed 1ˢᵗ *position situation type*, and S₂ 2ⁿᵈ *position situation type*. Through perception and cognition we find specific individuals for all the free occurrences of parameters in the structure of the 1ˢᵗ position situation type and the 2ⁿᵈ position situation type, then we obtain *infons* that are made true by the instance of the 2ⁿᵈ position situation type. We call this process the instantiation of a pair of situation types that are connected by an *info connection*. This is how information is created and flows.

Using the set of concepts described above, we can formulate information flows in an elementary actvity. Figure 1 illustrates an 'information flow view' of an elementary activity. For each elementary activity in a 'human activity system', we create a unit like this that visualises the relevant situations and the relationships between situations whereby information and its flow can be captured.

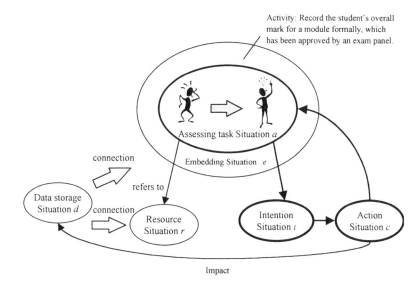

Figure 1: An 'information flow view' of an elementary activity 'Recording students' overall marks for a module, which has been approved by an exam panel'

5 Implications for IS Methodologies

This work may be seen as an enhancement to existing theories and frameworks for semantic information, such as Deretske's [22], Stamper's [23], [24] and in particular Mingers' [8] work, by integrating the theoretical work of Barwise and Devlin and predicate logic into them, which adds a 'mathematical formulation dimension' to them.

As a result of the above, commonly used rather intuitive concepts and terms such as *situation, data, information, meaning, type, instantiation, abstraction* and so on are now given a mathematical model or a mathematics based definition. Rigorously defining basic concepts that we use for information systems design should increase the exactitude of the work.

This work shows that before semantic data modelling is employed to specify data requirements, the required meaning should be investigated and formulated first. Through formulating semantic information flow, information requirements are the meaning that is required by the actors for their activities, rather than a synonym of data requirements. This should serve as a reference point for ascertaining that an information system to be built is a 'sign system' that is indeed capable of carrying the information from which the meaning can be derived. Some work has been done on the information bearing capability of an entity-relationship schema [28]. A schema is analysed in terms of its topological structures and its representation of information with regard to the original information requirements, which should ascertain that the information system built upon the database be able to serve the information needs of the users.

Two prominent problems with conventional semantic modelling, apart from its ontological and epistemological assumptions, are the identification of data entities [18], [29], [30] and what Brodie [31] calls 'semantic relativism', which permits different views of data to coexist and evolve. For example, a marriage could be considered to be: an object consisting of two people, an attribute of one or both of the two people, a relationship between two people, or a function mapping between two people. While this supports logical data independence and modelling flexibility, semantic relativism also cause confusion and uncertainty in semantic modelling. The problem here is to find the most appropriate constructs to model some perceived reality. Our work provides the foundation for a possible solution to these two problems. The idea is this as follows. Through information flow formulation, raw data are identified from the 'data storage situation'. Then raw data are flattened and consolidated by identifying their overlapping and one's inclusion of another. Then the usage of raw data are formulated by using a set of parameters and then analysed whereby data entities and their inter-relations are revealed. These give us a basis for the creation of a conceptual data schema in terms of a semantic data model [32], [33].

6 Conclusions

Semantic models were originally developed for capturing more meaning of data than primitive record-oriented data models do. But they are now employed as an approach to information systems development. Semantic modelling is used as an inquiry into a problem situation, to collect information requirements, and to specify the structure of the information base of an information system. The greatly increased duty shows some inadequacies of semantic modelling due to its tacit realistic-positivist philosophical assumptions and the lack of constructs for human inquiry.

Theories and frameworks for semantic information can and should be used to complement semantic modelling for information requirements analysis. Among others, Mingers' framework seems the most convincing one in that it clarifies the concepts *sign*, *information* and *meaning* and their relationships.

To apply these theories on information systems design requires some enhancement in terms of concrete forms and exactitude, which are provided by the situation theory of Barwise's, the information flow theory of Devlin's and predicate logic. This work shows that by integrating these mathematics based theories into the former, semantic information flows within human activities can be formulated. As a result, some light was shed on the information aspect of human activities and their revelation, and mathematical rigour was injected into early stages of information system development, namely the formulation of information requirements and the design of the conceptual data schema for an information system.

References

1. Avison D. and Fitzgerald G. Information systems development: methodologies, techniques and tools, McGraw-Hill, London, 1997

2. Ashworth C. and Goodland M. SSADM - a practical approach, McGraw-Hill, London. 1990

3. Yourdon Inc. Yourdon systems method: model-driven systems development, Yourdon Press, Englewood Cliffs, New Jersey, 1993

4. Coad P. and Yourdon E. Object oriented analysis, 2nd ed., Prentice Hall, Englewood Cliffs, New Jersey, 1991

5. Avison D. and Wood-harper A.T. Multiview: an exploration in information systems development, McGraw-Hill, Maidenhead, 1990

6. Barwise J. and Perry J. Situations and attitudes, Bradford Books, MIT Press, 1983

7. Devlin K. Logic and information, Cambridge University Press, Cambridge, 1991

8. Mingers, J. Information and meaning: foundations for an intersubjective account. Info Systems J, 1995; 5:185-306

9. Barwise J. and Seligman J. Information flow – the logic of distributed systems, Cambridge University Press, Cambridge, 1997

10. Chen P.P. The entity-relationship model – Toward a unified view of data. ACM Trans Database Syst 1976; 4, 4: 397-434

11. Buneman P. and Niknil R: The Functional Data Model and its uses for interaction with databases. In: Brodie et al (ed) On conceptual modelling. Springer-Verlag, New York, 1984, pp 359-384

12. Hammer, M and McLeod, D. Database description with SDM: A semantic database model. ACM Trans Database Syst 1981; 6: 351-386

13. Elmasri R. and Navathe S.B. Fundamentals of database systems, 2nd ed., Benjamin/Cummings, Redwood City, California, 1994

14. Flynn D. J. Information systems requirements: determination & analysis, 2nd ed. McGraw-Hill, London, 1998

15. Shlaer S. and Mellor S.J. Object-oriented systems analysis: modelling the world in data, Yourdon Press, Prentice Hall Building, Englewood Cliffs, New Jersey, 1988

16. Klein H.K. and Hirschheim R.A. A comparative framework of data modelling paradigms and approaches. The Computer Journal 1987; 30:8-15

17. Lewis P. Information-systems development, Pitman, London, 1994

18. Lewis, P: New challenges and directions for data analysis and modelling. In: Stowell F. (ed) Information systems provision: the contribution of soft systems methodology. McGraw-Hill, London, 1995, pp 186-205

19. Klein H. K. and Lyytinen K: Towards a new understanding of data modelling. In: Floyd C. et al (ed) Software development and reality construction. Springer-Verlag, Berlin, 1992, pp 203-19.

20. Wood-Harper A. T. and Fitzgerald G. A taxonomy of current approaches to systems analysis. The Computer Journal 1982; 25:12-16

21. Checkland P. Systems thinking, systems practice, John Wiley & Sons, Chichester, 1981

22. Dretske F.L. Knowledge and the flow of information, Blackwell, Oxford, 1981

23. Stamper R: Semantics. In: Boland R. and Hirschheim R. (ed) Critical issues in information systems research. Wiley, London, 1987, pp 43-77.

24. Stamper R: Organisational semiotics. In: Mingers J. and Stowell F. (ed) Information systems: an emerging discipline? McGraw-Hill, London, 1997, pp 267-283

25. Ringland G.A. and Duce D.A., ed. Approaches to knowledge representation – an introduction, RSP, Taunton, Somerset, England, 1988

26. Date C.J. Introduction to database systems, 6th ed., Addison-Wesley, Reading, Massachusetts, 1995

27. Tsichritzis D.C. and Lochovsky F.H. Data models, Prentice-Hall, Englewood Cliffs, 1982

28. Feng J.-K: An analysis of some connectedness problems in an EER schema by using a set of 'info concepts'. Computing and Information Systems, University of Paisley, 1998; 5:64-72

29. Feng J.-K: A method for entity identification. In: Ellis, K. et al (ed) Critical issues in systems theory and practice. Plenum, London, 1995, pp 303-308

30. Feng J.-K: Can "entity identification" be disciplined? In: Wrycza S. and Zupancic J. (ed) information systems development - ISD'96 methods & tools, theory & practice, Fundacja Rozwoju Uniwersytetu Gdanskiego Zaklad Poligrafii, Sopot, ul.Armii Krajowej, 1996, pp 163-174

31. Brodie M.L: On the development of data models. In: Brodie et al (ed) On conceptual modelling. Springer-Verlag, New York, 1984, pp 19-47

32. Feng J.-K: Function-oriented data modelling. In: Stowell, F. West, D. and Howell, J. (ed) Systems science: addressing global issues. Plenum, London, 1993, pp 331-342

33. Feng J.-K: Data handling: a perspective of sign, information and meaning. In: Zupancic J. and Wrycza S. (ed) Information systems development - ISD'94 methods & tools, theory & practice. Moderna Organizacija, Kranj, 1994, pp 153-162

Using the Multiview2 Framework for Internet-Based Information System Development

Richard Vidgen
School of Management, University of Bath
Bath BA2 7AY

Abstract

Internet-based information system development is booming. There is the possibility that traditional IS analysts will be left behind, marooned with their structured (and even Object-Oriented methods) while technophiles and graphic designers join forces to hack out Internet applications at an ever increasing rate using technologies that change and grow week on week. Using the Multiview2 framework as an organizing scheme, this paper considers the role and relevancy of traditional methodologies for Internet-based IS development. The first stages of an action research project are used to illustrate how Multiview2 could contribute to the development of a strategic Internet marketing application.

1   Introduction

We are experiencing a staggering rate of growth of the Internet, in both the infrastructure of computers and networks and the uses and applications to which it is put (see, for example, Tapscott, 1996 and Davis & Meyer, 1998). This rapid growth threatens to leave information system (IS) developers and their traditional methods behind, unable to cope with either the severely foreshortened development timescales or with the strategic and transformational implications of IT applications that stretch out beyond the traditional boundaries of the organization. The first aim of this paper is to consider if and how traditional IS development methods might need to be adapted to address strategic Internet applications effectively. The second aim is to see what traditional development wisdom might be able to contribute to Internet-based IS development. To this end we will use the Multiview2 framework (Avison & Wood-Harper 1990; Avison et al., 1998) as a guide to the development of an Internet marketing application for a market research company. The structure of the paper is as follows. In the second section Internet marketing is introduced, followed by an overview of the Multiview2 framework in section three. In the fourth section the research method and a case study are described and the application of the Multiview2 framework is reported. In the last section reflections on the role of IS developers and IS methods in the age of the Internet are made.

390

2 Internet Marketing

The Internet is enabling electronic commerce (e-commerce) for business to business and business to consumer applications (see, for example, Kalakota & Whinston, 1997). We will take a simple definition of marketing (Vassos 1996): to increase sales; to decrease the cost of doing business; and to improve communications with stakeholders. Within this definition of marketing a number of stages of Internet development can be identified (figure 1).

At the most basic level a presence is created on the Internet to publicise an organization's existence and activities, moving through further levels of sophistication to strategic alliances and transformation. The Internet reconfiguration model in figure 1 is not intended as a stage model such as the software capability maturity model (Humphrey 1989) where progress is supposedly made by moving stepwise from one level to the next. For example, an organization could start its Internet activity at level 3a in figure 1 and then move to a 'higher' level while omitting intermediate levels. At the time of writing, Internet applications are moving rapidly out of levels 1 and 2 and into the middle age of levels 3 and 4. As a consequence of this maturation, it is no longer sufficient to have good graphical design skills and a hyperlink-generator. Database design, communications, security, interface/form design and good old-fashioned programming skills (e.g., JavaScript and Java) are all needed for the effective design of middle period Internet applications.

3 The Multiview2 Approach to IS Development

The foundations of Multiview (Avison & Wood-Harper 1990) as an *enquiring framework* for IS development rest on a recognition that the needs of computer artefacts, organizations, and individuals must be considered jointly. An IS development exercise should generate robust technical artefacts that support purposeful organizational activity and take into account the needs and freedom of the individual. This concern with negotiating between the technological, organizational, and personal aspects of IS development has constituted a central theme in the Multiview framework and differentiates it from other IS development approaches (Bickerton & Siddiqi, 1992). The core components of the Multiview2 framework are shown in figure 2.

Multiview2 is a framework for IS development rather than a methodology per se; a methodology must take into account the Multiview2 interpretive scheme (figure 2), the situation (together with its rich history), and those wishing to instigate change in the problem situation. The local and contingent methodology may make use of IS development methods - indicative methods appropriate to each of the four quadrants are:

Maturity	Type	Sub-type	Level	Characteristics
Low	Data provision	Presence	1a	The organization creates a web-presence to publicise their existence and activities. This is often done out of fear of being left behind.
		Data	1b	Product details are added to support and promote the sales of the organization's offerings.
	Information support	Information	2a	A searchable database of products is implemented on the server, allowing customers to search for products using keywords. Basic ordering facilities may be added. Information such as industry commentaries is added to attract visitors and to provide added value.
		One-to-one marketing	2b	Mass customization - web page content is customized based on customer-defined criteria, transforming the site to a one-to-one marketing vehicle. Users may be issued with IDs and passwords to make them identifiable.
Medium	Process support	Internal coordination	3a	Intranets are established to aid coordination and communication within an organization.
		E-commerce	3b	Ordering and shopping cart software, secure payment facilities, and integration with back office databases and legacy transaction processing systems.

Figure 1: levels of Internet-enabled reconfiguration (adapted from Venkatraman 1991; Vassos 1996)

Maturity	Type	Sub-type	Level	Characteristics
	Product redesign	Product redesign	3c	Offer new combinations of products and services and a wider range of varieties of existing products. For example, Dell computers allow users to 'build' their own PC to their precise specification.
	Business process redesign	Business process redesign	4	Reengineer internal business processes and extend the reach of corporate applications through extranet and intranet integration (e.g., suppliers access their customers' stock control systems and deliver stocks where and when needed).
High	Network redesign	Network redesign	5	Create strategic alliances between organizations in the value chain (this is more than electronic data interchange - EDI).
	Transformation	Transformation	6	Deliver new products to new markets through Internet-enabled technologies.

Figure 1 (continued): levels of Internet-enabled reconfiguration (adapted from Venkatraman 1991; Vassos 1996)

Organizational analysis: this activity, described by Vidgen (1997), is concerned with understanding the organizational needs for an information system. Organizational analysis involves gaining an appreciation of the purposeful activity that the information system is to support. Approaches such as soft systems methodology (Checkland, 1981; Checkland & Scholes, 1990; Checkland & Holwell, 1998) and stakeholder analysis (Mason & Mitroff 1981) are used to cater for complexity and pluralism of interests respectively. A radical view of organizational requirements in support of business process redesign might also be incorporated (Wood et al. 1995).

ANALYSIS

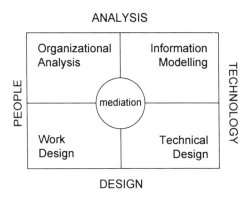

Figure 2: Multiview2 and IS definition (adapted from Avison et al., 1998)

Information modelling: the aim here is to develop a representation of the information system in technical terms using object-oriented analysis (Fowler 1997) and business process modelling techniques such as role activity diagrams (Ould 1995). These methods have tended to replace traditional analysis methods such as data flow diagrams and entity-relationship models used in Multiview1 (Avison & Wood-Harper 1990).

Work design: the IS modelling activity is counter-balanced by a sociotechnical analysis that draws from ETHICS (Mumford, 1995), and also ethnography (Randall et al., 1994; Avison & Myers, 1995), as well as the Scandinavian School of participatory design (Greenbaum & Kyng, 1991) and a general concern with how work is accomplished in actuality (Sachs 1995).

Technical design: this activity is the traditional province of the computer scientist (for example, Somerville, 1997) and involves the design and, ultimately, construction of software, hardware, and communications technologies. The internal design of the software includes functions and data in structured methods (Elmasri & Navathe, 1998), classes and methods in O-O programming (Booch, 1994) and can be contrasted with the external design of the human-computer interface (Schneiderman, 1998).

In practice the IS developer needs to mediate between the four elements of figure 2, accepting that there is no absolute primacy of one quadrant over another and indeed no particular temporal ordering of how the quadrants might be tackled. However, figure 2 does represent the Multiview2 interpretive scheme - we do propose that all four quadrants should and need to be considered in any IS development. Each of the quadrants will be addressed with greater or less formality and greater or less rigour, depending on the methodology adopted (which should emerge from consideration of the problem situation and the change agents).

4   The Fieldwork

Action research is used to test the theory that Multiview2 is an appropriate framework for organizing Internet development (Checkland 1992; Baskerville & Wood-Harper 1996). The framework of ideas to be tested in the action research is the application of Multiview2 to strategic Internet marketing. The area of application is a small to medium enterprise, Acme International. The methodology for the intervention is emergent and developed through the use of Multiview2 in the action research domain.

The research was initiated as a result of MSc coursework at the University of Bath. Students worked in groups to produce a business strategy for Acme and a proposal for how Acme should introduce Internet technology. As part of the project each team produced a prototype web-site for Acme. As a result of this work, Acme decided to continue with the initiative and create a live web-site. The author is assisting in the development and implementation of the web-site.

Acme International carries out specialist market research and consultancy for the food, drinks, and packaging industries worldwide. Acme was founded in 1985 and has its head office in Bristol, with a satellite office in Dusseldorf. The primary activities of the company are: market research reports; bespoke research; and consulting (technical and strategic). Together these activities constitute an annual turn-over of £1.5 million, generated by twenty staff. Around three quarters of the income is generated through selling market research reports at an average price of £1500 per copy. The market research reports often lead to bespoke research and wider consulting opportunities. Acme recognizes that its clients are becoming more global and is responding by forging global alliances.

4.1   Information System Development Methodology

Two planning workshops were held with Acme personnel: the chairman, the managing director of Acme Projects, a market research analyst, and the IT manager. It was agreed that a basic site, **Stage 1**, should be developed within three months, with ideas for future developments, **Stage 2** and beyond, being recorded but not implemented.

On the basis of the planning workshop and taking into account the analysis of Acme's business strategy reported by the MSc students the Multiview2 framework was adapted to the specifics of the situation (figure 3). The emergent methodology was pragmatic and constituted a considerable reduction of the indicative methods in the Multiview2 framework (for example there would be no explicit soft systems analysis). The dynamic view of the IS development process was seen as incremental with interdependencies between IS definition, IS implementation, and particularly IS operation (figure 3b).

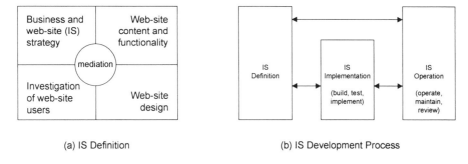

(a) IS Definition   (b) IS Development Process

Figure 3: the emergent methodology for Stage 1 Internet development at Acme

4.2 IS Definition

4.2.1 Business Strategy and Web-site (IS) Strategy

The original impetus for the development of a web-site was the need to respond to a new technology that was unknown and slightly threatening. As the analysis proceeded it became apparent that the Internet could be a significant factor in shaping and furthering the organization's strategy. The strategic aims of Acme are: to create a global presence; to broaden the product range; and to develop complementary skills (e.g., a synergy of market intelligence reports and consultancy). Globalization is concerned with extending the research and analysis activity to all countries and is a response to the recognition that Acme's principal customers are multi-nationals competing in global markets. Acme intend to achieve this through building up a network of researchers and consultants and by strategic alliances - although they have an office in Paris there is no intention to increase staff on the payroll or to acquire further offices. The product range is predominantly focussed on soft drinks and Acme want to expand its offerings to other areas of the food and drink sector. This is viewed as important due to the cross-over between sectors and Acme believe that it will be more and more difficult to survive as a soft drinks niche specialist. Acme are also keen to develop further their reputation for putting resources back into the food and drink industry through activities such as journals, training, education, and information services. This is important since the collection of data that constitutes a market intelligence report is to a large extent reliant on the goodwill of the companies that constitute that industry.

Acme's strategy is to expand its products and market (figure 4). A significant proportion of Acme's business is concerned with information, whether it be packaged as reports or as consultancy, or even as conferences. Information technology is clearly an important factor as it is medium through which Acme's products are created and delivered. The Internet is for Acme a strategic technology that will allow existing products to be packaged in different ways. For example, through automation

Acme could sell smaller chunks of data at a lower price due to lower transaction costs. Acme could also leverage its data banks and sell cross-report data (such as all data on soft drinks relating to Brazil). From a strategic perspective Acme must consider products, markets, and technology jointly.

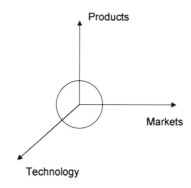

Figure 4: strategic analysis (Venkatraman 1990)

Stage 1 of the project is to create a web presence and to provide marketing information about Acme companies and their services and products. Report contents pages and sample pages will be available on the Internet, but not full electronic copies of reports. Analysis of competitors shows that market research companies are making reports available online (e.g., Gartner, Datamonitor) and issuing user ids and passwords to customers. This is a stage 2 development for Acme. However, customers will be able to search for Acme products and place orders online. An information service was identified as a key requirement that would help to attract visitors to the site and, through the Chairman's newsletter, would promote the reputation of Acme as industry leaders. Overall, the aim was to make a site that addresses levels 1a, 1b, 2a, and 3b of figure 1.

Stage 2 aims were collected and considered for future development of the web-site. In the longer term Acme will look to deliver all of its reports online through the Internet. New products could be generated from existing data, such as an extract of all the data that pertains to a single country or product across all the current reports (level 3c in figure 1). Pricing structures could also change since it will be possible to sell smaller amounts of more highly targeted data at lower cost. This is possible because data extraction, formatting, and order processing can all be automated and delivered via the Internet. Advertising for suppliers to the food and drink industry could be carried on the site and global directories produced and sold. The globalization of Acme will need coordinating communication systems, such as an Intranet (level 3a and level 4 in figure 1). An Intranet would also provide a basis for knowledge sharing and knowledge management, which is a particularly important to virtual organizations. The raw data that is processed by analysts into saleable reports could be collected via the net, from searching for data on the Internet to having questionnaires completed online. Acme also make data available to students for project and research work; standard briefings could be made available on the web so that there is less demand on staff time and to show the company's commitment to supporting the industry.

Stage 2 ideas indicate that Acme may need to change the way it does business in the short to medium term. Currently, Acme produces hard-copy products. The reports can be seen sitting on a shelf and have a tangible physical presence. In the future it is likely that all aspects of market intelligence can be conducted electronically: the collection of raw data, the processing of the data into market intelligence, the formatting of the processed data into reports (of varying granularities) based on customer requirements, and the delivery of the product. This is both a threat and an opportunity for Acme and the Stage 1 web-site represents an important first step.

4.2.2 Web-site Content and Functionality

The content of the web-site follows standard practice and is organized around the categories: 'Information Services', 'Reports, 'Consulting', 'Conferences', 'About Acme', and 'Contact us'. The content includes details of the market intelligence reports, including contents pages and text from the paper-based brochures. The 'Information Services' category will include press releases and news of upcoming reports, but will also have a section for data of interest to the industry, such as statistics on inflation and GDP for different countries. The aim is to provide a value-added service so that market researchers could use the site as a standing resource and thus be encouraged to make return visits. Information for the press will also be provided. The major business process functionality of the site is the implementation of an online ordering service. The information analysis has been documented using ad hoc diagramming notations to show the data and processes supported. As more business functionality is added it is expected that more sophisticated methods might be appropriate, such as the universal modelling language (UML).

4.2.3 Web-site Users

With a traditional information system the users tend to be internal to the organization and can be identified and consulted (or not). With an Internet marketing application the users are external and to a large extent anonymous. The Acme business development manager is currently conducting a questionnaire of customers to gain deeper insight into their requirements of Acme. Questionnaires are to be followed up with telephone interviews and some of the data collected will be concerned with Internet usage and the demand for Acme to supply online services. In a sense the problem is the same as with traditional information systems - to understand the purposeful activity the users are engaged in and to provide appropriate IT support. Monitoring of actual usage is of particular importance in this scenario since the users are to a large extent anonymous. The understanding of the web-site users' work will help to inform the content of the information services area of the web. The aim is to make the site a useful support to Acme customers' in carrying out their work so that they view the site as a resource as well as a marketing initiative.

4.2.4 Web-site Design

The web-site design must address the following issues:

- aesthetics of design;
- usability (e.g., navigability, download times, browser compatibility);
- maintainability (e.g., adding new reports to the site).

Multimedia-intensive pages were considered (e.g., Macromedia's Flash) but excluded from Stage 1 in the interests of fast download times that do not require plug-ins. This policy will be reviewed for Stage 2. Examples of good and bad web-site design were considered (see, for example, Suck, 1998). The aesthetics of design were to portray the clean and professional image of Acme's paper-based marketing materials with an emphasis on ease of use and speed. The web-site design would therefore not be a cutting edge site in terms of multi-media and creative graphics, but it would require reasonably sophisticated programming to implement the ordering subsystem. A site map was created to show how the pages linked together and mock-ups of the pages were made showing the buttons and navigation paths.

4.3 IS Development Process

4.3.1 IS Implementation

For the implementation of the web-pages Macromedia's Dreamweaver was chosen. The reasons for this choice were that this software has had good reviews in the press, is a mid-range professional web development toolkit, and familiarity (the author has used it before!). Adobe Acrobat will be used to make sample pages of reports available to prospective purchasers. It was clear that server side programming would be needed for stage 1 for orders and registrations to be recorded. Access to a CGI directory was needed on the server to email the contents to the Acme order processing clerk. A database of products was also need to be available to support searches by customers of reports. A shopping cart metaphor for report ordering was adopted and implemented using client-side JavaScript programs. This gave a degree of independence from the service provider since only minimal server-side facilities were needed.

4.3.2 IS Operation

At the time of writing the web-site is being put into production operation. It is not therefore possible to report on the operation of the site. Acme have acquired a domain name, and although they did not previously have a web-site they have been using email for the last two years. These services are currently hosted by an independent service provider, Frontier. The new web-site will be implemented with the current service provider (ISP), but the choice of ISP may need to be re-evaluated in the light of development and operational requirements.

In assessing the success of the site some metrics will be required. For example, we need to know: are customers visiting the site? Who else is visiting the site and why? Do they come back to the site? Are reports being sold? Are these additional sales that are achieved as a result of a web presence or would they have been made anyway? Which pages are most popular? Where do the users come from (analysis by country, industry sector, etc.)? Is the image of Acme in the market place being strengthened? We are putting together a set of key success factors using ideas based on Buchanan & Lukaszewski (1997).

5 Reflections

One might argue for a number of different stances concerning the role of traditional methodologies, such as SSADM (CCTA 1990) or Euromethod or even the newer Object-Oriented methods, such as the universal modelling language (UML). Firstly, one might argue that there is nothing different about the Internet and traditional and post-traditional methodologies are as relevant (or irrelevant) to this type of system development as they are to any other type of information system. Alternatively, we might take the approach that Internet applications are intrinsically different from traditional IS applications and need new and different methodologies. More radically still it might be argued that Internet applications are inherently amethodological, needing to grow and evolve through the skills, creativity, and nurturing of talented designers. Lastly, we might try and make a case for some hybrid of these different stances. However, it is a mistake to focus too narrowly on the role of methodology. The Multiview2 framework emphasizes the interaction of the change agents (users and analysts), the situation, and an interpretive scheme. From this triumvirate a contingent methodology, or indeed a non-method, should emerge that is suitable for the development of a locally-situated and specific information system. An analyst familiar with structured methods might indeed attempt to apply traditional methods to web-site development, while we would expect a graphic designer to approach the problem rather differently. From a Multiview2 perspective it is possible that in some situations an amethodological approach would be indicated, whereby a web-site is allowed to evolve and grow by accretion with a minimum of rules (the Internet itself has developed somewhat in this fashion). To some extent, any IS development must be opportunistic, making use of the skills, tools, and techniques that are available.

Although a developer versed in SSADM would probably be ill-equipped (in methods, at least) to design and build a web-site for marketing and projecting a corporate image where visual appeal and immediate impact are important, it seems likely that business applications involving electronic commerce need to be handled differently from promotional web-sites. Business applications need access to product and order databases with a corresponding increase in concerns about software quality factors such as robustness, maintainability, and security. These middle period web-sites require many of the traditional technical skills in database design, programming, structured testing, and communications. One challenge for Internet-based IS development will be the integration of graphical design skills with traditional IT/software engineering skills. As we move into higher levels of sophistication then a focus on business processes will be needed and analysis methods such as the universal modelling language (UML) can be expected to have a role.

It is difficult to imagine how the activities in figure 3b can be reduced. Any IS, whether Internet-based or not, needs to be defined, implemented, and operated. One cannot operate an IS that has not been built, but it might be argued that implementation can take place without a formal process of definition. This is indeed so; any IS can be built on the basis of implicit assumptions, but there is no guarantee that it will in some way further organizational aims, other than by happenstance. To make the IS definition explicit some mental framework is needed, such as Multiview2 (figure 3a). With regard to IS definition, experience with the Acme project to date suggests that the concerns of the four quadrants will be as relevant to Internet-based IS development as to any other type of IS project; there will still be a need to balance the interests of business strategy, information modelling, technology, and work.

At the general level of the Multiview2 framework we are arguing that there is no difference between an Internet-based IS development and a traditional IS project. However, at the level of practice there are differences, and these may be significant. Firstly, from the organization analysis point of view, an Internet application will typically have significant strategic implications, reaching out to new customers, enabling the provision of new product offerings and improved levels of service. To omit this level of analysis is to lose a significant opportunity. Even if the organization is not going to re-invent itself in its first web-site implementation, thinking about the long-term implications sets the scene for future developments and can help to avoid the closing-off of alternatives. IS planning is still needed and may need a network rather than firm-centred approach (Finnegan et al., 1998). Secondly, the IS users of a strategic marketing site are external to the organization and largely anonymous, which makes the monitoring of site statistics of fundamental importance. This means also that attracting the target audience to the site and then getting feedback on how to improve the site takes on a greater significance. Of course, all these things are true of traditional information systems, but they seem rarely to have been taken seriously. Internet sites, in common with any other technical artefact, need to persuade people (and other things) to use them. Since there is unlikely to be mandated usage (as there might be with a traditional IS that is internal to an organization) the web-site developer needs to pay attention to the marketing of the site itself. Thirdly, the relationships between definition, implementation, and operation are much more tightly coupled than with traditional information systems. One might argue that this aspect can be addressed by rapid applications development (DSDM, 1995), a popular theme in traditional IS development currently. However, the focus with RAD is still too often on the process of IS definition with the aim of constructing a stable software artefact that can be reviewed periodically and updated. Internet applications need to be more responsive, changing and evolving as they adapt to their environment and try to retain user interest. In some cases a successful Internet application is an unstable mix of continual re-definition, re-implementation, and monitoring of operations - this might be taking place from day to day or even from hour to hour.

This paper represents some early thoughts on the role of methodologies in Internet-based IS development. Unsurprisingly, we have found that it is all too easy to focus on the right-hand side of the Multiview2 interpretive scheme (technology) with an accompanying downplaying of the organizational and work aspects of IS development. Although this might be acceptable in Stage 1, it is unlikely to be so for Stage 2, which will be concerned with business transformation and moving Acme toward being a virtual organization. Since any transformation must involve a fundamental reconsideration of the purpose of the enterprise it is expected that the soft systems methodology will be particularly relevant to planning for Stage 2.

References

Avison, D.E., & Myers, M., (1995). Information Systems and Anthropology: an anthropological perspective on IT and organizational culture. *Information Technology & People*, 8(3): 43-56.

Avison, D. E., & Wood-Harper, A. T., (1990). *Multiview: An Exploration in Information Systems Development.* Blackwell Scientific Publications, Oxford.

Avison, D. E., Wood-Harper, A. T., Vidgen, R. T., & Wood, J. R. G., (1998). A further exploration into Information Systems Development: the evolution of Multiview 2. *Information Technology & People*, 11(2): 124-139.

Baskerville, R., & Wood-Harper, A.T., (1996). A critical perspective on action research as a method for information systems research. *Journal of Information Technology*, 11: 235-246.

Bickerton, M., & Siddiqi, J., (1992). The classification of Requirements Engineering Methods. *IEEE*, 182-186.

Booch, G., (1994). *Object-Oriented Design with Applications.* Second edition. Benjamin Cummings, Redwood City, CA.

Buchanan, R. W., & Lukaszewski, C., (1997). *Measuring the Impact of your Web Site.* Wiley, New York.

CCTA, (1990). *SSADM Version 4 Reference Manual.* NCC Blackwell.

Checkland, P., (1981). *Systems Thinking, Systems Practice.* Wiley, Chichester.

Checkland, P. B., (1991). From Framework through Experience to Learning: the essential nature of Action Research. In: Nissen, H. -E., Klein, H.K., & Hirschheim, R., editors. *Information Systems Research: Contemporary Approaches and Emergent Traditions.* Elsevier Science Publishers (North Holland).

Checkland, P., & Howell, S., (1998). *Information, Systems and information Systems – making sense of the field.* Wiley, Chichester.

Checkland, P., & Scholes, J., (1990). *Soft Systems Methodology in Action.* Wiley, Chichester.

Davis, D., & Myer, C., (1998). *Blur: the speed of change in the connected economy.* Capstone, Oxford, UK.

DSDM, (1995). *Dynamic Systems Development Method.* Tesseract Publishing, UK.

Elmasri, R., & Navathe, S., (1998). *Fundamentals of Database Systems.* Third edition. Benjamin/Cummings, Redbridge, CA.

Finnegan, P., Galliers, R., & Powell, P., (1998). Systems Planning in an Electronic Commerce Environment in Europe: Rethinking Current Approaches. *Electronic Markets Journal,* 8(2): 35-38.

Fowler, M., (1997). *UML Distilled: applying the standard object modelling language.* Addison-Wesley, Reading MA.

Greenbaum, J., & Kyng, M., editors (1991). *Design at Work: cooperative design of computer systems.* Lawrence Erlbaum Associates, NJ.

Humphrey, W.S., (1989). *Managing the Software Process.* Addison-Wesley.

Kalakota, R., & Whinston, A., editors, (1997). *Readings in Electronic Commerce.* Addison Wesly, Reading MA.

Mason, R., & Mitroff, I., (1981). *Challenging Strategic Planning Assumptions.* Wiley, New York.

Mumford, E., (1995). *Effective Systems Design and Requirements Analysis: The ETHICS Approach to Computer Systems Design.* Macmillan, London.

Ould, M., (1995). *Business Processes: modelling and analysis for re-engineering and improvement.* Wiley, Chichester.

Randall, D., Hughes, J., & Shapiro, D., (1994). Steps towards a partnership: Ethnography and system design. In: Jirotka, M., & Goguen, J., editors, *Requirements Engineering: social and technical issues,* pp 241-258, Academic Press, London.

Sachs, P., (1995). Transforming Work: collaboration, learning, and design. *Communications of the ACM,* 38(9): 36-44.

Schneiderman, B., (1998). *Designing the User Interface* (third edition). Addison-Wesley.

Suck, (1998). *Web Sites That Suck.* http://www.webpagesthatsuck.com/

Tapscott, D., (1996). *The Digital Economy: promise and peril in the age of networked intelligence.* McGraw-Hill, NY.

Venkatraman, N., (1991). IT-Induced Business Reconfiguration. In: Scott Morton, M. S., editor. *The Corporation of the 1990s: Information Technology and Organizational Transformation,* Oxford University Press, New York.

Vassos, T., (1996). *Strategic Internet Marketing.* Que Corporation. Indianapolis, IN.

Vidgen, R., (1997). Stakeholders, soft systems and technology: separation and mediation in the analysis of information system requirements. *Information Systems Journal,* 7: 21-46.

Web Programming, (1998). *Netscape DevEdge Online.*
http://developer.netscape.com/viewsource/index_frame.html

Wood, J.R.G., Vidgen, R. T., Wood-Harper, A. T., & Rose, J., (1995). Business Process Redesign: radical change or reactionary tinkering? In Burke, G., & Peppard, J., editors, *Examining Business Process Reengineering: current perspectives and research directions.* Kogan Page.

Author Index